GAY LIVES

OTHER BOOKS BY PAUL ROBINSON

The Freudian Left (1969)

The Modernization of Sex (1976)

Opera and Ideas: From Mozart to Strauss (1985)

Freud and His Critics (1993)

Ludwig van Beethoven: "Fidelio" (1996)

PAUL ROBINSON

GAY LIVES

Homosexual Autobiography from John Addington Symonds to Paul Monette

THE UNIVERSITY OF CHICAGO PRESS   CHICAGO AND LONDON

PAUL ROBINSON is Richard W. Lyman Professor in the Humanities at Stanford University. He is a member of the American Academy of Arts and Sciences.

The University of Chicago Press, Chicago 60637
The University of Chicago Press, Ltd., London
© 1999 by The University of Chicago
All rights reserved. Published 1999
08 07 06 05 04 03 02 01 00 99   1 2 3 4 5
ISBN: 0-226-72180-9

Library of Congress Cataloging-in-Publication Data

Robinson, Paul A., 1940–
    Gay lives : homosexual autobiography from John Addington Symonds to Paul Monette / Paul Robinson.
        p.   cm.
    Includes bibliographical references and index.
    ISBN 0-226-72180-9 (alk. paper)
    1. Gays—Biography.   I. Title.
HQ75.2.R63   1999
306.76'62'0922—dc21
[b]   98-24460
                                                                        CIP

For Jim and Joan Robinson

I want to thank

the Stanford Humanities Center,

where I enjoyed a stimulating year while

writing this book.

Contents

Introduction

⚭ NOT ALL FOURTEEN OF the autobiographers I examine in this book would call themselves gay men. Depending on the period, the author's views, or even his mood, other labels might be preferred: invert, pederast, bugger, or homosexual, although "gay" increasingly became the self-designation of choice after the Second World War, until it was recently challenged, in radical circles, by "queer." I use the phrase "gay autobiographer," sometimes anachronistically, to identify writers who make attraction to their own sex a central theme of their autobiographies. That is the first criterion by which I have arrived at my cast of characters: they are not just homosexuals who happened to write autobiographies, or who perhaps mention their sexual lives in passing, but autobiographers whose chief concern is to describe and explain their love of men.[1]

The criterion has led me to exclude a number of books that, on first blush, might seem to qualify. A case in point is Gore Vidal's *Palimpsest* (1995). Although he gives a frank, elegiac account of his early love affair with a beautiful blond boy, Jimmie Trimble, Vidal's primary interest, in this long and entertaining memoir, is not his sexual life or his evolving identity as a gay man. Rather *Palimpsest* is the story of Vidal's literary and political friendships—or, more often, enmities. It is a piece of higher gossip, often wickedly funny, about the rich, the powerful, and the famous. In short, it is not a gay autobiography in my sense of the phrase. Similar considerations have led me to exclude other distinguished memoirs written by gay men, such as James Merrill's *A Different Person* (1993), Lincoln Kirstein's *Mosaic* (1994), and Ned Rorem's *Knowing When to Stop* (1994). All of them contain information about their authors' sexual experience, but the treatment is glancing; their main concern lies elsewhere.

---

1. Christopher Isherwood's first autobiography, *Lions and Shadows* (1938), might not seem to measure up to this standard, but I argue in chapter 2 that the book in fact begs to be read as a coded gay autobiography.

My second criterion was to select autobiographies written by artists and intellectuals.[2] In the case of the earlier autobiographers I had no other choice: until very recently only artists and intellectuals wrote such books. But in the past decade gay autobiography has become a growth industry. Now there are dozens of books that meet my first criterion: autobiographies written by gay FBI agents, gay Olympic divers, gay baseball umpires, gay politicians, and—a particularly large category—gay soldiers who've been kicked out of the military. In general these books are concerned less with their authors' erotic history and identity formation than with the struggle against prejudice. Often they are cowritten by journalists. As a result they seldom boast the rich subjectivity of autobiographies by artists and intellectuals. Put another way, they lack the literary texture that invites the kind of analysis I am interested in. I am by profession an intellectual historian, a close reader of (preferably) complex writings, and I've looked for works whose strategies, modes of argument, and inner tensions will respond gratefully to such readings. Of course, because my sample consists of artists and intellectuals, I have had to be cautious in drawing conclusions about the lives of gay men more generally. The stories of my fourteen autobiographers are, I believe, highly suggestive about the experience of the broader gay population, but I am aware that the sexual lives and self-conceptions of intellectuals are not necessarily representative.

Two further concerns have dictated my choice of authors. The first was a desire to cover as broad a chronological range as possible. As just mentioned, the great majority of gay autobiographies have been written in the past decade. Nonetheless, I have found suitable writings from over the full century. My earliest text, John Addington Symonds's *Memoirs,* dates from 1889 to 1890, and the most recent, Paul Monette's *Becoming a Man,* from 1992. I have been able to push the chronological boundaries back as far as I have only by making some strategic compromises. Symonds's *Memoirs* were not published until 1984, although Symonds always intended for them to appear sometime after his death. Likewise, the autobiography of Goldsworthy Lowes Dickinson, written mostly in 1921, didn't see print until 1973, though Dickinson, too, made careful arrangements for its eventual publication. I have had to practice a similar stretching—in this case not just chronological but generic—with the two American diarists, Jeb Alexander and Donald Vining, treated in chapter 5. To my knowledge there are no

2. The two American diarists treated in chapter 5, Jeb Alexander and Donald Vining, are, I argue, artists manqués.

American gay autobiographies (in my sense) written before the 1970s. So in order to talk about the self-presentation of gay Americans in the first half of the
century I have turned to my two diarists. Jeb Alexander's diary, treating the years
from 1912 to 1964, was edited and published by his niece in 1993. Donald Vining's
diary, from 1933 to 1982, was published in a reduced form by the author himself
in five volumes between 1979 and 1993.

My second concern was to find autobiographers from more than one country. I didn't begin with any preconceptions about which countries, except that I
wanted to end with the Americans. As it happened, the British and French autobiographers urged themselves on me because they so ideally met my criteria of selection: I quickly found a substantial number of accounts by artists and intellectuals,
often quite eminent, focused on their sexual experience and identity. I was surprised that no obvious German candidates came to light, given the extravagant
gay life for which Germany became famous during Weimar and which attracted
a number of Englishmen—among them W. H. Auden, Christopher Isherwood,
and Stephen Spender—to pursue their sexual liberation in Germany. There are,
of course, gay autobiographies by writers of other nationalities—the Australian
Patrick White's *Flaws in the Glass*, the Cuban Reinaldo Arenas's *Before Night
Falls*, for example—but the concentration of British and French texts gave me
the sort of national range I wanted to complement the chronological range.

Although my autobiographers are all intellectuals and artists, that does not
mean I am primarily interested in the more high-minded aspects of their stories—how they conceive of their identity, what kind of politics follow from their
erotic circumstances, the significance of being gay for their work. These and
other such questions will be attended to, but I am, if anything, even more interested in just exactly what they tell us about their sexual lives: what they did in
bed, what they wanted to do, what they didn't want to do. David Halperin says
somewhere, "There is no orgasm without ideology." I know what he means and
even agree, up to a point: every sexual act has an imaginative dimension; it exists
in the mind as well as the flesh, and thus it engages our socially constructed ideas
about gender, desire, the self, and even politics, broadly construed. But sex is
never just ideological; it is also a rudely physical, indeed animal, need for the
pleasure we get doing particular things with particular parts of our bodies. This
is as true for intellectuals as it is for anyone else. Sex is an often humbling experience for intellectuals precisely because it reminds them, so unconditionally, of the
extent to which they are not pure Geist. In fact much of the interest in sexual

autobiographies written by intellectuals lies in the author's awareness of the tension between the brute demands of his body and the ethereal aspirations of his thought. So I have studied my autobiographers with a sharp eye to the way they describe their sexual practices and fantasies. Sometimes I even grow impatient with them (Stephen Spender and Julien Green come to mind) when they seem unnecessarily coy or deceptive about what they were up to, although I hope I make proper allowance for the historical constraints under which they wrote.

WHEN I BEGAN WORK on this book I had no hypothesis about what general story it might tell—what overarching pattern it might reveal. And in the end no such story has emerged, or, if one exists, I have failed to detect it. But even though I propose no hypothesis, I have reached a conclusion. More than anything else, I have been impressed by the extraordinary differences in the lives led by my gay autobiographers and in the stories they tell about those lives. They differ, often widely, in their sexual behavior, their desires, the meaning they attribute to their predicament, the happiness or misery it brings them, and the implications they draw from it for the rest of their experience. The differences are so radical that I sometimes wonder whether it makes any sense to speak of "gay autobiography" as an identifiable literary phenomenon, or whether, by implication, there is such a thing as a "gay life," even within the restricted confines of the past century and in the three countries I look at. Not surprisingly, the further back one goes, the greater the distance from the lives (and stories) of gay men today. In fact I hope one of the uses of this book will be to expose the provincialism of our current notions about what a gay life is or should be. The autobiographical record shows that in other times and other places homosexuals have often done quite different things and entertained different ideas about the meaning of their orientation. Nor have they necessarily been unhappy with their fate, as we perhaps too smugly assume with our enlightened views about coming out.

Admittedly, if one stands back far enough and considers the broadest trajectory, the story, as revealed in the autobiographical record, is a progressive one. I would not deny that the earliest autobiographies show us lives hemmed in by prejudice, often limited in their erotic choices and actions, sometimes burdened with guilt, while, as we move closer to the present, gay men seem to get more accomplished sexually and to feel better about it. There is some truth, in other words, in the Whig interpretation of the modern gay experience, and I, for one, am happy to be living at the end of the twentieth century rather than at the previous fin-de-siècle or anywhere in between. But the autobiographies examined here suggest that the progress toward self-affirmation has been neither smooth nor inexorable. I have been surprised to find that the older autobiographers sometimes had the more reasonable sex lives and tell their stories with less embarrassment. André Gide, although born three decades before his fellow novelist Julien Green, had more fun and felt less guilty about it than did the younger man. Green published his autobiography in the 1960s and 1970s, yet he is not nearly so forthcoming about his sexual life as either of his French predecessors—Gide, whose autobiography appeared in 1920–21, and Jean Genet, who published *Journal du voleur* in 1948. History also seems to be running backwards when we compare the pre–1950s entries in Donald Vining's diary with the story Martin Duberman tells, in *Cures* (1991), about his life in the 1950s and 1960s: both men had lots of sex, but Vining (who was born in 1917, thirteen years before Duberman) enjoyed himself thoroughly, while Duberman suffered through two of the most miserable decades imaginable, as he went from one psychoanalyst to another trying to get changed into a heterosexual. The same "backwardness" is evident, if less spectacularly, in the accounts of my first two autobiographers, John Addington Symonds (b. 1840) and Goldsworthy Lowes Dickinson (b. 1862): Symonds had by far the fuller homosexual life.

Although my book has no master narrative, I have paid attention, in all the autobiographies I analyze, to three issues that have been much on the gay mind of late. They might be called "identity," "masculinity," and "solidarity." To the extent the texts allow, I have taken the temperature of my authors in terms of how they conceive of their sexual selves, what those conceptions imply for their position on the gender continuum, and the degree to which they embrace, or reject, other men who share their tastes. On all three questions, once again, I have been struck by the range of views expressed by these fourteen men.

In recent years discussions of gay identity have been dominated by the controversy between "social constructionists" and "essentialists." The debate has been rich and complex, but, simply put, essentialists hold that homosexuality is a transhistorical phenomenon, deeply embedded in the structure of the self, indeed probably grounded in biology, while constructionists hold that it is a contingent identity, invented in the past century. (David Halperin's authoritative defense of the constructionist position is entitled, aptly, *One Hundred Years of Homosexuality*.) The argument is not about behavior but about self-conceptions. Essentialists imply that men who regularly have sex with other men have always thought of themselves as gay—as persons defined by a certain kind of desire, although, of course, they have used different words or perhaps no words at all to describe themselves. Constructionists, on the other hand, draw a sharp distinction between acts and identities. They argue that, while same-sex acts have always occurred, men and women have come to think of themselves as homosexual persons only since the late nineteenth century. The writings of psychiatric authorities like Richard von Krafft-Ebing, Havelock Ellis, and Sigmund Freud are usually assigned a central role in the "invention" of homosexuality in the modern sense.

At a somewhat less theoretical level, the essentialist-constructionist debate had played itself out in terms of opposing ideas about the role of volition and fate in homosexual lives. The constructionists protest that this reduction of the controversy to a question of free will versus determinism distorts their views: their argument is meant to describe a cultural process; it is not a statement about psychology or philosophy. But their protests have been in vain. Constructionism has been taken to imply that sexual identity is malleable and therefore that individuals can, in some sense, choose to be homosexual or heterosexual (or both). Essentialists of course insists that sexual identity is profound, enduring, and inalterable. They also believe that the essentialist doctrine is politically superior: it makes prejudice against homosexuals seem to condemn people for what they are rather than what they do. Surveys show that the public is inclined to be more tolerant if it believes homosexuality is a state of being rather than a choice; conversely, conservatives, like former Vice President Dan Quayle, often insist that homosexuality is in fact "a lifestyle choice."[3] But constructionists are unwilling to cede the political high ground: they maintain that their position is the genuinely radical one, because it implies that gays need not apologize for themselves by appealing to an inalterable destiny (whether caused by genes or early conditioning). Rather, they should be proud to affirm the lives they have chosen.[4]

Of course only the most recent of my autobiographers, Martin Duberman and Paul Monette, are alert to the essentialist-constructionist debate. But, with

3. During the 1992 presidential campaign Quayle said (in his inimitable way), "My viewpoint is that it's more of a choice than a biological situation. . . . I think it is a wrong choice." *New York Times*, September 14, 1992, p. A17.

4. The historian John D'Emilio, very much a constructionist, makes the radical argument in his 1983 essay "Capitalism and Gay Identity":

> *There are more of us* than one hundred years ago, more of us than forty years ago. And there may very well be more gay men and lesbians in the future. Claims made by gays and nongays that sexual orientation is fixed at an early age, that large numbers of visible gay men and lesbians in society, the media, and the schools will

varying degrees of explicitness, the earlier authors reveal whether they consider their sexuality innate or chosen, and, wherever possible, I have tried to measure their views on this hotly contested issue. The majority of them are what might be called "natural essentialists": they speak of their desires as deep, lasting, and unchangeable. Stronger yet, they occasionally speak of them as something they would gladly be rid of but regret that it is not within their power. Even gay men like Duberman or Monette who try to convert to heterosexuality are apt to be pessimistic about their chances. Still, two of my autobiographers, Stephen Spender and Jean Genet, might be invoked for the constructionist cause. Spender officially gave up on homosexuality in the mid-1930s, when he decided to marry and (later) raise a family, and in *World within World* he mounts a case for the superiority of the heterosexual choice. Genet, for his part, makes the proposition that he "chose" to be a homosexual (just as he chose to be thief) the intellectual centerpiece of *Journal du voleur.*

The other issues I have watched for, "masculinity" and "solidarity," are not always easy to disentangle. In one form or another all my autobiographers wonder whether being homosexual compromises their manliness. They stake out a wide range of opinions. In chapter 3 I have paired the autobiographies of J. R. Ackerley and Quentin Crisp, both published in 1968, mainly because Ackerley and Crisp occupy such extreme positions on just this question. Ackerley presents himself as an entirely masculine (and thus invisible) homosexual, while Crisp makes a display of his effeminacy, raising it to the level of principle and even denying that figures like Ackerley are really homosexuals at all. Most of the other autobiographers, especially the earlier ones, take the "masculinist" position, if not so vehemently as Ackerley. André Gide is typical: his autobiography shows him as a normal child, rambunctious and athletic, who in no way gave up his claim to manliness when he later went to North Africa to chase after native boys. In fact, Gide got married (to the woman he had been in love with, he contends, since they were children), and he drew a sharp distinction between his emotional

---

have no influence on the sexual identities of the young, are wrong. Capitalism has created the material conditions for homosexual desire to express itself as a central component of some individuals' lives; now, our political movements are changing consciousness, creating the ideological conditions that make it easier for people to make that choice.

Reprinted in *The Lesbian and Gay Studies Reader,* ed. Henry Abelove, Michèle Aina Barale, and David M. Halperin (New York, 1993), pp. 473–74. D'Emilio's references to the influence of the media and the schools, as well as his final mention of "choice," make explicit the voluntarist implications of the constructionist stance.

attachment to women and his purely physical interest in men. Some of the more recent autobiographers, notably Andrew Tobias and Martin Duberman, entertain the same masculine self-image, but, in keeping with the shifting ideological winds, they are more politic about asserting it and are usually careful not to malign their fellow gays who happen to be effeminate. Here we sense how the issues of masculinity and solidarity intersect with one another.

A substantial number (but still a minority) of my autobiographers are more tractable about effeminacy, their own and others'. Goldsworthy Lowes Dickinson, for example, speaks candidly of his sexual femininity, even while insisting on his psychic masculinity. Likewise, Stephen Spender and Christopher Isherwood are less anxious than either Symonds or Gide about maintaining a butch image, although Isherwood had to grow into this more flexible view. The most intriguing case is Jean Genet, who, like Quentin Crisp, makes a great show of his youthful femininity, including his desire to be sodomized, but who also pretends to have undergone a process of "virilization" in later years. If I had to generalize, I would say that the historical trend is toward greater suppleness on the gender question, but with a masculine bias lingering throughout.

The issue can also be measured in terms of erotic choice, as opposed to self-image: the qualities these writers looked for in the men they pursued. J. R. Ackerley again stakes out the extreme position: any sign of effeminacy was a turn-off; he had no sexual tolerance for "pouffs" and "queans," even though they might be his ideological allies. Martin Duberman and Andrew Tobias share the same erotic prejudice. But in other autobiographies we sometimes find a tension between the author's own intense masculinity and the femininity of the men they wanted: both John Addington Symonds and André Gide, though male-identified themselves, preferred young adolescents—"ephebes," in Symonds's term— whom they considered at least implicitly feminine, certainly passive. In Quentin Crisp we find the reverse pattern: his own effeminacy meant that the men in his life had to be masculine, even heterosexual. The remaining autobiographers share a masculine bias, but they tend to be more relaxed and undogmatic about the issue. Again I am impressed by the wide range of views we encounter.

"Solidarity"—my third theme—is not just a question of sexual politics. It begins at the level of self-image: the degree to which these men suffer from what has come to be called "internalized homophobia." In each of the autobiographers I have been on the lookout for evidence of self-contempt and have sometimes inferred it from their critical remarks about other homosexuals. A degree of internalized homophobia is present in all the books, but it varies, often greatly, from individual to individual. In the coming-out autobiographies written by Americans in the recent past, transcending self-hatred is a major theme, as it is in Isherwood's *Christopher and His Kind* (1976), which, significantly, appeared thirty-seven years after Isherwood emigrated to the United States. The older autobiographers tend to suffer more from the disorder, though, as always, generalizations are hazardous: one can't imagine fiercer self-loathing than Martin Duberman endured in the 1950s and 1960s, while Donald Vining, in the preceding two decades, was a paragon of self-esteem.

The very act of writing a gay autobiography implies a degree of identification with one's fellow homosexuals. At some level it is a political act. I argue that this sort of implicit solidarity inspired the *Memoirs* of John Addington Symonds and the diary of Jeb Alexander: both men, I believe, recorded their erotic travails (in the late nineteenth and early twentieth centuries) with a notion of benefiting homosexuals in the future, when the documents would finally be published. At the other end of the historical record, the ideal of gay solidarity is the express goal to which the coming-out narratives of Christopher Isherwood, Martin Duberman, and Paul Monette are dedicated: they all move in the direction of identity politics.

Many of my autobiographers, however, betray contradictory impulses: they might intend their stories as a call to arms, but they often draw sharp lines between their own legitimate brand of homosexuality and the disreputable brand of others. Gide is the most striking example. His autobiography, *Si le grain ne meurt,* was written to complement his theoretical defense of homosexuality in *Corydon,* yet he excludes the more extravagant and effeminate homosexuals, notably Oscar Wilde, from his apology. In their diaries Jeb Alexander and Donald Vining sometimes make similarly invidious distinctions—between their own restrained behavior and the excesses of "the gay world" (in Vining's phrase) or "all that queer stuff" (in Alexander's). For his part, Quentin Crisp, although intensely political in the 1930s, eventually abandoned politics for entertainment, and in any case his sense of identification was limited to his fellow "bitches." Julien Green's attitude toward homosexuality—his own and others'—is so hostile that it precludes any feeling of gay solidarity, except that implied by his decision to write an account of his sexual life. There is another kind of opposition in J. R. Ackerley: he distinguishes between the masculine (often straight) men he desired and the more various homosexuals with whom he socialized and felt a political bond;

indeed, he was so worried the two worlds might contaminate one another that he took great precautions to keep them apart. As usual, the most contradictory politics are found in Jean Genet's *Journal du voleur,* which at once celebrates Genet's deep sense of union with his fellow queers, including the most abject and feminized among them, and shows him gleefully rolling bourgeois homosexuals in Antwerp.

The organization of the book—which begins with six British autobiographers, followed by three Frenchman, and concluding with five Americans—implies that I have also been concerned with a further question: whether there are national differences in the stories gay men tell about their lives. Fourteen cases are hardly the sort of sample to justify bold generalizations about national character. But I have nonetheless probed the autobiographies for what they suggest about British, French, and American ways of being homosexual. And, in the event, several patterns have emerged.

The British stories typically involve a sexual fascination with the lower classes. I am hardly the first to notice the phenomenon: it has become a commonplace in discussions of British homosexuality. Nonetheless it is clearly evident in four of my six British autobiographies, ranging from John Addington Symonds's infatuation with lower-class choristers to Christopher Isherwood's satirical account of lusting after proletarian teenagers in Berlin. The phenomenon reflects the intense class-consciousness of British society, where everyone seems to be acutely aware of the fine gradations of hierarchy and of his or her exact place in the scheme. Even the two British autobiographers who don't go in for cross-class romances, Goldsworthy Lowes Dickinson and Quentin Crisp, are attuned to social distinctions. In Crisp's story, for example, all the sex takes place among fellow down-and-outers, but Crisp is perfectly conscious that he himself is really middle class and a bohemian only by courtesy.

I focus on two distinct proclivities among the French autobiographers. The first is their weakness for abstraction: they tend to put their stories through a philosophical wringer. Unlike the British and the Americans, they are not satisfied simply to *be* homosexual; they have to rationalize their preference in terms of some grand metaphysical scheme, whether it be Gide's dualism of body and soul (the former homosexual, the latter heterosexual), Genet's existential doctrine of radical transgressive freedom, or the theological tug-of-war between God and the Devil that Green uses to organize his narrative in *Jeunes années.* The other striking feature of the French texts is the erotic importance they assign to national and ethnic difference. All of my French autobiographers went abroad to find their quarry: Gide to Tunisia and Algeria, Genet to Spain and Eastern Europe, Green to Italy, Germany, and (most improbably) the American South, where he spent three crucial years in his sexual education as an undergraduate at the University of Virginia. One is tempted to see in this association between desire and otherness a kind of sexual variant on the phenomenon Edward Said has called "orientalism": the world outside France is treated as a kind of erotic colony. National difference, we might speculate, plays a role in the French autobiographies similar to class difference in the British autobiographies.

In contrast to the British and French cases, the three American autobiographies (though not the two diaries) are organized as coming-out stories: they end in the author's decision to make a (more or less) public declaration of his homosexuality. In this regard they are entirely typical of the flood of American gay autobiographies written in the last decade. They invite comparison with the conversion narratives that figure so prominently in the Western cultural tradition, from St. Augustine to Malcolm X: the old closeted man gives way to the proudly reborn gay. There is a curious purity of spirit about these American tales, which have little tolerance for the ambiguity and compromise Europeans seem able to live with. Americans, one might say, are fundamentalists even in their perversity.

I must repeat that my sample is not broad enough to consider these generalizations any more than suggestive. The patterns I have identified are not even exclusive national possessions in the fourteen writers I treat. The link between homosexual desire and national difference, for example, can also be found in some of the British stories, most obviously in Isherwood's and Spender's erotic forays to Germany but also in John Addington Symonds's decision, after his marriage, to pursue his bliss among Swiss peasants and Venetian gondoliers. Likewise, Martin Duberman might be considered an honorary Englishman in view of his obsessive cultivation of lower-class young men, often hustlers. And Christopher Isherwood became a spiritual American, at least from an autobiographical perspective: *Christopher and His Kind*, composed in Los Angeles in the 1970s, is a celebration of the "tribe" of homosexuals; it is as much a coming-out narrative as Andrew Tobias's *The Best Little Boy in the World*, Martin Duberman's *Cures*, or Paul Monette's *Becoming a Man*.

∞ SOME FINAL PRELIMINARY THOUGHTS. I have often been asked if my study would include women. At first I thought it would. In fact I spent much of the summer of 1995 reading lesbian autobiographies, in particular Violette Leduc's *La Bâtarde* (1964), Kate Millett's *Flying* (1974), Audre Lorde's *Zami* (1982), Jill Johnston's *Mother Bound* (1983) and *Paper Daughter* (1985), and, among more recent works, Margarethe Cammermeyer's *Serving in Silence* (1994) and Meredith Maran's *What It's Like to Live Now* (1995). I've since read others: Rosemary Manning's *A Time and a Time* (1971) and *A Corridor of Mirrors* (1987) (the second more exclusively lesbian than the first), Linda Niemann's *Boomer* (1990), Mab Segrest's *Memoirs of a Race Traitor* (1994), Kim Chernin's *My Life as a Boy* (1997), and Claudia Bepko's *The Heart's Progress* (1997). Clearly someone ought to write a book about lesbian autobiography, and even a comparison of the men's and women's stories would be illuminating.

But in the end I decided to limit myself to the men. At a practical level I began to see that I had more than enough book on my hands already. The more serious inhibition was that the lesbian stories seemed so utterly unlike their gay male counterparts as to belong to an alien universe. The most remarkable difference was the greater sexual fluidity of the women's narratives. In the male autobiographies homosexual desire announces itself early and unambiguously: the compulsion is first felt at adolescence or before, and, with rare exceptions (whose good faith I am inclined to doubt), it stays fixed. In the female autobiographies, by contrast, attraction to other women often begins later and it doesn't necessarily put an end to the author's heterosexual life. In many cases a sense of emotional and political bonding with women is as important as sexual intimacy, lending support to Adrienne Rich's notion of a "lesbian continuum" embracing all "woman-identified women."[5] The two patterns conform to the most striking difference Alfred Kinsey found in the erotic development of men and women: in men, according to Kinsey, sexuality explodes at adolescence, reaches a peak before eighteen, after which it gradually declines, whereas women's sexuality emerges more gradually, arrives at a kind of plateau in the late twenties, and remains there well into middle age. Of course the female pattern may be as much socially determined as biological. Likewise, the fact that all the lesbian autobiographers I've read, except Rosemary Manning and Mab Segrest, got married and the majority of them had children may also reflect social pressures, as Adrienne Rich has again suggested. There are two further intriguing differences. The lesbian autobiographers are romantics, far less willing than the men to separate sex

---

5. Adrienne Rich, "Compulsory Heterosexuality and Lesbian Existence" (1980), in *The Lesbian and Gay Studies Reader*, pp. 227–54; Audre Lorde, *Zami* (New York, 1982), p. 225.

from emotion. Neither are they so sexually preoccupied with youth: the men are much fiercer "ageists."

Kate Millett's *Flying* is characteristic. Even when, in her thirties, Millett got involved with a number of women, she continued to be attached to her husband, both emotionally and sexually. (Her lesbian initiation took place as a college senior, but there had been no women in her life during the first eight years of her marriage.) From the book's often candid descriptions we sense that her attraction to women was more emphatic ("bisexuality" would imply greater evenhandedness), but it was not exclusive in the way known to gay men. A related pattern can be found in Violette Leduc's *La Bâtarde*. Leduc's lesbianism manifested itself earlier than usual—in splendidly recreated scenes from girls' boarding school—but her adult life was dominated by involvements with men, most of them homosexual, including Maurice Sachs and Jean Genet—although she also fell in love with Simone de Beauvoir. Lesbian autobiography, I am inclined to say, belongs to a different order of things. In terms of the current theoretical wars, if gay men are natural essentialists, lesbians are natural constructionists.[6]

I was also inhibited, frankly, by my sense of the indelicacy, or, better, inappropriateness, of a man's pronouncing on the intimate lives of women, especially women sexually attracted to other women. As will become evident, I have felt free to complain about the behavior, sexual and otherwise, of my gay male authors without a sense of undue presumption. But I didn't think I could bring the same critical spirit to bear on lesbians. In effect, I am the victim (or the beneficiary) of the kind of restraint that identity politics has taught us to exercise when speaking about the experience of people different from ourselves, especially when the difference involves race, gender, or sexual orientation.

I also need to say something about the relation of my study to the scholarly literature on autobiography, which has grown enormously in recent years. This scholarship has mostly been the work of literary critics. Its master question has been how to define autobiography as a literary genre, above all how to distinguish it from the novel. At one end of the spectrum Georges Gusdorf argues that there is no categorical difference between autobiography and fiction. Both in-

---

6. The formula is a deliberate overstatement. Of the lesbian autobiographers I've read, Margarethe Cammermeyer and Claudia Bepko speak in essentialist language. The following, from Cammermeyer, is typical: "Some unchangeable part of myself felt that sex with a man was an invasion and I resented it. Over fifteen years of marriage, those feelings only got stronger. At the age of forty-six, I finally had to face that fact that being straight wasn't a choice I had." *Serving in Silence* (New York, 1994), p. 219.

volve a selection of incidents, and both receive their overarching shape from the author's imagination: autobiography, in this view, is as much about self-creation as self-reporting. At the opposite extreme Philippe Lejeune (who has built an entire career writing about the genre) holds that autobiography is separated from fiction by the author's sincere effort to give an accurate account of his or her experience.[7]

In a sense I can't enter into this debate impartially, because I have chosen my autobiographers on the basis of a presumed fact about their "real lives," namely, that they were homosexual. Almost by definition, I am on Lejeune's side of the argument. Nonetheless I have paid attention to the literary strategies at work in the texts I write about, especially when I think they raise doubts about the author's reliability. An obvious example is the three coming-out narratives treated in the last chapter, where I argue that the structural imperatives of the form result in certain distortions, above all a tendency to paint a blacker picture of the closet years than seems warranted. I also make an effort to show how an autobiographer's tone of voice can have a decisive effect on the story he tells, especially when the tone is ironic or humorous. Thus I suggest that Christopher Isherwood's self-satirizing in *Christopher and His Kind,* Quentin Crisp's stand-up routine in *The Naked Civil Servant,* and Andrew Tobias's nonstop slapstick in *The Best Little Boy in the World* pose hazards for the unwary reader. In other words, I have tried to keep formal issues in mind. But they have not been my main concern. This is a historian's book, not a literary critic's.[8]

I have sometimes been urged to begin with an account of my own gay his-

---

7. Georges Gusdorf, "Conditions and Limits of Autobiography" (1956), in *Autobiography: Essays Theoretical and Critical,* ed. James Olney (Princeton, 1980), pp. 28–48. Philippe Lejeune, *On Autobiography,* trans. Katherine Leary (Minneapolis, 1989).

8. One of my surprising discoveries was how seldom gay autobiographies reveal evidence of what literary critics call "intertexuality": the influence of one text on another. In Harold Bloom's version of the idea, "the anxiety of influence," Bloom argues that literary works are typically written in an "agonistic" effort to overcome, even defeat, their significant predecessors (thus Wordsworth's *The Prelude* is a reworking and cancellation of Milton's *Paradise Lost*). Gay autobiographers write as if they never read the autobiographies of their sexual forebears. In part, I suspect, their apparent ignorance stems from the sense that autobiography is, we might say, "self-authorizing": because it is the story of one's own life, there is no need to look over one's literary shoulder to compare it with the stories told by other gay men.

A striking illustration of this absence of intertextual influence is Julien Green's *Jeunes années.* Green was a friend of André Gide's. Yet nowhere in *Jeunes années* does Green even mention Gide's autobiography, *Si le grain ne meurt,* though he speaks (critically) of Gide's homophile tract *Corydon.* The only exceptions to the rule are Christopher Isherwood and Stephen Spender. As close lifelong friends, they not only read each other's autobiographies but even quote (and correct) their respective versions of events in which both were involved.

tory—the idea being that in a study of this kind the author ought to put his sexual cards on the table. It is the erotic version, I suppose, of Max Weber's injunction that the scholar be candid about his values. I have resisted the advice, partly for literary reasons, but more because I am allergic to the self-advertising that such a gesture would entail. Still, I recognize that writing a book about autobiography is, at some level, an autobiographical exercise: one is always conducting a kind of mental comparison between the authors' stories and one's own.

Almost in spite of myself, I have found a solution to my dilemma by insinuating some of my personal story into the final chapter, which treats the autobiographies of Andrew Tobias, Martin Duberman, and Paul Monette. These men, I found, were part of my life in a way not true of the others. They are close to me in age as well as being fellow American intellectuals. Andrew Tobias's *The Best Little Boy in the World* was the first gay autobiography I read, and, in my discussion of the book, I talk about the difference between my reaction to it back in the 1970s and my reaction today. Martin Duberman was my teacher as an undergraduate at Yale, and we have been in touch, off and on, over the years since. In writing about *Cures* I make several comparisons between Duberman's gay life and my own, especially regarding our very different experience of the closet. I did not know Paul Monette, though he was a friend of my Stanford colleague Marjorie Perloff, and through Marjorie I corresponded with him briefly. But as a novelist living in Southern California, one whose work I began reading in the 1970s, he has been a figure in my imagination for many years, and in the discussion of *Becoming a Man* I again make some of my implicit mental comparisons explicit. I hope these interventions are modest enough not to undermine the book's generally disinterested tone.

In effect, I have settled on a compromise between discretion and full disclosure. My own proper autobiography will have to await another day. In what follows the attention will be on the remarkably varied lives of these fourteen men who have told their stories over the course of the past century.

1

THE MAN OF LETTERS
AND THE DON

John Addington Symonds

and

Goldsworthy Lowes

Dickinson

I WANT TO BEGIN with two English autobiographies that give us some purchase on the nineteenth century, as a point of reference for the otherwise almost exclusively twentieth-century stories with which this book is concerned. John Addington Symonds (1840–1893) describes homosexual experiences that date from the 1860s to the early 1890s, while Goldsworthy Lowes Dickinson (1862–1932) focuses on the three decades before the First World War. André Gide's autobiography, *Si le grain ne meurt*—which culminates in Gide's sexual initiation in the 1890s—is the only other document that takes us outside the confines of our own century. Neither Symonds's nor Dickinson's autobiography was published in the author's lifetime; Dickinson's did not appear until the 1970s, Symonds's until the 1980s.

As one might expect, both Symonds and Dickinson recount homosexual lives pursued under highly unfavorable conditions. Those conditions, moreover, were often self-imposed and not merely the result of the legal prohibitions and social disapproval to which homosexuality was then subject. Their stories, accordingly, have a very different texture from the stories of the four English autobiographers examined in chapters 2 and 3—Christopher Isherwood, Stephen Spender, J. R. Ackerley, and Quentin Crisp—men who were born around or after the turn of the century and thus launched their homosexual careers under less oppressive circumstances in the 1920s and 1930s. Symonds's and Dickinson's lives were dominated by agonizing compromises, as they tried to reconcile their desires with the values of their society, values they often shared. Both suffered from internalized repressions that were only gradually and imperfectly overcome. Yet, in their different ways, both also managed to achieve an accommodation with their sexual condition, even a degree of contentment.

The sexual histories they recount take an essentially romantic form, which distinguishes them from their successors in the twentieth century. Both men tell their story in terms of a sequence of great loves, of profound attachments that often lasted for years but seldom achieved full erotic expression. Of the two, Symonds, although twenty-two years older than Dickinson, actually made more sexual progress. But Dickinson's loves had a greater psychological intensity, and his account of them is more affecting, perhaps because he had to be satisfied with largely emotional and one-sided relationships. Both men were autobiographical pioneers: they command our attention—and our respect—less for the lives they led than for their extraordinary decision to leave an account of their often painful sexual odyssey.

John Addington Symonds soon after his marriage in 1864.
By permission of the University of Bristol Librarian.

The Memoirs of John Addington Symonds

OHN ADDINGTON SYMONDS may have been the first homosexual to write an autobiography focused on his erotic life. Symonds was an eminent Victorian. When he penned his *Memoirs* in 1889–90 he ranked among England's foremost men of letters. He was the author of numerous books, including a seven-volume study of the Italian Renaissance as well as two of the earliest homophile pamphlets, *A Problem in Greek Ethics* and *A Problem in Modern Ethics*. Although, as noted, the autobiography remained unpublished in his lifetime, he made arrangements for it to be issued when it would no longer be "injurious to my family."[1] It is a remarkable work, at once deeply foreign to the experience of homosexuals today yet often anticipating the issues that have preoccupied gay autobiographers throughout the twentieth century.

Symonds's account of his life is informed by a number of tensions. The central tension, not surprisingly, is between his imperious sexual desires and the moral ideals of respectable society—ideals that, as the scion of a well-born professional family, he fully endorsed. He was heir to the staunch tradition of English Puritans—what Matthew Arnold, in *Culture and Anarchy*, called "Hebraism"—a tradition that had been both softened and enriched in the nineteenth century by a liberal cultivation of art and literature (Arnold's "Hellenism"). Symonds considered his father the perfect embodiment of this Victorian synthesis. From the Puritans came a particularly exigent ideal of moral self-discipline: "To

---

The Memoirs of John Addington Symonds (London, 1984) were edited by his biographer Phyllis Grosskurth, who cut about a fifth of the text, "confined mainly," she writes, "to Symonds's execrable poetry and to self-conscious nature descriptions quoted from his own letters" (p. 11).

1. Letter to H. F. Brown (December 29, 1891), appended to *The Memoirs of John Addington Symonds*, p. 289.

live purely and act uprightly, to follow honour, to postpone mundane and selfish interests to duty, to deal mercifully, sympathetically, tenderly, justly with his brother men, to be unsparing in condemnation of rebellious evil, painstaking and long-suffering with struggling good." From the liberalism of his own time came a tempering devotion "to culture, to art, to archaeology, to science, to literature." But whether Hebraic or Hellenic, Symonds's conception of personal development was relentless high-minded and thus incompatible with any indulgence of his homosexual passions, no matter how imperious. We will not do justice to the poignancy of his autobiography if we fail to recognize the powerful hold of this Victorian ideal on his thinking or to acknowledge that it was in many ways deeply admirable.

The central problem of Symonds's life was to negotiate an accommodation between his moral convictions and his erotic needs. It found expression, above all, in his effort to rationalize homosexuality in terms of two powerful—and related—nineteenth-century ideas, Hellenism and democracy. The Classical Greek culture so central to the Victorians' conception of themselves was, he argued, based on homoerotic relationships, notably between older men and adolescent boys. Symonds embraced this idea ecstatically when he read the *Phaedrus* and the *Symposium* at seventeen, and, as Linda Dowling has shown, it was richly amplified by the Victorian Hellenism he absorbed at Oxford. Thus, in theory at least, his wayward sexual desires, if properly realized, were the logical fulfillment of everything the nineteenth century held dear. At the same time, he portrayed homosexual relationships as transcending the boundaries of class in a Whitmanesque ideal of comradeship; they thereby contributed to a more perfect democracy. Both of these notions invested homosexuality with something of the dignity and spirituality of romantic love between men and women. But because they set such high standards they made the mundane task of having a reasonable sex life excruciatingly difficult for Symonds, as he himself came to recognize and, at least on occasion, regret. His autobiography tells the long and painful story of the gradual easing of those standards, as the claims of the body gradually made inroads on those of the mind.

Inevitably Symonds's story also engages the gender conceptions of his culture. Stefan Collini and others have shown that the Victorians subscribed to an unusually strenuous ideal of manliness. Symonds, as a good Victorian, was unwilling to forego his birthright to so precious a psychic commodity. "Morally and intellectually, in character and taste and habits," he writes, "I am more masculine than many men I know who adore women." Indeed, the ideal of manliness shaped his sexual desires, both whom he was attracted to and what he hoped to do with them: he was nearly always the sexual aggressor, and the men he desired were both younger than himself and socially beneath him. At the same time he recognized that homosexuality—even Hellenized homosexuality—could never be fully reconciled with the cult of manliness, and he seemed prepared to jettison at least some of its tenets. He was unembarrassed, for example, by his lack of physical vigor or athletic skill, both of which were central to the manly ideal. Even in the sexual realm there was a tension between his usual assertiveness and a desire to be possessed, perhaps overwhelmed. In his earliest fantasy he imagined himself "crouched upon the floor amid a company of naked adult men," whom he describes as "shaggy and brawny sailors, . . . such as I had seen about the streets of Bristol."

In Symonds's account of the sexual imaginings of his childhood these sailors are the only figures from the real world. Otherwise his erotic education appears to have been an entirely literary affair, setting the intellectual stage for the strenuous idealizations of his maturity. Shakespeare's "Venus and Adonis" supplied the first image of a type of adolescent that became his *idée fixe*. Later he read the *Iliad* and became obsessed with the description of Hermes disguised as a mortal, "like a young prince with the first down on his lip, the time when youth is the most charming." This figure of the ephebe inspired Symonds's early crushes, and it never lost its powerful sexual charm for him. But it had to complete with an image descended from the shaggy and brawny sailors of his childhood fantasies. "What I really wanted at this period," he confesses, "was some honest youth or comrade, a sailor or a groom or a labourer, who would have introduced me into the masculine existence for which I craved in a dim shrinking way," and he regrets that one of his father's footmen did not "take me into his bed."[2]

2. In the case history he prepared for Havelock Ellis's *Sexual Inversion*, Symonds describes two youthful sexual experiences that are suppressed in the *Memoirs:* "Between the age of 8 and 11 he twice took the penis of a cousin into his mouth in the morning, after they had slept together; the feeling of the penis pleased him." "He was in the habit of playing with five male cousins. . . . They sat round the room on chairs together, each with his penis exposed. The boy went round on his knees and took each penis into his mouth in turn. This was supposed to humiliate him."

The case history also provides a more graphic version of Symonds's "brawny sailor" daydream: "He fancied himself seated on the floor among several adult and naked sailors, whose genitals and buttocks he contemplated and handled with relish. He called himself the 'dirty pig' of these men, and felt that they were in some way his masters, ordering him to do uncleanly service to their bodies." *Sexual Inversion* [1897], Case 17, reprinted in *The Memoirs of John Addington Symonds*, appendix 1, pp. 284–88. Although the *Memoirs* were

∞ SYMONDS EXPERIENCED the full force of his predicament at school. In 1854, when he was thirteen, he was sent to Harrow. The reader of the *Memoirs* is not surprised to learn that he there encountered the institutionalized homosexuality for which English public schools were notorious. Yet he left Harrow four years later without having had a single sexual adventure. Already he was so completely in the grips of his idealized conception of same-sex love that the unsentimental couplings of his fellow students appalled him:

> One thing at Harrow very soon arrested my attention. It was the moral state of the school. Every boy of good looks had a female name, and was recognized either as a public prostitute or as some bigger fellow's 'bitch'. Bitch was the word in common usage to indicate a boy who yielded his person to a lover. The talk in the dormitories and the studies was incredibly obscene. Here and there one could not avoid seeing acts of onanism, mutual masturbation, the sports of naked boys in bed together. There was no refinement, no sentiment, no passion; nothing but animal lust in these occurrences. They filled me with disgust and loathing.

The disgust and loathing were not sustained without a struggle. The *Memoirs* also record his intense attraction to the displays of "animal lust" about him. He was "both fascinated and repelled" by a student who "resembled a handsome Greek brigand. . . . His body was powerful, muscular, lissome as a tiger. The fierce and cruel lust of this magnificent animal excited my imagination." In another narrow escape he had to summon the full rhetorical force of his moral vision—which to the contemporary gay man sounds suspiciously like internalized homophobia—to withstand the temptation:

> A very depraved lad, whom I had known for three years, on one occasion finding me alone in my room, suddenly dared to throw his arms round me, kissed me, and thrust his hand into my trousers. At that moment I nearly gave way to sensuality. I was narcotized by the fellow's contact and the forecast of coming pleasure. But in this, as in all other cases, the inclination for vulgar lust was wanting. That saved me from self-abasement and traffic with the unclean thing.

---

intended for publication only long after his death, Symonds clearly wished to maintain a certain decorousness even from the grave.

In these two boys Symonds saw not merely the dangerous physical reality of sex but also a threat to his precarious masculinity. To yield would betray both his ideals and his position as the subject, rather than the object, of desire.

The contradiction between Symonds's barely repressed passions and his romantic idealism came to a head in an episode known as "the Vaughan Affair." The headmaster of Harrow, Dr. Charles Vaughan, was courting one of Symonds's fellow students, a boy named Alfred Pretor, who showed Symonds Vaughan's love letters. After much agonizing, Symonds reported the matter to his father, who in turn confronted Vaughan and forced him to resign. Symonds's account of the episode in the *Memoirs* reveals a nice awareness of his own priggishness, while not entirely relinquishing the moral high ground. He submitted the matter, he writes, to "casuistical analysis." He was disgusted to find that "this species of vice," far from being confined to "a phase of boyish immaturity," could infect "a man holding the highest position of responsibility." But he also recognized that Vaughan had sinned "by yielding to passions which already mastered me." Indignation got the upper hand, he suggests, only because he still hoped "to overcome the malady of my own nature." But in hindsight his youthful idealism appears to him more than a little inhumane. He may have been inspired by a genuinely elevated conception of homosexual love, but that conception, he seems to appreciate, came at an exorbitant cost to himself as well as others.

Exactly how exorbitant is revealed in Symonds's account of his first *amour*, a Bristol chorister named Willie Dyer, whom he met in the spring of 1858 during his last term at Harrow. Willie was in some respects the quintessential ephebe: at fourteen he was three years younger than Symonds. His association with music also echoed the Platonic ideal. In fact, Symonds claims to have fallen in love with Willie's voice.

Symonds wrote Willie and arranged to meet. The sexual content of their relationship was established at once: "I took Willie's slender hand into my own and gazed into his large brown eyes fringed with heavy lashes." Over the course of the following months he saw or wrote Willie every day. But "more than a year elapsed before I dared to do more than touch his hand." What was it Symonds did after the year of hand-holding? Twice—and twice only—he kissed Willie. "Good heavens! What an uproar in the city of my soul those kisses wrought, as we lay together couched in ivy and white wood anemones upon the verge of the red rocks which dominated the Avon!" The uproar was an erection: he writes of "the tumult of my blood, the quickening of my heartbeats, and the rising of my flesh." But he also records that "these symptoms annoyed me; I strove to put them aside, and evaded the attempt to formulate their significance." So stringent was his idealism that it could barely manage a couple of kisses, and then only when their erotic significance was driven from consciousness. Inevitably our primary reaction to this story is astonishment at the sheer meagerness of it all. Yet Symonds continued to regard the relationship with Willie as the defining event of his life.

No less important than the sensual repression and romantic inflation of the affair was its class character, which set the pattern for Symonds's later relationships—indeed, one is tempted to say, for the history of British homosexuality in the modern era. Whether chorister or sailor, the beloved was nearly always a member of the lower orders. In contrast to the Greek model, where the beloved is, to be sure, younger but nonetheless a social equal, Symonds's inamorati tended to be workers or peasants. He justified this preference by appealing to the democratic ideal of comradeship: it made him an enemy of snobbery and a proponent of equality.

Nevertheless Symonds yielded to his father's plea to end the attachment with Willie Dyer. Moreover he did so not for sexual but for social reasons: his father persuaded him of the unseemliness of "an ardent friendship" between "a young man, gently born, bred at Harrow, advancing to the highest academical honours at Balliol" and "a Bristol chorister, the son of a Dissenting tailor." At the same time we are bound to wonder whether the very intensity of class consciousness in British society did not, by a complex unconscious process, result in the eroticization of class for homosexuals like Symonds. Social difference seems to have supplied something of the "otherness," the mystery, that sexual difference supplies for heterosexuals. If one were to take a polemical view of the matter, one could even argue that Symonds's infatuation with choristers, sailors, and peasants was merely a sexual variant of class exploitation. Far from being an expression of social solidarity, it is the old story of the rich having their way with the poor.

While Symonds was at Oxford Willie Dyer was succeeded in his affections by another chorister, Alfred Brooke. In one respect this new love marked a retreat—hard as that may be to imagine—from the sexual territory staked out with Willie: they did not even hold hands. But the Alfred who emerges in the *Memoirs* is a decidedly more physical creature than Willie. Symonds's imagination, it seems, was growing distinctly (and inexorably) sexual, even if his body hung back. No less revealing is the way Symonds's description of Alfred—which he quotes from a "prose dithyramb" written in 1865—descends from an ephebe-like head to an athletic lower torso reminiscent of the muscular sailors of his early dreams: "Light hair; bright purple-blue eyes; pale delicately flushed complexion; firm bold level gaze, square white forehead; large red humid mouth; vibrating voice; athletic throat and well-formed breast; broad hard hands; poise of trunk upon massive hips; thick and sinewy thighs; prominent and lusty testicles; brawny calves; strong well-planted feet." Alfred is less seen than imagined, but Symonds insists that the young man knew exactly what was happening and was in fact just as "lascivious" as Symonds himself. He took Alfred on midnight drives and gave him money. Yet Symonds remained sexually paralyzed, much to the boy's contempt. In the *Memoirs* he upbraids himself for his timidity. He blames his failure not only on his "dread of the world's opinion" (especially in view of his role in the Vaughan affair) but, with withering insight, on his over-wrought "ideal of purity in conduct." He was the victim as much of his own conceptions as of society's hostility.

IN 1864 SYMONDS TRIED TO ESCAPE his predicament by marrying. He was inspired to this unhappy decision by contradictory motives. His first notion was that, with enough effort, he could redirect his desires from men to women. As he puts it, "I firmly expected that some extraordinary and ecstatic enthusiasm would awake in me at the mere contact of a woman's body in bed." He tried assiduously to cultivate such a passion for a Swiss girl named Rosa Engel, but his feelings for her remained categorically less intense, less "tyrannous" (to use one of his own favorite words), than they were for Willie or Alfred or the "visionary beings in male forms of beauty" that filled his imagination. This failure became an important source of the conviction that his homosexuality was congenital. The doctrine of the congenital nature of homosexuality was to form the cornerstone of *Sexual Inversion,* written with Havelock Ellis and published after Symonds's death as the first volume of Ellis's monumental *Studies in the Psychology of Sex.* In this matter Symonds anticipated the experience of most modern gay autobiographers, who, with few exceptions, have viewed their sexual orientation as a deep, enduring, and inalterable condition. Symonds, one might say, was the original essentialist.

At the same time, he persuaded himself—or allowed himself to be persuaded—that marriage need have nothing to do with intense sexual feelings. Rather it was a social institution. Or, to the extent that it was a sexual relationship, it provided a purely mechanical outlet, a reliable and convenient means of erotic release. Symonds's physician, Sir Spencer Wells, advanced this singularly unromantic conception: "He impressed upon me the theory that marriage ought not to be regarded as a matter of idealized passion, but as the sober meeting together of man and woman for mutual needs of sex, for fellow service, and loyal devotion to the duties of social and domestic life in common."

Armed with this doctrine—and the masculinist prejudices he shared with his heterosexual contemporaries—Symonds married Catherine North, a woman of his own class and three years his senior. Despite a catastrophic wedding night—it was, he notes, his first sexual act with anyone—he found himself quite capable of functioning sexually according to Dr. Wells's minimalist formula: "The organ of sex was vigorous enough and ready to perform its work." Catherine gave birth to four daughters—three of them in relatively short order—to whom Symonds was a doting father. But while intercourse brought relief from tension, it was, from the start, a joyless experience.

Symonds coped with the sexual failure of his marriage through various practical and intellectual strategies, which inevitably sound as if they were devised to soothe his conscience. First, he tried to convince himself that Catherine liked sex even less than he did. So great was her aversion to pregnancy, he writes, that she developed "a strong feeling of repugnance for the marriage bed." The *Memoirs* also insist that as the sexual relationship ended, he and Catherine grew closer emotionally: she became his confidante as she ceased to be his lover. When, after four years of marriage, he took up with another young man—Norman Moor—Symonds made Catherine party to the affair. "I had a long talk with my wife. The points were these: our common wish to beget no more children, chiefly for her sake; the consequent difficulty of my position; my increase in health since I knew Norman, [and] the uncontrollable bias of my nature in this direction." He gives contradictory accounts of Catherine's reaction. On the one hand, he quotes from his diary at the time to suggest that she accepted the arrangement: "She comprehends the situation, and understands me completely about Norman." On the other—and to his credit—he concedes that it hurt her deeply: "She could not help being jealous of Norman, especially when she found some letters written by me to him in strains of passion I had never used to her." He recognized in effect that his homosexuality did not excuse treating another human being so shabbily. But he remained divided between this recognition—that he was guilty of using Catherine—and his insistence that the marriage was, in some sense, a moral success.

During the first four years of the marriage Symonds was homosexually abstinent. But his repressed desires continued to assault his imagination in ever more vivid form. He began writing homoerotic poetry, which he describes in the *Memoirs* as "a kind of mental masturbation." He quotes from "a prose poem," whose high-flown language shouldn't prevent us from noticing that he was now contemplating a good deal more than hand-holding and chaste kisses:

> Golden hair, and white neck, and breast brighter than twin stars, and belly softer than the down of doves, and dewy thighs, and awful beauty of love's minister beneath the tuft of crispy curls, and slender swelling legs, and rosy feet, and long lithe languid arms. I had them all pressed to my body there, flank to flank—kissed every part and member of the lad—with wandering hand tasted them one by one, and felt the fervour of smooth buttocks glowing and divine.

At the same time he provided his imagination with ample stimulation. He took early-morning walks to Hyde Park, where he could "feed [his] eyes upon the naked men and boys bathing in the Serpentine," and he lingered over a "rude *graffito*" of two penises ejaculating, "'Prick to prick, so sweet'; with an emphatic diagram of phallic meeting, glued together, gushing." He also surmises, shrewdly, that his sexual experience in marriage, however unsatisfactory, contributed to the shift from "vague and morbid craving" to "a precise hunger after sexual pleasure."

When he could no longer confine his impulses to benign sublimations and voyeurism, Symonds renewed his homosexual life along two fronts, one sentimental the other frankly physical. The first was his affair with Norman Moor, whom Symonds considered the great love of his life. It represented a continuation of the sort of relationship he had enjoyed earlier with Willie Dyer and Alfred Brooke. Norman was a member of the sixth form at Clifton College who later went up to Oxford. He was thus less clearly a social inferior than either Willie or Alfred. But the fact that he was only seventeen when they met, and hence more than ten years younger than Symonds, strongly suggests that he belonged to the ephebe type. In the *Memoirs* he is described as having "the sort of face which seemed made to be cast in bronze."

Sexually the relationship with Norman was still relatively buttoned-down, although Symonds labored agonizingly to invest it with something of the physical concreteness of his fantasies during the preceding six years. "It was romantic, delicately sentimental," he writes, "but at the same time passionate and tinged with unmistakable sensuality." He adds immediately, "Nothing occurred between us which the censorious could rightly consider unworthy of two gentlemen." What this huffy assertion seems to mean is that their sexual repertory avoided the grosser embraces that would have led to orgasm. He quotes from his diary:

> I have had two perfect midnight hours with him. . . . We lay covered from the cold in bed, tasting the honey of softly spoken words and the blossoms of lips pressed on lips. . . . I stripped him naked, and fed sight, touch and mouth on these things. Will my lips ever forget their place upon his breast, or on the tender satin of his flank, or on the snowy whiteness of his belly? . . . Shy and modest, tender in the beauty-bloom of ladhood, is his part of sex *now longing for passion* [in Greek]—fragrant to the searching touch, yet shrinking: for when the wandering hand rests there, the lad turns pleadingly from my arms as though he sought to be relieved of some delicious pang. . . . How his head drooped on one shoulder, and how his arm lay curved along flank and thigh, and how upon the down of dawning manhood lay his fingers, and how the shrinking god was covered by his hand!

The contemporary reader is apt to be annoyed by Symonds's evasions and suspicious of his diction, which instead of naming body parts and physical acts envelops everything in saccharine and inflated circumlocutions. But Symonds deserves a certain historical indulgence—he was, inescapably, a creature of his time and culture—and, I would argue, some credit for struggling against his own inveterate idealizing to come to terms with the concrete and messy realities of sex. After all, he did manage to make a significant advance on his affairs with Willie and Alfred: he had gotten his lover into bed, naked, and was launched into what would later be called serious petting. Perhaps just as important, he was willing—again within his aestheticizing vocabulary—to record the scene in his diary and reproduce it in the *Memoirs*.

He also records his retrospective judgment that he had sabotaged the affair by his unwillingness to accept it for what it was. Instead of simply enjoying Norman, Symonds remained in the grips of his merciless abstractions, demanding more from the boy (and from himself) than either could deliver. Once again he had allowed his ambitious romanticism to interfere with his pleasure. But he appears to have taken the lesson to heart. "This episode," he concludes, "closed the period of idealism; and certain experiences which I shall relate in another chapter led me to seek a new solution upon lower and more practical lines of conduct."

The most important of these "lower and more practical lines"—and the second front along which Symonds's homosexual life advanced after his marriage—was male prostitution. He discovered this possibility when, in 1877, "an acquaintance of old standing asked me one day to go with him to a male brothel near the Regent's Park Barracks." The remark draws our attention to two matters very little discussed in the *Memoirs:* first, the robust homosexual subculture in nineteenth-century London and, second, the circle of like-minded friends who connected Symonds to that subculture. Admittedly, he sometimes mentions fellow students or colleagues who shared his "Arcadian" proclivities, but for the most part he gives the impression of confronting his sexual predicament alone.

On this occasion, however, he accepted the acquaintance's invitation, "out of curiosity." "Moved by something stronger than curiosity," he continues, "I made an assignation with a brawny young soldier for an afternoon to be passed in a private room at the same house." The telltale adjective ("brawny") returns us to the fantasies of his earliest childhood and promises a sexual experience stripped of the idealizations and masculine prerogatives of his affairs with Willie, Alfred, and Norman. The element linking these two otherwise very different erotic realms is, of course, their similar class character.

Symonds's account of his afternoon with "the strapping young soldier" aims to convey an impression of innocent pleasure and fellowship. Its matter-of-factness contrasts pointedly with the intense emotion of his previous relationships:

> He was a very nice fellow, as it turned out: comradely and natural, regarding the affair which had brought us together in that place from a business-like and reasonable point of view. For him at all events it involved nothing unusual, nothing shameful; and his simple attitude, the not displeasing vanity with which he viewed his own physical attractions, and the genial sympathy with which he met the passion they aroused, taught me something I had never

before conceived about illicit sexual relations. Instead of yielding to any brutal impulse, I thoroughly enjoyed the close vicinity of that splendid naked piece of manhood.

Reduced to its essentials, Symonds's arrangement with the soldier (and presumably with other male prostitutes) appears to have consisted of masturbating himself in front of the nude young man, while the soldier himself indulged in nothing more "shameful" than a healthy narcissism. But even as Symonds engineered this modest escape from his ruinous idealism, the *Memoirs* cannot allow the episode to be seen as a purely physical—or economic—exchange. There is still the need to lend it ideological respectability by associating it with the Whitmanesque notion of comradeship: "I made him clothe himself, sat and smoked and talked with him, and felt, at the end of the whole transaction, that some at least of the deepest moral problems might be solved by fraternity." Symonds is unable to sustain this apology without qualification. Relations with a prostitute, he admits, never overcome the "false position" on which they are based. Thus he left his friendly soldier "shaking the dust and degradation of the locality off my feet," even though over the remainder of his life he was to return to brothels hundreds of times.

〇 IN 1877 SYMONDS AND HIS FAMILY left England for Switzerland, ostensibly (like Hans Castorp) for the sake of his health but in reality to find a more satisfactory accommodation of his sexual needs. From then until his death in 1893 he divided much of his time between Davos and Venice, pursuing young peasants in the former and gondoliers in the latter. His decision to go abroad set a pattern for British and especially French homosexuals in the twentieth century. The immediate attraction of a foreign country was to escape the stifling surveillance and internalized repressions of the homeland. But more complex (and less defensible) motives were also at work: a Swiss peasant or a Venetian gondolier offered the sort of exotic enticement that an "orientalizing" homosexual like André Gide would later find in North African boys. Symonds's enterprise, in other words, cannot be divorced from the logic of empire—from the presumption that the world beyond the Channel is an Englishman's natural erotic hunting grounds. It is the geographical counterpart, so to speak, of his obsession with the lower orders at home, a further variation on his quest for otherness.

There is also an affinity between Symonds's overseas adventures and his trafficking with prostitutes in England: money was involved. In the *Memoirs* he struggles to persuade himself that the relationships were redeemed by the genuine affection of the young men. In the case of Christian Buol—the main object of his attentions in Davos—Symonds helped out the boy's family to the tune of several thousand pounds. But Christian, he asserts, was not the sort "to give anything whatever of himself in return for pecuniary considerations; he understood . . . that I had conceived a real and disinterested liking for his family."

Symonds's excuse would seem hopelessly lame were it not for the fact that his dealings with Christian, in contrast to those with London's male prostitutes, conformed to the pattern of repression and idealization established with Willie Dyer, Alfred Brooke, and Norman Moor. Indeed, the affair was, if anything, even more voyeuristic:

> We often slept together in the same bed; and he was not shy of allowing me to view, as men may view the idols of their gods, the naked splendour of his perfect body. But neither in act nor deed, far less in words, did the least shadow of lust cloud the serenity of that masculine communion. . . . I have never enjoyed a more sense-soothing and more elevated pleasure than I had with him—sex being nowhere—drowned and absorbed in love, which was itself so spiritually sensual that the needs of the body disappeared and were forgotten.

Symonds also insists that when Christian decided to marry, it in no way altered their relationship: "He accepted me for what I was; and I asked nothing except his proximity." But Symonds immediately undermines this innocent picture with an angry outburst against the denial of his desires. The passage—among the most eloquent in the *Memoirs*—mercilessly identifies the contradictions of his erotic and emotional life:

> Alas, while writing this, I must perforce lay the pen aside, and think how desolate are the conditions under which men constituted like me live and love. . . . The best we obtain is friendship grounded on the intimate acquaintance with our character derived from long experience in extraordinary circumstances. Love for love we cannot get; and our better nature shrinks from the vision of what a love aroused in the beloved (and corresponding to our love for him) would inevitably involve.

He had so fully internalized the ideals of Victorian culture that the notion of sexual arousal in the beloved was positively distasteful to him. His boys seem never to have erections.

Symonds's liaisons with Venetian gondoliers, and in particular his long alliance with Angelo Fusato, were at once more orientalized and more frankly venal than those with Christian Buol and other Swiss peasants. While hardly satisfactory from a modern gay perspective, they nonetheless managed to overcome the harsh dichotomy between love and lust, sentiment and desire, that had crippled his earlier romances. The Italian affairs might be regarded as a synthesis of his bucolic Swiss idyll with the earthiness of the London brothel, and they brought the middle-aged Symonds "a moderate degree of satisfaction." The phrase is unmistakably deflationary—given the high romantic expectations with which he began—but he deserves credit for fashioning an erotic modus vivendi under unfavorable historical conditions and against great psychic odds.

Angelo Fusato—whom Symonds met on the Lido in 1881—emerges from the *Memoirs* as a decidedly more exotic creature than any of his predecessors. Indeed, as a Mediterranean, he enjoys a marked alienness, which Symonds confounds with the Venetian environment: "He took hold of me by a hundred threads of feeling, in which the powerful and radiant manhood of the splendid animal was intertwined with the sentiment for Venice, a keen delight in the landscape of the lagoons, and something penetrative and pathetic in the man." There are echoes here of the brawny sailors and brothel soldiers of earlier years. Significantly, at twenty-four, Angelo was more mature than the adolescent choristers, though still much younger than Symonds himself. The *Memoirs* present him as heir to the Rousseauist tradition of noble savagery: "proud and sensitive, wayward as a child, ungrudging in his service, willing and good-tempered, though somewhat indolent at the same time and subject to explosions of passion."

Symonds confesses that the liaison had from the start—and never relinquished—a commercial dimension. Later the exchange of money for sex was regularized (and softened) by employing Angelo as his personal gondolier. Symonds even notes that his "pecuniary assistance" enabled Angelo to marry the girl with whom he already had two sons (and who eventually became Symonds's housekeeper). Doubtless Angelo's heterosexuality, like Christian Buol's, increased his attractiveness to Symonds.

The relationship with Angelo, and with other young Italians ("they have been very numerous"), involved a delicate negotiation between the erotic and the sentimental. The sex—though not described in detail—appears to have resembled that with London prostitutes. "It is not to be supposed," he writes with asperity, "that I confined myself to sitting opposite the man and gazing into his fierce eyes of fiery opal." He had finally tamed his savage idealism, aided by a comfortable sense of distance—both social and geographical—from his chosen objects. But he firmly rejects equating his Italian affairs with prostitution. In the case of Angelo and the other Italians, he contends, an element of consideration, even affection, always tempered the commercial transaction. "He gave what I desired, as a token of friendliness. It cost him nothing, and he saw that I took pleasure in it." Angelo visited him in Davos, and they often traveled together. Perhaps Symonds was deluding himself. At one point in the narrative he suggests as much by providing Angelo with an imaginary soliloquy that neatly deflates the author's Whitmanesque pretensions: "At the back of his mind the predominant thought, I fancy, was to this effect: 'Had I not better get what I can out of this strange Englishman, who talks so much about his intentions and his friendship, but whose actual grasp upon my life is so uncertain?'" Nonetheless I am reluctant to belittle Symonds's achievement. Judged against the erotic wasteland of his earlier loves, the relationship with Angelo seems altogether reasonable, both sexually and emotionally. It may have been illusory, but at least the illusion was functional.

⊘ THE GREAT THEME OF SYMONDS'S autobiography is ambivalence. He presents himself throughout as a man divided. The central division—and the one of most interest to the historian of gay self-representation—is in the way he judges his sexual constitution. The dominant emphasis in the *Memoirs* is on the essential pathology of his condition. Repeatedly he speaks of his "malady," of "the congenital aberration of the passions which . . . has been the poison of my life," of the "deeply rooted perversion of the sexual instincts (uncontrollable, ineradicable, amounting to monomania)." We should not forget that this conception, while at some level a product of self-hate and thus distasteful to modern gay sensibilities, was deployed by Symonds (and his ally Havelock Ellis) to criticize society's treatment of homosexuality as a vice—an act of willful impurity. Stripped of its tendentious psychiatric rhetoric and repackaged in the neutral language of "sexual orientation," it has become the main argument by which modern homosexuals have defended themselves.

Still, one mustn't minimize the harshness with which Symonds judges his condition. Its cruelest consequence, he laments, was that his sexual feelings could never be reciprocated. He was without any hope of enjoying the experience that, like his heterosexual contemporaries, he regarded as life's greatest good. He cannot even imagine the possibility of mutual homosexual desire, in part because the idea didn't exist in his society's cultural repertory, but also because he was so fixated on much younger men, who were unable to "return his passion." Symonds's predicament might be considered an extreme version of the modern gay man's obsession with youth—the manner in which the homoerotic imagination lags behind the homosexual body.

He also complains that his disposition has condemned him to a fruitless pursuit of his desires and a no less fruitless effort to repress them. Energies that might have been invested in friendship, marriage, or work have been squandered in an exhausting dialectic of lust and guilt:

> What hours and days and weeks and months of weariness I have endured by the alternate indulgence and repression of my craving imagination. What time and energy I have wasted on expressing it. How it has interfered with the pursuit of study. How marriage has been spoiled by it. What have I suffered in violent and brutal pleasures of the senses, snatched furtively with shame on my part, with frigid toleration on the part of my comrades, and repented of with terror.

But self-lacerating passages like this one must be set against others in which Symonds pleads the fundamental innocence of his feelings and their compatibility with a dignified and worthwhile existence. Not instinct but society, he contends, has made him a criminal. His desire is "natural, instinctive, healthy in his own particular case—but morbid and abominable from the point of view of the society in which he lives." Again, it is a "spontaneous appetite," "a natural instinct reputed vicious in the modern age" (in contrast to its celebration in ancient Greece).

No less striking is Symonds's ambivalence about his life as an intellectual and a writer. Here he establishes a pattern we will observe in other gay autobiographers, most strikingly in Martin Duberman. Sometimes he invokes his literary achievements as evidence against the charge of depravity. But more common, and more disturbing, is a tendency to deprecate his work as a frivolous sublimation, even a cowardly avoidance, of his true passion. He recalls lecturing on "Florence and the Medici" at the Royal Institution in London just as he made his first visit to a male brothel. "Very dull lectures they were, for my soul was not in them; my soul throbbed for the soldier."

The incident becomes the basis for an attack on the Arnoldian gospel of culture. "I am, above all, a believer in culture," Matthew Arnold had written in *Culture and Anarchy,* the central intellectual document of the age. But Symonds—in many respects no less quintessential a Victorian than Arnold himself—dissents. His homosexual agony has led him to conclude—with almost Nietzschean ferocity—that culture must be subordinated to life:

> In my heart of hearts I do not believe in culture except as an adjunct of life. Life is more than literature, I say. So I cannot, although I devote my time and energy to culture, . . . regard it otherwise than in the light of pastime, decoration, service. Passion, nerve and sinew, eating and drinking, the stomach and the bowels, sex, even money-getting—the coarsest forms of activity—come, in my reckoning, before culture.

Yet in the end Symonds wrote his *Memoirs*—and arranged for their publication after his death. So he is unable to maintain that all intellectual labor was useless, a mere distraction from the serious business of living. On the contrary, he expresses the hope that his book—the final effort of a prolific literary career—will ease the affliction of others like himself:

> It seemed to me, being a man of letters, possessing the pen of a ready writer and the practiced impartiality of a critic accustomed to weigh evidence, that it was my duty to put on record the facts and phases of this aberrant inclination in myself—so that fellow-sufferers from the like malady, men innocent as I have been, yet haunted as I have been by a sense of guilt and a dread of punishment, men injured in their character and health by the debasing influences of a furtive and lawless love, men deprived of the best pleasures which reciprocated passion yields to mortals, men driven in upon ungratified desires and degraded by humiliating outbursts of ungovernable appetite, should feel that they are not alone, should discover at the same time how a career of some distinction, of considerable energy and perseverance, may be pursued by one who bends and sweats beneath a burden heavy enough to drag him down to pariahdom.

Admittedly, the declaration is heavily burdened with the self-loathing that gay men would spend the next century trying to overcome. But it also suggests— with full Victorian eloquence—that the author's unhappy tale might contribute to a better life for homosexuals in the future. In its own hesitant and contradictory way, Symonds's autobiography is an emancipatory work.

Goldsworthy Lowes Dickinson in middle age.

The Autobiography of G. Lowes Dickinson

OLDSWORTHY LOWES DICKINSON was a generation younger than Symonds and outlived him by nearly four decades. Over half of Dickinson's life was passed in the nineteenth century, and many of his early experiences closely resembled Symonds's. But he is, by comparison, a distinctly more modern figure. Curiously, however, his autobiography does not mark the clear sexual advance that a Whig historian might expect. His account of his homosexuality is certainly different from Symonds's. Yet in some ways it involves a retreat, even if it boasts its own peculiar grandeur and pathos. Dickinson, we shall see, resolved his homosexual predicament on a decidedly more ethereal and sublimated plane than Symonds.

Like Symonds, Dickinson was a man of letters, but with an important difference: he was also a devoted teacher. He spent most of his life at King's College, Cambridge, where he had been an undergraduate and where he was elected a Fellow in 1887. He was in fact the classic homosexual don, whose emotional life was vicariously invested—sometimes overinvested—in his young charges. Cambridge undergraduates play a role in his story similar to that played by choristers, peasants, and gondoliers in Symonds's. As an intellectual, his interests were more political and philosophical than Symonds's (although both men wanted desperately to be poets and wrote a good deal of homoerotic verse). Politically he was a radical, much of whose early work concerned the issue of poverty, and he achieved his greatest notoriety as an opponent of the First World War and an advocate of the League of Nations.

Dickinson's autobiography followed a torturous route to publication. The manuscript of the "Recollections," as he called them, was left with his friend and biographer E. M. Forster, who, according to the terms of Dickinson's will, was "to be at liberty to publish them or withhold them from publication as he may in his uncontrolled discretion think fit."[3] Forster followed the manuscript closely in composing his biography, but he suppressed the story of Dickinson's four great loves—which take up the central chapters and are the source of the work's historical importance—as well as the candid account of his early sexual propensities. Forster and Dickinson had been friends since the turn of the century, although, somewhat surprisingly, there is no account of the friendship in the autobiography. One suspects a certain sexual incompatibility: Forster, as we know from *Maurice*, shared Symonds's working-class tastes, in contrast to Dickinson's obsession with undergraduates.

When Forster died in 1970 he in turn left the manuscript with Dennis Proctor, Dickinson's last love (from the period after the composition of the autobiography). "Nothing was said on either side about eventual publication of the writings," notes Proctor, "but it was understood that there would devolve on me the expressed provision of Dickinson's will." Although the bulk of the text dates from 1921, it is a patchwork affair, with substantial later additions and changes (mainly from 1927 and 1931) and incorporating a large number of letters. Proctor also discovered forty handwritten pages, mostly from 1910 and entitled "A chapter in my autobiography—Privatissimum," that give a more circumstantial account of Dickinson's affair with Oscar Eckhard, which was in its early (cataclysmic) stages at the time. Proctor incorporated large sections of the chapter into the Introduction to the published autobiography, making the chapter, in effect, an integral part of the document. Yet for all the work's randomness it is often curiously moving.

☙ DICKINSON'S ACCOUNT OF HIS childhood in the country village of Hanwell is generally idyllic, although he has a sharp eye for the rigid class distinctions of English society. His mother (rather like John Stuart Mill's) is little mentioned, and he describes his father, a portrait painter, as "a Liberal and Gladstonian" as well as "a man of remarkable charm." To be sure, the father played the familiar enforcer when, at sixteen, Dickinson wrote from school confessing to masturbation: "My father wrote back a very kind but very alarming letter, in which he dwelt on the frightful consequences of this act. One grew up, he said, 'ashamed in the presence of women and unable to hold up one's head among men'. I remember the phrase, because it made a tremendous impression." But Dickinson's father was merely doing his duty by passing on received Victorian wisdom on

3. Dennis Proctor, preface to *The Autobiography of G. Lowes Dickinson*, ed. Dennis Proctor (London, 1973), p. ix.

the topic. More important is how little the senior Dickinson resembles the tyrannical and repressive *pater familias* of Samuel Butler's *The Way of All Flesh* or Edmund Gosse's *Father and Son* or other representative texts of the period. The same is true, incidentally, of John Addington Symonds's father, of whom the *Memoirs* draw an entirely admiring portrait. Nor does Dickinson's father receive the narrative attention that is so striking a feature of J. R. Ackerley's *My Father and Myself*. Whether intentionally or not, the text conspires to inhibit a Freudian reading, with its stress on hostile (or distant) fathers and suffocating mothers.

As in Symonds's case, everything changed dramatically when, in 1874, Dickinson was sent away to school. He spent the first two years at Chertsey and the next five at Charterhouse. "Boarding school!" he moans. "What a flood of black memories!" He found himself bullied, alone, and often physically cold. Like Harrow, Charterhouse was "what would be called a 'hothouse of vice'." "As I write," he continues, "there comes back to me a picture, in the room where we changed for exercise, of a bigger boy masturbating against a smaller, amid a crowd of admirers." But unlike Symonds—who struggled heroically against the temptations presented by his fellow students in order to defend his elevated conception of homosexual love—Dickinson was indifferent to the sexual carryings-on and "perplexed" by their significance. Indeed, his ultimate regret is that he passed through these years "with not one of those passionate friendships or loves which redeem school for many boys." In effect, the young Lowes Dickinson was not a homosexual. There are no figures in his history comparable to Willie Dyer and Alfred Brooke in Symonds's. After Dickinson discovered his attraction to men— at the surprisingly advanced age of twenty-four—he spoke of his desires as natural, profound, and inalterable. But his early indifference suggests a certain pliability in his sexual constitution. His story, in contrast to Symonds's, invites an anti-essentialist reading.

Although without homosexual (or heterosexual) interests, the adolescent Dickinson was far from ascetic. His sex life, real and imagined, centered on two things: foot fetishism and masturbation, both of which were to remain lifelong staples of his erotic repertory. The foot fetishism predated his years at school. "My earliest remembrance of sexual feeling was connected with boots. . . . What I actually remember is lying on the floor in our little drawing room, and my father patting me with his feet. It was, as it still is, from this earliest time, boots rather than feet, and polished boots that moved my feelings." He adds: "I used, later, to get my brother to tread upon me, or my sisters. I don't know whether he, at that time, had any sex feeling about it, but imagine he may have had. At night, when I had gone to bed, I used to steal out to my father's dressing room, and excite myself over his boots."

Dickinson insists that his fetishism was entirely impersonal and thus, by implication, unrelated to his later homosexuality: "Neither at this time, nor during all my school life, nor even in the first years of my university life, were these sex feelings connected in any way with love. And in these early days they were not connected specially with either the female or the male sex, for I was at first indifferent between them." He also makes a show of dissociating himself from turn-of-the century sexological ideas about fetishism, including presumably Freudian ideas. But he conveniently ignores his own revelation that the fetish was in fact originally attached to a person, indeed a male person—his father.

His reflections about his fetishism in the autobiography raise troubling questions about gender for him. Like his heterosexual contemporaries (including Freud), he accepts the conventional equation of masculinity with activity and femininity with passivity, and he acknowledges that his desire to be tread on betrays a feminine disposition. He even embraces the idea, developed in the nineteenth century by Karl Heinrich Ulrichs, that the homosexual is in some essential sense female. His boot fetishism, he writes in the "most private" chapter of 1910, is "part of a general 'femininity' in my physical feeling towards men." "My dream is always to be dominated, not to dominate. I have, so far, a woman's soul; and the only thing for which I should like to be a woman is that I might experience the dominating and aggressive love of a man." He also speaks deprecatingly of his timidity, especially at school, where he was warned to "resist and resent being treated like a girl." But while his sexual desires cast him the role of woman, he nonetheless insists that emotionally and intellectually he never relinquished his masculine authority, not even with his beloveds. The wish to be dominated sexually, he writes, "has never given to the key to my relations to men, because, on the spiritual side, I have a much more imperious need to preserve my independence and self-respect." Dennis Proctor, who as the last beloved speaks with some authority, supports Dickinson's contention (while also asserting his own heterosexuality): "There was certainly nothing feminine about Goldie's *mind*, and I should not myself have said that his soul was feminine either. I do not recognise anything in my own intimacy with him that seems in any way akin to those which I have had with women."

Dickinson also began masturbating before he was sent off to boarding school, but there the practice intensified, "perhaps to excess." At school—and indeed for the rest of his life—he masturbated "under the stimulus of the idea of boots." After his father's intervention, astonishingly, he gave up the practice until his mid-twenties. Dickinson thus lived through what Alfred Kinsey later showed to be the peak years of male sexual desire in complete chastity. Eventually, however, the masturbation resumed, and in fact it was to become Dickinson's sole sexual activity in adulthood. He adopted the modern doctrine, enunciated by Havelock Ellis in *Auto-Erotism* (1899), that it was fundamentally innocent. It was a purely mechanical outlet (comparable to what Symonds claimed to find in marital intercourse), without psychological significance, and the only sensible choice for a homosexual, like himself, unable to consummate his desires with another man: "In itself it is merely a relief. . . . It keeps a man of my temperament free from physical trouble, while leaving him open to emotional experience. That, at least, has been my experience for nearly forty years, and I commend it to whoever may have to adapt himself to similar circumstances."

CAMBRIDGE CAME AS A GREAT RELIEF after the tortures of boarding school. Dickinson describes his undergraduate years as a time of sexual abstinence and intellectual excitement. His interests quickly took a philosophical turn, introducing him to a kind of cosmic mysticism that left its mark on all his subsequent work and even invaded his masturbatory fantasies. "My mind was in ferment," he writes. "What I saw was a dim and moonlit scene, infinite, exciting, perilous, full of adventure. It presented itself to me as the problem of existence." At Cambridge he also discovered his political radicalism, first through Shelley and then through Henry George. And Cambridge provided him with a model of sorts for his future career as a homosexual don in the person of the "notorious" Oscar Browning, "who had, beyond a doubt, the homosexual temperament" and whose influence was greater than that of any of Dickinson's other teachers. The model was perhaps not an entirely comfortable one, for Dickinson also notes that, as secretary of the swimming club, Browning's "corpulent person was constantly to be found in the state of primitive nudity which, in those early and happy days, was characteristic of Cambridge bathing."

Both intellectually and, as it turned out, sexually, the most important event of the early Cambridge years was his election in 1884 to the Society of Apostles, the progenitor of Bloomsbury. The Society's Saturday night paper-readings and discussions intensified his philosophical bent. There is, moreover, an unmistakable homoerotic tug in the autobiography's account of the Apostles' meetings: "When young men are growing in mind and soul, when speculation is a passion, when discussion is made profound by love, there happens something incredible to any but those who breathe that magic air." The Society united him with two lifelong friends, the future neo-Hegelian philosopher John McTaggart and the future classicist (and King's colleague) Nathaniel Wedd. Most important, it united him with his first great love, Roger Fry.

Four years younger than Dickinson, Fry was elected to the Apostles after Dickinson had graduated but was still in residence at Cambridge, desultorily pursing a medical degree. Their friendship began "in a common interest in things intellectual." The way to homosexual romance was prepared by the familiar route of the Greeks: "One evening, in a talk with a student of Classics, I discovered that the Greek love, as I had read of it in Plato, was a continuous and still existing fact." The Platonic theme forms an obvious link to Symonds and the entire homoerotic heritage of Victorian Hellenism, though by Dickinson's time the tradition had lost some of its original force, and it figures much less centrally in his account than it does in Symonds's. Nonetheless it still had enough residual strength to bring about a revolution in Dickinson's thinking: the discovery of the homoerotic Greeks "set free a current of feeling that was natural to me."

The affair with Roger Fry, though it lasted only "a year or two," established the pattern for the more extended and traumatic relationships that followed. The beloved was a younger scholar, heterosexual, if somewhat ambiguously so, who shared Dickinson's intellectual interests. The sex never progressed beyond kisses and embraces, because Dickinson put on the brakes. But, surprisingly, it allowed for some expression of his foot fetishism. At the same time, the relationship was invested with extravagant emotional, even metaphysical, significance. And as the passion waned (or was settled on a new object), it transformed itself into friendship, which lasted a lifetime. Dickinson often writes of feeling "married" to his former beloveds.

The romance began with an innocuous kiss and a profound realization: "The next thing I remember [after discovering the homoerotic Greeks] is going one night to Roger's bedroom to say good night, and stooping down to kiss his forehead. This was a decisive moment. I went back to my lodgings strangely excited, lay awake reading (I think, Heine's *Reisebilder*), and said to myself 'I must be in love'." In the following academic year (1887–88, Fry's last) they took breakfast and lunch together daily, "and every night I used to see him to bed and then kiss him passionately." Fry's attitude is hard to discern from the autobiography. Dickinson reports, "His feeling for me was different from mine for him," and the affair in fact ended when Fry fell in love with a woman and married. Yet he seems flirtatious, or, if not that, then remarkably broad-minded. The idea that passionate kissing, or embracing, was compatible with a heterosexual identity sounds improbable to the modern reader, but apparently the boundaries were differently drawn in nineteenth-century England. We recall John Addington Symonds's passionate kissing of Norman Moor, even while maintaining that they had done nothing together that was "unworthy of two gentlemen."

Dickinson resisted the impulse to do more, even as he maneuvered to satisfy his fetishism. "The feeling of sex was now strong, but I did not indulge it, and should have thought it wrong to do so. There recurred also the old childish, I suppose really infantine, tick about boots, and I used to lie on the floor and get him to put his feet on me." It was the nominally heterosexual Fry who proposed that they might venture beyond kissing. "Bathing at Weymouth, we lay naked on the sand, I holding Roger's hand. We slept in the same bed. And I recollect him saying to me, as we embraced, should we not go further? I said No, and did not want to. Why? I don't know. I believe I thought it would lower our love." In one important particular, however, Dickinson did "go further": after an especially frustrating evening with Fry he returned to his room and masturbated for the first time in eight years. All the elements of his adult sexual life were now in place: an intensely romantic attachment, passionate kisses and warm embraces (with a hint of fetishism), followed by relief through masturbation.

Roger Fry of course was to become a great figure in Bloomsbury, its elder statesman, most famous as the organizer of the Post-Impressionist Exhibition of 1910 that marked such a watershed in its history. We might be inclined, therefore, to place Dickinson himself somewhere in the Bloomsbury firmament, all the more so because of his membership in the Society of Apostles (which later claimed Leonard Woolf and Lytton Strachey, among others) and his friendship with E. M. Forster. And indeed there were certain affinities, including homosexuality, although Dickinson's erotic predilections were decidedly more repressed than those of the bed-hopping Bloomsburians. The most important affinity, I would argue, was their shared commitment to friendship as the supreme good. But, on the whole, the temptation to situate Dickinson in the prehistory of Bloomsbury should be resisted. Through Fry and Forster he was acquainted with its central figures (nearly all of whom were a generation younger than he), but their names, other than Fry's, are noticeably absent from the autobiography. Nor was it merely a matter of age. Dickinson's concerns were always more public, more political, than Bloomsbury's. He did not share their cult of introspection, and he notably rejected their interest in psychoanalysis. In this regard he is a less modern figure, closer in intellectual style, and even in sexual manners, to a Victorian romantic like Symonds. For their part, Bloomsbury viewed Dickinson with some condescension, speaking dismissively (in Leonard Woolf's words) of "a weakness, a looseness of fibre" and "a thin vapour of gentle high-mindedness."[4] For them he belonged to the slightly discredited past.

FERDINAND SCHILLER ENTERED Dickinson's life almost as a footnote to Roger Fry. Along with John McTaggart, Schiller had been a contemporary of Fry's at Clifton School, and it was through the two younger Apostles that Dickinson "became intimate" with Schiller during his undergraduate years at Cambridge. In the summer of 1888 Fry and McTaggart accompanied Dickinson on a visit to Schiller's family in Gersau, on Lake Lucerne. Although Dickinson was still more attached to Fry, the visit set a pattern that was to repeat itself nearly a half-dozen times over the next sixteen years: a summer month spent together with Ferdinand and his family at one of their Swiss vacation spots. Dickinson became especially attached to Ferdinand's mother, "the kindest, humanist, most pagan woman I have ever known." The episodes, with their Alpine climbing and fellowship, contain more than a hint of the Central European odysseys of John Addington Symonds before and Christopher Isherwood after.

Although Dickinson sensed already in 1888 that he might fall in love with Ferdinand, there ensued a hiatus of five years during which Ferdinand went out to India to follow his father into business while Dickinson remained in Cambridge and led "a curiously solitary life" writing his book on the history of modern France. In 1893 Ferdinand returned for the first of a series of summer holidays (others were to follow in 1895, 1899, and 1902). Again the two men went to Gersau, where once more there was much climbing, including an ascent of the Rigi, and where the "passion fixed itself." From the start the relationship was veiled in a philosophical penumbra, which the autobiographer, now grown more cynical, finds rather alien: "The kind of mysticism I then had I derived from McTaggart, but my love for Ferdinand gave it body. I cannot now recover it;

---

4. Leonard Woolf, *Beginning Again* (London, 1964), p. 190.

cannot understand how I thought that this personal passion in transitory individuals could be the key to the universe." The mysticism was complemented by his devotion to Wagner, in whose music he found a perfect echo of his passion and his grief. Over the two years following the visit of 1893 he composed a set of twenty-five love sonnets to Ferdinand, which are appended to the published autobiography.

Sexually the relationship was even less venturesome than the one with Roger Fry. It centered around a ritual good-night kiss, which, Dickinson concedes, didn't have the same significance for Ferdinand that it did for himself. "Every night he kissed me good night. And that little ceremony, nothing no doubt to him, was a kind of sacrament to me." Otherwise Dickinson had to be satisfied with sitting on the balcony "our arms around one another, reading Dante." The chapters on Ferdinand contain no mention of foot fetishism.

It was a curious love affair, but in a sense a great one. It took what might be considered the ideal form for a romance in which one of the parties was (nominally) heterosexual: between the brief summer visits the two men carried on a grand correspondence. From 1893 to 1904, still posted in India, Ferdinand wrote a letter every two weeks, while Dickinson responded weekly. Writing and receiving the letters became the emotional centerpiece of Dickinson's existence: "To me these letters, coming upon my then solitude, were the principal events of my life. I waited for them, week by week, and often have let them lie upon my table, while I worked, postponing the pleasure of opening them in that it might not too quickly pass." It is the language of delayed erotic gratification, and indeed the correspondence, in a profound psychological sense, *became* Dickinson's love life. Appropriately, his account of it occupies the two central chapters of the autobiography.

Dickinson interrogates the letters for evidence of Ferdinand's true feelings—and ultimately, one senses, to figure out his sexuality. The letters have a marked ambiguity, as if they were asking to be decoded. Dickinson notes their pervasive pessimism. One suspects (and one wonders whether Dickinson suspects) that their general world-weariness serves to cover a more specific malaise. There is also the theme of Ferdinand's "asceticism," which Dickinson takes to explain his failure to marry, despite being officially attracted to women. Marriage, Ferdinand writes, is an "'abyss'" that he would prefer to avoid—even though, Dickinson notes, "some women certainly attracted him and he has usually had about him one, at least, who was devoted to him and he to her." In fact Ferdinand never did marry, and the only woman to whom he was truly devoted—increasingly so as he grew older—was his mother. Dickinson never says as much, but all the signs—including the classic Freudian one—point toward repressed homosexuality. Perhaps Dickinson's infatuation was not so irrational after all.

Ferdinand's sexuality puzzles him. "Ferdinand's own attitude to sex I have never felt that I understood. . . . I do not think he was ever homosexual, in the sense of feeling physical attraction to those of his own sex." Yet the letters are full of ambiguous signs. At one point Ferdinand writes concerning a friend, "'He is one of the people whose faces I feel in love with and curiously I have never had that experience except with men's faces.'" During the Oscar Wilde scandal (which otherwise goes unmentioned in the autobiography), Ferdinand teasingly begins his salutation: "'My . . . (mustn't use the words since the Oscar Wilde trial).'" He enters upon a carefully managed discussion of Edward Carpenter's pamphlet on "Homogenic Love": "'On one point I think Carpenter is wrong. I don't believe the "outward and visible sign" is necessary and essential, or even stimulating, except at very rare intervals. I have a kind of notion that you and I don't agree on this point, and it is very likely that my asceticism (which is constitutional) is au fond responsible for this. . . . Only, my dear, if we don't agree about this I don't see that it really matters.'" The passage seems to grant Dickinson the right to his homosexuality, while excusing Ferdinand himself on somatic grounds. For Dickinson it "shows that Ferdinand knew that my feeling was, on the physical side, more urgent than his." Dickinson is also eager to clarify Ferdinand's understanding of what was involved sexually: "When . . . he refers to the 'outward and visible sign', he is, I am sure, not thinking of more than kisses and embracing, which in fact we used to do. I did not myself, at that time, desire anything more, or think it would have been right." We have the impression of watching a delicate erotic minuet.

As the correspondence evolved, Ferdinand's understanding of the situation grew more explicit and his declarations of affection more open. Admittedly, the conventions then governing correspondence between men tolerated greater emotional extravagance than they would later. Nonetheless one increasingly has the sense of reading love letters, if slightly uncomfortable ones. After the month together at Gersau in 1993, Ferdinand writes, "'I need not hesitate to tell you how much and how often I have been wanting you ever since your departure.'" His letters now begin "'My beloved,'" which Dickinson interprets as a sign of "the closer character which our relation had assumed"—and which Ferdinand, as noted, satirized in his allusion to Oscar Wilde. In 1894 he is saying "'I can't conceal from myself, confound it, that my letters mean much to you,'" and he adds, in another letter, "'If it is any mitigation, I will tell you that I want you almost as much as you want me, only, as I am ascetic by nature, the provocation keeps me going.'"

Dickinson greatly looked forward to Ferdinand's return from India in 1904. Apparently, however, their affair depended on long absences interrupted by short, ecstatic summer reunions. The return led not to an embarrassing confrontation, as one might have feared, but, as with an old married couple, to a prosaic waning of the passion. "I say, of the passion, not of the love. For I feel that, behind walls, the old feeling still exists on both sides. For we both have faithful natures. Still, for many years now I have not craved for his presence, as I used to." Once again the romance devolved into a lifelong friendship.

Years later, in 1927, Schiller returned a batch of Dickinson's letters from 1896. With them he sent a letter of his own, the final one quoted in the autobiography. It is a kind of painful apology, deeply sad, in which he finally acknowledges the significance of the relationship and regrets his lost opportunity:

"I spent a good portion of this afternoon re-reading your letters to me. . . . Looking back I of course see that I really had it in my power to end the frustration and torture that it involved, although at the time it seemed to me that I was caught in an iron coil of circumstances. I ought to have burst through that bond and counted the world well lost for love, yours and my mother's. The torment of that thought I must carry to the grave, and no tears can wash out what Fate has written. . . . And believe that, however undemonstrative I may have seemed, it was not really so, and I want you to know—if indeed you have not known it all along—that I always realised—from my undergraduate days— that your love was an incredibly precious possession. I well remember that when I first read the sonnets they took my breath away, and it seemed to me incredible that they could have been written to me, as I could discover nothing in myself that entitled me to such a great and overwhelming affection. Well, all I can say is that that feeling is true and alive today, and that it is the only comfort and solace that I now have."

Dickinson calls the letter "the last word about our friendship."

It was not, however. Less than a month later Dickinson learned that "another episode has begun." Schiller, at sixty-one, had fallen "desperately in love" with a lady novelist. But he remained a less than fully satisfactory heterosexual, for the young woman loved someone else and offered no prospect of ever marrying him. Dickinson ends the two chapters devoted to the great romance of his life with an enigmatic sentence, added the year before his death: "The episode continues, but has led to nothing further." Their affair had been a "veritable *grande passion*," as Ernest Jones said of Freud's courtship of Martha Bernays.[5] But because of its sexually asymmetry, it had also been profoundly frustrating.

∞ THE RELATIONSHIPS WITH Roger Fry and Ferdinand Schiller, when Dickinson was in his twenties and thirties, were succeeded by those with Oscar Eckhard and Peter Savary, when he was in his forties, fifties, and sixties. Not only were the beloveds now much younger than Dickinson—half his age in the case of Eckhard, more like a third in the case of Savary—but, unlike Ferdinand, they were no longer separated from him by half a globe. As a result the sexual pressure increased, just as its objects became less appropriate, and there was more resistance on the part of the young men and more unhappiness for Dickinson. By his own admission the affairs were tinged with sordidness, especially the one with Peter Savary, even though Dickinson got more accomplished sexually than he ever did with Ferdinand.

Oscar Eckhard came up to King's in 1908, when Dickinson was forty-six. "A close intimacy" soon formed. The middle-aged don and the fresh undergraduate talked, went riding, and attended concerts and plays together. Eventually Oscar became his student. At first, Dickinson insists, there was "no element of passion." But the sublimation could not be sustained. "I began to find an irresistible attraction in his face, his mouth, his eyes, and his voice, all his ways and manners. I thought a day wasted in which I did not see him. Finally, the desire to come into physical contact with him grew more than I could resist."

Dickinson's erotic folly kept him from taking adequate notice of Oscar's reluctance. Indeed, he constantly misunderstood the young man. A crisis was precipitated early in 1910, when he wrote Oscar a long letter explaining his "temperament" (Dickinson's euphemism for "homosexuality") and "the character of my love for him." He then went abroad, to Sicily, where he received "a short rather stiff note," intended by Oscar to end matters but interpreted by Dickinson "as an indication that we could resume relations as before." Letters, which had been the

5. *The Life and Work of Sigmund Freud* (New York, 1953), vol. 1, p. 109.

vehicle of his love for Ferdinand, now produced only confusion and self-deception. The denouement came later that year in Baden Baden, where Dickinson had pursued Oscar and his family. This time Oscar's note breaking off relations was so unambiguous that not even Dickinson could misconstrue it. "I was more overwhelmed with distress than I have ever been in my life. I left Baden Baden by the next train and arrived shattered in England."

A reconciliation was arranged through Oscar's mother, with whom Dickinson became even friendlier than he had with Ferdinand's. The next year they were again close, "and in the Easter term of 1912 I first kissed him." But Dickinson also records Oscar's continued resistance: "He had no answering passion and was constantly swept back by strong reactions."

Ironically the relationship was given a reprieve by the First World War, which in effect recreated the elements of Dickinson's romance with Ferdinand: long, anxious separations sustained by correspondence and interrupted by brief but ecstatic reunions. Oscar was stationed on the Western Front, and Dickinson's fears and hopes about his beloved doubtless fueled his intense opposition to the War.

Those brief reunions seem to have brought Dickinson closer to a satisfactory sexual relationship than anything he had yet known, and certainly they made him happier than ever before. Examined closely, however, the text is ambiguous. "On his first return he came into bed with me, and we embraced with a passion of happiness on my side and with content on his." What exactly happened? A note from 1915, included in the same envelope with the "most private" chapter, reveals that the event was more emotional than physical, although Dickinson's foot fetishism managed to find expression: "The first night I lay on the floor by the fire and held his naked feet. The second night he came into bed with me. I felt almost no sexual passion; only deep happiness and love. I think he was happy too."

Oscar's return after the War, exactly like Ferdinand's return from India over a decade earlier, brought not the hoped-for bliss but a renewal and heightening of the familiar prewar tensions. Oscar—also, like Ferdinand, a somewhat troubled heterosexual—now entered on "one of his miserable affairs, with a typewriting girl, a flirtation without her becoming definitely his mistress." Despite Oscar's growing impatience, Dickinson somehow managed to keep the relationship afloat for another four years, into the period of the autobiography's composition. They continued to go to bed together, and Dickinson even succeeded in getting Oscar to satisfy his fetishism: "According to the tick I have referred to, I liked him to stand upon me when we met. I think this rather bothered him, though he used not to seem to object." Eventually, however, came a repeat of Baden Baden: Oscar wrote and again broke off relations. Dickinson was hurt and angry, though still hoping for a reconciliation. Yet he concedes, "I suppose this is the best thing that could happen. . . . I expect that really he was never easy, in face of feelings like mine, and I cannot blame him. Most people, indeed, would blame me, and perhaps rightly." Two final entries, from 1927, note that Oscar, now thirty-eight, has finally married. Dickinson visited him and his wife on their farm in Gloucestershire. "I find fortunately that I can see him without disturbance and leave him without grief." The old pattern had reasserted itself, as Dickinson himself observes with satisfaction: "Here too my troubled and at times very distressing relation has subsided into a friendship."

The affair with Peter Savary was a darker, more pathetic, variation on the one with Oscar Eckhard. Dickinson met Peter, then only sixteen, though Roger Fry: he was the nephew of a Swiss woman teaching Fry's children. In contrast to John Addington Symonds, Dickinson seems to have been uninterested in adolescents, and the affair with Peter did not begin for another seven years, in 1922, just as the relationship with Oscar was ending. Despite his connection with Fry, Peter was the only one of Dickinson's loves who had never been a Cambridge undergraduate.

When Peter fell ill with influenza, Dickinson spirited him off to the Isle of Wight and there briskly initiated him into the sexual routine that had taken years to evolve with Ferdinand and Oscar: "After a brief explanation, he was willing enough to let me kiss him and embrace him, though he was averse from any further intimacy." Dickinson was now sixty and Peter twenty-three. When, not surprisingly, things didn't go well, Dickinson preposterously attributed their troubles to Peter's being straight: "He has no physical feeling for me, being entirely heterosexual." The account of their sexual accommodation is painful to read. Dickinson tries desperately to convince himself that, even in the absence of desire, there was at least genuine affection. But the text reeks of bad faith. As for the young man, one can't tell whether he was merely confused or subtly exploiting the situation. He was, once again, a less-than-fully-successful heterosexual, "discontented with casual relations," whom Dickinson helped get a job in the London office of the League of Nations. Looking back in 1927, after the passion had cooled, he admits that the affair now "surprises and rather disgusts" him. Yet even in this most improbable instance he manages to salvage something enduring from the erotic shipwreck: "I see him often, and we are on very friendly terms."[6]

⚭ DICKINSON'S MISTAKE WITH Peter Savary, and to an only slightly lesser extent with Oscar Eckhard, was to have imposed a physical relationship on much younger, heterosexual, and above all unwilling men. In the case of Oscar, moreover, the younger man was a student of his and thus especially vulnerable to an abuse of power. Dickinson was not insensitive to his mistake. As noted, he expresses "disgust" over his dealings with Savary, and he begins his account of the affair with Oscar by calling it "the only one with regard to which I feel I have something to reproach myself," because of the subject's being "a full generation younger" than himself. John Addington Symonds's solution, while hardly ideal, was more satisfactory, both morally and sexually: a kind of elevated prostitution, whereby Christian Boal and Angelo Fusato (and numerous others) were paid, directly or indirectly, for their sexual services yet appear to have developed a genuine fondness for their benefactor. Certainly the final chapters of Symonds's autobiography convey a sense of contentment quite opposite from the agony and gloom of Dickinson's.

No more than any other human being was Dickinson responsible for whom he desired or fell in love with. His attraction to undergraduates was simply a given of his psychic constitution, at least in adulthood. Moreover no teacher who happens to be homosexual will fail to recognize something of himself and his own sexual situation in Dickinson's circumstances. I would even argue that some sort of erotic involvement, however sublimated, is involved in nearly all teaching. One thinks of Socrates, the teacher *par excellence,* who was also of course a lover of young men.

Dickinson's engagement with Peter and Oscar, with whom he played something of a masher, must, I think, be set against the background of his long career as a teacher and a more properly disinterested lover of young men. The most evocative passages in the autobiography conjure up images of his profound devo-

6. One of Dickinson's last infatuations, unmentioned in the autobiography, was with young J. R. Ackerley, whose own memoir, *My Father and Myself,* is discussed in chapter 3. Ackerley, too, was a Cambridge undergraduate, although Dickinson didn't meet him until three years after he had left the University. The relationship was entirely chaste (Ackerley was interested exclusively in younger men, preferably soldiers and sailors). Its novelty lay in the fact that Ackerley was the first true homosexual in whom Dickinson seems to have taken an erotic interest. Despite more than a thirty-year difference in age, the two men became friends. See Peter Parker, *Ackerley* (New York, 1989), pp. 84–88, 96–97.

tion to the undergraduates he taught in his thirty-five years at King's. Often set in a pastoral landscape—on a bicycle ride, or simply in the gardens of the University (perhaps the most beautiful in the world)—they are tinged, as he recognizes, with a hint of eroticism, but an eroticism that has been carefully contained:

> Last night I spent the evening with some undergraduates listening to the gramophone. I am not the least in love with any of them, nor likely to be. But the subtle charm of them to me pervaded all the atmosphere. It is only when this mild radiance blazes up that trouble begins.

> I do feel that Cambridge in Spring, with its young men, is very lovely. Last night (24 May [1927]) I sat out in the College garden with three of them, till 10:30—one of those rare English nights when one can do that. And I was delighted, as so often, by the candour, sensitiveness, and intelligence of these boys—a small minority, no doubt, in the whole mass of athletes and womanisers, but still very charming.

> Only a week or two ago I bicycled out there [to Overcourt] with an undergraduate. We crossed by ferry and wheeled our machines along the green road on the dyke that leads to Holywell, and had tea there, sitting out and looking at the slow river. The meadows were full of buttercups and the hedges of hawthorn. The young man, charming as they always are, faintly stirred my sensibilities, and interested my mind. We rode home to a late supper and smoked for an hour in my rooms, looking at Japanese prints. 'And so to bed!'

Here we have Dickinson's authentic "love life," for which, in contrast to the tortured entanglements with Oscar Eckhard and Peter Savary, he had nothing to reproach himself. It is, one might say, the legitimate "teacherly," or "donly," solution to the homosexual predicament. Noel Annan, who provides a Forward to the autobiography and who himself went up to King's in 1935, recalls Dickinson in just this fashion: "He holds a special place in the golden age of friendship between dons and undergraduates." The final chapter of the autobiography, after rehearsing Dickinson's bitter disappointment with the "international anarchy" of the postwar decade, concludes elegiacally with a haunting image of the University and its students: "I am getting very old and have little left to do but to keep myself innocently occupied so long as I can, or must. I still enjoy myself much and often. This term in particular Cambridge had been so lovely in the almost perpetual sunshine that it has been enough to be alive and look at it. And still the young men exercise their perennial fascination."

2

AUDEN & CO

Christopher Isherwood

and

Stephen Spender

W. H. Auden, Stephen Spender, and Christopher Isherwood
on Ruegen Island, 1931.

Spender: With a masturbatory camera designed for narcissists I took—or it took—the most
famous photograph in the history of the world, of US THREE.

Isherwood: Stephen, in the middle, with his arms around Wystan and Christopher and an expression on his
face which suggests an off-duty Jesus relaxing with "these little ones." Christopher, compared with the others,
is such a very little one that he looks as if he is standing in a hole.

From *Christopher and His Kind* (New York: Farrar, Straus, Giroux, 1976), pp. 81–82. Photograph reprinted with the permission of The
Poetry/Rare Books Collection, University Libraries, State University of New York at Buffalo.

∞ THE NAMES OF Christopher Isherwood (1904–1986) and Stephen Spender (1909–1995) are intimately linked in modern literary history. Along with their mutual friend W. H. Auden (1907–1973), they were the foremost representatives of the Thirties generation—sometimes, following Samuel Hynes, called "the Auden Generation"—which introduced a new political urgency into British literature in response to the rise of fascism. Isherwood, Spender, and Auden in fact formed a kind of literary triumvirate, whose lives and work were richly interwoven throughout the decade (and who remained friends until death). Isherwood and Auden had been schoolmates in the closing years of the First World War. Then in the late 1920s Auden befriended Spender when they were fellow undergraduates at Oxford, and in 1928 Auden introduced Spender to Isherwood.

They were united first by a shared literary sensibility—Auden as a poet, Isherwood as a novelist, and Spender as a kind of polymath, writing poetry, fiction, and political essays. In the case of Auden and Isherwood, this affinity led to their actual collaborating on three plays and a travel diary in the later 1930s. Although there were subtle and ever-changing differences in their political views—with Spender the most militant of the three and Isherwood the least—they also shared a common response to the political crises of the Thirties, first to the poverty and injustice of the Depression and then, increasingly, to the threat posed by fascist dictators, especially Hitler. Spender was briefly a member of the Communist Party, and Isherwood and Auden happily described themselves as fellow-travelers. All three, like so many of their generation, were deeply engaged by the Spanish Civil War, which they considered the great antifascist cause of the decade: Spender and Auden actually went to Spain, and Isherwood was sorely tempted to. Most important, for our purposes, they were united by their homosexuality. Indeed, they were as much a sexual as a literary triumvirate, intensely preoccupied with "buggery" (as they chose to call it) and influencing one another in its pursuit and in their reaction to the homophobia of their society. (Although not romantically attached, Auden and Isherwood were also occasional bedmates for at least a decade.) Auden generally took the lead in their sentimental education: his example persuaded the other two to pursue their erotic adventures in Berlin in the late 1920s and early 1930s, where Isherwood and Spender were close neighbors for the better part of three years. Most strikingly, Isherwood and Spender found themselves, in the mid-1930s, involved in long-term relationships with working-class men, and both of those relationships ended in dramatic political adventures.

The autobiographical record of this story is fascinatingly complex. Auden wrote no autobiography, although he suggested that his commonplace book *A Certain World* was "a sort of autobiography."[1] Isherwood, however, wrote two (and arguably three) autobiographies, in addition to his many autobiographical fictions.[2] The first, *Lions and Shadows*, was published in 1938. It treats his life in the 1920s, from his last two years at public school, through Cambridge, to his decision to leave for Berlin in 1929. It is a deeply closeted work—despite being composed during his five-year international romance with Heinz Neddermeyer—which nonetheless invites a homosexual reading, at least for the cognoscenti. The second, *Christopher and His Kind*, written four decades later in Southern California, picks up the story in 1929 and ends with Isherwood's departure for America, with Auden, in 1939. In contrast to *Lions and Shadows*, *Christopher and His Kind* is very much "out" and expressly concerned with Isherwood's sexual life (just as the earlier work had been expressly concerned with his literary life). It is in fact a product of the militant political consciousness of American Gay Liberation in the 1970s, as its title already suggests, yet its no less militant irony and self-satire clearly link it with

---

1. W. H. Auden, *A Certain World* (New York, 1970), p. vii.

2. *Kathleen and Frank* (1971), Isherwood's elaborately annotated version of his mother's diaries, focuses on the years before his father's death in the First World War but naturally becomes, in its latter half, more concerned with Isherwood himself. It might be considered a preparatory exercise for *Christopher and His Kind*. *My Guru and His Disciple* (1980), Isherwood's account of his relationship with Swami Prabhavananda, is also a partial autobiography of his life from 1939 to 1976, the year in which the Swami died and Isherwood completed *Christopher and His Kind*.

the earlier work and confirm our sense of the literary and psychological identity of its author.

Spender's autobiography, *World within World,* was published in 1951 and thus represents a curious intermediary between the two Isherwood autobiographies. Its chronological focus is virtually identical with *Christopher and His Kind:* the 1930s, although it contains brief accounts of Spender's childhood and his activities—notably in the National Fire Service—during the Second World War. Naturally many of the same figures and episodes appear in both books, and both are centrally organized about an account of their working-class homosexual romances and the political intrigues those romances gave rise to. But the differences are even more interesting than the similarities: differences in the language and tonality of their treatment of homosexuality and, above all, the radically different life choices made by the two men toward the end of the decade. Isherwood came to America to pursue his homosexual identity and eventually to find a permanent mate in Don Bachardy; Spender stayed in England and married. *Christopher and His Kind* thus becomes an apology for homosexuality and, despite its winning self-deprecation, a call to arms, while *World with World* becomes, depending on your point of view, a retreat back into the closet or a rallying-cry for bisexuality.

There is a fourth document, though not strictly speaking an autobiographical one, that is now very much a part of the Isherwood/Spender story: David Leavitt's novel of 1993, *While England Sleeps*. It is closely based on Spender's account of his love affair with Jimmy Younger in *World within World*, indeed so closely that the elderly Spender—in almost his last significant literary-political act—managed to get the book suppressed in England (several thousand copies were actually "pulped"), and Leavitt's American publisher agreed to discontinue selling it anywhere in the world. Although Spender sued Leavitt for plagiarism, what truly enraged him about the novel was that it supplemented the Jimmy Younger story with the element so spectacularly absent in the original: sex. The novel and Spender's reaction to it offer eloquent testimony to the historical transformation of gay sensibilities over the past half century. In the latest, and perhaps final, installment of the saga, Spender's cause has been taken up by the literary critic Marjorie Garber in her book *Vice Versa: Bisexuality and the Eroticism of Everyday Life* (1995), where Spender's postmodern erotic suppleness is championed against the oppressive essentialism of David Leavitt.

I will be concerned in this chapter with the variations, grand and subtle, that distinguish these renderings of a homosexual existence, focused on the 1930s but written over the course of nearly sixty years. One underlying reality, as yet unmentioned, categorically separates all of them from the autobiographies of John Addington Symonds and Goldsworthy Lowes Dickinson: they were written to be published, and published promptly upon completion, with the author taking full public responsibility for his actions. This fundamental difference is especially crucial for appreciating *Lions and Shadows,* which is less overtly forthcoming than either Symonds or Dickinson, but it should also affect our tolerance for the reticences and obfuscations that still afflicted Stephen Spender in 1951. We have entered an intellectual world where a homosexual life can now be narrated, if not always with full candor.

Lions and Shadows

HRISTOPHER ISHERWOOD IS a deceptively straight-forward writer, as much in his autobiographical works as in his fiction. His unfailing lucidity and his eagerness to entertain can distract us from attending to his deeper—and often deeply serious—purposes. Just as important, they can dull our sensitivity to the sometimes dizzying authorial posturing and self-ironizing that create multiple levels of meaning and invite complex, even contradictory, interpretations.

Part of Isherwood's deviousness is precisely his seeming straightforwardness: on the opening page of *Lions and Shadows* he announces—in what sounds like a joke on Rousseau—that his autobiography does not even pretend be truthful: its characters are "all caricatures" and its incidents have been dramatized with "a novelist's licence." And in fact many passages in it read like set-piece discarded from the several unpublished novels described in the book. But Isherwood's honest dishonesty puts us on notice that the author is not above a certain trickery.

The wickedest literary trick of *Lions and Shadows*, I am convinced, is its invitation to a double reading. It is ingeniously contrived to be perceived differently by two different imagined audiences: the general public, which is properly heterosexual, and an audience of sympathetic "conspirators," essentially homosexual, who will respond with recognition and pleasure to the author's carefully coded secret history. It thus represents a distinct moment in the history of gay literary consciousness, when an author—who, as we will see from *Christopher and His Kind*, was leading an openly homosexual life—feels he can give a public airing of his sexuality if only it is adequately disguised. Indeed, much of the fun and funniness of *Lions and Shadows* derives from the ingenuity of Isherwood's performance of this acrobatic act of self-exposure and self-effacement.

Perhaps the simplest example of the tactic is the narrator's gender-neutrality: on the rare occasions when his own desires are alluded to, either no object is mentioned or its sex is left unspecified. "Always, when I walked along this crescent, I should experience a slight but delicious nausea of sexual desire." "I had returned from a romantic holiday by the sea." Innocuous remarks, which for most readers simply confirm that the narrator is a sexual being—that is, a heterosexual being like the reader himself—but which insiders will note are gender-neutral and unelaborated. A more complex instance occurs when the author describes the quarters in Romilly Road to which he moved in January 1927:

> Mine was the rigid tidiness of the celibate: that pathetically neat room, as I
> now picture it, seems to cry out for the disorderly human traces of cohabita-
> tion—the hairbrush discovered among your papers in the drawer, the unfamil-
> iar queer-feeling garments in the dark cupboard, the too small slipper you
> vainly try to pull on when half awake, the wrong tooth-brush in your glass, the
> nail pairing in the fender and in the tea-cup the strange lustrous single hair.
> But the room, as long as I occupied it, remained virgin, unravished.

The passage is fiendishly devious. It puts us firmly in mind of sex, opening with "celibate" and "cohabitation" and ending with "virgin, unravished." To the in-attentive heterosexual reader the imagined companion will automatically seem to be female: there are the "too small slipper" and the "strange lustrous" hair. But the slipper, the insider will note, is not so small that the narrator doesn't confuse it with his own and try to put it on. The insider will further note that the "garments" and "toothbrush" are gender-neutral and the "nail pairing" is distinctly masculine. He may also be inclined to wonder how the author—who throughout the book has not a single sexual adventure—knows so much about "the disorderly human traces of cohabitation." We are being told—at least some of us are being told—that, despite his apparent claim to be, like his room, an "unravished virgin" (another inside joke), he has had or will have sexual experiences, of an unspecified character, that go unreported in the text.

A closely related device is to comment on the erotic activities of heterosexuals while failing to identify with them or even subtly distancing himself from them. Chatting with a flirtatious salesgirl in a sweetshop, he recalls his randy friend "Philip Linsley": "At this point Philip would undoubtedly have given her a long glance in the celebrated 'certain way'"—which, by implication, the narrator cannot. Watching bathers at the beach, he observes: "The majority of the men were secretly embarrassed at finding themselves practically naked in the presence of a lot of semi-naked and (presumably to them) attractive girls"—the parenthetical "presumably to them" strongly implying, for the attentive reader, "but not to me." At the same beach he befriends a working-class boy he calls Tim (who looks suspiciously like a trial-run for Heinz Neddermeyer, including Heinz's "snub nose" and "monkey-like" appearance):

> Together, we visited the local cinema, picked up a couple of girls and cuddled with them throughout the performance. I found that I was particularly good at cuddling; especially after three or four "dog's noses" (gin and beer) at the pub. Indeed, my very inhibitions made me extremely daring—up to a point. Tim, who really meant business, was often curiously shy in the opening stages. Once or twice, having pushed things farther than I had intended, I was scared to find myself committed to a midnight walk over the downs. But, on these occasions, I always discovered an excuse for passing my girl on to Tim.

Perhaps the passage tips the balance too far in an unabashedly homosexual direction, with the terrified narrator turning his girl over to the reliably heterosexual Tim. But the lazy straight reader will simply see a man successfully engaged in petting, although still too "inhibited" to go further, and likely overlook the narrator's surprise at his own technical facility (aided by liquor) or the implicit contrast between "Tim, who really meant business," and "me, who was just pretending."

The narrator also alludes repeatedly to some vague unhappiness, some unmentionable problem, in his life, which the straight reader is invited to interpret as generalized sexual repression but the insider will recognize as altogether specific. He quotes three startling entries from a 1924 diary: "'Too miserable to write any more . . .'" "'All the same symptoms . . .'" "'This is the end . . . .'" He then deploys his narrative authority to make fun of his younger self and throw the straight reader off the scent: "I wasn't dying of an obscure kind of paralysis—though in reading some of my more desperate entries, you would hardly suspect it. . . . By these outbursts, I meant, as a rule, simply that I was bored."

A variation on this theme is the recurring complaint about his isolation, or, more pointedly, his "sense of exclusion," which he claims to share with a small group of like-minded and similarly-suffering friends. The straight reader can interpret the isolation as political and intellectual—and, as we shall see, much of the text supports such an interpretation—while the cognoscenti will sense the familiar alienations of a homosexual ghetto. Again contemplating the summer guests enjoying themselves at the beach, he writes:

> People like my friends and myself, I thought, are to be found in little groups in all the larger towns: we form a proudly self-sufficient, consciously declassed minority. We have our jokes, we amuse each other enormously; we are glad, we say, that we are different. But are we really glad? Does anybody ever feel sincerely pleased at the prospect of remaining in permanent opposition, a social misfit, for the rest of his life?

He returned from the beach, "overcome by a profound melancholy," to his "lonely bed."

The subtitle of *Lions and Shadows* is "An Education in the Twenties." Its purpose, Isherwood writes, is "to describe the first stages in a lifelong education—the education of a novelist." Appropriately, a good deal of the book is devoted to discussing the six novels Isherwood wrote in the 1920s, only two of which were ever published. These discussions provide another opportunity for a double-edged exploration of the author's mysteriously shameful problem. This is especially true of the first novel, written while he was still at Cambridge, to which, significantly, he assigned the title *Lions and Shadows*.

The treatment of the story is a perfect example of Isherwood's double-speak. Its ostensible subject was the shame he felt for not having been old enough to serve in the Great War, a shame so terrible, he says, that it had to remain "subconscious" and "suppressed by the strictest possible censorship." "Had I become aware of it and dared to bring it up to the light, to discuss it, to make it the avowed motif of my story, *Lions and Shadows* would have ceased to be a curiosity for the psycho-analyst and become, instead, a genuine, perhaps a valuable, work of art." Doubtless Isherwood, like many of his generation (George Orwell and C. Day-Lewis come to mind), did bear a burden of survivor's guilt for having missed the War, a subject he in fact explored in his second published novel, *The Memorial*. But the repeated assertion that the guilt was somehow so overwhelming that it had to remain unspoken seems exaggerated. It invites the suspicion—intentionally, in my view—that his truly unspeakable "problem" was something entirely different.

That suspicion is confirmed by what Isherwood says about the novel's proposed title, *Lions and Shadows*. The phrase, he reports, came from C. E. Montague's *Fiery Particles*, but it was not chosen for any substantive reasons. Rather "it was simply an emotional, romantic phrase which pleased me, without my consciously knowing why, because of its private reference to something buried deep within myself, something which made me feel excited and obscurely ashamed." And why was the War invariably associated with "this feeling of guilty excitement," with "terrors and longings"? Because "'war,' in this purely neurotic sense, meant The Test. The test of your courage, of your maturity, of your sexual prowess: 'Are you really a Man?'" Here he comes about as close as he decently can to confessing that his real problem was homosexuality. There is, furthermore, a meta-issue here as well: Isherwood's elaborate discussion of his first novel telegraphs the message that the very book we are reading is also about homosexuality. For why else has it inherited a title chosen solely for "its private reference to something buried deep within myself, something which made me feel excited and obscurely ashamed"?

More typical of Isherwood's coded style than bathetic complaints about his problem or heavy-breathing analyses of The Test is his frequent resort to one-liners that both entertain and reveal. "Polly," the fiancée of his friend "Roger East," does yeoman's work as a veritable stand-up comic with an unfailing eye for Isherwood's (or, as she prefers, "Bisherwood's") true self. Polly, the author implies, has his number. She hints broadly at his effeminacy: "'Do you always flap about with your hands, like that? Hasn't anybody ever told you how funny you are?'" After her wedding she congratulates herself on avoiding an unimaginable fate: "'I was only thinking how awful it'd have been if I'd married Bisherwood, by mistake.'" And observing Isherwood's "celibate" quarters in Romilly Road (which had previously been rented by Roger and which were, presumably, a place of romantic clutter), she asks, "'What's Bisherwood done to this room? It's quite different from when you had it, Roger. He's made it all sort of respectable—like a public park.'" But the narrator reserves the best joke for himself. Visiting the French Alps with his schoolmates in the summer of 1922, he ends an account of the Baudelairean sexual views of his chum Allen Chalmers with a zinger: "Needless to say, Chalmers and myself were both virgins, in every possible meaning of the word." All readers can laugh at this emphatic put-down of teenagers whose sexual ideas far outstrip their experience. But the cognoscenti will also find a coded message in the joke: there is, it implies, more than one way to be a virgin.

◯ *LIONS AND SHADOWS* is organized about two great friendships: the first with "Allen Chalmers" (the future novelist Edward Upward), who became Isherwood's inseparable companion during his last years at public school (Repton) and in the two years they overlapped at Cambridge; the second with "Hugh Weston" (W. H. Auden), whom Isherwood had known as a boy in prep school (St Edmund's) and met again seven years later, in 1925, after Isherwood had left the university but while Auden, three years younger, was still at Oxford. Isherwood's relationships with both men are presented as essentially literary (since *Lions and Shadows* is ostensibly the story of his coming of age as a novelist), but with Chalmers the emphasis is on politics whereas with Weston it is on sex.

The story of Isherwood's friendship with Allen Chalmers is told, in the first instance, as one of shared political alienation, culminating in their joint creation of a utopian fantasy that was published many years later as *The Mortmere Stories*. Isherwood introduces Chalmers as "a natural anarchist, a born romantic revolutionary," who led young Christopher (one year his junior) into a private cult of opposition to the philistinism and snobbishness of their school and, ultimately, to the entire society for which it was a training ground. Chalmers is very much the mentor, initiating Christopher into his latest literary discoveries, while Isherwood presents himself—as in all his later political apprenticeships—as somewhat timorous and given to backsliding. Isherwood gets considerable comic mileage out of recounting the pair's youthful extremism. When they visited Les Invalides—which "Chalmers had denounced . . . in advance—a shrine to war!"—they decided the only proper response was to spit on Napoleon's tomb, which they proceeded to do, "mentally." Later they took a steam-tram up the French Alps, but "Chalmers and I refused to look at the view at all, much less to admire it; we had passed a resolution that morning consigning mountains to the great rubbish-heap of objects and ideas admired by our adversaries, 'the other side,' and therefore automatically condemned."

At the same time the story of the relationship is also told in Isherwood's patented double-edged manner: for the general reader there is the narrative of political and cultural alienation, but for the cognoscenti there is a coded romance, albeit a one-sided romance. Young Christopher was clearly smitten by the "strikingly handsome" Chalmers, with his "dark hair and dark blue eyes." "Never in my life," he confesses, "have I been so strongly and immediately attracted to any personality, before or since. Everything about him appealed to me." To be sure, the "attraction" was mainly ideological, but we are invited—at least some of us are invited—to recognize that Christopher's feelings, as the Freudians say, were overdetermined: the expressly erotic language permits, indeed encourages, a double reading.

During their travels in France in the summer of 1922 Chalmers revealed the secrets of *Les Fleurs du mal*. "His suppressed excitement set me, as always, instantly on fire." Later, in the Alps, Chalmers read Christopher a poem he had written. For Isherwood the comedian it is another instance of adolescent extravagance, but it is also a love-scene of sorts: "I tell him that this is his best poem and that now I am certain, absolutely convinced, that he is going to be a really great poet, the greatest of our generation. My voice trembles with excitement; I keep my eyes fixed on the roofs of the distant village, because they are full of tears. Chalmers is moved, too. "'Do you honestly like it? I'm glad. . . .' After this, we are too happy and excited to say any more."

Chalmers then went up to Cambridge, a year ahead of Christopher, and they corresponded. Christopher looked forward to the letters with the same romantic anxiety, and indulged in the same rituals of delayed gratification, as had Lowes Dickinson with Ferdinand Schiller's letters from India. "The mere sight of my address on the envelope would thrill me in anticipation," he writes. "I sometimes carried the letter about with me for hours, waiting for a quiet moment to enjoy it to the full."

The following year they were united at the University, where they became an inseparable couple, sharing unspoken private understandings, singing, as it were, a private duet. Their "semi-telepathic relationship" was sheer bliss for Christopher (as Isherwood reports in lines, we remind ourselves, written in the midst of his love affair with Heinz Neddermeyer): "Looking back, I think that those first two University terms have been amongst the most enjoyable parts of my whole life. . . . As long as I could be together with Chalmers, which was all day and most of the night, the word boredom didn't exist. I was in a continuous state of extreme mental excitement." No doubt the excitement was indeed "mental," but "excitement" (the attentive reader will notice) is also an erotic term, and it becomes a leitmotif in Isherwood's account of the friendship. At Cambridge Chalmers also introduced Isherwood to alcohol: "The icy layers of my puritan priggishness, which were far thicker than he ever suspected, had begun, very slowly, to thaw." Again we are in the presence of a sexual metaphor: under Chalmers's ministrations the frigid Christopher had begun to melt.

The friendship cooled in their second year at Cambridge. The main reason

was the firm emergence of Chalmers's heterosexuality. Part of Isherwood's strategy in telling the Chalmers story is to leave the matter of the young man's sexual
identity murky for as long as possible. At first we get only a hint: in public school
"[Chalmers's] nervous energy made him extremely good at football." When in
1922 he spent a term in France, the signals remain mixed: he read du Maupassant
and Flaubert, "thinking of . . . Madame Bovary being seduced in the closed black
cab," but his main guru was Baudelaire, from whom he "knew all about *l'affreuse
Juive,* opium, absinthe, negresses, Lesbos" and the doctrine of sexual love as
"the torture-chamber, the loathsome charnel-house, the bottomless abyss." At
Cambridge, the next year, matters began to clarify themselves: for all his alienation, Chalmers couldn't fully resist the enticements of the "hearties," who valued
his football skills and included him in their sexual predations. Finally, in Christopher's second year, the sexual issue became more exigent for Chalmers and
brought the relationship into crisis: "He was sexually unsatisfied and lonely: he
wanted a woman with whom he could fall in love and go to bed—not any more
of these shopgirl teasers and amateur punt-cuddling whores." Isherwood adds
that his own misery was of a different sort and did not admit of the same solution:
"I was unhappy, too; but less consciously so because, being in a much more complex psychological mess than Chalmers himself, I had evolved a fairly efficient
system of censorships and compensations." The cognoscenti will have no trouble
recognizing here an allusion to his homosexuality. The end of the one-sided romance (though not the friendship) left Christopher with an erotic hangover: he
suffered through "days of depression, when I huddled in my armchair, empty as
a burst paper-bag."

Much of Isherwood's attention in the Chalmers section of *Lions and Shadows*
is given to recounting the elaborate private fantasy the two young men created.
In part he does so because the fantasy was the first significant effort in Christopher's literary development, and the main subject of the book is his emergence
as a novelist. He also does so because the fantasy is often quite funny (the emerging writer, after all, will be a *comic* novelist). But he has a serious purpose as well:
for both Isherwood and Upward, the fantasy represented the earliest formulation
of an ideological worldview, an embryonic version of their adult political consciousness, though in the end the two drew significantly different conclusions
from the exercise.

The basic idea of the fantasy is that the world is divided into two opposing camps: "us" (Isherwood and Chalmers) and "them" (everybody else, but

especially everybody else at Cambridge). The fantasy is introduced in *Lions and Shadows* when they go up to the University for their scholarship exams: "We were venturing, like spies, into an enemy stronghold. 'They,' our adversaries, would employ other tactics down there; they would be sly, polite, reassuring; they would invite us to tea. We should have to be on our guard. 'They'll do everything they can to separate us,' I said darkly." In the event nobody tried to separate them. Instead they were lavished with "an enormous tacit bribe" of food and drink, against which they privately fortified themselves by "swearing never to betray each other, never to forget the existence of 'the two sides' and their eternal, necessary state of war."

Later, as undergraduates, they filled their private world with an ever-expanding cast of characters, headed by "the Watcher in Spanish" and "the Laily Worm," an imaginary don, "the typical swotter, the book-worm, the academic pot-hunter." They referred to their antagonists as "the Combine" or "the Poshocracy," "a word [Chalmers] had coined to designate the highest of our social circles." They also invented imaginary allies for themselves—the enemies of their enemies. They called them "the Other Town," then "the Rats' Hostel" (after the menagerie portrayed in three Dürer prints on Chalmers's wall), and finally the village of "Mortmere," whose "anarchic, eccentric freedom" stood in eternal opposition to "the University system" and whose denizens became their familiars.

One feature of Mortmere (which is often genuinely amusing in a vaguely P. G. Wodehouse fashion) requires our attention: its plot has two expressly homosexual subthemes. The first centers on the figure of Reverend Welken, the village Rector, who "had been guilty of moral offenses with a choirboy"; the second involves a young man, Anthony Belmare, "whose extraordinary beauty was a source of perpetual jealousy" between the College Headmaster, Shreeve, and Mr. Wherry, a local architect. Homosexuality, in other words, is treated with an amused condescension that doesn't endanger the authors' heterosexual credentials: it is a silly (if harmless) infatuation of old men with young boys from which we can all get a good laugh. At the same time, Isherwood's inclusion of even these arch homosexual elements in his retailing of the Mortmere story has a faintly subversive effect: it reminds readers of the reality of homosexuality even while keeping it at arms length. In this respect it performs the same double function as an anecdote Isherwood tells, early in the book, about his final term at public school: "For the first time, I had a study of my own, and two fags to keep it clean. The fags were both new boys, their names were Berry and Darling. I caused my friends much amusement whenever I shouted down the passage: 'Berry, darling!' or 'Darling Berry!'" Like Christopher's schoolmates, all of us are properly (and safely) amused, but a few of us (and doubtless a few of Christopher's schoolmates as well) are more than just amused.

Isherwood reports that, as the "telepathic relationship" waned, the Mortmere stories became an increasing obsession for Chalmers, who tried (sometimes with Isherwood's reluctant help) to turn them into a book, one that would link Mortmere to his growing concern with the social injustices of his society: "He was to spend the next three years in desperate and bitter struggles to relate Mortmere to the real world of the jobs and the lodging-houses; to find the formula which would transform our private fancies and amusing freaks and bogies into valid symbols of the ills of society and the toils and aspirations of our daily lives." And eventually Chalmers did find the formula. He found it, Isherwood writes, "not hidden in the mysterious emblems of Dürer or the prophetic utterances of Blake, not in any anagram, or cipher, or medieval Latin inscription, but quite clearly set down, for everybody to read, in the pages of Lenin and of Marx."

Edward Upward, in other words, became a Communist. In retrospect, we are made to see that the "us-them" fantasy of Mortmere served as an intellectual apprenticeship for Upward's adult politics—for the dialectical binarism of Marxism-Leninism. But what, we might wonder, was its upshot for Isherwood, who of course did not become a Communist? In the official story of a young man's literary education it seems mainly to provide an opportunity for him to hone his comic skills. But might it not have had another function as well? Might it not have been the primordial version of the very different worldview Isherwood would articulate in *Christopher and His Kind,* where the universe is divided, not between capitalists and workers, but between the "tribe" of homosexuals and their straight oppressors? I would be stretching matters to claim that Isherwood's gay identity had achieved such settled self-consciousness by 1938. Clearly it hadn't. Nonetheless, Mortmere symbolized for him a deep and abiding sense of his isolation and exclusion. Toward the end of *Lions and Shadows* there is a strange incident, a kind of negative epiphany. Heavily sedated with drink and wandering over sand dunes at the beach, Christopher suddenly found himself wrestling with "the wind": "As I fought my way down towards the sea, the wind assumed a physical shape. It was the Enemy, the Laily Worm, Cambridge; it was the embodiment of my most intimate and deadly fears." Here his "most intimate and deadly fears" are linked directly the oppositional fantasy of Mortmere. One suspects it had lodged itself in his unconscious, or perhaps in his semi-conscious, as a code for his oppressed sexual condition.

∽ "HUGH WESTON" IS INTRODUCED IN *Lions and Shadows* just as the infatuation with Chalmers withers, and, along with it, the preoccupation with Mortmere. Weston appears not merely as Chalmers's replacement but in certain ways his opposite. In particular, he is not an object of desire: he was only ten years old when he and Christopher got to know one another at prep school, and, in contrast to the "strikingly handsome" Chalmers, he is described as "a sturdy, podgy little boy, whose normal expression was the misleadingly ferocious frown common to people with very short sight." Indeed, he seems downright unprepossessing: "untidy, lazy and, with the masters, inclined to be insolent."

Nonetheless, young Weston is immediately associated with sex—and, what's more, with a profoundly antiromantic, one might say materialistic, view of sex:

> To several of us, including myself, he confided the first naughty stupendous breath-taking hints about the facts of sex. I remember him chiefly for his naughtiness, his insolence, his smirking tantalizing air of knowing disreputable and exciting secrets. With his hinted forbidden knowledge and stock of mispronounced scientific words, portentously uttered, he enjoyed among us, his semi-savage credulous schoolfellows, the status of a kind of witch-doctor. I see him drawing an indecent picture on the upper fourth form blackboard.

In his earliest incarnation Weston is a kind of boy-positivist, a home-grown Krafft-Ebing or Frank Harris, whose ambition, significantly, was to become a mining engineer.

They met again seven years later, when, "by purest chance," a mutual acquaintance brought Weston to tea just before Christmas 1925. In the interim Weston had discovered his vocation as a poet, and a good deal of *Lions and Shadows* goes to recounting their literary relations. In artistic matters Christopher was very much the teacher, to whom Weston looked for approval—"a sort of literary elder brother." But sexually Weston remained the unchallenged authority. By now his sexual materialism had evolved into a full-fledged ideology—and practice as well—that quite terrified the older Christopher even as it entranced him.

Six months later, in July of 1926, Weston paid Christopher a visit at the seaside. Isherwood sets the unapologetically physical Weston to minister to Christopher's unnamed sexual malaise, in language carefully coded to telegraph a diagnosis of repressed homosexuality:

> Weston left nothing alone and respected nothing: he intruded everywhere; upon my old-maidish tidyness, my intimate little fads, my private ailments, my most secret sexual fears. . . . I had found myself answering his questions, as one always must answer, when the questioner himself is completely impervious to delicacy or shame. And, after all, when I had finished, the heavens hadn't fallen; and, ah, what a relief to have spoken the words aloud!

Isherwood follows his by-now well-established technique of presenting Weston's irreverent erotic philosophy in a way that carefully fails to specify the sex of his partners, thereby sending a familiar double message, one for ordinary readers, another, as it were, for gnostics: "Weston's own attitude to sex, in its simplicity and utter lack of inhibition, fairly took my breath away. He was no Don Juan: he didn't run round hunting for his pleasures. But he took what came to him with a matter-of-factness and an appetite as hearty as that which he showed when sitting down to dinner." Weston's lascivious talk left Christopher "excited and disturbed." He continued to rehearse the "shameless prosaic anecdotes" as he "lay restlessly awake at night, listening to the waves, alone in my single bed."

The meeting, with its aggressively frank discussions, inspired a guilty reaction in the puritanical Christopher: "During the next three of four months, I suffered all the acute mental discomfort of a patient who has been deserted by his psycho-analyst in the middle of the analysis. . . . I ran away . . . to a cottage in Wales [rather like Ludwig Wittgenstein escaping to a cabin in Norway to wrestle with *his* homosexual demons], where I sat at the window, looking down the road towards the mountains and trying to read the first volume of Proust"—another wink to the cognoscenti. He even contemplated suicide, going so far as to buy a gun and make a will (in which, revealingly, he ordered Chalmers "to burn my manuscripts and diaries unread"). Typically, however, Isherwood turns the matter into a joke by noting that Christopher's family refused to take his despair seriously: "They knew me too well: everybody knew me too well—that was my supreme humiliation."

Were Weston's sexual lectures perhaps accompanied by demonstrations? In *Christopher and His Kind* Isherwood reports that he and Auden did indeed have sex together—sex very much in the antiromantic spirit of Weston's erotic philosophy. Describing a visit Auden paid him in Paris in January 1937, on the way to the Spanish Civil War, he writes:

> Their friendship was rooted in schoolboy memories and the mood of its sexuality was adolescent. They had been going to bed together, unromantically but with much pleasure, for the past ten years, whenever an opportunity offered itself, as it did now. They couldn't think of themselves as lovers, yet sex had given friendship an extra dimension. They were conscious of this and it embarrassed them slightly—that is to say, the sophisticated adult friends were embarrassed by the schoolboy sex partners.

The passage is chronologically confusing. If they were "schoolboy sex partners," they must have been going to bed together for more like twenty years. But if "ten years" is accurate, their casual screwing didn't begin until 1927, more than a year after the tea-party reunion of December 1925 and at least six months after the fateful seaside visit that left Christopher so profoundly "excited and disturbed." Most likely the initiation had to await Christopher's recovery from suicidal guilt and the retreat to Wales. Perhaps it occurred when he visited Auden at Oxford in early December 1926, after which Christopher's guilt continued to attack him in the form of a bad cold every time they met: "During the next two years, these psychological attacks became one of our stock jokes. . . . Were they . . . a manifestation of my tireless Sense of Guilt? Was the analyst-patient relationship between Weston and myself far more permanent and profound than either of us realized? Honestly, I can't say. Or perhaps I won't say." The final enigmatic remark is, once again, an encoded signal to his sexual fellow travelers.

Weston, we sense, was destined to win their sexual argument. His final triumph, and the moment of Christopher's full conversion, came after Weston introduced his pupil to the doctrines of "the great psychologist" Homer Lane, whose central precept (in the manner of Wilhelm Reich) was that "there is only one sin: disobedience to the inner law of our own nature." Weston had absorbed this revolutionary teaching through Lane's disciple the anthropologist John Layard (called "Barnard" in *Lions and Shadows*) on a visit to Berlin, where Weston established an erotic beachhead for the pilgrims, Isherwood and Spender, who would follow him there in the next two years. By this point—the end of 1928—Christopher had reached such depths of self-loathing that he was more than ripe for the Lane-Layard gospel of sex without guilt:

I hadn't advanced an inch, really, since those Cambridge days. "Isherwood the
Artist" was still striking an attitude on his lonely rock. But his black Byronic
exile's cloak failed to impress me any longer. I knew what was inside it now—
just plain, cold, uninteresting funk. Funk of getting too deeply involved with
other people, sex funk, funk of the future. I was eternally worrying about what
was going to happen to me—in 1930, in 1940, in 1950; eternally building up
defenses against attacks which were never launched.

Those frightening but unspecified attacks, the gnostic reader will know, were the
public humiliations that he must expect if he embraced a queer life. But Christopher heard the insinuating voice of great Homer Lane—Weston's Homer
Lane—urging him to follow the imperious call of his desires:

> "You're afraid—afraid to trust your deepest instincts, afraid to take the
> plunge! . . . We know what you want, all right! The voice of your heart has
> told us already. You want to commit the unforgivable sin, to shock Mummy
> and Daddy and Nanny, to smash the nursery clock, to be a really naughty little
> boy. Well, why not start? Time's getting on. It's your only hope of ever grow-
> ing up, at all. If you stick to your safe London nursery-life, you never *will*
> grow up. You'll die a timid shrivelled Peter Pan."

The "internal struggle continued—to its inevitable conclusion": the decision to
leave England and go to Germany, where Weston had already invited him to visit
and where he could meet John Layard himself.

On March 14, 1929, Christopher Isherwood left London by afternoon train
for Berlin—where his autobiographical journey would be resumed almost forty
years later.

World within World

THIRTEEN YEARS SEPARATE *Lions and Shadows* from Stephen Spender's *World within World*. That historical distance, one might anticipate, should enable the later autobiographer to be more frank about his homosexuality. And indeed it does. *World within World* contains long, circumstantial accounts of Spender's homosexual affairs, as well as extended reflections about the advantages and disadvantages of love between men. Its centerpiece is the narrative of Spender's nearly four-year-long relationship with "Jimmy Younger" (Tony Hyndman) and the dramatic events that led Spender to try to rescue Jimmy from prison (and, Spender feared, death) in Spain during the Spanish Civil War. In this respect the book marks a clear advance in candor on *Lions and Shadows*. It is the logical-next-step, one might say, in the emergence of gay autobiography from the closet.

But in reality the frankness of *World within World* is highly circumscribed. Indeed, it is so hedged about, both rhetorically and substantively, that the book often seems emotionally more closeted, more anxiety-ridden, than its predecessor. It gives the impression of a painfully embarrassed admission, whereas *Lions and Shadows* has the effect of a wickedly subversive revelation.

A good deal of *World within World* is in fact written in the coded manner we have become familiar with from *Lions and Shadows,* where sexual realities and relationships are disguised in language that is both gender-neutral and emotionally unspecific. But because Spender's book appeared almost a decade and a half after Isherwood's and because, in contrast to *Lions and Shadows*, it describes several relationships whose homosexual character is transparent, Spender's resort to these euphemisms and circumlocutions—which have a piquant double-edged effect in Isherwood—seems merely evasive. The reader (or perhaps I should say the gay reader) is not charmed or amused by the author's ingenuity, as he is with Isherwood, but merely exasperated. Why, that reader is inclined to ask, if Spender is willing to describe his love affairs with men, does he persist in speaking vaguely of "a troubled period of my adolescence" or "my problem" or "the person to whom the [love] poem was addressed" instead of identifying his feelings and actions with honesty and precision? A technique that was mildly seditious in 1938 seems reactionary in 1951. But, in Spender's defense, we should remember that 1951 is not yet 1976 (the year *Christopher and His Kind* was published): the awkward compromise he strikes is a perfect reflection of a time when homosexuality could be spoken of only apologetically. One might even argue that the increased homophobia of the post-War years, in England as in America, made his backpedaling inevitable.

The coded style of *Lions and Shadows* is not, however, Spender's preferred device for talking about homosexuality in *World within World*. Rather, he invents a manner distinctly his own. It might be called "coy frankness." It uniquely combines candor with obfuscation, and it has the dubious distinction of allowing Spender to talk about homosexuality in such a way that it almost feels as though he were *not* talking about it. He achieves this curious effect above all by virtually eliminating desire from the text. Men are shown engaging in elaborate and often agonized relationships without so much as a hint as to what brought them together in the first place. Instead Spender indulges in airy philosophical speculations about "identification" and "otherness," long passages of sub-Sartrean existential blather that take us ever further from the physical and emotional specifics of homosexual love. Desiring bodies evaporate into abstraction. The systematic repression of sex in *World within World* must have constituted an open invitation to David Leavitt to write *While England Sleeps*.

A significant difference in plot, and ultimately in sexual ideology, underlies the stylistic choices that make *World within World* at once more advanced and more regressive than *Lions and Shadows:* the story reaches its climax in Spender's decision to marry Inez Pearn. That decision ended the love affair with Jimmy Younger and precipitated Jimmy's departure for Spain, with all its melodramatic consequences. The decision, we come to recognize, has been carefully prepared textually: women have been insinuated as objects of desire almost from the start. What might be called the sexual architecture of the book now reveals itself as a grand movement from "unrespectable" homosexuality (associated with Isherwood, Auden, and Berlin) to "normal" heterosexuality (associated with Inez, his literary ambition, and London). I am reluctant to call the book a plea for bisexuality, because the term implies a kind of sexual evenhandedness, an openness to erotic and emotional relations with both sexes, quite foreign to Spender's ultimately tendentious apology for marriage. Rather, the message of *World within World* is that the author has put his homosexual adventures behind him—not, to be sure, with the vengefulness of a convert (he remained close to Isherwood, both personally and artistically) but with an adult appreciation of their immaturity and inevitable unsatisfactoriness.[3]

⚭ SPENDER'S ACCOUNT OF HIS childhood and adolescence in *World within World* is written entirely in the coded style of *Lions and Shadows*. It centers on young Stephen's revolt against the "Puritan decadence" of his parents, especially his father. His family, Spender writes, was obsessed with the fear of being perceived or exposed as immoral: "In all their relationships there was the sense of something which might turn up and which could never be mentioned, . . . a fear of discovering something horrible . . . about ourselves." He carefully avoids naming the particular "horrible something" whose discovery in his own case would have been most catastrophic. Likewise his youthful rebellion against the family's Puritanism is cast in entirely general terms. "My revolt against the attitude of my family led me to rebel altogether against morality," he writes. "Secretly I was fascinated by the worthless outcasts, the depraved, the lazy, the lost"—where "the depraved," one imagines, serves as an acceptable stand-in for "the homosexual." He continues in this bowdlerizing vein: "[My] reaction was doubtless due to the fact that I wanted to love what I judged to be the inadmissible worst qualities in myself." In the same passage he complains that his father "turned everything into rhetorical abstraction, in which there was no concreteness, no accuracy." One cannot imagine a more exact description of Spender's own intellectual manner, especially in treating his sexuality.

Spender also recounts his important childhood relationship with his grandmother, Hilda Schuster, who had married a Jew. The narrative is vaguely Proustian, with the grandmother serving as a confidante who indulged his taste for "modern painting, theatre, [and] literature," in contrast to his father's hidebound Victorianism. The grandmother was also the earliest source of his leftist

---

3. I make no claim about Spender's actual sexual behavior after his marriage, only about the argument he advances in the text.

political views. At the same time, the relationship with the grandmother became, Spender recognizes, a model for the emotional dependencies of his adulthood—in particular, one suspects, that with Isherwood during their Berlin years, although Isherwood is not mentioned specifically. Spender and the grandmother "discussed everything," including "sex": "she was quite unshocked by anything I said." But of course nothing is mentioned about the content of their shocking discussions. Still, Spender manages to telegraph the suggestion (in the *Lions and Shadows* manner) that his Jewishness—inherited from his grandmother's husband—became a kind of metaphor for homosexuality: "At school, where there were many Hampstead Jews, I began to realize that I had more in common with the sensitive, rather soft, inquisitive, interior Jewish boys, than with the aloof, hard, external English." "The only trait common to most Jews," he concludes, "is that of feeling 'different.'"

Spender's evasiveness is raised to a high art in the account of his adolescence. Bland generalizations and circumlocutions abound. As puberty hit he was afflicted with a series of psychosomatic complaints. "These illnesses," he writes, "were . . . a means of escape from certain problems." He and his friend Maurice Cornforth exchanged confidences: "We were both traversing crises in our adolescence. We made frightful confessions to one another which left me shaken." In this "troubled period" of his adolescence art became a more or less acceptable outlet for coping with his "problem": "To state my taste for poetry, painting, and friends at this time was an act of passionate self-revelation. One day, in the fruit garden of a house in Surrey, I told Caroline that I liked Michelangelo and the Elgin Marbles. It was the trembling revelation of a terrifying truth." The last sentence is in his best *Heart of Darkness* imitation, while the mention of Michelangelo drops a strategic homoerotic hint.

The account of childhood and adolescence in the opening pages of *World within World* contains no mention of the sort of boarding school homosexuality that is such a fixture of British autobiography—and that figures so prominently in the memoirs of John Addington Symonds and Goldsworthy Lowes Dickinson. At the very end of the book, however, Spender returns to his childhood. Why he does so is not satisfactorily explained. Perhaps he wants to lend the volume a literary symmetry, echoing the circular movement that Proust achieves at the end of *Le temps retrouvé*. "Childhood is like wheels within wheels of this book, which begins, and revolves around, and ends with it," he writes, in a sentence that, whether intentionally or through negligence, he repeats word for word within five pages. When he revisits his childhood at the close, the repressed schoolboy episodes make their reluctant appearance, displaced from their natural location and cast into the book's outer limits. There are only two of them; they are remarkably tame; and Spender's account is thoroughly understated. One took place right after his arrival at boarding school, at age nine: "On my second morning at school I was told to go and take a cold shower. I entered a room where I saw a number of boys, some of them pubescent, completely naked. It was the first time I had ever seen any nakedness, outside my own family, and it made a strong impression on me." The other was less innocent, even though it occurred when he was only seven. After protecting his flank by noting that he had fallen in love with a girl named Penelope, he introduces a boy he calls Forbes, with whom, one day, he got into a wrestling match: "Suddenly afraid, I lay on top of him and held him very closely in my arms, and at that moment I experienced a sensation like the taste of a strong sweet honey, but not upon my tongue, and spreading wave upon wave, throughout my whole body." Almost unbelievably, this childhood orgasm, carefully enveloped in metaphorical drapery, is the only description of sexual arousal in the entire autobiography.

The elaborate avoidances of the opening sections of *World within World* seem all the more preposterous when we come to the book's first explicitly sexual episodes, which occur on a Continental vacation during the summer before Spender went up to Oxford. Suddenly he drops the *Lions and Shadows* style in favor of his "coy frankness." He introduces the new manner by relating three fantasies he entertained while in Nantes. They acknowledge the attractions of the male body, even while directing the nineteen-year-old's efforts into safely heterosexual channels:

I would populate the scene with passionate fantasies: of a bare-throated poet as beautiful as Shelley approaching me with a book under his arm which he wished to open between us, like the unfolded wings of a bird, as we lay under a hedge. Or of a handsome couple whom I would meet in a copse, of whom the husband would say: "Monsieur, we have a great sorrow. I cannot give my wife a child. Therefore I implore you to sleep with her behind this hedgerow, then get up and walk out of our lives for ever." Or I imagined that I met a youth who wished to learn English and to teach me French. We began by naming all the parts of the body, beginning with the head and working downwards: until this anatomy of the bodies entered into the anatomy of the language and became a passionate love-making of French with English.

In the last fantasy the heterosexual protections are abandoned. In their stead Spender resorts to a technique—which he will perfect in the remainder of the book—of aestheticizing his urges: not bodies but languages make love. Homosexual desire is at once coyly admitted and nervously deflected.

The fantasies serve as a prelude to Spender's first homosexual romance, with an English boy he met in Lausanne. His account displays the full armory of his defense mechanisms, and it anticipates several of the features of his later relationship with Jimmy Younger. Spender describes the boy, whom he calls "D" and who was exactly his own age, as at once physically attractive and intellectually repellent: "D" was "well-bred and ignorant, delicate and uncultivated, beautiful and vapid." Desire is thus insulated by aversion, as the desired object is condescendingly assigned to a lesser category of being. In the case of Jimmy Younger the demotion will be not just intellectual but social as well. Nonetheless the same process of distancing, of "othering," is at work in Spender's presentation of "D" as an intellectual lightweight.

The infatuation with "D" is further sanitized by setting it in competition with a heterosexual romance, Spender's "love" for a young woman, Caroline, whom his grandmother Schuster had brought into the Spender household to care for the children after both parents had died. The situation perfectly foreshadows the more epochal homosexual-heterosexual struggle for Spender's soul between Jimmy Younger and Inez Pearn: "This was my first experience of the feeling that I had betrayed my love of one person, by being too deeply involved with another. What distressed me most was to realize that even when I cared most intensely for Caroline I was not released from my obsessive fascination with D." The message here is that the young Spender was not really a homosexual. His deepest feelings remained attached to a worthy heterosexual object awaiting him at home; he was merely "involved with" or "obsessively fascinated" by the "spoiled favourite" in Lausanne, whose frivolousness disqualified him as a serious romantic interest.

Spender's account of the infatuation with "D" is fundamentally passionless. He speaks of his "love," even, as we've seen, of his "obsessive fascination," but never of his desire. Nor does he provide any of the circumstantial detail or reconstructed dialogue that make Isherwood's relationships with Chalmers and Weston so unforgettably vivid. Instead he remains vague, both physically and emotionally. We have to be satisfied with mystifying generalizations. "Our relationship," he comments typically, "remained at a stage of mutual frustration and irritation because we were both afraid."

Spender wrote a story based on his Lausanne adventure. At Oxford, in the fall, he showed the story to his new undergraduate friend W. H. Auden, who judged it "'very good indeed.'"[4] Auden in turn showed it to Isherwood, and thus this little homoerotic narrative became, appropriately, the vehicle through which Spender and Isherwood were introduced at the end of 1928. In *Lions and Shadows* Isherwood gives a typically colorful account of the moment when the florid Spender descended upon them in Auden's rooms at Oxford: "A few weeks later, Weston arranged a meeting with the author. He burst in upon us, blushing, sniggering loudly, contriving to trip over the edge of the carpet—an immensely tall, shambling boy of nineteen, with a great scarlet poppy-face, wild frizzy hair, and eyes the violent colour of bluebells." The cognoscenti will have no difficulty recognizing a noisy gathering of young queens: "In an instant, without introductions, we were all laughing and talking at the top of our voices." Isherwood's account, which bristles with secret messages, differs remarkably from the staid version in *World within World,* where, even though we now know that the meeting was occasioned by Spender's homosexual story, not a word is uttered about its subject: "Isherwood made me a quite formal little speech saying he had read my manuscript, and that he regarded it as one of the most striking things he had read by a young writer for a long time, and so on."

Remembering the beginnings of the friendship with Isherwood apparently so raises Spender's homosexual anxiety level that he temporarily reverts to the coded language he had used to narrate his childhood and adolescence. Even though homosexuality was clearly a major theme of their discussions, Spender can't bring himself to say the word. Instead he falls back into evasive circumlocutions. "After this [the meeting in Oxford] I saw Isherwood in London. He simplified all the problems which entangled me, merely by describing his own life and his own attitude towards these things." There is moreover an interesting discrepancy between Spender's and Isherwood's versions of this period. Isherwood, we

4. *Lions and Shadows,* p. 279.

recall, had described himself as a sexual basketcase, desperately throwing himself into the arms of his "psychoanalyst" Weston, who plied him with the liberating doctrines of Homer Lane and Berlin. In Spender's account Isherwood is transformed into the sexual master, preaching the Lane-Layard gospel with all the sovereign confidence and authority of an experienced erotic adventurer: "The whole system [of Oxford and Cambridge] was to him one which denied affection and which was based largely on fear of sex. . . . He spoke of Germany as the country where all the obstructions and complexities of [middle-class] life were cut through. . . . By the end of our conversation on the edge of the Serpentine, I was longing to be cured by this method of being allowed to do whatever I liked." But Spender immediately adds (still in his generalized language), "I secretly doubted whether my desires, if fulfilled and even organized, would be less agitating." Homosexuality, although unmentioned and apparently unmentionable, clearly made him nervous.

At Oxford Spender adopted an affected persona whose effeminacy (so strongly hinted at in Isherwood's description) he is eager to mute and apologize for in *World within World*. His "eccentricity," as he calls it, was motivated by his opposition to the "hearty" culture of undergraduate life, with its exclusive interest in sport and women and its contempt for art and intellect. "When I found that [the hearties] cared only for games, drinking and girls, I was disappointed. Worse than this was their intolerance for everyone not like themselves. I took revenge on them for disappointing me, by becoming self-consciously their opposite. I became affected, wore a red tie, cultivated friends outside the college, was unpatriotic, declared myself a pacifist and a Socialist, a genius." The mention of his pacifism and socialism in this context is significant. One might be tempted to construe Spender's political radicalism as a displaced form of homosexual protest (which in Isherwood's case it sometimes was, by his own admission). But *World within World* gives the firm impression that Spender's political convictions were the most genuine thing about him, distinctly more forthright and emphatic than his tortured sexual convictions. I am thus disinclined to question his *bona fides* when he attributes his oppositional stance at Oxford to his detestation of the class prejudice of his fellow undergraduates.

Still, he is eager to explain away his affectation as the external sign of some deeper and somehow more respectable psychological process: "Affectation," he asserts, "is an aping of hidden outrageous qualities which are our real potentialities." And he adds, "I aped my own exhibitionism, effeminacy, rootlessness and lack of discipline." At the same time he nervously distances himself from the full-fledged sissies among the undergraduate population—"sickly young men" who "called one another 'dear' and burned incense in their rooms"—"esthetes" whose effeminacy was both too extravagant and without the political and intellectual inspiration that justified his own deportment.

While at Oxford he managed to fall in love with an undergraduate who was a perfect clone of his Lausanne boyfriend, with the singular difference that "Marston," unlike "D," seems to have been heterosexual. He was beautiful but dumb—"unassuming and yet dazzling"—thus recreating the intellectual distance that Spender apparently found sexually attractive. "Marston was someone with whom I had few interest in common. He was not talented or intellectual or even strikingly intelligent. What was extraordinary about him was the purity of his ordinariness." His only passions, in fact, were games and flying: he was training to become a pilot. Amusingly, Spender confesses that his hopeless infatuation led him to feign interest, even expertise, in Marston's utterly practical concerns.

As in his account of the affair with "D," Spender can't bring himself to say a word about the physical charms or manner that attracted him to Marston, except that "there was something watchful, withdrawn, in his attitude" that separated him from his fellow hearties. Once again, desire is obliterated from the text. Spender writes as if he chose the young man entirely at random: "I first noticed him—I remember—in the train to Oxford, at the beginning of my second term. . . . At that moment I made a decision to get to know him, when I quite well might not have done so. There was a moment of pure arbitrariness when I thought: 'I need not do this, but I will do it.'" We have to turn to a letter he sent Isherwood the following year, after the passion had subsided, to catch a glimpse of his true feelings. "I have stopped being in love with Marston," he writes, "but I still catch my breath when he comes into the room."[5] *World within World* contains not a single line of such erotic candor.

He is better at recreating the lunacy of the courtship, as he put himself through ever more hysterical contortions, while Marston responded with uncomprehending passivity. His "attachment" reached a crisis when he decided to write Marston a letter "stating my feelings towards him," a gesture that unwittingly repeated Goldsworthy Lowes Dickinson's imprudent letter to the young Oscar Eckhard in 1910. When they met, Marston "explained that he in no way re-

5. *Letters to Christopher: Stephen Spender's Letters to Christopher Isherwood 1929–1939* (fall, 1930), ed. Lee Bartlett (Santa Barbara, 1980), p. 36.

sponded to my emotion," but "he said he would like me to explain matters and make him understand. When I had done so, he looked at me with a dazed expression and said naively: 'Do you know, old son, this is the first time you've ever talked to me that I haven't been completely bored?'" Only the self-deprecatory wit and specificity of the story prevent us from growing annoyed at its parade of decorous circumlocutions: his "enthusiasm," his "feelings," his "attachment," his "emotion," the "matters" he must explain—anything but his "desire" or his "passion." "The friendship with Marston," he concludes in his airy philosophical manner, "was one phase of a search for the identification of my own aims with those of another man." Happily, it also inspired him to compose a series of love lyrics, the so-called "Marston" poems, which, almost forty years later, Christopher Isherwood still judged among Spender's best.

Embarrassed perhaps that he has recounted a homosexual romance—albeit an unreciprocated one—without ever mentioning the word, Spender follows the Marston story with a little discourse on sexual "labels." He presents himself as a postmodernist *avant la lettre,* refusing to be straitjacketed by the rigid sexual categories invented by psychiatry in its misguided effort to stabilize the fluid reality of erotic attraction. The speech is interesting both for its continued repression of the physical facts of homosexual sex (which are bowdlerized here as "certain of its aspects") and for its easy equation of heterosexuality with "the normal," whose comforts Spender is unwilling to forgo:

> I suspect that many people feel today that a conception of friendship which can be labelled homosexual, on account of certain of its aspects, excludes normal sexual relationships: and conversely that the heterosexual relationship should preclude those which might be interpreted as homosexual. As a result of this tendency to give themselves labels, people feel forced to make a choice which, in past times, was not made. It also follows that since a relationship of the highest understanding can be between two people of the same sex, some who have experienced this relationship renounce a normal way of life. Yet when we look into the lives of men and women in the past we see that relationships which today would be labelled abnormal existed side by side with the normal.

Given a few modifications, the passage might have come right out of David Halperin's *One Hundred Years of Homosexuality* (1990) or some other critique of the essentializing labels of modern sexology. One also understands why Spender has been taken up by Marjorie Garber in her defense of bisexuality, *Vice Versa*.

In effect, Spender here articulates the notion—recently advanced by some queer theorists—that sexual identity is a matter of choice rather than destiny. The body is a kind of infinitely malleable vessel, which can pursue different plea-sures with different objects, finding one sort of physical and emotional satisfac-tion with the same sex and (perhaps later in life) another with the opposite sex. Homosexuality, according to this view, is a "sexual preference"—with the impli-cation that one's tastes might change—rather than a "sexual orientation," which suggests desires so profoundly ingrained (whether biologically or through the experiences of early childhood) as to be inalterable. Spender's championing of what I've called the "postmodern" doctrine of sexual indeterminacy has, ironi-cally, given rise to the suspicion that his early homosexuality was more a social than an erotic phenomenon: that he was driven by a "peer pressure," notably that applied by his heroes Auden and Isherwood, to make the choice. In the Oxford of the 1920s, according to Isaiah Berlin, it was "chic to be queer," and "many students who weren't had to pretend the be, if they wanted to be socially success-ful."[6] Homosexuality, in this unfriendly interpretation, appears as merely an arti-fact of Spender's relentless careerism—which is also the view taken by his biog-rapher Hugh David. My own opinion is less cynical, though damning in its own way: Spender's same-sex desires were, I'm persuaded, authentic; the dishon-esty—or the self-deception—lay in his repression of them in the text of *World within World*.

I should not imply that David Halperin or Marjorie Garber would fully en-dorse Spender's critique of modern sexual "labels" in the passage I just cited. In particular, they would reject his tendentious characterization of heterosexuality as "normal" and his embarrassed denigration of his homosexual urges as "certain limitations in myself" that he had only reluctantly learned to accept. He has sought, he writes, "to go beyond those qualities which isolated me from com-monly shared human experience, towards the normal," "adjusting my acceptance of my own nature to the generally held concept of the normal." To abandon "the normal" means "to put oneself outside a concept which has a saving value of sanity in most people's minds." For the artist, in particular, it means "to feel cut

6. Quoted in Ian Hamilton, "Spender's Lives," *The New Yorker*, February 28, 1994, p. 76.

off from this warm flow of the general normal life," and "such isolation is a grave disadvantage." In these assertions one senses the profound sexual conservatism and conformity that separate Spender from Isherwood and Auden. Indeed, one suspects that his sentiments here were intended precisely for Isherwood's and Auden's consumption. According to Spender's strictures, his two friends had clearly made the wrong choice, both personally and artistically.

⊘ FROM 1929 TO 1932 Spender spent about half of his time in Germany, first in Hamburg and then, with Isherwood, in Berlin, pursuing the kind of homosexual life that Auden had pioneered there in 1928 and that Isherwood would describe much more candidly a quarter century later in *Christopher and His Kind*. The account of these years in *World within World* makes the homosexual character of Spender's adventures perfectly clear, but it goes to great lengths to blur their outlines and divert our attention from them. In part he achieves this effect by continuing to deploy the techniques he used to recount his infatuations with "D" and "Marston": he keeps to safely generalized language and, whenever possible, introduces heterosexual episodes to muddy the erotic waters. But he supplements these tried-and-true devices with two innovations, one political the other aesthetic. First, he consistently interprets the German homosexual scene of the late 1920s and early 1930s as an ominous metaphor for the coming Nazi revolution. The concrete sexual reality is thus allegorized into the story of Germany's political collapse. Here he imitates Isherwood's technique in *Goodbye to Berlin*—that conflation of sexual deviance and political madness ironically hinted at in the novel and then blatantly exaggerated in its movie-musical adaptation, *Cabaret*. More subtly, he associates Germany's homosexual subculture with artistic modernism: it becomes the acting-out of the decadent impulse implicit in avant-garde literature and painting, to the point where love-making between men seems merely the bodily counterpart of expressionist canvases or Danish-modern furniture.

Spender first went to Hamburg in the summer of 1929, before his last year at Oxford. In the account of this visit he manages, almost in spite of himself, to create a sense of the strong erotic pull he felt from the bronzed young men disporting themselves in the summer sun: "Thousands of people went to the open-air swimming baths or lay down on the shores of the rivers and lakes, almost nude, and sometimes quite nude, and the boys who had turned the deepest mahogany walked amongst the people with paler skin, like kings among their courtiers." But when he socializes with these young people, the sex of the participants is unspecified (although, of course, we imagine them to be indoor versions of the male bathers we have just seen), and the nakedness of their bodies is equated with the nakedness of their souls and thus linked to Germany's political disorder. At the same time Spender describes himself as properly detached from the scene and hence sexually "unscathed." Apparently he remained unscathed because no one—again we presume he means "no man," though he avoids being explicit— made a pass at him.

He links his friends' troubling display of sexuality to the artistic modernism that has conquered Germany. "Their lives flowed easily into the movements of art, literature and painting, which surrounded them"—the clean vertical and horizontal lines of the new architecture, the "experiments in the theatre and opera," the cinema. In effect, he identifies the erotic carryings-on of his young acquaintances with "the nihilism, sophistication and primitive vitality which was so dangerously attractive in the beginning of the Weimar Republic." Even as he places himself in what is clearly a homosexual environment he contrives to preserve the impression of his own aloofness and to imply that its deeper meaning was not erotic but cultural and political.

The main embodiment of this fusion of homosexuality with modernist art and political decadence was a young man Spender calls "Joachim." Tall and bronzed, with "raised, sexual, expressive nostrils," Joachim is introduced as the complete hedonist, dedicated to "living," where "living was bathing, friendship, travelling, lying in the sun." He is paired with his blond boyfriend, Willi, whose "utter devotion" Spender claims to find "sad." Both men are situated in Joachim's modernist apartment, surrounded by "beautiful things," above all huge photographs celebrating the sun-drenched homoeroticism of the New Germany. "The photographs were like an enormous efflorescence of Joachim's taste for 'living', a great stream of magnificent young people, mostly young men, lying on the sand, standing with their heads enshadowed and pressed back as though leaning against the sun, rising from bulrushes and grasses, swimming in seas and rivers, laughing from verandas, embracing one another." Again Spender rushes to equate the eroticism being portrayed in these photos with its "modern" artistic representation: "About the appearance of them all and about the very technique of the photography, there was the same glaze and gleam of the 'modern' as in the room itself and the people in it." In case we have failed to get the point he inserts a portentous aside to remind us of the political apocalypse that it is all leading to:

"(I imagine all these photographs now, sodden under sweet-smelling rubbish from which weeds grow behind broken window frames: and where is this army of the young?)"

In Spender's account Joachim appears as something of a priapic Hitler, ruling over the "court of those who loved him." He was also cavalierly unfaithful to Willi. When he took Spender on a Rhineland walking tour he picked up a boy named Heinrich—with a "body . . . liked carved polished wood"—whom he immediately pronounced "the great attachment of his life." Spender made this walking tour the subject of his novel *The Temple,* which he left unpublished until the late 1980s.

He says nothing about his own sexual activities, although in a letter to Isherwood he had written, "I am in love and going away with a German friend on the Rhine."[7] Indeed, the only erotic adventure he describes from his first Hamburg summer is safely heterosexual. At one of Joachim's parties he met a "slim and boyish" girl called Irmi. "She danced in an inviting way, pressing her body close to mine, and holding her warm brown face almost against my lips," after which she ran off to Joachim, "threw her arms around his neck and kissed him." Spender, it appears, is eager to present the Hamburg world as one of generalized erotic abandon, not exclusively or even expressly homosexual. "I seemed to be moving," he concludes the Irmi episode, "in a trance of sensuous freedom where everything was possible and plausible and easy." Accordingly, when he reports on his visit to a gay bar, he takes care to distances himself from its monstrous denizens, just as he had from the fairy esthetes at Oxford: "Men danced with men. Several freakish febrile men were dressed as women. Singing weirdly, rolling their eyes, chucking staid citizens seated at their tables under the chin, these lolled from table to table." "This decadence," he asserts, was simply "the reverse aspect" of "the swimming, the sun-bathing, the rather facile pleasure in beautiful things."

Spender returned to Hamburg the following summer and took up with a young man named Walter, who was, in effect, an amateur prostitute. The episode, although more sordid, is reminiscent of John Addington Symonds's relationship with Angelo Fusato. It also has certain marked affinities with Isherwood's exactly contemporaneous relationship with the boy Isherwood calls Otto Nowak, in both *Goodbye to Berlin* and *Christopher and His Kind:* it is presented

7. *Letters to Christopher* (April 17, 1929), p. 31.

against the background of the Depression, and it is ultimately sabotaged by its venality.

Walter was in fact an unemployed worker, thus marking a significant departure from the social equals who were Spender's first two inamorati. But in sexual terms, Spender still can't bring himself to say what has attracted him. Just as with Marston, he writes as if the decision to pick up the young man were utterly random: "At one *Lokal* I met an unemployed young man called Walter, in whom I rather arbitrarily decided to take an interest." Indeed, Walter is as much an economic as an erotic project for Spender: he becomes the personification of the Depression, and Spender's involvement with him is made to seem more political than sexual. Thus when Walter repeatedly borrowed money from him—supposedly to visit his relatives—and then promptly claimed to have lost it, Spender was prepared to forgive him on political grounds. In retrospect he criticizes his attitude as "sentimental." But he still struggles to persuade himself—as had John Addington Symonds—that the relationship was not merely an exploitative sham but contained some element of genuine feeling. It represented, he insists, his first significant escape from the Puritan decadence of his family into "something denser, less pure, but out of which I could extract and refine little granules of affection."

After Spender had been in Hamburg (on this second visit) only a few months, Isherwood invited him to become his neighbor in Berlin. Thus began the period of their most sustained and intimate friendship, as they walked through the city together, visiting its famous forests and cafes, and engaged in endless conversation. "About three years of my life," Spender writes, "were lived precariously off the excitement of being with Isherwood. I told him everything, I showed him every letter of any interest I received, I looked to his judgment of my friends and activities." But those "friends and activities" are never called by their real names in *World within World*. Astonishingly there is not a single word about the subject with which they were most preoccupied. Instead, Spender reverts to the bland generalizations and circumlocutions of his *Lions and Shadows* imitation. He was drawn to Isherwood not by his bold incursion into Berlin's homosexual underworld but by "the adventurousness of his life." Together they pursued an existence "in which we used Germany as a kind of cure for our personal problems." To be sure, he mentions "the relentlessly handsome German youths" they saw on their walks through the *Grünewald*, and he archly records Fräulein Thurau (Isherwood's legendary landlady Frl. Schroeder in *Goodbye to*

Berlin) rolling her eyes when she announced he would have to wait in the entrance hall because "*Herr Issyvoo hat Besuch.*" But otherwise homosexuality is simply banished from his account of their Berlin years. It contains no figure comparable to Joachim or Walter in Hamburg.

Spender established a pattern of spending six months a year in Berlin and six months in London. In London his life became intensely social, as the young writer threw himself into a routine of "parties, luncheons, dinners, teas" with which he sought to launch his literary career. But the pace was so hectic that, ironically, he got less accomplished "than when I was leading an unrespectable life in Berlin." He even contrives to suggest that he returned to Berlin not to pursue his sexual escapades but for the sake of his work. Berlin was a place not to find boys (as Isherwood would memorably define it in *Christopher and His Kind*) but to escape from social distractions. Spender even contends—with some justice—that his sojourns in Berlin were an artistic success.

In the Winter of 1932, Spender and Isherwood suffered a temporary falling out, which ended Spender's Berlin adventure and began the gradual parting of their ways. The cause of their disagreement was remarkably trivial. Spender reports that when he and Isherwood came to London at the same time that winter, Isherwood was incensed to find that Spender had already told their friends "most of his stories" and that he had been "indiscreet." "I received a letter from him saying that if I returned to Berlin he would not do so, that my life was poison to him, that I lived on publicity, that I was intolerably indiscreet, etc." In *Christopher and His Kind* Isherwood endorses Spender's account, but adds two significant items. First, he speculates, self-deprecatingly, that his deeper (if unconscious) motive for quarreling with Spender was "to get him out of Berlin altogether." "Christopher regarded Berlin as his territory. He was actually becoming afraid that Stephen would scoop him by writing Berlin stories of his own and rushing them into print!" More intriguingly, he recalls a moment from their London confrontation that suggests a growing sexual-ideological opposition between the two. "Stephen, annoyed by Christopher's evasiveness, exclaimed, 'If we're going to part, at least let's part like men.' To which Christopher replied, with a bitchy smile, 'But, Stephen, we *aren't* men.'" The quarrel might be seen as adumbrating the eventual separation of their lives. Spender's immersion in London literary society represented a pull toward normalcy—i.e., heterosexuality—to which he would finally succumbed and whose pompously macho conventions he apes in this exchange. Isherwood responded by aggressively, if indirectly, reminding him

of their shared homosexual existence in Germany, from which Spender now resolved to free himself.[8] As a result of Isherwood's letter Spender decided not to
return to Berlin, in order to "break with my habit of dependence on Christopher."
The homosexual experiment was not yet over, but it would enter a new phase.
Isherwood's letter forced Spender to realize that "at the age of twenty-four I
had still succeeded in forming no intimate relationship." The quarrel (which was
quickly repaired by mail) thus set the stage for his grand romance with Jimmy
Younger.

SPENDER APPEARS TO HAVE met Jimmy Younger early in 1933, after Isherwood
had returned to Berlin. The affair began in an act of sheer willfulness: Spender
simply decided he no longer wanted to live alone, and he "did not consider marrying"—as if it were a real choice. "I was in the mood when people advertise for
a companion in the newspapers. I used to enquire of my friends of their friends in
case they knew anyone suitable." Like Marston and Walter before him, Jimmy
appears to have been chosen in a monumental act of arbitrariness, in which, once
again, neither the young man's physical charms nor his qualities character are
allowed to play a role. Spender says only that he was "pleasant-looking" and
"friendly."[9] He describes the moment as if he were hiring a secretary rather than
taking a lover: "When by chance I met a young man who was unemployed, called
Jimmy Younger, I asked him to live in my flat and work for me." Elsewhere he
refers to "this very arbitrary decision of mine to take him as a companion."

Jimmy of course was a member of the working class. Spender fully recognizes the romantic significance of this economic fact. Indeed, he articulates more
clearly than anyone before him what might be called the social logic of British
literary homosexuality: "The differences of class and interest between Jimmy

8. Many years later Spender complained to Brian Finney that Isherwood "advances as treachery on the
part of a homosexual or a bisexual, if he doesn't choose to be homosexual but chooses to be heterosexual." Brian
Finney, *Christopher Isherwood: A Critical Biography* (New York, 1979), p. 79.

9. Much later in the story, when Spender has gone to Spain in search of Jimmy, we finally get a physical
description of him, and it is deeply patronizing. Spender and his friend Cuthbert Worsley were stopped in the
road by a donkey:

> I discerned something in the donkey's appearance which reminded me of Jimmy! Jimmy had a flat brow
> beneath thick, wiry, reddish hair which stood up in a brush-like way. Sometimes his eyes had an expression of
> unflickering patience under the loads of ideas, of music, of literature, of politics, which I forced on to him. His
> nose had a squarish base, and his mouth turned upwards at the corners in a way which recalled some patient
> animal.

Photographs suggest that he was decidedly more prepossessing.

and me certainly did provide some element of mystery which corresponded almost to a difference of sex. I was in love, as it were, with his background, his soldiering, his working-class home." As with Walter in Hamburg, Spender describes the relationship as a "social phenomenon": "through him I had taken into my home the purposelessness of the life of the Depression outside."

Despite the class difference, he endows Jimmy with greater intelligence and taste than any of the previous men in his life, including those who were his social and educational equals. Jimmy was "quickly intelligent" and "capable of learning"; he also "read a good deal and had a response to poetry which often astonished me." Still, Spender cannot avoid creating an impression of deep condescension in his portrait of Jimmy, who is made to seem both womanish and savage, "out of his depth" and inclined to "lose his head." He was a Welshman—a kind of semi-colonial—and suffered from "the Welsh passion for arguing about things of which he knew little." The division of labor in their domestic economy mimicked the conventional male-female, or master-servant, antithesis; as Spender puts it, with unconscious prejudice, "Jimmy cooked, I worked."

We learn very little about the character of the relationship other than that they fought almost continuously. Needless to say, there is not a word about sex. On the rare occasions when Spender suggests what held them together he speaks in flat generalizations about "our need of one another," "our bonds of affection," the "real interest in our life together," and sometimes of their "happiness." Jimmy has barely been introduced before Spender begins his long lament about their incompatibility. The main source of tension was Jimmy's having nothing to do. His "life was empty"; he was "living in a way which seemed to lead to no better future." Spender alternated between pitying him as a victim of the Depression and being incensed by his "indolence." Their fights, he suggests, were caused by Jimmy's pigheadedness. But Spender acknowledges that a deeper source of their difficulties was the profound asymmetry of the relationship. With his superior education, his famous friends, his money, and his bright young career, Spender exercised an oppressive domination that threatened Jimmy's sense of self-worth, indeed his very identity. Beneath Jimmy's contentiousness and hostility, Spender admits, one could hear his "real voice . . . saying, 'You have helped me at the price of taking away all possibility of my having any self-respect. I have been moved into your world where everyone must think of me as your creation, and no one as having any existence independently of you.'"

Spender is not satisfied, however, to attribute their troubles solely to a clash of temperaments or the deep inequalities that divided them. He interrupts his narrative to deliver a long speech about the general psychological impossibility of love between men. Homosexual alliances, he argues, are sabotaged by the logic of sameness: "We had come up against the difficulty which confronts two men who endeavour to set up house together. Because they are of the same sex, they arrive at a point where they know everything about each other and it therefore seems impossible for the relationship to develop beyond this." Love between men is thus condemned to "sterility." Only with a woman, Spender concludes, can one find the necessary differences—physical, emotional, intellectual—on which a relationship can hope to flourish:

> At this time . . . I became vividly aware of an ambivalence in my attitudes towards men and women. Love for a friend expressed a need for self-identification. Love for a woman, the need for a relationship with someone different, indeed opposite to, myself. I realized that self-identification leads to frustration if it be not realized; destruction, perhaps, if it be half-realized; a certain sterility if it be realized. The relationship of a man with the "otherness" of a woman is a relationship of opposite poles. They complete, yet never become one another, never reach a static situation where everything which is possible to be known between two people is known, every gesture a repetition of one already performed, where little development, except loss of youth, seems possible beyond this.

Feminists would be quick to note that Spender's analysis here rests on threadbare stereotypes of sexual difference, according to which women are mysteriously other, a "Dark Continent" in Freud's notorious phrase. But what is surely most remarkable about this speech is once again its complete repression of desire. The choice between homosexuality and heterosexuality turns on a grand metaphysical opposition between "identification" and "otherness." The urgent and entirely specific demands of the body simply don't figure in the equation. As happens so often in *World within World,* the concrete experience of sexual attraction dissolves into vague abstractions.

David Leavitt must have shared my exasperation with Spender's repressive evasions when he was inspired to compose the sex scenes between Brian (Spender) and Edward (Jimmy) in *While England Sleeps.* Leavitt doesn't transform the two men into rank sybarites. In fact he nicely imagines the mutual reticences, the feelings of embarrassment and delicacy, that inhibit their erotic progress. But, most emphatically, the progress *is* erotic: two men with bodies desire each other intensely:

> Edward kissed me. The record stopped. I bent onto my knees, I started kissing his chest, his stomach, going further down. . . . What I wanted to do I knew was depraved. I should have been thinking, It will shock Edward, he'll run screaming away . . . but his indrawn breaths, as I kissed his body, encouraged me, and then there was his cock, hard and springy as a mushroom, the tip pearled with glistening dew, just inches from my lips. God knows I felt ashamed—really, I thought, I should go and hand myself over to the sexologists right away—and so I started making my way back up his stomach, toward his mouth, but he pushed my head down again, and said, "Do it," his voice raspy.[10]

Ultimately Leavitt establishes them in a sexual routine that appropriately mirrors Spender's social and intellectual domination: Spender becomes the active partner in anal intercourse. But even as Leavitt makes this political point, he still insists on the irreducible reality of the physical needs that are being met. Sex may be a metaphor, but it is also a fact:

> I liked to fuck Edward against a particular wall where the sun came down in louvered columns. Bars of light bisected his rump while he leaned there, hands in the air, his mouth against the wallpaper. . . . I'd take him like that, bugger him relentlessly, until he came in a wet patch against the wall. . . . It is curious to me, in retrospect, that though I fucked him routinely, Edward showed little interest in doing the same to me. . . . I hadn't experienced anything like the paroxysms of pleasure that claimed Edward, those afternoons against the wall— paroxysms so intense I couldn't help but wonder what I might be missing.

In an article in *The New York Times Book Review* Spender accused Leavitt of having imposed his own "lubricious" fantasies on the relationship: "I resent my biography being mixed up with David Leavitt's pornography."[11] But in all the huffing and puffing he doesn't deny the reality Leavitt has imagined. He merely

---

10. David Leavitt, *While England Sleeps* (New York, 1993), p. 94. In 1995 Leavitt published a revised edition of the novel, in which he "deleted or reworked those details that the man who sued me found objectionably close to his own experience." But, he adds, "The sex scenes remain intact. I haven't changed one word" (p. xii).

11. Stephen Spender, "My Life Is Mine; It Is Not David Leavitt's," *The New York Times Book Review*, September 4, 1994, p. 11.

dismisses it as irrelevant to a proper account—whether novelistic or autobiographical—of human relations: "Knowledge of what people do when they are in
bed together may be true, but it is not true to what we know or wish to know
about them." I am inclined to feel that Leavitt has simply provided a much-
needed corrective to the radical desexing of the affair—and indeed of all homosexual relationships—in *World within World*. No one expects Spender, writing at
midcentury, to give a nuts-and-bolts description of the sexual acts between
Jimmy and himself. But he has done something more fundamentally dishonest
than Leavitt by contriving to obliterate all evidence of physical attraction from
the relationship. At the very least we can agree that the erotic discrepancy between these two texts marks a revolutionary change in literary sexual manners
over the latter half of the twentieth century.

The constant antagonism with Jimmy and the reflections it inspired pointed,
according to Spender, to a single, inescapable conclusion: he would have to abandon homosexuality for heterosexuality. "My relationship with Jimmy had . . .
made me realize that if I were to live with anyone it could not be with a man.
Through this very relationship I began to discover a need for women, to think
about them, to look for them." Actually *World within World* implies that the heterosexual option had long been in the back of his mind. He blames his family for
having suppressed his natural heterosexual inclinations (and thus inadvertently
driven him to homosexuality). In his adolescence, he complains, "older people
guarded me from having any love relationship with a woman." He mentions in
particular not being allowed to go on a romantic outing with a nurse whom, at
sixteen, he enjoyed kissing. Even as he became aware of his homosexual desires,
he continued to imagine a heterosexual future for himself.

Little more than a year after he began living with Jimmy he had his first
heterosexual affair. While Jimmy was hospitalized in Vienna for an appendec-
tomy, Spender began sleeping with their host, "Elizabeth" (Muriel Gardiner),
who was there completing her medical and psychoanalytic training. It was a thoroughly modern arrangement, with Elizabeth fully aware of Spender's attachment
to Jimmy (though Jimmy himself appears to have been kept in the dark). Indeed,
they agonized together over the choice Spender faced: it was "unthinkable" that
he should abandon Jimmy, especially now that he was ill, yet Elizabeth offered
the possibility of escape from the miseries of his homosexual existence.

Spender's account of the affair with Elizabeth reveals, almost in spite of himself, its sexual artificiality. He gives the unmistakable impression of play-acting.

Instead of succumbing to erotic abandon (which, presumably, he knew about from his experiences with men), he remained external to their love-making, almost as if he were a clinician observing his own performance: "I failed at any moment to lose myself completely in the life with her. . . . It was as though I were standing outside and watching experience even while I partook of it." We are thus not surprised to learn that he was satisfied to carry on the affair at great intervals, visiting Elizabeth for only a few weeks once or twice a year from 1934 to 1936. He also experienced a palpable sense of relief when she found a more satisfactory lover in one of her Austrian socialists colleagues. Spender in fact became fast friends with her new husband, toward whom, one suspects, he felt a considerable burden of gratitude.

A virtually identical pattern, if on a larger scale, manifested itself in his relationship with Inez Pearn, whom he married only weeks after deciding to live apart from Jimmy in the autumn of 1936. "Whirlwind romance" fails to do justice to the precipitateness of Spender's action: he proposed to Inez the day after he met her. "I certainly felt strongly attracted," he assures us, although he admits that the decision was brought on by his horror at finding himself alone, now that he had broken up with Jimmy and ended his affair with Elizabeth: "I was forced to act because I had reached that stage were work is not enough to fill the emptiness of living alone, friends had failed, and therefore marriage seems the only solution." Not surprisingly, given the blind desperation to which he here confesses, he fell into a mood of "intense depression" as the wedding approached. He had, after all, reached the great parting of the ways that would forever separate him from Auden and Isherwood. "Blackness and desolation seemed the truth and all else an evasion and escape. My day-to-day activities seemed a process of flight from an awareness of horror. . . . My marriage now seemed like a prison sentence."

Like the affair with Elizabeth, the marriage itself had an "as-if" quality. It was a pretend marriage, with Spender once again assuming the role of participant-observer, watching himself with the clinical detachment of Isherwood's camera. Even as he kissed Inez after the ceremony, he writes, "part of my mind stood aside and, as it were, recorded the moment without letting her know how much it meant to me." When he tries to characterize the relationship he struggles to find the appropriate word: "It is difficult to define exactly the emotion which existed between us. But, in the sense in which the term is used nowadays, I think it would be true to say that we 'adored' one another." It is a feeling one imagines entertaining for a child or a pet. When Inez eventually took a lover, Spender reacted at first with "stupefying anger and jealousy." But, as had happened in the same situation with Elizabeth, he also appears to have felt relieved. They separated in the summer of 1939. Spender insists, defensively, that they were "by no means unhappy together," but he doesn't conceal that the marriage had been fundamentally counterfeit: "We did achieve a certain kind of life when we were alone together, but this was of a play-acting, almost childish kind."

When he comes to relate his second marriage, to the pianist Natasha Litvin, in 1941, Spender is prudently circumspect, saying nothing about his motives, sexual or otherwise. In fact he limits his remarks about Natasha to one brief, uninformative paragraph. All we learn is that she had no tolerance for his guilty obsession with the failure of his earlier relationships. "'From now on,'" he reports her saying, "'there is no question of blame. There is only us.'" Spender seems to have concluded that it is best to keep quiet about his desires.

Because he is so unforthcoming about his sexual feelings, I have been forced to construct an erotic profile of Spender from such hints as *World within World* supplies. I am inclined to share David Leavitt's assumption that his homosexual urges were fairly imperious, despite his systematic effort to eliminate all direct evidence of them from the text. Why else would he have devoted such energy to their pursuit—with "D," Marston, Walter, Jimmy, and who knows how many unnamed others while living near Isherwood in Berlin—when it meant a constant, guilty struggle against the conventions of his society and, in the case of Jimmy, three years of painful squabbling? At the same time, the textual evidence, as we've just seen, inspires little confidence in the genuineness of his heterosexual feelings. His decision to pursue women was no doubt the result of weighty psychological—even philosophical—considerations, but the text strongly suggest that it was a decision taken not because of, but in spite of, his desires. That is the clear implication of the attack of despair he suffered just before his marriage and the sense of clinical disengagement he conveys in describing his relationships with both Elizabeth and Inez.

But there is an important piece of evidence that might seem to contradict this interpretation. During the affair with Elizabeth he wrote Isherwood a letter in which, after insisting that he was still "fonder of [Tony] than I could be of any woman I know of," he makes a startling assertion: "But I find sleeping with a woman more satisfying." He adds, "It also means that our relationship isn't something we tire of when we tire of it sexually."[12] One possible explanation is that, after a year and a half of living (and fighting) with Tony/Jimmy, the passion had begun to fade. But I think it more likely that we are dealing here with a discrepancy between desire and performance. Spender, I suspect, may have found that, for all the excitement he felt, the mechanics of homosexual sex remained awkward or embarrassing or in some other way disappointing—in contrast, if we are to believe his statement, to having sex with women. The experience is not unheard of. As we will see later in this book, Andrew Tobias's *The Best Little Boy in the World* is devoted in large part to recounting a similar predicament—the difficulty of having gay sex—and the author's sometimes hilarious efforts to overcome it. Sex with women may have been easier for Spender, but I'm far from persuaded that it was what he really wanted.

When Spender returned from visiting Elizabeth in autumn 1936, he and Jimmy moved into separate places, though they continued to see each other. Spender is no more revealing about the end of the affair than he had been about its beginning. All he says is, "My personal life seemed a failure. I decided that I must separate from Jimmy." When, within a matter of weeks, he had got engaged and married, Jimmy proceeded to become a Communist, join the International Brigade, and depart for Spain. Spender is not embarrassed to claim full credit—or responsibility—for all these actions: Jimmy, he insists, was simply reacting to his romantic disappointment: "Without my influence he would never have become a Communist, and unless I had decided to live apart from him, and had then married, he would certainly not have joined the Brigade." All this may be true (we have only Spender's word for it), but there is something deeply patronizing in the way he so confidently treats Jimmy in the text (and probably in life) as an emotional and intellectual dependent, psychologically feminized to the point that his political acts are seen simply as displaced longing for Spender.[13]

Soon after he arrived in Spain Jimmy had a falling out with the Communists. The appalling violence convinced him that he was a really a pacifist, and before long he found himself imprisoned by the Loyalists as a deserter. The news caused

---

12. *Letters to Christopher* (October 21, 1934), pp. 67–68.

13. In his article attacking David Leavitt, Spender concedes that he may have "blamed" himself too much. He quotes a letter, dated December 27, 1936, from Isherwood (who had just been visited by Jimmy): "'You can set your mind absolutely at rest about one thing: [Jimmy] is not going to Spain on account of your marriage.'" *The New York Times Book Review*, September 4, 1994, p. 11.

Spender "the greatest distress" of his life. "Someone I loved had gone into this war as a result of my influence and of my having abandoned him. A problem which should have been solved by our gradually becoming independent of one another, might well be solved by his death." Much of the fourth chapter of *World within World* is devoted to recounting his efforts in Spain, over the course of several months, to secure Jimmy's release. David Leavitt makes the Spanish adventure the occasion for Spender to repent the error of his heterosexual ways. A letter Spender sent to Isherwood gives some support to this interpretation: "All I know is that I love him & that whenever he comes back, I shall be extremely happy and that I wish he were now here, and that I miss him very much."[14] But in the autobiography Spender presents his rescue mission as inspired not by passion but by loyalty. Jimmy had become a political responsibility rather than a romantic object. The emphasis falls squarely on Spender's objective sense of moral responsibility: because his actions had initiated the unhappy chain of events now threatening Jimmy's life, he was ethically bound to save him. Moreover, he found the chance to play the role of heroic and selfless rescuer psychologically liberating: it put an end to his self-torturing doubts—his feeling that his "personal life seemed a failure." One might say that his sexual guilt was consumed in a blaze of principled action.

IN *WORLD WITHIN WORLD* Spender says that Isherwood attended his wedding with Inez Pearn. But Isherwood himself makes no mention of it in *Christopher and His Kind*. In fact, he gives the firm impression that his feelings at the time were distinctly hostile. He quotes Spender's self-justification, in a letter, to the effect that Isherwood should appreciate his need for "'a permanent and established relationship,'" because Isherwood himself enjoyed just such a relationship (with Heinz). But the appeal failed: "This was clever pleading but it didn't placate the implacable Christopher. However, he gave Stephen no hint of his reactions— until much later—and only showed them by an increased warmth toward Jimmy." Indeed, Isherwood clearly regarded the decision to go straight as a betrayal of what he would later call "the tribe." He had, he confesses, "a rooted horror of marriage" and found the marriages of even his heterosexual friends "slightly distasteful." "When his basically homosexual friends got married—declaring that they were really bisexual, or that they wanted children, or that their

---

14. *Letters to Christopher* (ca. December 30, 1936), p. 129.

wife was 'someone who understands'—Christopher expressed sympathy but felt disgust." He showed his disgust by inviting Jimmy to stay with Heinz and himself in Brussels. Two years later, in August 1938, he upped the ante: he traveled to Ostende with Jimmy, and they had a brief affair. "Christopher now found him desirable as well as companionable. They made love often, with the warmth of friendly affection."

Isherwood considered Spender's turn to heterosexuality more than a categorical betrayal of the "tribe." It also violated their commitment to parallel lives. Their correspondence documents that they viewed their working-class romances of the mid-1930s almost as a shared experiment in a new kind of homosexual domesticity. They were two couples moving in tandem; their letters are filled with paired greetings and references to their analogous situations. Jimmy wants to find a proper job, Spender writes, "just as Heinz wants it." "Tony and I talk much of you, because, as he says, you and Heinz are the only people 'like us.'" [15] Most remarkable of all, they actually made an attempt at living as a foursome in Portugal in late 1935 and early 1936. Spender doesn't mention the episode in *World within World*. But Isherwood gives a full—and often amusing—account of it in *Christopher and His Kind*. Apparently there was considerable "domestic friction." The arrangement ultimately came to grief over the seemingly inconsequential matter of Heinz's treatment of his dog, Teddy. Spender and Jimmy accused Heinz of being cruel to the animal. When they decided to leave, putting an end to the three month experiment, Isherwood wrote in his diary, "It's all very friendly and we are perfectly pleasant about it, but of course we all know that our attempt a living here together has been a complete flop." Just how much he regretted the failure can be appreciated only when we retrace our steps and consider the full saga of Isherwood's homosexual life in the 1930s.

15. Ibid. (July 12, 1935), p. 77; ibid. (September 6, 1933), p. 63.

Christopher and His Kind

HE MAIN DIFFERENCE BETWEEN *Lions and Shadows* and *Christopher and His Kind* is of course that Isherwood's first autobiography is closeted while his second is out. Isherwood himself introduces this distinction in his opening sentences: "There is a book called *Lions and Shadows,* published in 1938, which describes Christopher Isherwood's life between the ages of seventeen and twenty-four. It is not truly autobiographical, however. The author conceals important facts about himself. . . . The book I am now going to write will be as frank and factual as I can make it, especially as far as I myself am concerned." In particular, he says, *Lions and Shadows* misrepresented the truth about Christopher's motives for going to Berlin in 1929. He did not go primarily to meet the anthropologist John Layard. Rather, "It was Berlin itself he was hungry to meet; the Berlin Wystan had promised him." And he concludes, in the book's most famous line, "To Christopher, Berlin meant Boys."

But the issue is trickier than at first appears. The problem is already hinted at in Isherwood's satiric capitalization of "Boys." *Christopher and His Kind* is divided throughout between the author's self-ironizing on the one hand and his serious polemical objectives on the other. The tension is already implicit in the decision to refer to his former self in the third person (indeed the familiar third person). He adopts this strategy, first of all, because in many respects he is deeply critical of his ideas and actions as a young man in the 1930s. At the same time, he also wants to amuse, and "Christopher" often becomes the butt of his jokes. Isherwood, in other words, remains the comic author of *Lions and Shadows* and the novels, and *Christopher and His Kind* is in fact a very funny book—which no one could accuse *World within World* of being. But the self-critical impulse, like the comic impulse, is often at odds with the book's express political aim. There are even moments when the tone verges on self-loathing, and we find ourselves, ironically, back in the closet. Still, Isherwood never loses sight of his serious purpose, which assumes ever greater prominence as the book advances: the story of Christopher's growing sense of identification with his "tribe" and his opposition to its political enemies. That sense of identification is already captured by Isherwood's title.

Nevertheless, we mustn't underestimate the extent of the change and the advance in candor and self-confidence it reflects—not just over *Lions and Shadows* but, even more significantly, over *World within World*. Above all, homosexual desire is now spoken of directly and precisely. After Christopher has had his one and only sexual experience with a woman (aided by drink and a healthy dose of narcissism), Isherwood shows him reflecting on the episode's significance: "He asked himself: Do I now want to go to bed with more women and girls? Of course not, as long as I can have boys. Why do I prefer boys? Because of their shape and their voices and their smell and the way they move." The sentence is breathtaking in its conciseness, clarity, and psychological precision. We have traveled light-years from Spender's obfuscating ruminations about "self-identification," into an intellectual universe where homosexual attraction can be described without embarrassment.

It is not yet, however, the sexual universe of David Leavitt. Stephen Spender makes this point in his *New York Times* article. Isherwood, notes Spender, may have taken advantage of the more permissive atmosphere of the 1970s to talk about chasing boys in Berlin, but "he did not use that freedom to describe physical acts between him and his lovers"—which, Spender adds (to bolster his argument against Leavitt), "he would surely have done . . . had he thought such confessions really revealing."[16] But in fact Spender overstates the case. Admittedly, *Christopher and His Kind* contains nothing comparable to the steamier pages of *While England Sleeps*. Yet it is surprisingly frank about Christopher's erotic activities. In effect, Isherwood has liberated not just desire but sex as well, albeit always within the restraints appropriate to a gentleman of a certain age (his seventies) and provenance (the English upper classes) and consistent with the serio-comic tone he has adopted for his revelations (in contrast to Leavitt's high romantic tragedy)

16. *The New York Times Book Review*, September 4, 1994, p. 12.

By way of example we may cite the admirably matter-of-fact contrast he draws between his sexual behavior as a teenager and what he did with the boys in Berlin:

> At school, the boys Christopher had desired had been as scared as himself of admitting to their desires. But now the innocent lust which had fired all that ass grabbing, arm twisting, sparring and wrestling half naked in the changing room could come out stark naked into the open without shame and be gratified in full. What excited Christopher most, a struggle which turned gradually into a sex act, seemed perfectly natural to these German boys. . . . Many of them liked to be beaten, not too hard, with a belt strap.

He ends, typically, with a joke: "This rough athletic sexmaking was excellent isometric exercise. It strengthened Christopher's muscles more than all his years of joyless compulsory games at school." The passage may not describe body parts, but it goes some way toward specifying the "physical acts between [Isherwood] and his lovers" that Spender feels should not be mentioned. Later we learn—in a dignified metaphorical way—that he played both top and bottom in anal intercourse. Christopher, he writes, "was able to enjoy both the *yang* and the *yin* role in sex." He adds that he didn't consider being on the receiving end "a humiliation and a threat to his masculinity." Rather, "it was simply the *yin* role, which he enjoyed playing precisely because he knew himself equally able to play *yang*." This may verge on the coy—and we might prefer Leavitt's "fucking" and "buggering"—but it tells us a good deal more about Christopher's sex life than Spender thinks we ought to be allowed to know.

Christopher's growing awareness of the political significance of his homosexuality provides *Christopher and His Kind* with its central thematic thread. As Christopher passes through his various adventures, Isherwood is forever taking the measure of his gay consciousness—of his identification with the tribe and its oppression—until the book reaches its apotheosis in a long and heated denunciation of British homophobia and the decision to pursue his sexual destiny in America. The metaphor of the tribe plays deliciously on the conventions of anthropology, at once identifying gay men with the savages patronized by European imperialism and exploiting the modern critique of just such ethnocentric prejudice. Isherwood makes fun of the gay primitives yet ultimately takes them all—all, that is, but an irredeemable few—into his embrace.

At first Christopher was reluctant to be identified with the tribe, especially its more extravagant members, and Isherwood mocks his fastidiousness. When he took an apartment in Berlin next door to Magnus Hirschfeld's homophile Institut für Sexual-Wissenschaft, Christopher squeamishly distanced himself (and his presentable friends) from Hirschfeld's collection of queer monstrosities. Isherwood, however, holds his feet to the tribal fire:

> At last, he was being brought face to face with his tribe. Up to now, he had
> behaved as though the tribe didn't exist and homosexuality were a private way
> of life discovered by himself and a few friends. He had always known, of
> course, that this wasn't true. But now he was forced to admit kinship with these
> freakish fellow tribesmen and their distasteful customs.

When André Gide visited the museum and showed some aversion to Hirschfeld's crudity, Christopher suddenly discovered his own deep kinship with "the silly solemn old professor with his doggy mustache." But Isherwood (speaking from his superior historical vantage point) insists that Gide too was his brother: "They were all three of them on the same side, whether Christopher liked it or not. And later he would learn to honor them both, as heroic leaders of his tribe."

Isherwood takes an equally dim view of young Christopher's obsession with his manliness and his horror at being identified with the effeminate denizens of the Hirschfeld Institut, notably its second-in-command (and Hirschfeld's lover) Karl Giese, most of whose friends were "middle-class queens." When Hirschfeld diagnosed him as "infantile," Christopher was pleased to interpret the label as "boyish." "Far better to be boyish, he thought, than effeminate. He could never join the ranks of Karl's friends and play at nicey-nice third-sexism, because he refused utterly to think of himself as a queen." Isherwood comments, almost censoriously, that Auden "was much more mature than Christopher, in this respect. Labels didn't scare him."

An even more clear-cut instance of the tribal ideology is the account of Christopher's friendship with E. M. Forster. Here all irony is banished, as Isherwood risks bathos in a full-throated tribute. They met in September 1932, just as Forster was beginning his biography of Goldsworthy Lowes Dickinson (whom Isherwood doesn't mention). In 1933 Forster showed him the typescript of *Maurice* and sought his opinion of it. Christopher was bothered by its Edwardian diction, but his principal reaction was astonishment at Forster's boldness, which

Isherwood celebrates in a variation on the tribal metaphor: "The wonder was Forster himself, imprisoned within the jungle of prewar prejudice, putting those unthinkable thoughts into words. Perhaps listening from time to time, to give himself courage, to the faraway chop-chop of those pioneer heroes, Edward Carpenter and George Merrill, boldly enlarging *their* clearing in the jungle." In memory Isherwood pictures Christopher sitting together with Forster, "this great prophet of their tribe, who declares that there can be real love, love without limits or excuse, between two men."

Perhaps the clearest illustration of the theme occurs when a British customs official at Harwich prevented Heinz from entering England in January 1934 because of a compromising letter from Christopher found in Heinz's possession. Isherwood reports the official as remarking, "'I'd say it was the sort of letter that, well, a man might write to his sweetheart.'" After Heinz had been sent back to Germany, Auden observed, "'As soon as I saw the bright-eyed little rat, I knew we were done for. He understood the whole situation at a glance—because he's *one of us.*'" Later, Christopher broke down in tears when he was forced to recount the incident to his employer, the movie director Berthold Viertel, with whom he was working at the time on the film *Little Friend* and who (in a mild fit of anti-Semitism) Christopher imagined to be unsympathetic, having reserved all his compassion for his fellow Jews. During the next few days Christopher could barely endure Viertel's or his wife's presence. "It was like a lack of oxygen; his nature grasped for the atmosphere of his fellow tribesmen. As never before, he realized that they were all his brothers—yes, even those who denied their brotherhood and betrayed it—even that man at Harwich." Inevitably, one wonders whether Isherwood may not have refashioned Christopher's 1934 consciousness here to fit a 1976 muster. But in a way that is just the point: *Christopher and His Kind* is determined to tell a story of gay liberation.

The opposite side of Christopher's identification with his tribe was his growing hostility to the straight world, which he referred to as "Nearly Everybody." The capitalization, as in the case of "Boys," again introduces a hint of self-satire: the mature Isherwood takes a somewhat amused view of the paroxysms of anger that Christopher worked himself up into against heterosexual prejudice. After Christopher's one sexual experience with a woman (in summer 1929), Isherwood first has him reflect on how convenient it would if he were to perfect the practice: then he could escape his "problems" because society would accept him.

But in the next instant Isherwood shows him exploding in rage at the injustice of
it all:

> At this point in his self-examination . . . Christopher would become suddenly,
> blindly furious. Damn Nearly Everybody. Girls are what the state and the
> church and the law and the press and the medical profession endorse, and com-
> mand me to desire. My mother endorses them, too. She is silently brutishly
> willing me to get married and breed grandchildren for her. Her will is the will
> of Nearly Everybody, and in their will is my death. *My* will is to live
> according to my nature, and to find a place where I can be what I am.

In this passage genuine (and revolutionary) indignation is virtually inseparable
from Isherwood's satire of his own youthful excess. But by the end of the book
the balance will have shifted definitively toward indignation, and Isherwood will
deny himself the literary pleasure of his famous irony.

On just two occasions in *Christopher and His Kind* do we encounter homosexuals whom Isherwood judges beyond the tribal pale. Interestingly, both are
excluded mainly for political reasons. The first are the homosexuals who cast
their lot with the Nazis. Isherwood avoids Spender's glib implication of a secret
alliance between homosexuality and fascism. But he takes a dim view of some of
Karl Giese's "silly" friends who "fluttered around town exclaiming how sexy
Storm Troopers looked in their uniforms." Still, among Christopher's acquaintances only a single pair of homosexual lovers "fondly supposed that Germany
was entering an era of military man-love."

The other exclusion was closer to home: Christopher's queer uncle Henry,
on whom he depended for an allowance during his Berlin years. Isherwood
makes light fun of Christopher's opportunistic exploitation of this wealthy relative. "Christopher had decided to become Uncle Henry's favorite nephew; and
he had done so instantaneously, by making it clear to Henry that they had the
same sexual nature." But he felt no tribal solidarity with Henry, only contempt
for his snobbery, reactionary politics, vulgarity, and even his effeminacy. Henry's
"queenly arrogance" is played mainly for laughs, but the contrast with the treatment of Forster is nonetheless striking. Later, when mocking Christopher's sexual
boastfulness, Isherwood can think of no more telling put-down than to compare
him to his aged relative: he bragged, Isherwood writes, "with a vulgarity which
showed that he was truly Uncle Henry's nephew." But aside from these few

queenly philistines and sissy fascists Isherwood's homoerotic ecumenicism encompasses the gay brotherhood in all its splendid variety.

⌀ CHRISTOPHER'S FIRST VISIT to Berlin (he left London, we recall, on March 14, 1929) was brief: it lasted only a week or ten days. But Isherwood pronounces it "one of the decisive events of my life." It was just long enough for Christopher to plunge into Berlin's gay nightlife and fall in love. The story is told in Isherwood's archest comic manner. He satirizes Christopher's erotic fetishism and naive romanticism. Ironic capitalizations proliferate, italicizing the story as a fatuous myth of sexual liberation. Indeed, the treatment is so brutal that we fear Isherwood hasn't mustered sufficient sympathy for his former self, who, for all his foolishness, was nonetheless making a heroic effort to subdue his sexual demons. The account might almost have been written by an Enemy of the Tribe, so fierce is its irony.

The object of Christopher's infatuation was a young man named Bubi, whom he met at a boy-bar, the Cosy Corner, where he was taken by Auden. Bubi "had a pretty face, appealing blue eyes, golden blond hair, and a body which was smooth-skinned and almost hairless, although hard and muscular." In Isherwood's account Bubi emerges less a person than a bundle of abstractions—a collection of "othernesses"—that exactly met Christopher's fetishistic needs. First he was the Blond Boy. "The Blond . . . had been a magical figure for Christopher from his childhood and would continue to be so for many years." The only explanation Isherwood can imagine for this fixation is that it expressed an ancient desire to be sexually dominated by what Nietzsche called the Blond Beast: "Christopher chose to identify himself with a black-haired British ancestor and to see the Blond as the invader who comes from another land to conquer and rape him." He notes, however, that the explanation is contradicted by Bubi's actual behavior, which was "gentle, considerate, almost too polite." It is also contradicted by a second abstraction with which Christopher invested Bubi: the Lost Boy or the Wanderer, "homeless, penniless, dreamily passive," though at the same time somehow "tough, careless of danger, indifferent to hardship, roaming the earth." In this more feminized conception, Christopher, who was older and socially superior, assumed the masculine role for himself, as he took charge of Bubi's "vulnerability."

Isherwood is especially scornful of Christopher's romantic overinvestment in Bubi. In part this hostility simply reflects the materialistic sexual views he had

learned from Auden and generally embraced himself, although his antiromanti-
cism was never as resolute as Auden's and existed side-by-side with his search—
ultimately successful—for a lifetime companion. Isherwood is almost contemptuous of Christopher's infatuation: "Christopher wanted to keep Bubi all to himself forever, to possess him utterly, and he knew that this was impossible and
absurd. If he had been a savage, he might have solved the problem by eating
Bubi—for magical, not gastronomic reasons." He heartlessly mocks Christopher's delight when, on his departure, Bubi gave him "a cheap gold-plated chain
bracelet." Later, when Bubi, who was in trouble with the police, wrote to ask for
money to flee to South America, Isherwood observes snidely that "the letter
thrilled Christopher unspeakably." Altogether, one feels, he is too hard on his
younger self: he fails to enter with appropriate sympathy into the sense of emotional release and physical pleasure that this first affair must have given him after
twenty-five years of repression. The satire verges on self-hate. Apparently, gay
autobiography as comedy is a risky venture, as we will have occasion to observe
again with Paul Monette's *Becoming a Man*.

The satirical impulse serves Isherwood rather better in his analysis of the
social logic of Christopher's early Berlin adventures. As Isherwood recognizes
with perfect clarity, those adventures were not inspired solely by the historical
and geographical accident that a robust homosexual subculture happened to existed in Berlin (though we would err if we were to ignore the importance of that
fact entirely). Rather, his sexual desires, like those of so many of his friends, were
implicated in a mysterious need to find partners of a different rank and ethnicity:
"Christopher was suffering from an inhibition, then not unusual among upper-
class homosexuals; he couldn't relax sexually with a member of his own class or
nation. He needed a working-class foreigner." Isherwood eagerly dissects the
illogical motives at work in this obsession: "The fact was that Christopher, the
upper-class boy, was now trying to disown his class. Because he hated it, he despised the middle class for aping its ways. That left him with nothing to admire
but the working class; so he declared it to be forthright, without frills, altogether
on the path of truth." Berlin, we see, represented as much a social as a sexual
liberation for Christopher. He felt "a marvelous freedom" chattering with the
proletarian bar boys, amateur hustlers who frequented the working-class estab-
lishments in Hallesches Tor as much to gossip and play cards as to pick up tricks.

An exactly parallel illogic lay behind the sexual allure of the foreign. "By
embracing Bubi," he writes, "Christopher could hold in his arms the whole

mystery-magic of foreignness, Germanness"—although Bubi was in fact Czech. Even Christopher's wish to speak German was erotically inspired. "He had learned German simply and solely to be able to talk to his sex partners. For him, the entire German language . . . was irradiated with sex. . . . The difference between a table and *ein Tisch* was that a table was the dining table in his mother's house and *ein Tisch* was *ein Tisch* in the Cosy Corner." Here Isherwood's satirical perspective seems right on target: it wickedly skewers the irrationality of Christopher's social and national complexes. Isherwood even raises the satirical perspective to high literary art by inventing another anthropological metaphor, one that reverses the ideological poles of his tribal conceit. Christopher and his fellow expatriate Francis Turville-Petre are no longer oppressed natives but themselves marauding imperialists:

> In the bars, Christopher used to think of Francis and himself as being like traders who had entered a jungle. The natives of the jungle surrounded them— childlike, curious, mistrustful, sly, easily and unpredictably moved to friendship or hostility. The two traders had what the natives wanted, money. How much of it they would get and what they would have to do to get it was the subject of their bargaining.

Despite his generally unsentimental attitude toward sexual transactions, Isherwood doesn't hesitate to condemn the arrangement as "a colonial situation." In chasing after an eroticized "foreignness," embodied in Bubi and other Berlin boys, Christopher was following in the footsteps of John Addington Symonds, pursuing Swiss peasants and Venetian gondoliers, and André Gide, ravaging Arab boys in North Africa—with the saving difference that, in contrast to Symonds and Gide, Isherwood recognizes the psychological irrationality and political objectionableness of his quest.

Given the incisiveness and glee with which Isherwood satirizes the social and national motivations underlying Christopher's Berlin escapades, we might be surprised that he says nothing about another peculiarity of his desires: all the men he pursued—at least all those mentioned in the text—were much younger than himself, were indeed for the most part teenagers. To use modern critical jargon, Isherwood excoriates Christopher's classism and racism but is silent about his ageism. Now, one might argue that age, unlike class and nationality, is intimately related to sex. Sociobiologists, for example, contend that nubility is attractive for good Darwinian reasons, and not merely because of repressive social conventions. In Isherwood's case the greater attractiveness of the young is so much taken for granted that he never bothers to comment on it. In effect, we have here reached the limits of his critical consciousness. He may make fun of Christopher's irrational infatuation with workers and foreigners, but he treats his exclusive interest in very young men as entirely natural—unless, of course, we detect a faint hint of self-criticism in his repeated references to the German "boys" (or, rather, "Boys") he pursued so avidly. The pattern—if not in such exaggerated form—would last a lifetime: Don Bachardy, with whom Isherwood eventually settled down in California, was more than thirty years his junior. Isherwood pokes gentle fun at this weakness, as we shall see, on the final page of *Christopher and His Kind*.

After his first visit to Berlin Christopher returned again in July 1929 to look for Bubi, but only at the end of November did he decide to make his stay long-term, even thinking of emigration. He was to live virtually all of the next three-and-a-half years—until Hitler's seizure of power—in Germany, spending a total of only five months in England. His stay was thus both longer and more sustained than Spender's, who, we recall, divided his year equally between Berlin and London.

In Spring 1930 Bubi was succeeded in Christopher's affections by another boy, Otto Nowak (as Isherwood calls him in both *Christopher and His Kind* and *Goodbye to Berlin*). In many respects Isherwood treats the new romance with the same brutality as the first—the dominant tone remains satirical, as he eagerly punctures Christopher's illusions. If Bubi was the Lost Boy, Otto was the Narcissist. "Otto was perpetually admiring his body and calling Christopher's attention to its muscles and golden smoothness." Fundamentally heterosexual, Otto enjoyed having sex with Christopher because he could watch himself being desired. "Christopher could compete successfully with most women by showing more lust, more shamelessly, than they would. . . . 'I love the way you look when you're hot for me,' Otto used to say to him." But Isherwood concedes that sex with a narcissist has its compensations. Christopher may have made an unwise emotional investment, but erotically it was a great success. "When winter returned and Otto revealed himself bit by bit as he pulled off layers of thick clothes, his nakedness aroused both of them even more. His body became a tropical island on which they were snugly marooned in the midst of snowbound Berlin." This last romantic flourish breaks the satirical mood, hinting at deeper satisfactions.

Still, the main effect of the Otto story is to create a pitiable impression of

Christopher abjectly at the mercy of a preening teenager who cared nothing for him. The impression is reinforced by Otto's venality. In this respect, his function in the narrative resembles that of Walter in *World within World*. The difference is that Isherwood's touch is considerably lighter (there is no heavy breathing about "the Revolution"), and he nicely captures how "the higher prostitution," as we might call it, could become a form of sexual play. "When Otto was coaxing Christopher into buying him a new suit," Isherwood recalls, "Christopher enjoyed the game in spite of his misgivings. It was a kind of seduction and it always ended erotically as well as financially."

After the romance had been going on for half a year Christopher went to live with Otto and his working-class family in the Hallesches Tor district, providing the occasion for the chapter "The Nowaks" in *Goodbye to Berlin*, with its powerful account of a proletarian household during the Depression and its dire political consequences. Isherwood continues to make fun of Christopher's irrational confounding of social and sexual impulses, as he had with Bubi and the bar boys. Christopher, he implies, was again engaging in a silly game of reverse snobbery. Indeed, Isherwood's main purpose here seems to be to strip Christopher of the pretensions to social conscience and political foresight he advanced for himself in *Goodbye to Berlin*. Thus Otto's older brother Lothar, whose sullen conversion to Nazism served as an ominous portent in the novel, is shown in a more favorable light. Christopher's arrival meant that Lothar had to move out of the room he shared with Otto into the already crowded living room. It is thus not surprising, Isherwood now suggests, that Lothar "disapproved of Christopher as a degenerate foreigner who had turned him out of his bed in order to have perverse sex with his brother."

The incident points to the general strategy Isherwood engages in, not just in the Otto episode, but throughout *Christopher and His Kind*. He is eager to correct the misrepresentations in his fiction—to the point that for long sections the book becomes a form of self-inflicted literary criticism, an extended essay at unmasking his former practice. We learn a great deal about what Frl. Schroeder and Sally Bowles and the others were really like and what motivated the young author to take various liberties with them. But the single most persistent theme in this exercise is Isherwood's systematic exposure of the lengths to which he went to disguise his own homosexuality.

He takes almost masochistic pleasure in documenting his literary lies, which infected matters both large and small. Consider the case of Otto. The narrator

Christopher in the novel of course represses his own sexual involvement with Otto, implying falsely that he moved to the Nowaks because of his poverty, not because he wanted "to share a bedroom with Otto." In order to throw the reader off the scent, he gives a false account of Otto's appearance. After mentioning "'the beautiful ripe lines of [Otto's] torso,'" he adds that the torso "'taper[ed] away too suddenly to his rather absurd little buttocks and spindly, immature legs.'" In reality, Isherwood notes, Otto "had an entirely adequate, sturdy pair of legs." Christopher makes them "'spindly'" only to allay the suspicion that he might have found Otto sexually attractive. Natalia Landauer is even more shamelessly abused, once again to hide Christopher's homosexuality. In the novel she is made "a bossy bluestocking, desperately enthusiastic about culture, sexually frigid and prudish." In reality, Isherwood confesses, her original (Gisa Soloweitschik) was Christopher's faithful confidante, with whom he continually discussed his relationship with Otto.

The autobiography, in short, "outs" Christopher Isherwood the narrator. The assumption is that his literary closetedness led to misrepresentation, sometimes (as in the case of Natalia) to serious distortion. The impulse is entirely consistent with the "tribe" ideology, and it gives *Christopher and His Kind* the feeling of an "out-of-the closet" book—and, one might add, a very American book as well. This practice, as much as anything, separates it from the curious evasiveness of *World within World,* which is happy to treat the closet simply as a decorous acknowledgment of social proprieties. From a strictly literary perspective, of course, we are delighted that Isherwood did not achieve such ideological clarity until many years after he wrote his most famous fictions, above all *Goodbye to Berlin*. Its distinct narrative voice—officially sexless but with just enough hints to arouse suspicion—offers piquant and memorable testimony to a historical moment when the closet door was just cracking open.

Because irony is the dominant mood in Isherwood's retelling of the Otto story, he is unforthcoming about its emotional significance. His emphasis throughout is on Otto's shameless self-absorption and his heterosexual philandering, perhaps most famously on their visit, with Auden and Spender, to Ruegen Island in the summer of 1931 (a visit memorialized in another chapter of *Goodbye to Berlin,* "On Ruegen Island"). We see Otto, "animally beautiful," wearing a loincloth and "taking the pose of a Michelangelo nude on the Sistine Chapel ceiling." And we also see the two of them squabbling a good deal, mainly "because Otto spent his evenings dancing with beach girls at the local casino."

But when we recall that, despite its many ups and downs, the affair went on for at least two years—from Spring 1930 to Spring 1932—we begin to suspect that Isherwood has not done it full justice. To be sure, the experiment of living together with Otto's family lasted only a month, and Isherwood also reports that the holiday on Ruegen Island "wasn't a success." After Ruegen, Christopher wrote Spender of his resolve "'not to live with Otto again for a long time.'" But he added, in the same letter, "'These last days, when he's been in to see me for quite short periods, have been absolutely wonderful.'" It is one of the few times we get even a hint of the relationship's intensity. Isherwood, one sometimes feels, is Spender's exact opposite: frank about sex but embarrassed by his feelings. Despite the weighty satirical case mounted against him, Otto, I suspect, was less a sequel to Bubi than a prelude to Heinz—and ultimately, to Don Bachardy. He was in fact Christopher Isherwood's first lover.

CHRISTOPHER MET HEINZ NEDDERMEYER in the spring of 1932, as the romance with Otto was winding down. Significantly, Isherwood recalls the precise date: March 13. Like the original departure for Berlin (almost exactly three years earlier), it was an anniversary of sorts: the beginning of a love affair that more and more came to resemble a marriage. Perhaps at first it did not seem much different from the arrangement with Otto: both were from working-class families, and both were about seventeen (and thus about a decade his junior) when Christopher began sleeping with them. Moreover, Isherwood's treatment of the relationship does not immediately abandon the self-mocking manner of the Bubi and Otto episodes. In fact, the comic style predominates in his account of their first years together. But it is gradually—and inexorably—displaced by a more serious tone, as Christopher and Heinz established their domestic routine, only to have it disrupted by the Nazis.

A more romantic note is already sounded right at the start. They had gone to live in a village near the Polish border with Christopher's friend Francis Turville-Petre, who had hired Heinz as a housekeeper. But after Francis learned that Christopher and Heinz were going to bed together, he demanded that Christopher pay half of boy's wages, which Christopher happily agreed to do. When Heinz found this out, he burst into tears. "It was," writes Isherwood, "his declaration of love." The mention of "love" apparently makes the comic author feel slightly queasy, so he immediately adds, in his best ironic fashion, "Christopher had no hesitation in falling in love with Heinz." As with Bubi, he was still indulging his neurotic abstractions: Heinz appealed to him as "someone emotionally innocent, entirely vulnerable and uncritical, whom he could protect and cherish as his very own"—another version, so to speak, of the Lost Boy. But Isherwood then drops his ironic guard to intimate that this new affair will not be simply a replay of Christopher's earlier erotic farces: "He wasn't yet aware that he was letting himself in for a relationship which would be far more serious than any he had had in his life." Heinz's tears of love, we see, were a portent of something entirely new.

The most striking novelty was that they began living together, albeit episodically at first and later often on the run, as their peregrinations took them from country to country trying to find new citizenship for Heinz. More important, they succeeded, against all odds, in creating an alliance of remarkable contentment. "Christopher found himself keeping house with Heinz. This was a kind of happiness which he had never experienced before; he now realized that he had always desired it." In some respects, the relationship suffered from the same inequities that would later prove so disastrous for Stephen Spender and Jimmy Younger, above all a division of labor that assigned Christopher the manly role of intellectual worker while Heinz was relegated to the wifely duties of cooking and housekeeping. But whether because Heinz genuinely liked the tasks that Jimmy found demeaning, or because Christopher managed to suppress the superciliousness that made Spender's intellectual pretensions so galling to Jimmy, Isherwood reports none of the grinding daily hostility of the other household. "Heinz actually enjoyed work for work's sake. No lover, however literary, could have shared Christopher's work with him. But Heinz did the next best thing; while Christopher wrote, Heinz collaborated with him indirectly by sweeping the floors, tidying up the garden, cooking the meals." As with Spender, of course, we have only Isherwood's version of the story, but we are inclined to believe him, because of the brutal pleasure he takes elsewhere in debunking his own illusions.

Perhaps the most important difference between the two couples had to do with the matter of writing. Even for the most forbearant of partners, living with a writer is a heavy burden. It demands considerable tolerance for hours of silent withdrawal, with their invidious implication of a higher calling from which the nonwriter is excluded. Spender complains that Jimmy bore the burden ungraciously. "The uncreativeness of Jimmy's life," he remarks, "often left me with a feeling that my own work was a kind of disloyalty to him." Christopher sensed a similar resentment in Otto: "Whenever Christopher had written while Otto was nearby, he had been conscious of Otto's restlessness and boredom and had felt responsible for it. His effort to go on writing became an assertion of his will against Otto's." But Heinz showed no such impatience. He went about his chores uncomplainingly, "quite unaware how much he was helping Christopher" with his own labors. "This odd pair"—working, eating, and making love together— "were absurdly like the most ordinary happily married heterosexual couple."

I don't want to exaggerate the domestic bliss. There were often tensions, and Isherwood reverts to his ironic manner to describe them. The most sustained example comes in his account of the summer they spent in 1933 visiting Francis Turville-Petre in Greece, an episode later memorialized in *Down There on a Visit*. The trouble, it seems, was caused by the Greek boys Francis had hired to help him with his archaeological work on the island of St. Nicholas. Heinz apparently enjoyed their company too much for Christopher's taste. Jealous scenes ensued. In mid-August Heinz declared they had to part. Isherwood quotes from Christopher's diary: "'After lunch I talked to him again and shed tears, and finally he said: Well, all right, I'll stay with you, but we'll go to Paris at once. Since then we haven't spoken to each other.'" Three weeks later the diary reports the following exchange: "'After lunch, Heinz said: "If you give me six thousand drachmas, I'll stay with you." I said: "Certainly not. I'm not going to buy you."'" When they finally secured passage on a steamer to Marseille, Christopher noted, "'He's sitting about with a face like death and won't speak. I shall have to get rid of him as soon as I'm in Paris.'"

Significantly, no such divorce occurred or seems even to have been seriously contemplated. Moreover, in the midst of their troubles on St. Nicholas, the diary also records moments of erotic satisfaction and domestic tranquility: "'I should like to live with Heinz in this tent always. Heinz is my only support. He makes everything tolerable.'" In contrast to his usual practice, Isherwood offers no snide comment on this effusion. On the contrary, he adds to the picture of newlyweds on holiday: "Occasionally they spent a whole day alone together, rowing and sailing, or scrambling up the nearest of the coastal mountains." He also reports that they made three trips together to Athens, where "it was a treat to make love without the interruptions common on St. Nicholas." Even at its rockiest, the relationship exudes an aura of sexual rapture and emotional comfort strikingly absent from Spender's account of his life with Jimmy Younger.

In the fall Christopher took Heinz back to England, where they stayed with Christopher's mother, Kathleen. But when Heinz's tourist permit expired in late

1933 he was forced to return to Germany. It was the first chapter in the harrowing story that would absorb both their lives for the next three-and-a-half years and result finally in their separation. Already Christopher considered himself virtually married to Heinz: he was resolved to find the money needed to bring Heinz back to England "for a much longer period, perhaps for keeps." More was involved than just wanting to live together. Because Heinz refused to be conscripted into Hitler's army, he risked imprisonment, perhaps even death. Thus Christopher's efforts to get Heinz out of Germany—which included forcing his mother to loan him vast sums of money to buy Heinz nationality in another country—closely resembled Spender's campaign to rescue Jimmy Younger from the Communists in Spain. Although the story was not without its amusing aspects—especially when the notorious Gerald Hamilton (Mr. Norris) became their principal intermediary—the emphasis in Isherwood's account falls squarely on their growing anxiety, even desperation, as the noose tightened. It also has the effect of creating an ever more powerful sense of the emotional bond between the two men, struggling to find a place where they could live together as a couple. The self-ironizing manner is largely banished, and we find ourselves caught in the painful web of a marital tragedy. At the same time, we are witness to Christopher's growing hatred for his native England, whose homophobia—embodied in the queer customs officer who had turned Heinz away at Harwich—he blamed for their predicament. The decision to emigrate to America lies just over the horizon.

The drama took them, for longer and shorter periods of time, to Holland (twice), the Canary Islands, Spain, Morocco, Denmark, Belgium (again twice), Portugal (where, as we've seen, they lived for three months with Spender and Jimmy), France, and finally Luxembourg. In the meantime there were complex intrigues and financial transactions to secure Heinz permanent citizenship outside Germany. Quito, Tahiti, South Africa, and the United States were considered, but their most sustained effort went into a scheme that would have taken them to Mexico. Isherwood notes that Christopher was not always above playing to the gallery in these efforts. He took sadistic pleasure in torturing his mother (who, for him, came to symbolize "the England of Nearly Everybody") with the lengths to which he was prepared to go to save his homosexual lover. She was the foremost member of "that audience, partly real, partly imaginary, of which he was always conscious." But these self-mocking observations occur less and less often as the relationship came under ever greater external pressure, testing their devotion.

When the Mexican passport seemed about to materialize, Isherwood records their happiness without an ironic blush: "Now their long period of waiting—waiting to begin a new life—seemed nearly over."

The end is told in the bleak tones of high tragedy. Heinz was expelled from Luxembourg on May 12, 1937—another anniversary that Isherwood remembers exactly. Gerald Hamilton's lawyer persuaded them that Heinz would have to travel to Trier to get a short-term Belgian visa. On their way to the railway station Christopher thought he detected a look of reproach in Heinz's eyes: "'You're sending me away. We shall never see each other again.'" As we fully expect by now, Heinz was in fact arrested in Trier and put on trial as a draft evader. In the trial Christopher sought, through the lawyer, to exonerate Heinz by assuming entire responsibility himself. He was portrayed "as a totally debauched creature, too effete to be anti-Nazi even, who had seduced this silly German boy at an early age and had persuaded him to leave Germany and live abroad with him by giving him large sums of money." Admittedly, Isherwood can't resist making a joke about the particular sexual act to which they confessed: "*eine ausgesprochene Sucht zur wechselseitigen Onanie*" ("a pronounced addiction to reciprocal onanism"). "This," he intones, "was the name which their love was to dare to speak, in the face of its enemies!"

Isherwood does not try to disguise the misery into which the separation plunged him. He quotes from Christopher's diary:

> "Heinz is always the last person I think of at night, the first in the morning. Never to forget Heinz. Never to cease to be grateful to him for every moment of our five years together. . . . The most painful is to remember him with animals. I think of him stroking a rabbit, giving a new-born chicken its first drink of water, playing with Teddy. That's the worst. At mealtimes I remember him, too, and wonder what he's eating."

He would not be Isherwood, of course, if he didn't suspect his own motives. "In this mirror of a diary, Christopher reveals a few frank glimpses of himself. The rest is posing." And he wonders whether "his helpless behavior, that last morning in Luxembourg, [had] concealed a cold decision to let the police set him free from Heinz?" But he is happy to leave us with a touching final image of Heinz and their love. Fifteen years later he returned to Berlin and saw Heinz and his wife (whom Heinz had met shortly after his trial and conscription). Happily married and a lucky survivor of both the Russian and Western fronts, Heinz assured

Christopher "that he wouldn't, for anything, have missed their travels together. . . . He alone had the right to blame Christopher. It had never occurred
to him to do so."

⬭ WE DON'T GET THE IMPRESSION that either Christopher or Heinz ever set
much store by sexual fidelity. Not surprisingly, therefore, Christopher's broken
heart didn't prevent him from taking advantage of his new-found bachelorhood.
The period of "Christopher's widowerhood" (the phrase is typically double-
edged, at once accurate and ironic) brought a series of dalliances. But he seemed
determined not to take any of them too seriously, most likely, I suspect, because
the experience with Heinz had wounded him more than Isherwood cares to
admit. "He preferred to have two or three affairs running concurrently; in that
way, he felt less involved with any particular individual." The same spirit prevails
in his account of the three-and-a-half-month trip he took with Auden to China
in 1938. The purpose of the trip was to compile a travel journal about the Japa-
nese invasion. But in Shanghai they indulged themselves in "afternoon holidays
from their social consciences" by visiting a local bathhouse. Isherwood describes
their outings in his most disabused manner, which combines sexual materialism
with social comedy:

> You were erotically soaped and massaged by young men. You could pick your
> attendants, and many of them were beautiful. Those who were temporarily dis-
> engaged would watch the action, with giggles, through peepholes in the walls
> of the bathrooms. What made the experience pleasingly exotic was that tea was
> served to the customer throughout; even in the midst of an embrace, the atten-
> dant would disengage one hand, pour a cupful, and raise it, tenderly but firmly,
> to the customer's lips.

They returned to England by way of Canada and the United States. In New
York, where they arrived in midsummer, Christopher continued his erotic adventuring. Their host, the novelist and editor George Davis, "offered to make sexual
introductions for them." "'All right,' said Christopher, half in jest, 'I want to meet
a beautiful blond boy, about eighteen, intelligent, with very sexy legs.' Such a
boy was instantly produced." So enters the young man whom Isherwood calls
"Vernon." Christopher found him "wonderfully human-smelling, muscular,
hairy, earthy." As must be clear already, Vernon's entrance brings an emphatic

return to the comic style Isherwood had used to satirize his adventures with Bubi and Otto. Indeed, the analogy with Bubi is entirely explicit. Just as Bubi was the German Boy, Vernon was the American Boy, who, he adds, was also "the Walt Whitman Boy." Isherwood proceeds to make fun of Christopher's fatuous daydreams about entering on a "wander-comradeship with Vernon in the Whitman tradition."

But, in fact, Vernon had struck deeper chord than Bubi ever did, and, through Vernon, so had New York, under whose spell Christopher now fell. Back in England, he continued to think of Vernon (as well as Heinz), and he began to entertain the hope that "the New World . . . might be the homeland he had failed to find in Germany." When he returned to New York in early 1939, significantly, it was Vernon who met him. The previous summer's high-comedy with a mail-order boyfriend had given way, if not to true love, then to a sexual-romantic reunion untouched by Isherwood's ironic mocking. Vernon whisked him off from the icy port to "a place of warmth and joy, [where] the two of them would be in each other's arms." Thus is the arrival in America subtly—but ineluctably—linked to the theme of sexual liberation.

Isherwood records that Auden dated their mutual decision to leave England and settle in the United States to their brief stay there in mid-1938 at the end of the Far East tour. In the late 1930s Auden and Isherwood had grown even closer, collaborating on their three plays and the travel diary. One suspects, moreover, that Spender's marriage had further driven them together as the remaining homosexuals of the original triumvirate. Isherwood firmly hints as much, without naming names: "While nearly all of his other friends were gradually withdrawing from him, into long-term relationships or careers or both, life seemed to be binding the two of them together."

Isherwood presents himself as the passive partner in their epochal decision. "If Wystan chose to emigrate, then he would too." But he insists that, for all his seeming indifference, his motives were crystal clear: he was not so much embracing America as renouncing England. And England was being renounced expressly for its homophobia and for what it had done to Heinz and himself. "For him, it was still the land of the Others. And in rejecting Heinz, it had rejected him too." *Christopher and Its Kind* thus concludes in a scathing critique of prejudice against homosexuality and a burst of what we would now call "identity politics."

Christopher, Isherwood reports, finally recognized that the antifascism that had inspired his political opinions and actions in the 1930s was a kind of dodge: it failed to specify the exact form of oppression to which he and his friends were in fact subject. The failure, he now concluded, stemmed from internalized homophobia: because he was "embarrassed" by his homosexuality he felt compelled to disguise his oppositional views in a decorously generalized form. More precisely, he had been "wavering between embarrassment and defiance. He became embarrassed when he felt that he was making a selfish demand for his individual rights at a time when only group action mattered. He became defiant when he made the treatment of the homosexual a test by which every political party and government must be judged." A case in point was his reaction to the sexual policies of the Soviet Union, whose antihomosexual legislation of 1934 he had wrongly minimized in the name of left-wing solidarity. But all that was over now. There would be no more wavering: "He must never again give way to embarrassment, never deny the rights of his tribe, never apologize for its existence." As in his earlier account of the episode at Harwich, we may doubt that his views had in fact achieved such clarity by the late 1930s. Isherwood admits as much himself. "The above description of Christopher's reactions," he writes, "is far too lucid. . . . What had actually begun to surface in his muddled mind was a conflict of emotions. He felt obliged to become a pacifist, he refused to deny his homosexuality, he wanted to keep as much of his leftism as he could." Still, the important matter, once again, is Isherwood's determination to tell a story of gay liberation, even at the risk of anachronism.

Christopher and Its Kind ends with an envoi in which Isherwood bids farewell to his own and Auden's former selves, as they arrive in their new homeland, and foretells their future. It is reminiscent of the final page of *The Magic Mountain*, where Thomas Mann bids moving farewell to his everyman, Hans Castorp, whom he has grown to love and pity during his seven years of intellectual and emotional wandering on the mountain. Isherwood's leave-taking (to this reader at least) is no less moving than Mann's. But because it is distinctly "Isherwoodian" (and emblematic of the spirit of the book as a whole), it is also funny, from the mildly irreverent salutation to the wicked little joke, at his own expense, in the last line:

Yes, my dears, each of you will find the person you came here to look for—
the ideal companion to whom you can reveal yourself totally and yet be loved

for what you are, not what you pretend to be. You, Wystan, will find him very soon, within three months. You, Christopher, will have to wait much longer for yours. He is already living in the city where you will settle. He will be near you for many years without your meeting. But it would be no good if you did meet him now. At present, he is only four years old.

Isherwood's memoir is dedicated to that four-year-old.

3

THE DETECTIVE AND THE COMEDIAN

J. R. Ackerley

and

Quentin Crisp

∞ NINETEEN SIXTY-EIGHT—a year after the Sexual Offenses Act partly decriminalized homosexual relations in Britain—saw the appearance of two of the most remarkable "gay autobiographies," J. R. Ackerley's *My Father and Myself* and Quentin Crisp's *The Naked Civil Servant*. Both books focus on homosexual lives in London during the 1930s and 1940s, and both take advantage of the more permissive atmosphere of the 1960s to tell their stories with considerable sexual candor. Yet what is truly remarkable about the two stories—set in the same town at more or less the same time—is their utter obliviousness of one another. That Ackerley and Crisp appear never to have met is perhaps not surprising; London, after all, contained thousands of active homosexuals. But the worlds Ackerley and Crisp inhabited and the lives they pursued seem so alien from one another as to constitute virtually separate universes. One might say that they came from opposite sides of the sexual tracks and occupied opposite ends of the sexual food chain.

Although slightly older, J. R. Ackerley (1896–1967) belonged to the intellectual and social milieu of Isherwood and Spender. Educated at Cambridge, he was a friend of Goldsworthy Lowes Dickinson and E. M. Forster. In *Christopher and His Kind* Isherwood calls him "one of the handsomest men of his generation." For thirty years, starting in 1928, he worked for the BBC; he served almost as long as literary editor of its weekly magazine, *The Listener*, where, in the words of his biographer, "he created some of the liveliest and most authoritative arts pages to be found in any journal of the period"[1]; and he was also the admired author of a play, *The Prisoners of War* (1925), and a travel journal, *Hindoo Holiday* (1932).

By contrast, Quentin Crisp (1908–) was a bohemian (or, to use his own preferred term, a "hooligan"), living on the margins of society and supporting himself, when not on the dole, through a series of odd jobs in advertising and as an artist's model. To be sure, he also entertained literary ambitions and even succeeded in publishing a book about window dressing and a pamphlet in verse about a kangaroo. But only with the appearance of *The Naked Civil Servant* (and its translation into a television documentary) did he escape from Bohemia into the celebrity he has enjoyed for the past three decades. In other words, he had none of Ackerley's social, educational, and intellectual advantages. Nor his physical advantages either, for if Ackerley was "one of the handsomest men of his generation," Crisp, by his own estimate, was "very plain."

1. Peter Parker, *Ackerley* (New York, 1989), p. 1.

To the reader of *My Father and Myself* and *The Naked Civil Servant*, these differences, important though they are, will seem less striking than the disparity between what might be called the gender identities embraced by Ackerley and Crisp. Ackerley was the quintessential invisible homosexual, self-consciously masculine, whose erotic interests were confined to other equally masculine, indeed preferably "normal" (i.e., heterosexual), men. Crisp, by contrast, was an effeminate homosexual who raised his effeminacy—heroically—to the level of principle: he made a public spectacle of himself. He thus embodied everything about homosexuality Ackerley sought to deny. In a sense, Crisp returned the compliment: throughout his book he writes as if homosexuals like Ackerley did not even exist—or, to the extent he recognizes their existence, he hardly thinks of them as homosexuals at all. Yet, though they occupied opposite ends of the gender continuum, they were in a way "secret sharers" in the importance they assigned to this matter of gender: the whole of Ackerley's life was driven by a horror of effeminacy no less exigent than Crisp's seemingly compulsive need to celebrate it.

There is another surprising affinity in their otherwise radically dissimilar stories. Both men narrate homosexual lives in which sex plays a fundamentally negative role. They were engaged in completely separate sexual universes—in terms of what they wanted to do and whom they wanted to do it with—but for both of them sex turned out to be a disaster, leading to none of the satisfactions that Isherwood or Spender extracted from it.

Indeed, even John Addington Symonds and Goldsworthy Lowes Dickinson, for all their nineteenth-century repressions, enjoyed more reasonable sex lives. In the end Ackerley and Crisp in fact gave up sex, and both claim to have been happier without it. Not surprisingly, an aura of failure, even despair, hangs about their stories, abjectly in Ackerley's case, less transparently in Crisp's antic and irreverent account.

My Father and Myself and *The Naked Civil Servant* invite comparison in one further respect. Both are, from a literary point of view, extremely self-conscious, even artful, productions, though inspired by very different models. *My Father and Myself* is perhaps the most compellingly readable of homosexual memoirs. It is cast in the form of a mystery: Ackerley sets the account of his own sexual experience in the context of a search to uncover the scandalous secrets of his father's past, implying that the father's story contains the key to his own. He peoples the domestic drama with memorable characters, drawn with a fineness and wit worthy of Jane Austen, and he unpacks the story's mystery with a Dickensian control of foreshadowing, coincidence, and revelation, although the final enigma of his own sexual discontent, we feel, ultimately eludes him. Crisp's model is not Austen or Dickens but Oscar Wilde. He is a veritable stand-up comedian, always on stage, packing his book with naughty aphorisms, wicked allusions, and running jokes. Where Ackerley's text boasts the carefully controlled architecture of a whodunit, Crisp is indifferent to structural concerns but works overtime to keep his readers laughing with a string of one-liners. Both procedures, I would argue, run the risk of undermining confidence in the autobiographer's reliability. The striving for effect—for surprise in Ackerley's case, for amusement in Crisp's—leaves us wondering whether truth has not been sacrificed in the process. All autobiography, admittedly, refashions the past to tell an intelligible story: it is as much the creation as the recovery of the self. But the delicate balance between evidence and construction, or between recollection and narrative coherence, is at greater risk in autobiographies with such powerful literary agendas as those of Ackerley and Crisp than it is in the more casually assembled accounts of Isherwood and Spender, or the artless, even ramshackle, ones of Symonds and Dickinson.

J. R. Ackerley and his father, 1913.

By kind permission of Diana Petre.

My Father and Myself

"I WAS BORN IN 1896 and my parents were married in 1919." Ackerley's famous opening sentence introduces us to the book's mysterious theme. More exactly, it introduces us to the theme of mystery itself. Ackerley assumes the role of detective, giving us a precise and circumstantial account of the researches he has conducted to unlock the secrets of his father's past. From the start the suspense is brilliantly managed. By his own admission he has arranged the book's surprises—"perhaps I may call them shocks"—with a careful eye to effect. Most of those surprises occurred in a brief span of years after his father's death in 1929, but in the book they are carefully spaced to heighten tension. The biggest surprise of all—the story of his own sexual life—is reserved until past the halfway point, and the most shocking of his revelations is consigned to an Appendix, a seemingly casual addendum that in fact (as in all good mysteries) packs the greatest punch.

Mysteries, I would suggest, have a special resonance for homosexuals. They are built around the idea of a secret, whose disclosure gives us a not entirely unpleasant jolt. Their logic, in other words, is analogous to the logic of the closet. If they are honest, homosexuals will admit that, for all its obvious inconveniences, the closet has its hidden pleasures—the sly pleasure of bringing off a deceit and the more transparent pleasure of surprising one's friends, relatives, and enemies with a revelation. Of course, I have no idea whether Ackerley consciously chose to exploit this affinity between a homosexual life and the literary conventions of the mystery. But I believe it is altogether germane to the deep satisfaction produced by his memoir.

Underlying the book's suspenseful researches, and linking them to his own sexual story, is a large structural argument, namely, the proposition that father and son have led parallel lives. From Ackerley's viewpoint the parallel might be stated as follows: just as I have a secret life so my father, I have discovered, also had a secret life. From this parallel follows a significant moral deduction, which Ackerley presses with ever greater urgency as the narrative advances: father and son, he contends, tragically failed to achieve the shared confidences—the mutual unburdening of their sexual secrets—that would have been an enormous emotional boon to them both, but above all to Ackerley himself. One might say that the book's official argument is inspired by his friend E. M. Forster's celebrated injunction, "Only connect." Ackerley sadly recounts the missed opportunities when he and his father seemed right on the verge of such revelations but failed, through stubbornness or faintheartedness on one side or the other, to take the final step.

In Ackerley's own case, as the reader figures out soon enough, the secret is of course his homosexuality, although the real surprise is not homosexuality itself but the peculiarly obsessive nature of his active sexual life, knowledge of which, as noted, is withheld until we are quite far into the story. But what of the father? He had, Ackerley concludes, three great sexual secrets. The first—telegraphed in the opening sentence—was that he lived with Ackerley's mother for a quarter of a century and sired three children before bothering to legitimize the union—which he did finally, in 1919, at the prompting of his wife's sister and, Ackerley speculates, out of a sense of guilt over the death of Ackerley's older brother in the War. The secret was especially scandalous because his father seemed the very pillar of bourgeois respectability: a successful business man (known as "the Banana King" for the fruit importing firm in which made his fortune), a generous if slightly distant parent, and a man of such regular habits that Ackerley thought of him "more as a useful piece of furniture than as a human being." To be sure, he was no prude. In fact he was a great connoisseur of women ("'plump little partridges,'" he called them), and he liked nothing better than to swap smutty stories with his male cronies. Ackerley professes to have found these stories "perfectly disgusting," although he learned to tolerate them, even encourage his father to tell them, because they gave the older man such obvious pleasure. But Ackerley considered the stories to be psychic compensations for a sexual life that, in reality, was fully retired—"the reminiscent after-glow of a lost libido, that substitute amusement in the old for actions they are no longer able to perform." This conclusion, he later became persuaded, was true as far as sexual relations with his mother were concerned. But otherwise it was wide of the mark—which brings us to his father's second sexual secret.

Among his father's papers, when he died, Ackerley found two letters, dated 1920 and 1927; they revealed that his life contained, as he put it, a "'secret orchard.'" In the years before the War, he had, it seems, taken a second mistress: a woman named Muriel Perry, who became a decorated Red Cross Quartermaster and whom he continued to see, especially on his annual cures to Bad Gastein, until his death. She had given birth to twin daughters in 1910 and a third daughter in 1912, and this second family lived, for nineteen years, "within easy walking distance" of the Ackerleys in Richmond. The father's second secret, we might say, was a variation on the first: it betrayed a shocking disregard for the proprieties of bourgeois morality. But in terms of the parallel Ackerley is so eager to draw between his father and himself, the second secret was even more significant than the first: father and son were united not merely in illegality—a somewhat formal and abstract matter—but in the active pursuit of forbidden sexual pleasure. His father's "sin" was on a par with his own and hence ought to have been an even more compelling motive for the shared confidences Ackerley wished for so devoutly.

The father's third secret is, naturally, the most important and brings his life into even closer parallel with Ackerley's, to the point that they become virtually identified. It consists in Ackerley's hypothesis that his father had been a kept man in his youth—in other words, a homosexual like Ackerley himself. His formula has now become not, "We each have a secret" but, "His secret is the same as mine." The hypothesis is advanced in two stages, the first coming before, the second after, the central chapters treating Ackerley's own sex life. A crucial piece of evidence—which Ackerley regards as the clincher—is withheld until the second discussion, so the first must be conducted by way of provocative and tantalizing hints, inferences extracted from a few ambiguous documents, notably the letters provided by his father's old friend and business partner, Arthur Stockley. It gains some credibility—but again of a purely inferential sort—from his father's having told him, in a belated talk about the facts of life, "that in the matter of sex there was nothing he had not done, no experience he had not tasted."

The hypothesis rested on the indisputable fact that, for most of five years, from 1879 to 1884, his father had been a guardsman—a member of the Royal Horse Guards. No sooner has Ackerley introduced this piece of information than he draws an incriminating portrait (much of it, we later learn, based on his own experience) of the sexual temptations to which the guardsmen were notoriously subject:

Healthy and vigorous young men, often, like my father, the merest boys, suddenly transplanted from a comparatively humdrum provincial or country life
into a London barrack-room, exercised and trained all day to the bursting
point of physical fitness, and let loose in the evening, with little money and
large appetites, to prowl about the Monkey Walk in Hyde Park, the pubs, or
West End streets, in uniforms of the most conspicuous and sometimes provocative design—it is hardly surprising that their education in the seductions and
pleasures of the world should take rapid strides.

The Monkey Walk and the West End were well-known sites of the queer trade
and Ackerley's own favored haunts. In one of those venues, sometime in the mid-
1880s, he speculates, his father was picked up by James Francis de Gallatin, "a
Count of the Holy Roman Empire and descendant of a famous Swiss-American
family." Certainly by summer 1885 the Count de Gallatin had set up house in
New Brighton with Roger Ackerley (and two other young men, one of them,
like Ackerley's father, "strikingly handsome"), and he kept young Ackerley in
his employ, and a virtual member of his family, for the next three years. To a
large extent Ackerley deduces the nature of the relationship between the Count
and his father from a strenuous reading of a photograph of de Gallatin and his
three friends, a photograph revealing, Ackerley insists, that de Gallatin was
"clearly bowled over" by the former guardsman. To disinterested eyes, however,
the photograph is hardly incriminating, leaving the reader with the uneasy feeling that Ackerley seems determined to convict his father of homosexuality no
matter how slender the evidence.[2] Somewhat more persuasive, but still entirely
circumstantial, is a letter from the Count's mother complaining bitterly of Roger
Ackerley's disloyalty and ingratitude when, in 1888, he ran off with a young
woman named Louise Burckhardt, a family friend of the de Gallatins, who was
supposedly intended for the Count. "'His heart is broken,'" wrote Mme de Gallatin, and Ackerley assures us that "the loss the Count suffered was not the loss of
a bride."

2. Photographic "evidence" plays a remarkable role in Ackerley's argument. Of several photos of his
father as a young man, obtained from the father's brother and from Arthur Stockley in the 1930s, Ackerley
writes:

> The inherent absurdity of envisaging my father in the arms of another man had never really faded; it faded
> now. It is true that, studying the photograph of him in uniform, I decided that I would not have picked him up
> myself; but the picture was said not to do him justice. . . . From the photo of him as a young man-about-town
> it was not difficult to see why . . . de Gallatin had fallen for him.

The putatively solid evidence for the hypothesis was supplied only much later. It came in the figure of Ackerley's most Dickensian creation, an "old quean" named Arthur Needham, from whom—by spectacular coincidence—Ackerley just happened to rent a flat in 1925. Arthur Needham is a true grotesque, shuffling and giggling across Ackerley's pages and inhabiting a set of cluttered and musty rooms that Miss Havisham might have envied. In the midst of the clutter what should Ackerley discover but a large portrait of the Count de Gallatin, captured many years after his supposed infatuation with young Roger Ackerley, now grown pompous and tending to fat. Eventually Arthur Needham confessed that the Count was indeed a homosexual, and a notoriously predatory one at that. "'Good gracious me, he was *awful*! So unscrupulous! . . . He simply went straight up to any soldier he fancied.'" When Ackerley received this intelligence, in the 1920s, he was not yet much interested in his father's past, but he sought out Arthur Needham again a decade later to get an answer to the single question with which, by then, he had become obsessed:

> 'Arthur dear, do tell me, Did your friend the Count de Gallatin ever say anything about having made love to my father? . . . Did they go to bed together? *That* is what I want to know. Did the Count ever tell you anything?'
> 'Oh lord, you'll be the death of me! I think he did once say he'd had some sport with him. But me memory's like a saucer with the bottom out.'

This tentative recollection of Arthur Needham's is the hardest evidence Ackerley has, and he immediately undercuts it by admitting his suspicion that, in offering it, Needham had only been trying to please him and be rid of an importuning visitor. To be sure, the revelation confirmed Ackerley's suspicions about the Count's sexual preference. But it left the precise character of the relationship between the Count and Ackerley's father unclarified. As he admits, there was a perfectly innocent explanation: "The Count, like myself, may have started his emotional life . . . by falling for young men whom he was unable to touch but worshiped from afar; his active and predatory homosexuality could have begun later"—an explanation that fits much better with the father's subsequent sexual history and with the boastfully heterosexual letters he wrote to his friend Arthur Stockley at the very time of his association with the Count in the 1880s. Once again, Ackerley seems determined to find his father guilty of homosexuality, and not merely of the sentimental or sublimated variety. "What irony," he exclaims, "if it could be proved that he had led in his youth the very kind of life that I was leading!"

Beyond the thinness of the evidence supporting it, Ackerley's hypothesis of a parallel between his own and his father's life—the driving organizational principle of his book—invites skepticism on two grounds, one glaring, the other subtle and subject to debate. The glaring objection is that the most obvious parallel in the story is not between himself and his father but between himself and the Count de Gallatin. His father—if we accept Ackerley's most lurid interpretation—was more like his opposite: a hustler, playing the (uniformed) role in the relationship with de Gallatin that various sailors, soldiers, and indeed guardsmen were to play in Ackerley's own life. One might say that Ackerley was in love with his father (or with young men who closely resembled his father), but, logically, he should have identified with de Gallatin. Yet only rarely—as in the passage I quoted in the last paragraph ("the count, like myself")—does the text admit to this identification. For the most part Ackerley seems determined to ignore it. In fact, he is horrified at the prospect of seeing a version of himself in the aging sybarite the Count was to become, a sybarite closely associated with the world of "old queans" like Arthur Needham. Behind his failure to draw this obvious parallel (and his dogged insistence on drawing the false one with his father) lies, I'm convinced, the horror of effeminacy I spoke of earlier on. But my interpretation depends on evidence from Ackerley's own sexual history, which we have yet to examine.

The more subtle and debatable objection to Ackerley's hypothesis rests on what I consider the fundamental unpersuasiveness of the rationale he says has inspired his inquiry, the theme of "failed confidences." The theme is presented explicitly and often in the book:

> Our relationship was never what I think he would have wished, close and confidential, the kind of relationship I fancy he might have had with my brother. After his death, when I knew more about him and believed he may have guessed about me, I regretted this. Whether I could have achieved a nearer understanding with him must remain a question; I was only sorry, when it was too late, not to have put it more boldly to the test. It is the purpose of . . . this memoir to explore, as briefly as possible, the reasons for our failure.

A full chapter is devoted to examining the occasions when the opportunity for such an exchange of confidences presented itself and, Ackerley feels, was stupidly and tragically missed. Perhaps the most telling of those occasions occurred in 1924, when Ackerley went off to Turin for a rendezvous with an Italian sailor but lied to his father that he was staying with E. M. Forster in Weybridge. When the deceit was accidentally discovered, it provided his father, Ackerley believes, with an opening that, alas, he proceeded to muff:

> I said, 'I'm very sorry to have lied to you. I wouldn't have done so if you hadn't once said something about me and my waiter friends. But I don't really mind telling you. I went to meet a sailor friend. . . .' But he interrupted me with 'It's all right, old boy. I prefer not to know. So long as you enjoyed yourself, that's the main thing.' Thus did he close the door in my face. At that moment, perhaps through some guilty need to confess, I would, for better or for worse, have told him anything in the world.

In a famous review of *My Father and Myself*, W. H. Auden cited this very passage as evidence of Ackerley's inability to appreciate his father's magnificent tact. How grateful Ackerley ought to have been, Auden implies, to have had a father who not only refused to intrude into his private life but showed genuine humanity by giving him permission, in effect, to seek his own happiness.[3] Whether or not one accepts Auden's judgment, I am inclined to feel that the motive of shared confidences, while plausible enough at some level, is ultimately too rationalistic to account for the obsessive passion driving Ackerley's methodical researches into his father's past—researches that he began in the mid-1930s but that were brought to a satisfactory conclusion only in the last years of his life. Surely something more fundamental than a desire for a better understanding between father and son—admirable as that might be—was at stake. A clue to what that more fundamental something may have been is provided, I believe, by the timing of the book's composition: Ackerley began it when, after more than a decade of sexual adventuring and the failure of his most significant romantic relationship (a four-year affair with a Portsmouth sailor), he found himself in a state of despair of ever achieving sexual happiness. *My Father and Myself*, I am suggesting, was inspired not by regrets over a might-have-been intimacy with his father but by a profound desire to understand himself and the unhappiness that seemed to be his fate. Toward the end of the book he admits as much himself, writing that he began "to brood over this story of my father and myself" after

3. W. H. Auden, *Forewords and Afterwords* (New York, 1973), p. 458. The review originally appeared in *The New York Review of Books*, March 27, 1969.

moving to Maida Vale in 1934: "It germinated . . . out of a sense of failure, of personal inadequacy, of waste and loss." Behind the book lies the inchoate hope that finding out the truth about his father will bring him closer to the truth about himself. One could say that the deep logic of the book is psychoanalytic: it assumes that self-knowledge lies always by way of penetrating the mystery of our relations with our parents. In this sense, the book is a representative document of the twentieth century. Perhaps Ackerley's express aversion to psychoanalysis—his English empiricism and common-sense rationalism—kept him from pursuing the Freudian logic of his enterprise. Be that as it may, the elaborate and vastly diverting exploration of his father's secrets, to which most of *My Father and Myself* is devoted, serves finally to set the stage for his own sexual autobiography, which occupies the book's two central chapters (as well as the Appendix) and whose agonies he wants so desperately to comprehend. We must now turn to that disturbing story.

☙ THE OVERWHELMING IMPRESSION conveyed by Ackerley's account of his early sexual experiences—in preparatory and public school—is of their essential meagerness. "My sexual life was of the dullest," he writes. "Apart from [some] furtive fumblings . . . , I had no physical contact with anyone, not even a kiss, and remained in this virginal state until my Cambridge days." His erotic deprivation did not result from lack of opportunity. On the contrary, Ackerley was exceptionally beautiful, and his fellow students were constantly making advances. But he responded even more negatively than had John Addington Symonds half a century before, though he carried little of Symonds's Hellenistic baggage. The first schoolmate who asked to be allowed into his bed terrified him "almost to tears." "Later, a ginger-headed boy used to crawl across the dormitory floor to my bed after lights out and, lying on his back on my strip of carpet, beseech me in whispers to let him in, or, failing that, to stretch down my hand." When, after much cajoling, Ackerley did finally stretch down his hand, he "found the touch of his hot flesh and the smell of his stuff on my fingers more repugnant than exciting." Thus are we introduced to Ackerley's intense aversion to bodily odors, a squeamishness that was to have a ruinous effect on his adult sexual life. "For a long time," he confesses, "I disliked the smell of semen, unless it was my own; I have never been able to enjoy other people's smells—farts, feet, armpits, semen, unwashed cocks—as I enjoy mine." A psychoanalyst would diagnose a problem with anality—and relate the obsession to Ackerley's fear of effeminacy—but it may simply have been an exaggerated version of the English preoccupation with cleanliness; George Orwell admits a similar aversion to "noisome" smells in *Homage to Catalonia*. The prejudice also reveals Ackerley's fundamental narcissism: the same odors that repelled him in others were agreeable if they emanated from himself. The important matter is that adolescent sex was for him a deeply alien experience.

The one exception, significantly, was masturbation, the sexual haven of the narcissist. Like Quentin Crisp, Ackerley has only good things to say about the practice—"that delightful pastime"—in which he indulged early and vigorously. Ackerley's frigid inability to join in the sexual adventures of his fellow students reflected, then, not a lack of desire but a paralyzing anxiety about his proper role. He was caught on the horns of an insoluble erotic dilemma: on the one hand was his horror of effeminacy, on the other his utter inability to take the sexual initiative—that is, to assume the traditionally masculine part.

From the beginning, the issue of effeminacy is associated with his physical beauty, which, without ever saying so explicitly, he seems to consider a fundamentally feminine attribute. Beauty, in other words, was a curse, and not just in the superficial sense that it opened so many sexual doors and thus led to his becoming too choosy (a "difficulty," as Quentin Crisp observes, that the plain are spared). Because of his looks, he writes, he was given the nickname of "Girlie." "That I was a pretty boy I have already said and the illustrations to this book may confirm, too pretty I fear—beauty, among the gifts of fairy godmothers, is not the one most conducive to happiness." But he protests—perhaps too much—that, despite his nickname, he was never "in the least effeminate":

> I was far from girlish, physically or in my nature; there were no marks upon me as I matured from which my father could have suspected the sort of son he had sired; I did not lisp, I could throw overhand, and I could whistle. True, I disliked football and cricket and thought them dangerous recreations, but I was good at hockey . . . and an accurate marksman . . . ; I grew a mustache . . . during the war and took to a pipe: all manly accomplishments.

The fragility of his sense of manliness is confirmed by repeated allusions in *My Father and Myself* to his identification with his mother. It is a paradoxical identification, because his account of her, like those of virtually all the women in his memoir, is hostile and belittling. His favorite expression for his mother is "chatterbox." Although charming, she was, he insists, feckless, scatterbrained, and apprehensive, "the vaguest of creatures." He imagines her withdrawing from the marriage bed shortly after the birth of his sister, thereby sending his father in search of his "'secret orchard.'" In old age (she died seventeen years after his father) she sank into neurosis and alcoholism. Yet Ackerley writes, "When I think of her, as I sometimes do, or look at her photos with that sad face she always put on for photographers, I take much of her psychology to myself." He shared with her a number of "idiosyncrasies," including an anxiety about bad breath. Most intriguing, both were "martyrs to constipation," raising once again the specter of his anality. There is, I would hazard, an element of self-contempt in his contemptuous portrait of the mother he in many ways resembled, and the contempt is intimately related to his fear of effeminacy.

The immediate sexual consequence of Ackerley's worry about manliness was an intense aversion to being an object of desire. At the same time, the boys he found appealing also had to be masculine, indeed "normal," although (somewhat contradictorily) he had a weakness for a "kind of dewy prettiness" similar to his own. "The normal, manly boy always drew me most," he writes. "Certainly effeminacy in men repelled me almost as much as women themselves did." Isherwood and Spender, we may recall, took a much more indulgent view of the gender politics of homosexuality; Spender spoke candidly of his own effeminacy, and Isherwood prided himself on having overcome his early prejudices about playing "yin" or "yang." By contrast, Ackerley, throughout his life, found the sexual advances of other (usually less attractive) men not merely an inconvenience but an unnerving threat to his sense of wellbeing.

He speculates that a schoolboy romance might have been just what he needed to set him on a healthy sexual course, rescuing him from the pathology into which he eventually sank. But, with characteristic pessimism, he concludes that "happiness of that kind . . . was not a thing I was psychologically equipped to find." This brings us to the other horn of his erotic dilemma: his passivity. No less paralyzing than his aversion to being pursued was his own inability to take the sexual initiative, even when he felt strongly attracted. In his last term at school he fell in love with a boy named Snook, but, he reports, "I could not bring myself to touch him and it remained a pure and platonic ideal." A few years later, in Cambridge, the same inertia kept him from doing anything with a beautiful undergraduate who spent the night in his home: the following morning the entirely willing boy remarked, "ruefully," "'Every time one meets you, one has to start all over again.'" Even after Ackerley had become a practiced sexual adventurer, he continued to experience great anxiety about initiating any sexual encounter—in other words, about performing what he himself considered "the masculine role": "I had to feel an absolute degree of confidence. Industrious predator though I was, I was not a bold or reckless one." Inevitably one suspects that profound doubts about his own manliness lay at the root of this timidity. Again, as with his terror of being desired, his sexual predicament seemed to revolve about the issue of gender. Indeed, no autobiographer has given a more indelible account of pitfalls of gender identity in a gay man's life.

Ackerley served in the War from 1915. He was wounded (though not seriously) at the Somme and taken prisoner at the Battle of Cérisy, after which he spent eight months in German prison camps before his father arranged for him to be sent as an internee to Switzerland. The War was an important sexual experience for him, as it was for many British intellectuals of his generation. Ackerley is called as a witness in Paul Fussell's famous discussion of the "homoerotics" of the War, "Soldier Boys," in *The Great War and Modern Memory*.

Ackerley himself writes as if the War marked no change in the pattern of his sexual life. "The Army with its male relationships was simply an extension of my public school," he asserts. In certain obvious respects the statement is accurate. He continued to fall in love with young men whom he never touched—he mentions in particular a soldier he calls "the younger Thorne," "one of the most beautiful boys I ever saw"—just as he continued to deflect the sexual advances of older officers who fell for him. But the War introduced two important—indeed fateful—novelties: first, a sexual fascination with the lower classes, and, second, a closely-related fascination with men in uniform. In fact I am inclined to think that the War had a greater influence on his sexual imagination than anything that happened in the relationship with his father.

"The working classes," Ackerley writes, "now took my eye." They filled not only his imagination but also his immediate circle:

> Many a handsome farm- or tradesboy was to be found in the ranks of one's command, and to a number of beautiful but untouchable NCOs and privates did I allot an early sentimental or heroic death in my nauseous verse. My personal runners and servants were usually chosen for their looks; indeed this tendency in war to have the prettiest soldiers about one was observable in many other officers; whether they took more advantage than I dared of this close, homogeneous, almost paternal relationship I do not know.

From the War, then, dated Ackerley's addiction to what Quentin Crisp later dubbed "the Cophetua complex," after the imaginary African king who married a beggar maid. Ackerley of course did not invent the phenomenon: it was already, as we've seen, a well-established pattern in British homosexual life, exemplified in John Addington Symonds's *Memoirs* and E. M. Forster's unpublished novel *Maurice,* and it would become a prominent feature in the erotic experiences of Isherwood and Spender. But Ackerley embodied it so completely (and with such unhappy consequences) that Craig Seligman has referred to the phenomenon, quite simply, as "the J. R. Ackerley syndrome": "that peculiarly English ardor for barely schooled lower-class youths, dumb but pretty tabulae rasae on which older men can inscribe their fantasies." [4]

Ackerley makes some effort, in *My Father and Myself,* to comprehend the logic of his obsession. He surmises, not implausibly, that he may have been trying to "work off" his sexual guilt on his "social inferiors." As with Symonds before him, the line between infatuation and exploitation is a fine one. If he had been asked about it during the War, he writes, "I would probably have said that working-class boys were more unreserved and understanding, and that friend-ship with them opened up interesting areas of life, hitherto unknown." The ex-planation seems rather flat, but it does suggest that the intensity of English class-consciousness (which Americans always find so bemusing) left no realm of experience, including the erotic, untouched. The word he uses most often in describing young men of the working classes is "innocent." Indeed, no word in the language is more powerfully cathected for him. It conveys the contradictory impression of a person without sexual experience yet intensely erotic. As such, it reflected his own deep-seated ambivalence about sex as something at once dirty and desirable. "Innocence," in other words, implies a sexuality that is mysteri-ously both present and absent. Children, for example, are not innocent, just inert; adolescents alone embody the combination of sexual potency and inexperience that Ackerley found irresistible. But why the quality should be associated particu-larly with working-class youth, rather than youth in general, remains an enigma.

Ackerley offers no explanation for his fixation on uniforms. Yet, as we have seen, it provides one of the key elements in the erotic mystery he has fashioned about his guardsman father. He seems to think it sufficient to say of uniforms (as he does of those of the guardsmen) that they are "of the most conspicuous and

---

4. Craig Seligman, "Sex and the Single Man," *The New Yorker* (October 24, 1994), p. 96.

sometimes provocative design." Quentin Crisp makes the same point, less decorously, when he writes that the American forces stationed in Britain during the Second World War were "packaged in uniforms so tight that in them their owners could fight for nothing but their honour . . . ; their bodies bulged through every straining khaki fibre towards our feverish hands." Surely, however, uniforms were more symbolically than literally revealing, especially when we bear in mind that the first thing Ackerley wanted to do with a uniform was remove it. But what did they symbolize?

A deep reading—that is, a psychoanalytic one—would probably stress the link between uniforms and violence and suggest the presence of masochism, perhaps an unconscious wish to be punished for one's guilty sexual desires; uniforms, we know, play an important role in the rituals of gay sadomasochism.[5] But a more direct interpretation—one supported by Ackerley's text—returns us to the anxieties about masculinity that, as we have seen, were a leitmotif of his emerging sexual identity. Men in uniform are warriors, and, culturally speaking, warriors are unambiguously masculine. Soldiers, sailors, and guardsmen are thus not merely youthful and potent but, by sartorial definition, the unadulterated embodiment of the sexual "normality" Ackerley found so desirable.

Ackerley clearly considered the War a test of his manhood, a test that, by his own standards, he conspicuously failed. The theme to which his account of the War returns over and over is his fundamental cowardice. He tells how he faked being seriously wounded at the Somme, staying down in a shell-hole after he had been grazed when he should have got up and continued the assault. He is astonished that he received praise for his coolness and self-possession, when all he had really mustered was a "defensive mask" to cover "the sickening anxieties and nervous fears [of] . . . the rabbit within." His concerns about masculinity— one could even say his fear of emasculation ("My special private terror was a bullet in the balls")—came to focus on his older brother, Peter, who served briefly under his command. He gives a long account of their final meeting, the point of which seems to be that he judged himself guilty of having left his brother lying wounded in no-man's-land, from which Peter managed to crawl back on his own, only to be decapitated by a whizz-bang just before the end of hostilities

5. Ackerley's earliest sexual memory supports this masochistic reading as well as the anal fixation suggested by his aversion to odors. It was of a game played with his brother and a "shadowy" boot-boy: "In this game my brother, the boot-boy and I take down each other's trousers by turn and gently beat the bare bottoms that lie, warmly and willingly, across our laps."

in 1918. The brother thus came to symbolize the very qualities of courage and manliness he himself lacked. Ackerley also imagines his brother as the son with whom his father fully identified and for whom Ackerley himself became such a poor substitute. One significant detail confirms the link between his brother and the unambiguous masculinity Ackerley both fetishized and despaired of realizing: among his most vivid memories of his brother was "his abnormally long dark cock, longer than my own or any other I had seen." In Ackerley's erotic imagination, we might say, uniforms not only highlighted the visibility of that organ— the mighty phallus—but stood for a psychic realm unblemished by femininity. Their appeal for him, I suspect, was rooted, as was so much else, in his anxieties about effeminacy.

The two years Ackerley was in Cambridge after the War saw virtually no change in his sexual life, although he reports spending a couple of weekends in a seedy Piccadilly hotel pursuing "street prowlers and male prostitutes." He continued in his by now well-established pattern of falling in love with younger men—beautiful but heterosexual—whom he could not bring himself to approach, even when he sensed they might be receptive.

In one respect, however, Cambridge marked an important watershed. At Cambridge he befriended other acknowledged homosexuals and found his identity as a homosexual intellectual. Even before he arrived at Cambridge he had begun to read the homosexual classics, such as Otto Weininger and Edward Carpenter. Along with his homosexual friends he became a propagandist of sorts. The ideology he adopted was a watered-down version of Symonds's high Victorian Hellenism: "True love, equal and understanding love, occurred only between men. I saw myself therefore in the tradition of the Classic Greeks, surrounded and supported by all the famous homosexuals of history—one soon sorted them out—and in time I became something of a publicist for the rights of that love that dare not speak its name." His new-found ideology also contained a heavy quotient of misogyny. Girls were "vain, silly creatures" whose "smooth, soft, bulbous bodies" couldn't compare to "the muscular beauty of men." Ackerley's two literary successes of the following decade carried on this guerrilla warfare. *Hindoo Holiday* centers on a Maharajah whose homosexuality is made clear in the text, while his play, *The Prisoners of War*, is based on his own infatuation with a young RFC observer in Switzerland. "In neither of these works," Ackerley writes, "do 'plump little partridges' abound, the emotional feeling is all between men and boys." *The Prisoners of War* also contains an exchange that, he reports, "is gratefully remembered even today by elderly homosexuals":

> *Mme Louis:* You see, Captain Conrad, I hear you do not greatly care for the fair sex.
>
> *Conrad:* The fair sex? Which sex is that?

But Ackerley's "queer solidarity" was suspect from the beginning—suspect even to himself, as is suggested by the mocking tone in which he treats it in *My Father and Myself*. In particular, it must not be confused with Isherwood's "tribe ideology," because it excluded (or at least cast into a lesser category) all homosexuals who failed to measure up to Ackerley's standard of masculinity. "I did not care for the word 'homosexual' or any label," he writes. His objection was not that of modern gay radicals, who complain of the medical origins of the term and hence its implication of pathology. Rather he could not bear to be identified with the effeminate men that such inclusive "labels" embraced. As he says later, of his Portsmouth sailor, "I did not want him to think me 'queer' and himself part of homosexuality, a term I disliked since it included prostitutes, pansies, pouffs and queans."

Even more striking than the discriminatory exclusions of his homophile ideology was its utter separation from his own sexual feelings. There was for him absolutely no connection between the friends and convictions of his Cambridge circle and his passions. In fact, the two existed in radical opposition to one another. It was as if being an acknowledged homosexual constituted an inoculation against sexual attractiveness. In part, of course, this "disconnect" between ideological solidarity and erotic interest followed naturally from Ackerley's obsession with lower-class innocents, which his Cambridge friends, by definition, were not. But other homosexuals who shared his tastes did not necessarily make such an inflexible distinction between politics and sex. Isherwood and Auden, we recall, bedded down regularly. Such an arrangement would have been unthinkable in Ackerley's case.

The sharp separation of his ideological and sexual worlds was a constant source of difficulty for him. For one thing, his intellectual friends, not suffering from the same aversion (or at least not to the same degree), would often become infatuated with their handsome comrade-in-arms. "It was particularly embarrassing when my homosexual friends seemed to fall for me if they themselves had no physical appeal. I dodged and frustrated them and hurt their feelings."

Not a callous man, he sought to improve his manners, but to no avail. At the same time he was terrified that these intellectual homosexuals would invade his erotic garden and somehow contaminate it. They had to be kept strictly away from his beloved soldiers, sailors, and guardsmen, whom, as we've seen, he did not even think of as homosexuals. In the end he couldn't prevent some of his friends from meeting his Portsmouth sailor, but, he writes, "I was always on edge in case they talked in front of him the loose homosexual chatter we talked among ourselves."

By his own estimate, therefore, he was caught in a strange emotional and intellectual bind. On the one hand, he was a self-confident homophile propagandist, who admitted to no embarrassment about his proclivities, indeed who broadcast them to anyone who would listen. "I thought, wrote, and spoke the love of man for man and, among my friends, even among some intelligent normal ones, made no bones about my activities." As an intellectual he was—to use language that is both anachronistic and inappropriately American—out of the closet. On the other hand, there was his carefully segregated sexual life, which he kept largely to himself and conducted under a heavy burden of shame, even if unconscious. "Although I regarded myself as free, proud and intellectually unassailable as a homosexual," he concludes, "I was profoundly riddled with guilt." Ackerley, in sum, was a classic example of what would later be called "internalized homophobia." The only word that does justice to the radical division of his intellectual and emotional worlds, it seems to me, is schizophrenic.

ACKERLEY'S ACTIVE SEXUAL LIFE was launched in earnest when he left Cambridge and returned to live with his family in Richmond in the early 1920s. He describes his enterprise as "a long quest in pursuit of love through sex." The search lasted for twenty-five years, during which he worked his way through "several hundred young men, mostly of the lower orders and often clad in uniforms of one sort or another." Rarely has love been hunted with such grim determination or led to such meager results. For six months in the mid-1930s he kept a diary of his erotic life; its record of unqualified misery shocked even Ackerley himself when he read it fifteen years later: "It contained no single gleam of pleasure or happiness, no philosophy, not even a joke; it was a story of unrelieved gloom and despondency, of deadly monotony, of frustration, loneliness, self-pity, of boring 'finds', of wonderful chances muffed through fear, of the latchkey turned night after night into the cold, dark, empty flat, of railings against fate for the emptiness and wretchedness of my life." This was the desperate mood in which he began his researches into his father's past.

Because he is determined to paint the blackest picture of his erotic history—a history of alienated labor even more joyless than that described by Marx in the *Economic and Philosophical Manuscripts*—Ackerley, one suspects, rather misrepresents his state of mind at the start of the campaign. He writes that he can no longer remember how he felt when he began. But he concedes that much of what he did must have seemed fun at the time: "It certainly afforded pleasure and amusement, it was physically exciting, and in England it had the additional thrill of risk." Indeed, one wonders whether, in this generally harrowing tale, the real pleasures of Ackerley's sexual adventures, particularly in the early years, have not been short-changed. Some sense of the excitement and release he found—after a decade of repression at school, on the Western Front, and in Cambridge—comes across in his account of an episode that occurred on a rail trip with his father in the early 1920s:

> In the restaurant car where we were having lunch a good-looking young waiter was instantly recognised by me as a 'queer'. While my father studied the menu I exchanged smiles and winks with this youth. Towards the end of the meal, when the business of serving it was over, he passed me with a meaning look and backward glance and disappeared down the corridor. Excusing myself to my father for a natural need I followed him. He was waiting for me by the door of the toilet. We entered together, quickly unbuttoned and pleasured each other. Then I returned to finish my coffee. I had scribbled down my address for this amusing youth, but never heard from him again.

Not an edifying story, perhaps, but hardly despicable. A life devoted to erotic diversions of this sort should not automatically have led to the self-lacerating misery recorded in the diary of the mid-1930s.[6]

But Ackerley's diversions began to be hedged about by a set of desiderata and restrictions that ultimately made his life a waking nightmare. He became prisoner of an erotic fantasy—a private sexual ideology—to which he later gave the label "the Ideal Friend." In his sexual pursuits, he convinced himself, he was

6. In his superb biography of Ackerley, Peter Parker comes to the same conclusion: "One of the false impression given in *My Father and Myself* is that Ackerley's promiscuity in this period [the mid-1920s] was a hopeless, miserable and degrading quest. In fact he turned many of his adventures into splendid anecdotes for the amusement of Forster and others" (*Ackerley*, p. 121).

looking for the one perfect young man with whom he could live in enduring bliss. The criteria he established for the Ideal Friend amounted to a summa of all the positive qualities he had longed for and, especially, all the negative qualities he had fled from in the repressed attachments and deflected advances of his years at school, in Cambridge, and during the War.

By his own admission, the "disqualifications" prevailed. First and foremost, the Ideal Friend should not be effeminate; preferably he would be "normal." Education was not absolutely excluded, but it was undesirable because it "always seemed to get in the way." Naturally the Ideal Friend had to be physically attractive, which meant younger than Ackerley himself. Furthermore he ought to combine those generally incompatible qualities summed up in Ackerley's cherished notion of "innocence": that is, he should be "lusty" but inexperienced and interested in no one but Ackerley himself. Of course he also had to meet Ackerley's exorbitant standards of cleanliness and odorlessness: "no phimosis, halitosis, bormidrosis." If these requirement were not already stringent enough, Ackerley added that the Ideal Friend should be healthy, circumcised, and "on the small side." As he astutely remarks, "I had set myself a task so difficult of accomplishment as almost to put success purposely beyond reach." "The Ideal Friend" was in fact a perfect formula for failure.

Despite the poor odds, Ackerley almost found what he was looking for in the Portsmouth sailor he wooed in the late 1920s. The history of the episode provides the book with its most affecting moments—as well as its moments of greatest erotic power. The young man seemed to meet all Ackerley's "undefined specifications":

> He was a sailor, an able-bodied seaman, a simple, normal, inarticulate, working-class boy. . . . Small in stature and a lightweight boxer quite famous in the Navy, his silken-skinned, muscular, perfect body was a delight to behold, like the Ephebe of Kritios. . . . If he smelt of anything it was the salt of the sea. He had had no sexual experience with anyone before, but wanted it and instantly welcomed it with me.

Interestingly, his looks recall (or, better, anticipate) those of Isherwood's Heinz: a "slightly simian face, with . . . flattened nose and full thick lips." Ackerley patronizes him—"this inarticulate, monkey-like boy who could not express himself without the help of manual gesture"—in a manner similar to Spender's treatment of Jimmy Younger.

From the start the relationship was accompanied by a high degree of anxiety on Ackerley's part. "Idle callers of a 'contaminating' kind"—meaning his intellectual friends—"had to be warned off or turned away from the door." Then he had to master his desires so as not to betray an oppressive devotion. "I would have liked instantly to undo his silks and ribbons, but the conventions by which he lived required, I supposed, the delays of conversation, drinks, supper: sex should be postponed to its proper respectable time, bedtime." There were further anxieties about bad breath (he kept a pocket full of Red Lavender lozenges) and cleaning up the mess afterwards, "to prevent, if possible, stains on the sheets as a speculation for my char." There was, in addition, a final, humiliating anxiety whose consideration Ackerley delays to his Appendix. The miracle is that, for all the terrors the affair evoked, it was tremendously arousing: "He liked dancing with me to the gramophone, readily accepting the female role, and often when I had ascertained that he too was in a state of erection we would strip and dance naked, so unbearably exciting that I could not for long endure the pressure of his body against mine." The sentence—magnificent in a way—testifies to the powerful eroticism that made Ackerley willing to endure the frets and agonies that were never far from his mind. For once he does justice to a passion that, if ultimately self-destructive, was nonetheless intensely real.

In his review of *My Father and Myself*, Auden complains that Ackerley "is never quite explicit about what he *really* preferred to do in bed."[7] The charge is unfair and seems to have been inspired mainly by Auden's desire to be the first to discuss "Plain-Sewing" and "Princeton-First-Year"—gay slang for mutual masturbation and intercourse between the thighs—in print. These were in fact the practices Ackerley favored. Both anal intercourse and fellatio were beyond the pale. At Cambridge he had learned that one of his acquaintances indulged in fellatio with two older men he was seeing. "This seemed to my innocent or puritanical mind so disgusting that for a long time I thought of his friends with utter repulsion as monsters, lower than the beasts, and wondered that their faces, when at length I met them both, should look so ordinary." Even after his standards had been eased, he never found the practice—which of course triggered all his anxieties about dirt and disease—enjoyable.

How ironic, therefore, that just this sexual act—which he had not before performed—brought his affair with the Portsmouth sailor to a sudden end. "I

7. W. H. Auden, *Forewords and Afterwords*, p. 453.

suppose I acted towards my sailor thus because his body was so beautiful and desirable that I simply wanted to eat it," he explains. The sailor responded exactly as Ackerley himself had after he learned about his Cambridge friend. When Ackerley asked him why he had suddenly cut off their appointments, the sailor replied, "'You know what you did! You disgusted me!'" One might say that it was the price of having sex with a young man who was both "normal" and "innocent." Yet a deeper reason for the failure of the relationship was that boy had grown impatient with Ackerley's neediness. The difficulties increased after Ackerley rented a flat in Portsmouth so that they could see each other on a more regular basis. In large part, the arrangement lasted as long as it did only because the sailor was so often kept away by his job. Still, its end was devastating for Ackerley, who pined away "in the darkest dejection of spirit" for a year and a half and was ready to start all over again, even though by then the sailor had found "a new gentlemen friend . . . who took him for holidays to Nice and Cannes." At a final meeting, Ackerley was unable to control the emotion in his voice or the trembling of his arm as he put it around the boy's shoulders. "He did not want emotion, only fun. He then disappeared out of my life." Ackerley records that, although he had never shown any interest in girls, he eventually married.

With the departure of his sailor Ackerley's long season of sexual labors began in earnest. He gives an unsparing account of those labors, which occupied the next fifteen years of his life, reducing all his other activities—his friendships, his work at the BBC, his literary efforts—to mere distractions from the serious and time-consuming business of finding the Perfect Friend. He surmises, not unreasonably, that some deep masochistic impulse lay at the root of his punishing routine: "I sometimes wonder . . . whether the hardship of it all was the very thing I wanted, the frustrations, which often seemed to me so starveling and wretched, my subconscious choice." As often happens in the book, he stands right on the brink of psychoanalytic insight but doesn't follow through.

With the passing years he grew more desperate, and the anxieties attending his search increased. He was consumed with fretful imaginings, his mind exhausting itself in an endless calculus of sexual opportunities:

> I was rarely happy in any one place, for all the other places where I was not appeared, in my imagination, more rewarding than the one I occupied. The Ideal Friend was always somewhere else and might have been found if only I

had turned a different way. The buses that passed my own bus seemed always
to contain those charming boys who were absent from mine; the ascending
escalators in the tubes fiendishly carried them past me as I sank helplessly
into hell.

He spares himself no embarrassment in his excruciatingly precise recital of his
techniques of predation. Even as he entered middle age, he continued to suffer
from the faintheartedness and fear of rejection that had made him so timorous
as an adolescent, supplemented now by the very real danger he courted:

> I did not like boys to think I was pursing them, they might turn nasty; the
> safest thing was a quick 'open' exchange of understanding looks or smiles. For
> this it was necessary to meet people face to face, a problem if the particular
> boy was moving in the same direction. In such a case I would hasten after him,
> pass him without a glance (in the hope of not being noticed), and when I had
> reached what I considered to be an invisible distance ahead, turn about to
> retrace my steps for a head-on collision. If then I got a responsive look, a
> smile, a backward glance, if he then stopped to stare after me or to study the
> goods in the nearest shop-window (the more incongruous they were the safer I
> felt) I judged I might act, though still with caution in case he was luring me
> into some violent trap. The elaborateness of this manoeuvre often lost me the
> boy, he had gone into a house or disappeared up some side turning behind my
> back—and therefore remained in my chagrined thought as the Ideal Friend.

Pointedly, Ackerley records that his favorite venues were exactly those he
would later imagine his father prowling as a young man: Marble Arch, the Monkey Walk, and Hyde Park Corner. Even more pointedly, he reports spending
more and more of his time concentrating on the members of His Majesty's Brigade of Guards: "Though generally larger than I liked, they were young, they
were normal, they were working-class, they were drilled to obedience; though
not innocent for long, the new recruit might be found before someone else got
at him." Ackerley detested the "taint of prostitution" that inevitably accompanied
these transactions, and he gives a characteristically painstaking account of the
complicated "face-saving techniques" he developed to disguise the mercenary
reality.

   As he grew older, Ackerley's competitors—many of whom were acquaintances—became an increasing source of worry. When they met "on the job"

they would nod to one another but never converse. Everybody understood that this was "a serious occasion needing undistracted concentration [on] the business at hand." They might be friends elsewhere, but here they were rivals, eyeing "each other surreptitiously, perhaps registering the fact that, with so many eagles about, if any Ganymede did arrive we would have to work fast." The language of labor—indeed alienated labor—seems altogether appropriate to this grinding pursuit of pleasure.

His intense awareness of aging cast yet further gloom over the already morose proceedings. In Ackerley's mind aging seems to have brought with it a dread feminization, at least in the perception of his quarry: "As the years rolled by I saw these competitors of mine growing older and older, greyer and greyer and, catching sight of myself in the mirrors of saloon or public bars, would perceive that the same thing was happening to me, that I was becoming what guardsmen called an 'old pouff', an 'old twank', and that my chance of finding the Ideal Friend was, like my hair, thinning and receding." It was the ultimate humiliation, the fulfillment of the worst fears of his adolescence, but Ackerley, brutally honest to the end, spares himself nothing. In effect, he recognizes that he had become indistinguishable from Arthur Needham or the Count de Gallatin.

He sometimes met a young man who was far worthier of his affection than had been his Portsmouth sailor but who failed to pass one or the other of his imaginary tests and was thus discarded. He mentions in particular a Welsh boy with smelly feet—"some glandular trouble, and out of politeness he preferred not to take off his boots." In retrospect Ackerley saw that this young man was "the best and most understanding friend I had ever made . . . , gentle, kind, cheerful, undemanding, self-effacing, always helpful, always happy to return to me in spite of neglect." Like many of those Ackerley pursued in the final years of his labors, he was killed in the Second World War—a sad echo of the erotic conflagration of the First. In a glimmer of enlightenment, Ackerley recognized finally that his heart had been engaged, leading him to reflect on the many opportunities he had missed. The "saddest thing" he came across in his diary of misery from the mid-1930s, he reports, was his critical comments upon his first meeting with the Welsh boy, "now dead, his dullness and smelly feet."

In Ackerley's shocking Appendix we learn the particulars of his final erotic debasement as well as of his ultimate and even more surprising transfiguration. Actually, the first revelation is not entirely unexpected, as he has already alluded to the matter in passing: he suffered from premature ejaculation (or, as he likes to say, from "sexual incontinence"), which grew more severe with time. It was caused, as were most of his difficulties, by anxiety, "which," he observes, "I take to be a part of guilt, and might have been corrected by psychoanalysis." As is his fashion, he recounts the agonies it caused him with merciless exactness:

> Whenever I was emotionally aroused, whenever I was in the presence of some-one physically attractive whom I was wanting to embrace, or even when I was awaiting his arrival, I lived in a state of hot sexual excitement, the bulge of which in my trousers I was always afraid would be noticed. A kiss then, the mere pressure of an embrace, if I got as far as that, was enough to finish me off—and provide a new shame, that the stain, seeping through my trousers, might be seen.

What was truly shameful, however, is that the condition often led him to behave inconsiderately toward his tricks. He was not above abruptly dispatching them, especially if they were not very attractive, after a fully-clothed embrace had brought on his own orgasm.

Eventually premature ejaculation gave way to its ugly (if paradoxical) twin, impotence. Not the impotence of advancing age or sexual exhaustion, Ackerley writes, but, once again, a neurotic disorder that was the inevitable result of the multiple anxieties he brought to every sexual encounter. It was triggered by his apprehension about taking the sexual initiative—ultimately by insecurities about his masculinity—which, as we have seen, had been a feature of his psychic con-stitution from the earliest years. Even as he continued to be afflicted by premature ejaculation with new conquests, "things began to go 'wrong'" with his old steadies:

> The fret would enter. . . . Why had I taken him to the pub first? it was getting late, I must hurry. . . . Why had I not taken him to the pub first? he was bored, I must hurry. . . . Why had I let him have his own satisfaction first? he was tired, I must hurry. . . . I was taking too long, he was only being obliging and my sweat and the weight of my body must be disagreeable to him, I must hurry, hurry. . . . Then the slow collapse, and nothing that he could do, or I could do in the way of furious masturbation, could retrieve the wretched failure.

Freud examines what he calls psychical impotence in a famous essay, originally translated as "The Most Prevalent Form of Degradation in Erotic Life" (*Die allgemeinste Erniedrigung des Liebeslebens*). The word "degradation" nicely captures the deep humiliation that must attend this experience in a man, like Ackerley, for whom sexual desire was so imposing and sexual adventuring so central to the way of life he followed for a quarter of a century. Moreover, Freud's conclusion that impotence originates in a separation of the affectionate from the sensual current in libidinal development is amply confirmed by Ackerley's predatory history.[8]

Ackerley was suddenly and miraculous rescued from his sexual toils by a dog, an Alsatian bitch named Queenie (but called Tulip in his first book about her), who, after his twenty-five year ordeal, entered his life just before he turned fifty. From then until her death in 1961 she became the center of his emotional world, the sole object of his love. "She offered me what I had never found in my sexual life, constant, single-hearted, incorruptible, uncritical devotion, which it is in the nature of dogs to offer." One might almost say that Ackerley's saga ended in the happy marriage we expect at the conclusion of Jane Austen novel, which in odd respects his book resembles. Queenie herself became the subject two splendid volumes, *My Dog Tulip* (1956) and *We Think the World of You* (1960). Appropriately she is the dedicatee of *My Father and Myself*, occupying the same place in Ackerley's life, and at the front of his book, as Don Bachardy in Christopher Isherwood's.

"From the moment she established herself in my heart and home," Ackerley writes, "my obsession with sex fell wholly away from me." He continues:

> The pubs I had spent so much of my time in were never revisited, my single desire was to get back to her, to her waiting love and unstaling welcome. . . . I never prowled the London streets again, nor had the slightest inclination to do so. On the contrary, whenever I thought of it, I was positively thankful to be rid of it all, the anxieties, the frustrations, the wastage of time and spirit. It was as though I had never wanted sex at all, and that this extraordinary long journey of mine which had seemed a pursuit of it had really been an attempt to escape from it.

8. Sigmund Freud, "On the Universal Tendency to Debasement in the Sphere of Love" (1912), trans. Alan Tyson, in *The Standard Edition of the Complete Psychological Works of Sigmund Freud*, ed. James Strachey (London, 1953–1974), vol. 11, pp. 179–90. In Freud's analysis, the degradation or debasement actually refers to the sexual object, not to the sufferer himself. Freud thought such a tendency to debase the sexual object was widespread, perhaps universal, among civilized men, who preferred to have sex with prostitutes rather than with their wives.

Were Ackerley writing fiction he might have allowed this categorical assertion about the end of his sexual odyssey to stand unqualified. But one of the glorious inconveniences of autobiography is that messy facts must be allowed to disturb neat novelistic conclusions. After Queenie came into his hands, he stopped his cruising at home, but whenever he went abroad—to France, Italy, Greece, and Japan—he would resume his former practices: "I looked for sexual adventure and found it. Into it were once more imported all the old anxieties and worries, heartbreaks even, that had attended it throughout my life—with the latest anxiety, to which I have alluded, added: impotence." The division between chaste England and the lubricious outer world echoes a habit of mind we have seen John Addington Symonds and Christopher Isherwood, the main difference being that in Ackerley's case the division came only after a lifetime of carousing on native grounds.

A friend, puzzled by the extraordinary change in Ackerley's behavior, asked him if he ever had sexual intercourse with Queenie. The answer was no, but he confesses, "In truth, her love and beauty when I kissed her, as I often did, sometimes stirred me physically." He was obliged, however, to deal with Queenie's own sexual needs, "her burning heats." "The most I ever did for her was to press my hand against the hot swollen vulva she was always pushing at me at these times, taking her liquids upon my palm." It is perhaps the most moving sentence in Ackerley's book, as he managed to overcome the squeamishness that had blighted his own erotic history, from his schoolmate's repugnant semen to the smelly feet of his Welsh boy. And doubtless there is poignant justice in seeing this inveterate homosexual, often misogynistic and terrified by everything associated with women, ministering to the sexual needs of, in effect, the only female in his life.

Auden wrote that Ackerley failed to appreciate his good fortune, and not merely in the matter of his father's tact: "How many people have had so understanding a father? How many have found their Tulip?" "No," Auden concludes, "he was a lucky man."[9] Far be it from me to belittle the emotional satisfactions we obtain from our pets. But surely one must reckon as at least a partial failure a life that abdicated not only sex but also the richer and more complex forms of companionship—intellectual as well as emotional—that only a relationship with another human being can give. One might be inclined to respond that Ackerley

---

9. W. H. Auden, *Forewords and Afterwords*, p. 458.

treated the men in his life more like animals than people (we recall the "simian" good looks of his Portsmouth sailor). Ackerley himself is aware of the paradox, but in keeping with his psychological reticence, he passes over it quickly: "Looking at [Queenie] sometimes I used to think that the Ideal Friend, whom I no longer wanted, perhaps never had wanted, should have been an animal-man, the mind of my bitch, for instance, in the body of my sailor, the perfect human male body always at one's service through the devotion of a faithful and uncritical beast." The wistful sadness of this vision of an imaginary synthetic lover may stand as a final comment on Ackerley's hard journey through the troubled waters of eros to the shoals of chastity. I would not begrudge him his contentment, but neither should we ignore the price he paid for it.

Quentin Crisp, ca. 1980.
Photograph by Jean Harvey.

The Naked Civil Servant

"AS SOON AS I STEPPED OUT of my mother's womb onto dry land, I realized that I had made a mistake." If J. R. Ackerley's memoir introduces us to a world of mystery, Quentin Crisp's introduces us to a world of jokes. Crisp is in fact the classic unreliable narrator, whose passion to entertain is forever sabotaging his duty to inform. He is in constant danger of abrogating what Philippe Lejeune has called "the autobiographical pact,"[10] the tacit agreement, between author and reader, that the autobiographer will seek to give a sincere accounting of his or her life.

Consider Crisp's description of himself, berouged and hennaed, entering the establishment of a prospective employer:

> I found it necessary to develop a technique of being interviewed. This came into operation the moment I arrived at the reception desk. It began with not evincing any surprise as all the office boys fled through the doors nearest to them, firstly in order to fall about the corridors laughing without restraint and secondly so that they might spread to distant floors of the building the news of my advent. Then, while I waited for my appointment, I had to invent some artificial occupation for my attention so that it would seem natural for me not to look up as each member of the staff, carrying a meaningless piece of paper, came to speak to the receptionist. Finally there was the interview itself. At the start of this I must, by what actors call some piece of 'business', allow my client a good look at me while I was not looking at him. I did not always succeed in giving him time to put his eyes back in his head before I turned my gaze upon him.

10. Philippe Lejeune, *On Autobiography*, trans. Katherine Leary (Minneapolis, 1989), p. 13.

Here the exaggerations are broad enough that we are in at no great risk of being misled: we don't for a minute believe that "all" the office boys fled the room or that "each" member of the staff invented an excuse to get a closer look, any more than we take literally the final cartoon image of the employer's bugging eyes. But the passage's determined literariness and its propensity for slapstick make us nervous about its author's trustworthiness—more nervous, at least, than we are made by the autobiographers considered up to this point.

I have said that Crisp was literary heir to Oscar Wilde. As with Wilde himself, his literary manner is a highly complex phenomenon that serves a number of different (and perhaps contradictory) purposes. In an important respect, it is simply a linguistic extension of the self-dramatizing style of his life, a queenly prose to match his queenly person. Increasingly, as we shall see, Crisp came to think of his life as a performance, and the language of his autobiography continues this "performative" impulse. From early on the performance was ideologically motivated: it was an act of transgression, of defiance, through which, almost singlehandedly, he did public battle with the heterosexual prejudices of English society. Likewise with his prose: it is, on one level at least, the verbal counterpart of his hennaed hair and lacquered fingernails, wittily savaging the repressive convictions of his countrymen. Not for the first time, comedy becomes a vehicle of aggression, a weapon of social criticism.

But Crisp's comedic aggression is as often directed against himself as against society, giving rise to a different worry in the reader's mind, namely, that the text has been disfigured not just by the author's crusading zeal but by his internalized homophobia as well. "I started to shed the monstrous aesthetic affectation of my youth so as to make room for the monstrous philistine postures of middle age, but it was still some years before I was bold enough to decline an invitation to *Hamlet* on the grounds that I already knew who won." Here not only do we suspect that a one-liner has been fashioned without much concern for accuracy (Did he really decline an invitation to *Hamlet*? Did he actually produce the zinger about already knowing who won?), but, more important, we also wonder what motivates him to reduce his life to affectation and posturing. This is the language of self-caricature. His deeply ambivalent wit comes to focus above all on his effeminacy, which is at once a militant cause and a huge gag. His dyed hair, his plucked eyebrows, his jangling jewelry, and his wicked sashaying were, to be sure, serious and intentional affronts to the heterosexual establishment, but that does not prevent Crisp from milking them for laughs. Both truth and the dignity of his sexual identity are thus put at risk.

The note of self-contempt is already evident in Crisp's opening sentence: "From the dawn of my history I was so disfigured by the characteristics of a certain kind of homosexual person that, when I grew up, I realized that I could not ignore my predicament." Homosexuality is a disfigurement, a "crippling" liability. Sometimes, to be sure, these self-directed put-downs appear to be witty exaggerations, as when he writes, "I regarded all heterosexuals, however low, as superior to any homosexual, however noble." But elsewhere he sounds entirely serious in concluding that self-hate is the homosexual's inevitable lot: "To rob blackmail of its potency, it would be necessary to remove the homosexual's feeling of shame. This no power on earth can do." He does not exempt himself from the indictment: "The only difference between me and other outsiders was that I cried aloud for pardon."

We are not yet done with the complexities of Crisp's literary posture, for there is a meta-level to this issue as well: repeatedly in *The Naked Civil Servant* he draws attention to his unreliability, his addiction to performance, and his logorrhea. One of his funniest running jokes is precisely that he is a nonstop talker. A young woman asks him a question "during a silence that must have been caused by my having to pause for breath." She wants to know if he might be persuaded to speak to the patients in a mental hospital: "No opportunity to speak uninterrupted could be allowed to pass without investigation." Summoned to the medical board at the outbreak of the Second World War, he was asked by a doctor why he dyed his hair: "While I was filling my lungs with air in preparation for delivering one of my favourite speeches of self-justification he shrugged his shoulders and said, 'I suppose you prefer it red.'"

With equally self-deflating candor he tells us that his torrent of words gradually evolved into what was in effect a stand-up comedy routine, first in life and then in his book. Riding back to London from various state-run art institutes in the provinces, where he worked as a nude model (hence "the naked civil servant"), he labored "assiduously" on his "quips, gags, anecdotes and epigrams." When invited to a friend's house, if he found people he hadn't met before, he "plunged into a complete cabaret turn." His "discourse," he reports, came to be called "Crisperanto." Eventually this uncontained verbosity led to senselessness and put an end to communication: "In middle age I found that I had gone beyond my original aim of purging my speech of the dross of sincerity. I had robbed it of all meaning whatsoever. I became like a stopped clock. I was right about once every twelve years [hours?], but what good was that when everyone had ceased to look at my face?" Our unreliable narrator tells us, paradoxically, of his own unreliability, leaving us tied in epistemological knots.

The issue of literary manner, and its implications for Crisp's autobiographical trustworthiness, is ultimately inseparable from the issue of character. One might say that if Ackerley was a narcissist, Crisp must be considered a solipsist. The nonstop talker lived in a universe of which, psychologically speaking, he was the sole inhabitant. Other persons had no meaningful existence for him; they were merely the compliant audience for his monologues. Appropriately, all the characters in *The Naked Civil Servant* remain shadowy and insubstantial, often reduced to a single (unattractive) physical feature. As usual, Crisp complicates matters by being the first to diagnose his own condition, turning it into another of his running jokes. Stumbling on a pair of illicit love-makers (an older Czech and a young art student), he writes, "I was shaken by the revelation of two people, whom until now I had regarded only as reflections of my own existence, in violent relation to each other. For the first time I was forced to admit that other people existed. It was not a discovery that I welcomed." Crisp has created the apparently impossible paradox of a self-aware solipsist.

Occasionally he hints that something more sinister than a "deep-seated indifference to the fate of others" lay behind his egoistic discourse. He had not suffered a lifetime of abuse "without accumulating a vast unused stockpile of rage," which, he confesses, inflamed his imagination with "lurid daydreams of having my revenge on the world." Even as a schoolboy this Nietzschean impulse had prompted a desire to "subjugate, and, if possible, destroy the personality of others." The ultimate inspiration of his public display and nonstop talk, then, was not merely self-advertisement, not even reform, but the will to power: "I wanted dominion over others in order to redress the balance. A lifetime of being constantly at the mercy of others left me . . . crushed and seething with a lust for tyranny." Typically, his formulation is so extreme that we suspect him of self-parody, especially when we recall the exquisite politeness with which he invariably responded to his tormentors. Are we to believe that *The Naked Civil Servant* is at bottom an exercise in naked aggression, a prolonged outpouring of its author's *ressentiment*?

I'm tempted to declare that Crisp has produced the last word in indecipherability, that supreme postmodern virtue. No autobiographer in my experience is more elusive. Virtually anything one says about him risks being contradicted by a reading that stresses the seriousness beneath the jest or, alternatively, the joke that explodes the apodictic pronouncement. I am not seeking a blank check for my interpretation, only warning readers to be on their guard.

ONE OF THE MATTERS about which Crisp is characteristically elusive is class and its relation to sex. As already noted, he invented the label "the Cophetua complex" for the common English addiction to sexual slumming, best embodied in J. R. Ackerley's career. He also observes, in his usual overstated manner, that in England the classes "never mingled except in bed." Yet his own class situation and its sexual implications remain murky.

When, in 1926, he began his brief career as a hustler, he entered a social world that was sharply divided between "us" and "them": "There was 'them', who acted refined and spoke nice and whose people had pots of money, and there was 'us', who were the salt of the earth." Here we get the impression that Crisp lived on the wrong side of the sexual tracks. He places himself among the working-class boys who sold favors to their betters—implying that he was, in effect, Ackerley's social and sexual opposite. In fact, however, he earned his lower-class status (if one can put it that way) on the basis of his sexual identification with his fellow hustlers, who knew in their hearts that he was not really one of them. "They forgave me for my unfair advantages," he writes, "because I was in the same sexual boat as they."

He admits that he came from a middle-class family (with the familiar retinue of governesses, nurses, and servants), but he describes the family as sliding into genteel poverty in its losing battle to keep up with the Joneses. In marked contrast to Ackerley's father, who rose spectacularly from impoverished guardsman to Banana King, Crisp's father seemed condemned to downward mobility, retreating to ever smaller houses. When young Quentin—or Denis ("as my name was before I dyed it")—organized dress-up games with the little girls in the neighborhood, he was as much interested in playing upper-class as with playing a woman. "'This wheelbarrow is my carriage. I gather up my train as I get in. Get in the other side, you fool. I nod to the servants as I leave. No. I ignore them. I am very proud and very beautiful.'" "This kind of monologue," he adds significantly, "I could keep up for whole afternoons."

There is a similar elusiveness in the account of his education. One of his conceits is that, just as he was down-and-outer, he was also a dunderhead. He had, he writes, "no more than a crossword-puzzle mentality" and was unable to "infer results from causes." But in reality he enjoyed the education of his class and appears to have been a perfectly respectable student. He earned a scholarship to a public school (where he suffered the familiar humiliations of that time-honored English institution) and later attended London University, though he left without getting his diploma. Indeed, despite his many humdrum jobs and his marginal existence as a "hooligan," he was in fact an intellectual, if never a member the elite milieu inhabited by his contemporaries (or near contemporaries) Isherwood, Spender, and Ackerley. He devoted long hours to writing novels, stories, poems, musicals, and opera libretti, even though few of them saw the light of publication. Admittedly, he likes to play the philistine; it is another of his self-belittling jokes. "I don't hold with art," he intones. But the posture is belied by the intellectual pretensions on display throughout *The Naked Civil Servant*, whose highly groomed prose is festooned with literary and philosophical allusions, from Homer to Sartre.

The account of his childhood is a parody of the stock Freudian narrative about the genesis of homosexuality. As he says, "My parents and I constructed between us the classic triangle for all the world as if we had read the right books on psychology." He had a father who hated him and whom Crisp regarded with a corresponding Oedipal contempt. But perhaps even more noteworthy than their mutual hostility is Crisp's general lack of interest in his father, who, in striking contrast to Roger Ackerley, makes only a few desultory appearances in the text. At first his mother failed to provide the exclusive, smothering affection he craved. Or, to speak more accurately, this supposed slight provides the occasion another joke about his unbounded egoism: "I saw that my mother intended to reapportion her love and divide it equally among her four children. I flew into an ungovernable rage from which I have never fully recovered. A fair share of anything is starvation diet to an egomaniac." But, joke or no joke, his self-absorption was genuine: the three other children (two brothers and a sister) are barely mentioned again.

Eventually his mother more than made up for the early neglect. The particular form her indulgence took was to encourage his fascination with women's clothes. Crisp did not become a transvestite: central to his adult persona was the desire to look, unambiguously, like an effeminate man. He painted his face, dyed his hair, grew his nails long, and wore shoes several sizes too small, but he never

appeared in skirts or dresses or anything that might have led to his being mis-
taken for a woman (though that sometimes happened). On a single occasion he
attended a drag ball, which he found supremely boring. But as a child, his feminine identity expressed itself precisely through cross-dressing. It was his mother's
tolerance, he writes, that allowed him to perform in a student production of
A Midsummer Night's Dream wearing a green tulle dress, although the show "was
in no other way transvestite." He doesn't know whether she secretly wished he
were a girl or was just trying to keep him quiet. But she let him feel that dressing
up in women's clothes—playing the part of a female of the upper classes—"was
a taste we shared." In childhood, then, the central pillar of his adult psychology,
his inner femininity, was firmly established. In reality he might be a boy, but in
his imagination he was "a woman, exotic, disdainful."

Was he also a homosexual? Yes, but with neither the enthusiasm nor the
pleasure he derived from his games of female make-believe. From the start, gender identity preceded sexual preference, and it never abandoned its pride of place.
Yet in a number of surprising ways, Crisp's early sexual history closely resembled
Ackerley's, despite the "formidable natural chastity belt" created by his plain-
ness. Most important, his adolescent experience, like Ackerley's, was meager and,
to the extent it existed at all, disappointing. He spent a single night in bed with
another boy, an Indian, and then only as part of the school's ritual end-of-term
orgy. "I did not expect any pleasure," he reports glumly, "and there was none."
He proceeds to editorialize that effeminate homosexuals are the least apt to have
sex with other boys at school: "They seem to realized that these jolly get-
togethers are really only a pooling of the carnal feelings of two people who deep
down are interested in their dreams of girls. Otherwise they tend to be self-
congratulatory pyrotechnical displays of potency." If sex was not the shameful,
"soiling thing" it was for Ackerley, it nonetheless had little allure. Again Crisp
presents us with a paradox: that of the confirmed homosexual who invariably
describes sex in the most unglamorous terms.

But he can't entirely disguise the fact that he entertained romantic hopes. In
this regard he was again like Ackerley. He "longed to be the subject of a school-
shaking romance," though perhaps as much for the publicity as the sentiment.
After he had become a full-fledged adult cynic he liked to make fun of his adolescent search "for some sheet-music kind of love" that would fulfill the erotic
dreams he had learned from literature. Indeed, his adult cynicism was so brittle
that one suspects him of being in the grips of a reaction formation. Every now

and then, moreover, he lets down his guard and we can see the frustrated romantic still lurking beneath the hardened veneer. He admits, for example, that he despised the coarseness of his life as a hustler. But he refuses to wallow in self-pity. The cynic prevails. "What better proof of love can there be than money?" he asks. "A ten-shilling note showed incontrovertibly just how mad about you a man is."

There is a final similarity with Ackerley: he became a devoted masturbator and an even more eloquent defender of its charms. In masturbation, he writes, "I discovered the only fact of life that I have ever fully understood." It was the egomaniac's ideal sexual activity, especially if, like Crisp, he happened to be unattractive. Later this perception would be elaborated into a full-throated celebration of the practice. Masturbation was not a make-do, resorted to in the absence of sexual intercourse. On the contrary, sexual intercourse itself was "a substitute—and a poor one—for masturbation." Its unique virtue was that it liberated the mind from the body. It had the further advantage of doing away with all the prejudices that attend the search for a sexual partner: "It saves a person from judging others by the confused standards of male, female, old, young, beautiful, [or] hideous." If people would masturbate rather than fornicate, Crisp implies, the world might be rid of sexism, ageism, and lookism. The proposition is typically exaggerated, but if we recall the agonies to which Ackerley subjected himself searching for his Ideal Friend (that impossible roster of desiderata and prohibitions), we can appreciate the grain of wisdom in Crisp's recommendation. Masturbation creates no victims.

The Naked Civil Servant does not expressly consider the question—which has so exercised gay intellectuals in the past decade—of whether his sexual identity was innate or chosen. But the bulk of the evidence suggests that he was what would later be called an essentialist rather than a constructionist. "In major issues," he writes, "I never had any choice and therefore the word 'regret' had in my life no application." His preferred label for himself and others like him is "a homosexual person," implying a deep and abiding psychic condition over which neither individual initiative nor social circumstance had any influence. Although he sometimes uses the phrase strictly to denote a particular sexual orientation, more often "a homosexual person" means an effeminate man who desires other men. Hence my suggestion, at the beginning of this chapter, that a man like Ackerley didn't even count as a proper homosexual in his estimate: "I was over thirty before, for the first time, I heard somebody say that he did not think of himself as masculine or feminine but merely as a person attracted to other persons with male sexual organs." One doesn't quite believe him, but the claim accurately reveals his tendency to equate homosexuality with effeminacy.

As he implies in his opening sentence, the stigmata of effeminacy "disfigured" him "from the dawn" of his history. "I was from birth an object of mild ridicule because of my movements—especially the perpetual flutter of my hands—and my voice. Like the voices of a number of homosexuals, this is an insinuating blend of eagerness and caution in which even such words as 'Hallo' and 'Goodbye' seem not so much uttered as divulged." To the contemporary theorist, nothing would seem less innate, more obviously the product of social and psychological contingencies, than the "insinuating" tone of voice so marvelously captured in Crisp's remark. But, in his own view, such "mannerisms" were fundamental to his being. Once, during the Depression, when he appeared at the Labour Exchange for a handout, the supervisor asked why he went about looking as he did. "'Because this is the way I am'" was his response. In keeping with that conviction, *The Naked Civil Servant* generalizes freely about how homosexuals behave and how they "are." It betrays none of the caution we have learned to exercise as we have grown more sensitive to the dangers of stereotyping—of mistaking historical accident for genetic fact. Both sexually and otherwise, homosexuals are for him a natural kind, indeed "my kind."

Not every affectation, however, enjoys his indulgence. His own effeminacy, he insists, was natural. But he recognizes excesses. Rather surprisingly, they include a certain kind of effeminate camp of which one might have thought he was the complete embodiment. "About camp, with its strong element of self-mockery," he observes, "there seemed to me to be something undignified—even hypocritical." He mentions, by way of example, an invoice clerk with whom he briefly shared a flat: "If I came into the kitchen and found him washing his socks, he could not have refrained from uttering some such phrase as 'A woman's work is never done.' I longed to cry out, 'You are washing your socks because they are dirty. The situation needs no comment.'" One might say that Crisp's effeminacy, in his own estimate, was genuine, but other varieties might be willful or artificial. The episode also reminds us that, while he eagerly embraced femininity in his appearance and manner, he had no interest whatever in domesticity, in spite of its long association with the female sphere. On the contrary, he lived in perpetual squalor and never learned to cook. He also detested shopping.

Although he says he never had any interest in girls and can't even imagine such an attraction, he sometimes speaks of sexuality, in the modern fashion, as an undifferentiated continuum on which there are no fixed locations. "It is universally agreed," he asserts, "that men are neither heterosexual nor homosexual; they are just sexual." In the same vein is his observation that "human beings respond to almost any erotic stimulus. It was only while people still felt that God was watching them that they directed their impulses exclusively towards certain parts of certain people. In everybody the anus is at least as capable of sexual excitement as the lips. Sex acts are now termed masculine and others feminine only to keep the subject tidy." But these pronouncements have a certain academic quality (tempered by his familiar wit) and find little resonance in the sexual particulars recorded in the text. At most one might say that he "chose" to be what he already "was." Crisp himself invokes—how seriously, as usual, one may doubt—the authority of existentialist philosophy to explain himself: "Perhaps Jean-Paul Sartre would be kind enough to say that I exercised the last vestiges of my free will by swimming with the tide—but faster."

Crisp's fatalism extended beyond his personal circumstances to embrace the course of history, at least in sexual matters. Fatalism is not perhaps the right word, because in some respects his sense of historical inevitability was quite comforting. He believed that it was only a matter of time before his own extravagance would come to seem perfectly ordinary. As he puts it—in another of his crafted metaphors—"Those who once inhabited the suburbs of human contempt find that without changing their address they eventually live in the metropolis"— although, he adds, "in my case this took a very long time." The most important historical shift, on whose inexorability he comments repeatedly, was the collapse of the binary gender system—the sharp division, in manner and dress, between the world of men and the world of women—on whose existence his self-presentation as an effeminate man was radically dependent. As women abandoned the sartorial habits of their forebears—donning jackets, trousers, and "sensible shoes" and cutting their hair—"effeminacy" became an increasingly precarious mode of existence. "To homosexuals, who must, with every breath they draw, with every step they take, demonstrate that they are feminine," the withering of the visible differences between the sexes was a source of frustration and regret. It meant that Crisp had become "indistinguishable from a woman"— an intolerable development, because, as we have seen, he carefully defined himself as an effeminate homosexual, not a transvestite. He suffered a similar assault on his identity in the 1960s, when the countercultural generation adopted much of the garb with which he had distinguished himself as a flamer. "By an unlucky chance," he complains, "the symbols which I had adopted forty years earlier to express my sexual type had become the uniform of all young people. By wearing bright colors and growing my hair long I had by mistake become the oldest teenager in the business." History had its compensations, to be sure. In particular as the years went by he no longer had to put up with the verbal and physical abuse that was a constant threat in the 1930s and 1940s. But progress had a price. Most regrettably, it was abolishing the very categories that had defined his way of life.

⌒⌒ CRISP SPENT SEVERAL YEARS in the late 1920s and the early 1930s as a street hustler, mostly in the seedier areas around Piccadilly. He describes a world of commercial sex utterly separate from that of guardsmen and their "twanks" inhabited by J. R. Ackerley, less than a mile to the west, at precisely the same time. The other hustlers with whom he associated were, like himself, visibly effeminate: "We sat huddled together in a cafe called the Black Cat, . . . combing each other's hair, and trying on each other's lipsticks." Their sense of solidarity, in other words, was as much a matter of gender identity as sexual orientation. The supreme embarrassment was to be discovered working in a day job that was considered unfeminine: "One frail little thing was a plumber's mate. About this were many arch jokes and much rolling of blue-lidded eyes."

Just as the hustlers were themselves as far removed as imaginable from the manly, "normal" young men pursued by Ackerley and his fellow predators, their clients, too, belonged to an entirely different sexual universe. For the most part they were older men, often physically large, and ostensibly straight. In sexual terms these two hermetic worlds appear as perfect inversions of each other. In one (Ackerley's) older homosexuals pursued young heterosexuals, in the other (Crisp's) older heterosexuals pursued young homosexuals. A psychoanalyst might say that Crisp and his friends were looking for fathers, Ackerley and his for sons. We also get the impression that the hustlers and their clients belonged to the same milieu. There is little sense of the social distance so important to the dynamics of Ackerley's erotic adventures.

In Crisp's world, both as a hustler and later, the players were divided into two water-tight compartments. Crisp and the other boys were "bitches," the men who propositioned them were "roughs." The former were, in theory, "frail, beau-

tiful, and refined," the latter "huge, violent, [and] coarse." The opposition mimicked the division between the sexes in heterosexual society. It also resembles the
two categories of criminal homosexuals—butch and effeminate—described by
Jean Genet in *The Thief's Journal*. One might almost think that Crisp and his
fellow hustlers had purposefully constructed a cartoon version of the established
gender system in order to subvert it, such as happens, according to Judith Butler,
among the female impersonators in a film like *Paris Is Burning*.

But Crisp insists that this imaginary construction could never be fully realized. It was, from the start, impracticable, because neither party was able to live
up to its role. The roughs, in particular, were constantly failing to fulfill their
assigned part, which was "to embody the myth of the great dark man which
haunts the dreams of pathological homosexuals." The very fact that they were
interested in other men contradicted this fantasy: "A man who 'goes with' other
men is not what they would call a real man. This conundrum is incapable of
resolution, but that does not make homosexuals give it up. They only search
more frantically and with less and less discretion for more and more masculine
men." Similarly, the bitches could never completely escape their own maleness,
to which Crisp attributes their "unladylike" obsession with male genitals: "Because they themselves are, however reluctantly, to some extent masculine, their
judgment in these matters is for the most part physical. If you ask a homosexual
what his newest true love is like, you will never get the answer, 'He is wise or
kind or brave.' He will only say, 'It's enormous.'" In the end, the bitches were
"pseudo-women," just as the roughs were "pseudo-men."

As this disenchanted analysis implies, Crisp never threw himself with complete abandon into the world of hustling. What separated him from the other
boys—and ultimately made him a significant figure in the history of homosexuality—was that he decided to turn his circumstances into a public issue. In other
words, he raised the matter of effeminacy to the level of ideology. He became, in
effect, a sexual politician.

He dates the transformation from 1931, "the year in which I first pointed my
toes towards the outer world." He passed, as he says, "from admitting that I was
homosexual to protesting the fact." "From that moment on," he continues, "my
friends were anyone who could put up with the disgrace; my occupation, any job
from which I was not given the sack." He was ready at the drop of a hat to
rehearse the various arguments against the persecution of homosexuality. But,
above all, he made himself "into a test case." This meant not simply parading

about the West End in increasingly bizarre costume but carrying the message, like a missionary, to the wilds of heterosexual England.

Crisp's political stance was just the opposite of J. R. Ackerley's. Ackerley, we recall, prided himself on his advanced views, even on his readiness to advertise them, but he combined them with a personal manner of impeccable masculinity and considerable deference. For Crisp, mounting arguments in favor of homosexuality (although he knew them all by heart) was less important than a willingness to display it. His tactics were very much "in your face." He felt that "the entire strength of the club must be prepared to show its membership card at any time."

The particular manifestation of homosexuality to whose display he devoted himself was of course effeminacy—exactly the aspect of homosexuality from which Ackerley was so eager to separate himself. "The message I wished to propagate," he writes, "was that effeminacy existed in people who were in all other respects just like home. I went about the routine of daily living looking undeniably like a homosexual person." He claims that the start of his political career marked the end of his sex life (such as it was): "Sex was definitely out. . . . It wouldn't do to allow myself to be picked up by strange men. This would give people the opportunity to say that I had only adopted an effeminate appearance for this purpose. Actually, from the moment I began to look really startling, men ceased to make propositions to me." The statement is an exaggeration, but it reflects a real tension in his life between sex and politics. Once again, he was Ackerley's opposite: Ackerley was a nominal ideologue, but he was truly serious only about the pursuit of pleasure; Crisp, by contrast, happily subordinated his sexual interests to the cause. The sacrifice was not perhaps a very great one. Sex had never brought him much happiness, and, as we shall see, it never would. As he jokes, "Sex was not one of my A-level subjects."

Crisp's radical campaign on behalf of effeminacy was unrelated to any broader political protest. In general terms, J. R. Ackerley, who was a socialist and briefly considered joining the Communist Party, was far to his left. Crisp even boasts of his indifference to the great political issues of his day—the rise of fascism, the Second World War, international communism. One might say that he practiced identity politics before they had been invented. He cared only about advancing the interests of his "kind." He was dumbfounded by the "senseless and implacable hatred" that workers felt toward their employers, and he carried out his duties, however tedious, in the various jobs he held with unfailingly good humor. It is thus not so surprising that this homosexual guerrilla should have ended up writing a book on etiquette,[11] turning himself into a kind of gay Emily Post.

His confrontational stance as an effeminate homosexual often led to his becoming a victim of physical violence. These episodes provide *The Naked Civil Servant* with its most dramatic pages. In describing them he for once abandons his compulsive tendency to jokey exaggeration. Instead the writing becomes circumstantial, precise, and utterly believable. He does not linger over his suffering, but the accounts exhibit a quiet pride in his own courage. He was unfailingly polite in these confrontations. Dragged out of a taxi and beaten and kicked by a gang of boys, he responded, "'I seem to have annoyed you gentlemen in some way.'" His splendid dignity so discomfited his attackers that he was able to make his escape without further harm.

By the late 1930s Crisp had all but given up his career as a propagandist for homosexuality. Much to his "pained bewilderment," he found that the very individuals for whose benefit he had undertaken his campaign disapproved of it. The main critics appear to have been those "invisible" homosexuals like Ackerley who set a premium on their masculinity—who defined homosexuality strictly in terms of sexual desire. The homosexuals "who camped in private and watched their step in public" were as appalled by him as were the most conservative straights. By flaunting his outrageous effeminacy he was ruining their chances of achieving greater social acceptance. It is the same argument that Bruce Bawer, Andrew Sullivan, and other conservative gays use today against ACT UP or the more extravagant marchers in Gay Pride parades. With some asperity, Crisp identified the self-hatred—the internalized homophobia—implicit in this desperate need to pass. "One fact became inescapable," he writes, "homosexuals were ashamed."

When Crisp found that he had made himself into a political martyr for a bunch of timorous ingrates, his reaction was to abandon reform in favor of entertainment. Hence the note of self-mockery that often mars the account of his youthful idealism. His political efforts become another victim of his demeaning wit. There is still a residual note of protest in his story of being falsely arrested, in the early 1940s, for soliciting. But for the most part he plays the trial for laughs—as a theatrical rather than a political occasion. By the outbreak of the

11. *Manners from Heaven* (New York, 1984).

Second World War he judged his campaign an abject failure. In truth, it had found little resonance in his society, even, as we have seen, among those whose lot it was meant to improve. As a sexual politician he was simply too far ahead of his time. I'm tempted to say that he had much more in common with today's queer radicals than with the homosexuals who happened to be his contemporaries.

CRISP, AS NOTED, CLAIMED to have given up sex when he decided to devote himself to a career of "propaganda by the deed." Invariably he describes the experience as one of liberation: "For many years I was at least happy enough to live without sexual encounters at all. Sex is the last refuge of the miserable." Or, as he says later, "I was compelled to take the veil of abstinence, which suited me quite well."

In reality, sex continued to be a part of his life. He did not automatically become immune to its allure. But the overwhelming impression he leaves is that he found it disagreeable, even demeaning. In so far as he continued to have sexual experiences, he regarded them mainly as an affliction. Sex for him became what it often seems in the writings of contemporary feminists like Catharine MacKinnon or Andrea Dworkin: a form of harassment. Crisp, one might say, is at his most truly "feminine" in his critique of male sexual predatoriness.

A visit to the Labour Exchange, for example, was always an invitation to abuse. As he stood in line, "both hands were fully occupied in fending off the fumblers who were busy fore and aft." Similarly, a train trip meant coping with the importunings of exhibitionists: "I was surprised at the frequency with which I found myself sitting opposite some man who between stations decided to try to win fame, like Mr Mercator, for his projection." The insult, he writes, no longer bothered him, but he worried that "what seemed to be starting out as a frolic might easily turn into something quite different."

Crisp also shares the tendency of some modern-day feminists to equate sex with rape. Being bedded by a rough, he suggests, was a brutal experience: "Any attention that they paid to us had to be put in the form of an infliction. Such gestures as running their fingers through our hair were accompanied by insults about what a bloody awful mop it was. If they wished to make any more definitely sexual advances, these must be ruthlessly stripped of any quality of indulgence." More than one of his heterosexual partners told him "that, to be really satisfactory, all sexual intercourse must preserve the illusion of rape." In his mind, accordingly, there was very little distance between his sexual experiences and the violence to which he was subjected in the streets. He could never tell, he says, how much the roughs' interest in him "was due to sexual curiosity and how much was what it seemed—hatred."

Even when sex is not equated with aggression, it is made the object of studied contempt. A flasher, for example, exhibits not his penis but his "do-it-yourself apparatus." A similar anti-erotic tug is felt in any mention of his own body: "When stripped, I looked less like 'Il David' than a plucked chicken that died of myxomatosis." At the medical board, "From my hair, interest passed to my anus, with which two of the doctors tampered for some time." And on the rare occasions when he mentions sexual acts, they are always made to seem distasteful. The sense of erotic obsession that is such a powerful feature of Ackerley's *My Father and Myself* is completely absent from the pages of *The Naked Civil Servant*.

Emblematic of his sexual dilemma—both his predominant aversion and his continued underlying interest—was a trip he made to Portsmouth in the summer of 1937. Portsmouth of course was the town of J. R. Ackerley's great romance, and it was still a kind of homosexual Mecca when Crisp visited a decade later. His account of the visit begins by creating a high level of erotic expectation. The town's sailors, he tells us, were notoriously available: "The fabulous generosity of their natures was an irresistible lure—especially when combined with the tightness of their uniforms, whose crowning aphrodisiac feature was the fly-flap of their trousers." Except for the hint of derision, the sentence could have been written by Ackerley himself.

Crisp's actual experience in Portsmouth was anticlimactic, yet his account of it is curiously moving. He made his appearance after he had "clapped on as much make-up as the forces of gravity would allow." Almost immediately, he reports, he was surrounded by sailors. What followed, however, was not the grand sexual encounter for which we have been prepared but another vintage Crisp monologue. At first, there was a certain atmosphere of erotic play. He seems to have been an object of desire, even in his effeminacy, though one detects an undertone of raillery: "I quickly found that if I spoke directly to any one of my companions he blushed and the others hit him till he fell off the seat. There was a great deal of laughing and flopping about, but the conversation never fell below the level of the risqué." In the end, instead of making love to the sailors he gave them a lecture, with the inevitable result that the erotic bubble burst: "After a while, when it became obvious that there was going to be speech but no action, without becoming angry the sailors began two by two to drift away." He eventually spent the night in a dive with a couple of older men. In the morning he crept back to his hotel, after "speaking off and on (but chiefly on) for about eight hours."

Yet for some reason this apparently uneventful evening, which started out with such high promise, lodged itself in his memory as deeply significant. Crisp himself attributes its importance to the happy fact that he had not once felt any of the anxieties about his physical wellbeing that were a constant feature of his London existence. But I am inclined to think something more important had happened. The evening became, in retrospect, his farewell to the possibility of a meaningful erotic life. Such, at least, is implied by the elegiac tone in which he sums up his feelings: "All the quality of that evening, and all the evenings like it that never came, remained with me for many years until I no longer felt the need for this kind of relationship with this kind of person—until my desires had changed and my whole nature had coarsened in a way that on the night in Portsmouth I would have thought impossible." The sentence has an almost Proustian melancholy—a tone entirely foreign to the book's usual desperate comedy.

After the Portsmouth interlude, Crisp's sex life was reduced to a series of desultory affairs, mainly with older heterosexuals. To none of them does he attach a name or devote more than the skimpiest description, and what he does reveal is always unattractive. The first candidate, with whom he took up "after many years of happy celibacy," was an official in one of the ministries, a person so terrified of disgrace that he never once visited Crisp in the daylight. The most sustained relationship was with a large, irresolute man whom he derisively calls "Barndoor"—because he "was the size of a barn door and as easily pushed to and fro"—and with whom he lived for "three long dark years." Barndoor apparently was a fellow bohemian, and Crisp first took him home as an object more of charity than of desire. The sex was barely managed: "When, presumably to normalize our relationship, he suggested a little sex, I concurred. A year or so later, in the middle of a sketchy embrace, he said. 'Let's pack this in.' I said, 'Let's.'" He briefly entertained the hope that Barndoor might be the "great dark man" so coveted by his fellow bitches, but Crisp was soon enough disabused. Passive and feckless, the gentleman had fallen into the company of homosexuals only because he was so inept with women, though he eventually married. "There is no great dark man," Crisp concludes.

The War provided him with the last glimmer of sexual interest. It came in the form of the American forces stationed in Britain. His description of them echoes his account of the Portsmouth sailors a decade before, and the outcome, in his own case, was just as disappointing. The G.I.'s are introduced as eminently desirable: "Their voices were like warm milk, their skins as flawless as expensive indiarubber, and their eyes as beautiful as glass." Above all, like the Portsmouth sailors, they were generous and available. "Never in the history of sex," he quips, amending Churchill, "was so much offered to so many by so few. At the first gesture of acceptance from a stranger, words of love began to ooze from their lips, sexuality from their bodies, and pound notes from their pockets like juice from a peeled peach."

This time, in contrast to what happened in Portsmouth, Crisp was not satisfied merely to watch (and talk). One of the generous and desirable Americans actually became his lover. For a moment we are allowed to think that the long, bleak story of prostitution and bloodless affairs is going to be lit up by genuine passion, maybe even love. But by this point in his life Crisp had apparently become so hardened—so completely the victim of his various defense mechanisms—that he was incapable of responding to what was offered him. Or perhaps his self-preservative instincts warned him not to invest too heavily in a relationship without any real future. The soldier would be going back to America; he could not become Crisp's Heinz Neddermeyer or his Jimmy Younger. In any event, Crisp did not allow himself to feel more than diverted. "I was happy," he writes, though "no more so than if I had met someone who could do a Ximines crossword or play chess at my shaky standard. I learned to like my American . . . [and] was always pleased to see him." But, he adds immediately, "I could not have said that I loved him," and when the young man stopped calling, Crisp felt no great disappointment. The brutalities of his long career as a professional homosexual, one supposes, had left psychological scars that kept him from acting otherwise.

In the late 1940s and early 1950s, he turned finally to the anonymous encounters—in theaters and undergrounds—that had become ever more available during the War. As he explains, in typical downbeat fashion, he needed "some way of filling the time between now and the grave." So he "took to sex." But the experiment brought him only "discomfort and exhaustion." It inspires a withering analysis of the tedium of impersonal sex: "In theory the pursuit of strangers divested of the needless convolutions of romance—the indulgence of chance encounters stripped of the clash of personalities—leads to unfettered gratification.

In practice it leads rapidly to monotony and, for homosexuals, to danger and expense." No critic of modern promiscuity, not even Roger Scruton, is more severe.

As Crisp nears the end of his story, the mood darkens and the jokes begin to fade. "I was growing old" becomes a litany. "What happened? What went wrong?" He doesn't know. His life had been eventful and brave, but, as often occurs with those who passionately espouse causes, the personal cost was very high. Above all, as he realizes, it had been a life devoid of meaningful relationships, whether with parents, friends, or lovers: "No one has ever been in love with me even faintly—even for half an hour, or if they have, it was a well-kept secret." But that realization, he insists, causes him "nothing more than a feeling of wounded vanity," because he himself had never been in love either. In fact he doesn't even "clearly know what the expression means." The reader is not fully convinced. The closing pages of the book betray an unmistakable sense of failure. In its emotional emptiness his life had come more and more to resemble J. R. Ackerley's, despite the radically different sexual paths they had traveled. Indeed, in some respects it was even grimmer, because he never found his Tulip.

"I stumble towards my grave confused and hurt and hungry. . . ." His final despairing words are counteracted only by our knowledge—*hors du texte*—that Crisp has outlived Ackerley by three decades, during which he has enjoyed, if not love, then at least the fame that eluded him until the publication of his autobiography. A regular columnist for *Christopher Street* and the *New York Native*, the author of many books, the subject of Jonathan Nossiter's film *Resident Alien*, and an imperious Queen Elizabeth in the movie version of Virginia Woolf's *Orlando*, he has become a gay icon of sorts, especially for the outrageous feats of his youth recorded in *The Naked Civil Servant*. Perhaps he has had the last laugh after all.

4

THREE FRENCH NOVELISTS

André Gide, Jean Genet,

and

Julien Green

∞ THE SIX ENGLISH autobiographers examined in the first part of this book led remarkably various homosexual lives, and they tell their stories in no less remarkably various ways. To be sure, certain common themes emerge in their accounts, notably, the extent to which these middle- and upper-middle-class intellectuals were sexually fixated on the lower orders. But from the idealistic and quasi-mystical infatuations of Symonds and Dickinson, through the boy-chasing and proletarian romances of Isherwood and Spender, to the antic effeminacy of Crisp and the obsessive cruising of Ackerley, their writings convey a sense of the great range of homosexual experience and the equally diverse character of the responses—psychological, moral, and political—to that experience.

Only when the English figures are set against their French counterparts do we begin to appreciate the more subtle commonalities that link the former in an identifiable tradition. For the French, as we shall see, are truly different—different both from the English autobiographers we have already considered and from the Americans still to come. My overarching

concern in what follows will be to underline that difference.

Three great figures of modern French literature have left accounts of

their homosexual lives: André Gide (1869–1951), Jean Genet (1910–1986),

and Julien Green (1900–1998). Gide's *Si le grain ne meurt* (*If It Die*) ap-

peared in a limited edition in 1920–21 and was the first published book in

which a living author described his own homosexual history. As such, it

is arguably the most important gay autobiography ever written and has

probably exercised greater influence than any of the other works treated

in this study. Some critics consider Jean Genet's *Journal du voleur* (*The

Thief's Journal*) (1948) a novel rather than an autobiography, but it exhib-

its many of the features of autobiography and can, I believe, be usefully

distinguished from Genet's autobiographical fictions of the same decade.

Both sexually and philosophically it is perhaps the most radical of all ho-

mosexual life-writings. The four volumes of Julien Green's *Jeunes années,*

written largely in the 1960s but describing the novelist's experiences in the

first quarter of the twentieth century, constitute, at just under a thousand

pages, the longest gay autobiography yet published. It is at once more

circumstantial and, ironically, more repressed than the books by Genet and

Gide, which preceded it by nearly a quarter century and a half century re-

spectively.

What is most distinctive about the French autobiographies is their philosophical character. They are in the thrall of abstraction. Their sexual stories are filtered through the grid of ambitious conceptual projects that lend them a very different texture and feel from the less self-conscious narratives of the English. In the case of André Gide that grid consists of a severe metaphysical dualism, which distinguishes sharply between body and spirit, confining homosexuality to a purely physical realm from which emotion (notably, love) is banished. With Jean Genet a different, but no less abstract, preoccupation gives the narrative its overarching shape: under the influence of Jean-Paul Sartre, Genet describes his homosexuality as an existential choice, comparable to his decision to become a thief and inspired by a rejection of traditional morality, a kind of Nietzschean revaluation of all values. Julien Green, for his part, offers an extreme variation on Gide's dualistic ontology: as a Roman Catholic, he sets his fallen homosexual state against a higher religious calling that, to his shame, he has failed to answer, and within the homosexual realm itself he distinguishes between purely emotional attachments, which are acceptable, even elevating, and grossly physical indulgences, which are the work of the Devil. In all three authors the resort to philosophy, one sometimes suspects, is a form of avoidance, a way of lending intellectual respectability to their otherwise disreputable acts.

I should not imply that the English autobiographers are innocent of the philosophical impulse. On the contrary, we have seen a tendency to abstraction at work in a number of them. The clearest example is John Addington Symonds, whose life, I have argued, was dominated by a punishing idealism, the homoerotic vision of Ancient Greece, from which he liberated himself only with great effort. Something similar, if not so exigent, informed the Apostolic mysticism that Goldsworthy Lowes Dickinson imbibed as a Cambridge undergraduate and that lent his great loves an unearthly quality. I have also complained about a tendency to philosophical blather in Stephen Spender's *World within World,* where, in order to cover his homosexual tracks, Spender propounds a high-minded distinction between what he calls the need for "self-identification" and the need for "otherness." But with the possible exception of Symonds, a weakness for abstraction remains marginal in the English texts, many of which (in particular, those of Isherwood, Ackerley, and Crisp) are positively antiphilosophical. In the autobiographies of Gide, Genet, and Green, by contrast, philosophical conceptions are articulate, systematic, and central to the organization of the narrative. They are a point of pride, a badge of intellectual seriousness. One is tempted to see in them the long shadow that René Descartes has cast over French intellectual life in the modern era. I recognize that I am here guilty of recreating, in the realm of homosexual autobiography, one of the hoariest of cultural clichés: the opposition between English empiricism and French rationalism. But clichés are clichés because they express a certain truth, and I remain convinced that the most striking effect of reading the French and English autobiographies side by side is a vigorous sense of just how beholden the French are to phi-losophy.

A second notable feature of the French autobiographies—this time serving to set them off especially from the Americans—is a curious ab-sence of embarrassment (though not necessarily of guilt). Perhaps it re-flects the famous Gallic sophistication—especially in sexual matters—that is often contrasted with the puritanism of the English and the Ameri-cans. Even the Roman Catholic Julien Green writes that his homosexuality caused him no social discomfort; his aversion, he insists, was entirely tran-scendental: he feared only the flames of Hell, not the disapproval of his fellowmen. One need not be entirely persuaded by these professions of indifference to recognize that the concern with secrecy, which plays such a central (and crippling) role in the lives of the American autobiographers, is much less urgent for the French. Perhaps this fact helps explain why André Gide was able to publish his story decades before anything similar was attempted by an Englishman or an American. *Si le grain ne meurt* ap-peared nearly thirty years ahead of *World within World,* yet Gide's book is far more candid sexually than Spender's. In any event, the theme of the closet and escape from the closet, which becomes the principal trope in the autobiographies written by Americans, is deeply muted, in fact virtually nonexistent, among the French.

Another distinguishing feature of the French autobiographers is their fascination with national and ethnic difference. At crucial moments all of them pursue their homosexual adventures outside the borders of France, and the identification of desire with otherness often verges on the obsessive. We have already seen this tendency among the English, namely, in Symonds's removal to Switzerland and Italy and in the sexual forays of Isherwood and Spender to Germany. But with the French the pattern is both more insistent and, geographically speaking, more far-flung. The best known case in that of André Gide, who sought his homosexual liberation with Arab boys in the French colony of Algeria during the last decade of the nineteenth century, inviting recent critics (among them Edward Said) to condemn his story as simply a homoerotic variation on the logic of empire. (The same proclivity can be found in Roland Barthes's autobiographical jottings—published after his death under the title of *Incidents*—where the sexual marauding has been transferred to post-colonial Morocco.) Similarly, Jean Genet's sexual escapades in *The Thief's Journal* take place not in France but in Spain, across Eastern Europe, and, finally closer to home, in Belgium. Julien Green's sexual itinerary was, in some respects, the most exotic of all. During and after the First World War it included the familiar sojourns to Italy and Germany. But the central episodes of his sexual education occurred in the American South, where he attended the University of Virginia for three years in the early 1920s. To be sure, Green was technically an American (both his parents were Southerners and he himself remained an American national even after President Georges

Pompidou conferred French citizenship on him when he was elected to the *Academie Française* in 1971). But French was Green's first language, and before his stay in the South he knew about America only from the tales of his parents. Virginia in the early 1920s was thus as foreign to him as Algeria was to Gide or Spain to Genet. I'm tempted to say that ethnic or national difference plays a role in French autobiographies comparable to class difference among the English. In both cases a trait that is of no obvious sexual significance—being non-French or being poor—assumes great erotic power.

There is a final way in which the French are different. Unlike the Englishmen and Americans treated in this book, the three French autobiographers have been the subject of what is by now a large secondary literature. No doubt this massive work of analysis and criticism simply reflects their greater literary stature: even Julien Green, though nowhere near so well known outside of France as Gide and Genet, is regarded by the French as a major writer, and the critical literature on Green (never mind Gide and Genet) dwarfs that on even the best-known of the English figures, such as Symonds, Isherwood, or Spender. Sartre's 600-page study of Genet, *Saint Genet* (1952), is only the most spectacular case in point. Needless to say, some of this interpretive writing, especially in recent years, deals with the homosexual issues that are my chief concern, and I will have to consider it. The critical attention that has been given the French is not just a function of their perceived literary superiority. It is also related to the matter with which I began: their philosophical seriousness. One might feel (as I often do) that too much philosophy is as bad for autobiography as it is for fiction. But their philosophical pretensions help explain the greater interest the French have attracted and the reputation for intellectual gravitas they uniquely enjoy.

André Gide, 1891.

Si le grain ne meurt

NDRÉ GIDE'S AUTOBIOGRAPHY is a work of polemic. It was paired in his mind with his philosophical dialogue *Corydon,* written before but published three years after *Si le grain ne meurt,* which mounts a vigorous argument for the naturalness of homosexuality. The autobiography was meant to illustrate in a single life, and with the authority of confession, the doctrine advanced theoretically in its companion piece. But Gide is nothing if not crafty. Where *Corydon* is confrontational, *Si le grain ne meurt* is seductive. In its long First Part (taking up more than three quarters of the text) the reader is lulled into a comfortable and apparently harmless intimacy with the young author before being plunged into the torrid homosexual disclosures of the African trips in the Second Part. The often random pastoral scenes of the first two-hundred pages can seem rather pointless, but in fact they serve Gide's polemical purpose brilliantly, for they establish the young man's utter normality, his bourgeois ordinariness, thus making it impossible to dismiss him, after his revelations, as degenerate or psychotic. Put another way, they circumscribe his sexual orientation as a discrete phenomenon that in no way compromises his integrity or moral worth.

Gide's youthful normality is certainly the dominant theme in the first section of the book. But it is set against two counter-themes. One is the emphasis on the strict Biblical puritanism—associated always with his taskmaster mother—that

André Gide, *If It Die,* trans. Dorothy Bussy (New York, 1963). I have occasionally modified Bussy's translation on the basis of my own reading of the original, which I have consulted in the 1955 Gallimard edition.

Gide's title is based one of Jesus' proverbs: "Except a corn of wheat fall into the ground and die, it abideth alone: but if it die, it bringeth forth much fruit." John 12:24. There is considerable scholarly disagreement about its meaning. In *André Gide and the Art of Autobiography* (Toronto, 1975), C. D. E. Tolton examines the various theories and concludes, "The seed that must die is [Gide's] own reputation—which will bring a harvest of freer, happier people" (p. 26).

Gide came to embrace as his own in the religious paroxysms of adolescence. This motif establishes an invidious opposition between spirit and flesh, which the Second Part will work to undo, although, in reality, the opposition is merely reconfigured, not abolished. The second counter-theme consists of a sequence of deftly insinuated episodes foreshadowing his ultimate sexual fate. These episodes are not meant to explain Gide's homosexuality; they do not create a causal or etiological chain. Rather they are presented as veiled revelations of a natural and inalterable condition that the author must learn to accept.

Although Gide was raised in Paris, much of his account in Part One is devoted to the time he spent on vacation at the maternal family estate at La Roque in Normandy or with his father's relatives in Languedoc. These scenes take place in plush interiors, lovingly recreated by the author, or in the verdant countryside, where André and his young companions romp with abandon. They are also filled with affectionate and virtuous relatives, friends, and servants devoted to the boy's wellbeing—his beloved nurse Marie (apparently modeled on Proust's Françoise); his mother's governess, Anna Shackleton; his ancient paternal grandmother, forever stuffing him with food; his cousin Albert Demarest, who labored with admirable tact to curb Gide's egoism. The ensemble leaves the impression that no childhood could have been more bourgeois and that no boy should have been more inclined to lead a conventional life.

Admittedly, the young man we encounter in these idyllic pages will eventually become a writer, and some allowance has to be made for the idiosyncrasies of an artistic disposition. This is a delicate matter for the autobiographer, because a literary identity carries with it at least a hint of rebellion and perhaps even of sexual unorthodoxy. Gide works to diffuse these hazards in several ways. For one thing, the text pays very little attention to his early literary interests, stressing instead his devotion to music, especially the piano. Sometimes he responded to piano music with the suspect ecstasy of Thomas Mann's sickly and homoerotic Hanno Buddenbrook. But more often his piano lessons become yet another conventional feature of his bourgeois upbringing, the obligatory accumulation of cultural capital, as one amusing and slightly preposterous piano teacher succeeds another. We also learn that, while he was mad for the piano, he actively disliked opera and theater—thereby distinguishing him from little Hanno Buddenbrook and all other future opera queens.

Gide further insulates himself against the suspicion of an "artistic" temperament by emphasizing that his early interests were scientific rather than literary.

As a child he went on botany expeditions, collected beetles, built a herbarium, and studied flowers under the microscope. Later he kept silkworms, mice, turtle doves, and canaries, observed submarine flora, developed a "passion for entomology," and conducted chemical experiments (including one, amusingly recounted, that caused an explosion). Even when he is shown becoming obsessed with his kaleidoscope—in a scene that echoes Proust's Chinese lantern in the opening pages of *A la recherche du temps perdu*—the danger of aestheticism is countered by noting that, where his girl cousins were interested only in the beautiful patterns created by the toy, he, as a young scientist, wanted to know how it worked and proceeded to dismantle it.

This little anecdote suggests another function served by Gide's emphasis on his early scientific interests: it establishes his firm masculinity. One of Gide's master-themes in the autobiography—as in *Corydon*—is that homosexuality has nothing to do with effeminacy. It touches only on the sex of the desired object and otherwise leaves one's manliness in tact. He thus sets himself against the notion of "inversion," as advanced by Karl Heinrich Ulrichs, which held that homosexuality involved a female soul imprisoned in a male body. In the Second Part of *Si le grain ne meurt* Ulrichs's conception will be linked to Oscar Wilde and Alfred Douglas, from whose effeminacy Gide distances himself, precisely because of it confounded homosexuality with gender deviance. The little would-be scientist we meet in the First Part of the autobiography has impeccably masculine credentials.

Those credentials are secured through a series of episodes that show young André as an athletic, even aggressive, boy, not afraid to mix it up with his peers. His athleticism seems all the more remarkable in that he was not especially robust and suffered from a series of real or imaginary childhood illnesses that forced him to rely on private tutors for most of his education. We observe him playing marbles, climbing rocks, fishing, skating, riding horses, and running. Nor does he share the usual aversion to ball games, traditionally a source of embarrassment for the future homosexual. On the contrary, he was as devoted to his childish version of football as were any of the other youngsters in the Luxembourg Gardens. And although he insists that he was peace-loving, he derives obvious pleasure from recounting a youthful scrape that shows him as decidedly feisty:

> There was a great big, carrotty-haired boy with a low forehead . . . who really took too great advantage of my pacifism. Twice, three times, I bore with his

sarcasms; but suddenly I was seized with a holy rage; I rushed up and fell upon him while the other boys made a circle round us. He was considerably bigger and stronger than I; but I had the advantage of taking him by surprise; and then, to my own astonishment, my fury multiplied my strength tenfold; I punched him, I shoved him and in a moment I had him down. Then, when he was on the ground, intoxicated by my triumph, I dragged him after the manner of the ancients, or what I thought was such—I dragged him by the hair of his head until a handful of it came off in my hand.

The scene makes an interesting contrast with the boyhood tussle recounted toward the end of Stephen Spender's *World within World:* where Spender's wrestling match gives way to sexual arousal, Gide's presents a triumph of unadulterated masculine assertiveness. Even when he lost his fights, we are left with the unmistakable impression that little André was every inch a boy.

I should admit that not all students of Gide's autobiography would accept my sunny reading of his early years. There is an interpretive tradition, based on close attention to the book's metaphorical language, that sees Gide establishing a systematic contrast between the darkness of his repressive youth in France and the light of his sexual liberation in Africa. I don't think that this analysis holds up very well, for the liberation, as we will see, was not without its shadows, and the sorrows of his childhood were more than balanced by moments of almost Wordsworthian bliss. To be sure, Gide's childhood contained its agonies, associated especially with the experiences that portend his homosexuality. He is also merciless in retailing his faults: his occasional cruelty, his tendency to sulk, his dimwittedness, his vanity, and his overweening ambition. These "dark" passages, I would argue, serve two functions. The first might be called Rousseauist. Following the example of his great autobiographical forebear, Gide makes a great show of sparing himself no embarrassment, because such frankness is the main guarantor of the reader's trust. Rousseau begins the *Confessions* by proclaiming, "I have displayed myself as I was, as vile and despicable when my behaviour was such, as good, generous, and noble when I was so,"[1] and he follows through with candid accounts of his masturbation, exhibitionism, and stealing. Gide's text is dotted with similar announcements. After presenting his own masturbation scene on the opening page, he comments, "I perfectly realise . . . that I am doing myself harm by relating this and other things to follow; I foresee what use will be made of

1. Jean-Jacques Rousseau, *The Confessions,* trans. J. M. Cohen (Baltimore, 1954), p. 17.

them against me. But the whole object of my story is to be truthful." (The most important of the "other things to follow" is of course the revelation of his homosexuality.) Later he editorializes, "This is no romance I am writing and I have determined not to flatter myself in these memoirs, either by adding anything agreeable or hiding anything painful." Much of the supposed "darkness" of Part One, in other words, is strategic: it promotes the author's trustworthiness.

The second function is closely related to the first: the stories of bad behavior and childhood misery confirm our sense of Gide's ordinariness. They show that he was no paragon, no angel, but once again a perfectly unremarkable specimen, as capable of wrongdoing and as prone to childish grief as any other boy. Rather than constructing a trajectory from repressive darkness to liberated illumination, Gide's autobiography, I am suggesting, is arranged to show that the most ordinary human stuff—a familiar mixture of good and bad, joy and gloom—can conceal an extraordinary sexual destiny.

☙ IN TWO RESPECTS, HOWEVER, Gide's upbringing was atypical for a bourgeois son in late nineteenth-century France. His family was Protestant, and he was an only child. He was thus exposed to an unusually spartan religious tradition and to a potentially suffocating emotional investment on the part of his parents. After his father's death in 1880, his mother's austere piety in fact became the most significant influence in his life, and his ultimate homosexual rebellion was above all a rejection of that maternal inheritance. But during the first ten years of his life Madame Gide's tyranny was held in check by her husband's more tractable instincts. In the Gide family, it seems, the usual roles were reversed, with, as Gide puts it, "my mother holding that a child should obey without trying to understand, my father always inclining to explain everything to me."

When his father died the family dynamics shifted fatally. All of his mother's moralizing energy, as well as her emotional neediness, came to focus on the boy. Her influence was especially seductive because, as Gide recognizes, she was truly a woman of principle, capable of acts of great disinterestedness. She was no dragon lady, no moral hypocrite, but a person whose genuine goodness utterly disarmed the young man who became the primary object of her solicitude. In the text Gide must force himself to acknowledge her qualities, because so much of the autobiography is devoted to his revolt against her. Even his warmest encomia evolve gradually into resistance, as he moves from honoring her passion for self-improvement to complaining about her intrusion into other people's lives, above all his own. By the end of the book he can no longer restrain himself and issues a bill of particulars indicting her moral totalitarianism: "She had a way of loving me that sometimes almost made me hate her and touched my nerves on the raw. You whom I shock, imagine, if you can, the effect of being constantly watched and spied upon, incessantly and harassingly advised as to your acts, your thoughts, your expenditure, as to what you ought to wear or ought to read."

Under his mother's tutelage Gide suffered an adolescent religious conversion similar to that experienced later by Julien Green. He became an avid reader of the Bible; the Gospels in particular entranced him. So intimately did the Scriptures become associated in his mind with his youthful austerity that when he departed for North Africa in 1893 he pointedly left his Bible behind (though scholars have shown that he wrote from Montpellier asking his mother to send it to him). In fact, his devotion to the Bible survived his homosexual liberation, and he continued to draw on it for literary purposes, including of course the title of his autobiography. Nor did he ever fully abandon his sense of a religious calling: something of the convert's earnestness still informed his later campaign on behalf of homosexuality. Likewise, his tendency to think in abstractions, especially the sharp opposition between spirit and flesh, was carried over from the religious to the secular domain.

After his confirmation, at sixteen, Gide's enthusiasm became truly fierce, as he subjected himself to a brutal regime of self-mortification. He got up at dawn and plunged into an icy bath; he read from Scripture and prayed at hourly intervals throughout the day; and at night he slept on boards. Inevitably the secular reader is tempted to interpret this extravagant piety as a ritual of avoidance, an unconscious effort to subdue his inner demons. It put his homosexual urges beyond the pale by mounting a massive and indiscriminate attack on the body and all its works. Although at this point in his narrative Gide is not yet ready to divulge his secret, he hints broadly that he has come to view his adolescent religiosity as just such a reaction formation.

The most remarkable feature of Gide's youthful Christianity, however, was not its blanket hostility to the flesh but his apparent ability to reconcile his striving toward saintliness with the continued practice of masturbation. He managed this trick by categorically separating sexual pleasure from any emotional or intellectual meaning. Masturbation, in his view, was an innocent physical diversion that no parental threat succeeded in converting into a source of embarrassment. Likewise, the practice seems never to have been accompanied by fantasies: it was for him a purely mechanical release, if an irresistible one. In effect, he constructed a radical dualism of body and spirit.

Si le grain ne meurt records two masturbation scenes, both of which reflect this materialist conception and show Gide resisting every attempt on the part of his elders to attach moral significance to the act. In the first he masturbates under the dinning-room with the concierge's son:

> "What are you up to under there?" my nurse would call out.
> "Nothing; we're playing."
> And then we would make a great noise with our playthings, which we had taken with us for the sake of appearances. In reality, we amused ourselves otherwise, beside each other but not with each other; we had what I afterwards learnt are called "bad habits."

The passage is the first of many that foreshadow his homosexuality, because even though Gide says that he and the other boy were "beside each other but not with each other," this very phrase calls our attention to the homosexual possibility. The crucial point is that masturbation is presented here as an amusement (*"nous nous amusions"*) that others have chosen to condemn (*"qu'on appelait 'de mauvaises habitudes'"*). It belongs to the hermetically sealed realm of pleasure.

In the second scene he is caught masturbating at school when he was eight. The discovery of his "bad habits" was a simple enough matter, he notes, because he "was at no particular pains to hide them, not having grasped how reprehensible they were." Once again, he presents himself as an insouciant votary of pleasure, dumbfounded by the fuss he has caused. Even more pointedly, masturbation in this scene is equated with eating—that is, with a bodily function devoid of moral consequence:

> My parents had had a dinner-party the evening before; I had stuffed my pockets with the sweetmeats that had been left over from dessert, and that morning, while Monsieur Vedel was exerting himself at his desk, I sat on my bench, enjoying alternately my pleasure and my chocolates [*je faisais alterner le plaisir avec les pralines*].

His parents reacted by subjecting him to what can only be described as a threat of castration. They took young André to the famous Dr. Brouardel, who gave him a severe talking-to:

"I know all about it, my boy," he said, putting on a gruff voice, "and there's no need to examine or question you. But if your mother finds it necessary to bring you here again, that is, if you don't learn to behave, look behind you!" (and his voice became truly terrible). "Those are the instruments we should have to use—the instruments with which little boys like you have to be operated on!" And he rolled his eyes at me ferociously as he pointed out a panoply of Touareg spearheads hanging on the wall behind his chair.

The tone of mock horror is already broad enough to suggest that the incident carried little weight with the boy. As Gide says, "This threat was really too thin for me to take it seriously." And, although he adds that his parents' distress finally managed to penetrate his indifference, masturbation remained for him a morally neutral act and thus compatible with the strenuous piety to which he later succumbed. The almost schizophrenic duality that would govern the whole of his adulthood was thus firmly in place at a very early date. On one plane he led an arduous spiritual life, on an entirely different plane he was an unreflective hedonist. In an important sense, homosexuality would inherit the place in his psychic economy occupied by masturbation in childhood and adolescence: it too, Gide came to insist, was morally neutral, leaving his emotions free to be invested elsewhere.[2]

The most important of his early emotional investments was in his slightly older cousin "Emmanuèle" (Madeleine Rondeaux). In some ways his "love affair" with Emmanuèle is the most extraordinary experience recorded in the autobiography, precisely because of its radically psychological character. It was a meeting of pure souls, not only without a physical dimension but conducted largely by correspondence. For all practical purposes the two had no existence for one another as bodies. Gide's love for Emmanuèle, in other words, conformed to the radical dualism that let him segregate his masturbation from his religiosity.

Emmanuèle first emerges in the text as just one of several maternal cousins with whom Gide played as a boy in Normandy. Significantly, their bond was formed when, at thirteen, he became her comforter in the face of an unmentionable sexual tragedy: the infidelity of her mother. One might say that their alliance was anti-erotic from the start. It rested not on desire but on "a conscious commu-

---

2. Gide's biographer Jean Delay argues that Gide was more disturbed by masturbation than he lets on and made strenuous efforts to give it up. *The Youth of André Gide*, trans. June Guicharnaud (Chicago, 1963), pp. 114–15, 153, 162.

nity of tastes and thoughts." Gide's attachment is inseparable from a nineteenth-century association of women with sexual anesthesia. "I cannot imagine anything more cruel for a young girl all purity, love and sweetness," he writes, "than to have to judge and condemn her own mother's conduct." He became convinced that his destiny was linked to his cousin, the "mystic orient" of his life. The relationship inspires the text's most effusive rhetorical outpourings, linking Emmanuèle, in language reminiscent of Wordsworth, to the beauty and light of nature.

Before long Gide had resolved to marry his cousin, and he persisted in the resolution despite his family's opposition. At the same time he admits—in another significant foreshadowing—that he may have been too willing to conduct his great affair by mail. "Perhaps," he writes, "my love for my cousin was too easily content with absence." In the same meaningful vein he continues, "But could I possibly have understood so early the signification of what was shaping within me?" The curiously ascetic love affair with Emmanuèle thus becomes one of the coded messages through which Gide alerts to the reader to his emerging sexual nature.[3]

∞ IN CERTAIN RESPECTS THE elaborate anticipations or foreshadowings built into the First Part of *Si le grain ne meurt* complicate the picture I have been drawing of Gide's philosophical dualism, which consigns his religiosity and his love of Emmanuèle to a purely mental realm, his masturbation to a purely physical one. All of the foreshadowings have the same dramatic function: they lead us to expect a sexual revelation in the Second Part of the book. But the sharp opposition between physical and emotional impulses—the centerpiece of Gide's adult erotic vision—emerges only gradually in these episodes. Especially in the earliest of them, the sensual and the romantic intermingle promiscuously. One gets the impression that, far from being a natural dualist, Gide had to learn to separate sex from sentiment.

The most enigmatic and arresting of the foreshadowings are what Gide calls his "*Schaudern*" (shudderings)—a notion he borrowed from Schopenhauer—experiences that mysteriously combined anxiety with a feeling of Dionysian release. Because they were brought on by seemingly trivial events—or sometimes by nothing at all—they convey a sense of the boy's profound discontent, his

---

3. The marriage, which took place in 1895 and endured over four decades, apparently remained unconsummated. See Jean Delay, *The Youth of André Gide*, pp. 443–57.

inchoate awareness that, despite the manifest joys and comforts of his life, something was wrong. Thus one day, when still under ten, he learned about the death
of a young cousin, a boy he hardly knew, and suddenly he collapsed in sobs on
his mother's lap. A few years later the "tremors" were even more mysterious, for
Gide can no longer recall what, if anything, caused them. Once again he found
himself sobbing in his mother's arms. The only thing he remembers from the
attack points, almost too obviously, to his secret destiny: through his sobs he
hears himself repeating, "'I'm not like other people! I'm not like other people!'"

That these episodes signal sexual, and not just emotional, distress is implied
by Gide's account of their physical symptoms. They gave him a feeling of "over-
powering suffocation," a bodily reaction not unlike that caused by sexual excitement. Gide encourages this sexual reading by characterizing his *Schaudern,*
despite their painfulness, as outbreaks of Dionysian rapture. He speaks of
"drunkenness without wine," "the happy moment in which I was shaken by that
divine madness," "the very one in which Dionysus visited me." The phases may
be vague, but they lend his attacks a distinct erotic edge.

A complementary strategy informs his treatment of the childhood experiences (besides masturbation) that led to actual sexual arousal. Here Gide observes that he was excited by things that, on the surface, seemed entirely unerotic.
He gives the impression that his libido was unhinged from the stimuli a normal
boy would have responded to. Instead it was free-floating and, by implication,
vulnerable to becoming attached to an "inappropriate" object.

He speaks of two writings that excited him as a child: George Sand's story
"Gribouille" and Madame de Segur's play *Les Diners de Mademoiselle Justine.* In
the first a boy throws himself in the water and is transformed into "a slender,
graceful sprig of oak." The story may not be so innocent as Gide thinks, in that
it invites being interpreted as a symbolic erection. In the Segur play a girl drops
a pile of plates when a coachman throws his arms around her waist from behind.
The resulting crash caused young André to "swoon." This story too can be given
a sexual gloss, namely, as a symbolic deflowering. But Gide seems unaware of
these transgressive possibilities. On the contrary, he stresses the absurdity of his
having responded sexually to such innocent narratives. Moreover he contrasts
his lubricious reaction to Sand and Segur with his visits to the Musée du Luxembourg, where the nude statues (including, significantly, one of Mercury) aroused
his admiration but not, he insists, his desires. Thus a familiar site of the bourgeois
child's sexual enlightenment (and one that will figure prominently in Julien

Green's autobiography) was without erotic significance for him. His sexuality was dangerously labile, inert to the usual provocations but mysteriously excited by things that anybody else would have found innocuous. We begin to suspect that a strange sexual fate awaits him.

Many of the foreshadowings give us a more precise anticipation of that fate. Quite early in the book, for example, he describes his discovery of a lesbian relationship between his nurse Marie and the family cook Delphine. The episode recalls Marcel's discovery of the lesbianism of Vinteuil's daughter in *A la recherche du temps perdu*. After Delphine had become engaged to a neighboring coachman, young André was awakened in the middle of the night by the wailing voices of the two women in the next room, "a melancholy chant, interrupted spasmodically by sobs and cluckings and cries." The moment is important, in the first instance, simply because it plants the fact of homosexuality in the reader's mind. But even more crucial is Gide's account of his own reaction. While insisting that he was too young to comprehend what was going on, he stresses his intuitive awareness that it was nonetheless significant: "I listened for a long time, sitting up in the dark and feeling in some inexplicable fashion that this was the expression of something more powerful than decency or sleep or the darkness of night." He further implicates himself by revealing that "some obscure instinct" kept him from mentioning what he had heard to his mother, thereby linking him in a conspiracy of silence with the lesbian servants, and once again putting the reader on alert. The incident is also intriguing because the relationship between the two women appears to have been both physical and emotional, and thus contradicts Gide's mature tendency to separate the sexual and affective realms.

The most important of the foreshadowings are the many incidents showing (or implying) his infatuation with young boys and his concomitant aversion to women. Gide establishes the pattern in the very opening pages of the autobiography, where the potentially homoerotic story of masturbating with the concierge's son is immediately followed by an episode in which, invited to kiss his beautiful cousin, he instead bit her "dazzling" bare shoulder. When the wound bled—in what Freudians would diagnose as an "upward displacement" of sexual intercourse—little André began "to spit with disgust." The two opening scenes thus establish an almost antiphonal opposition between homosexual affinity and heterosexual revulsion.

Gide recounts several preadolescent crushes. In all of them—as in the affair between Marie and Delphine—he fails to discriminate between sensual and emotional attraction. He celebrates the boys' physical charms but also confesses, with remarkable frankness, to how deeply his feelings were stirred. Among the first was a Russian boy, "extraordinarily pale," with long hair and blue eyes, for whom he conceived "an absolute passion" and whose sudden disappearance from school, he writes, was "one of the first and deepest griefs of my life." A little later, at a children's dress ball, he "fell in love—yes positively in love" with a boy in a clown outfit, whose "slender figure was perfectly moulded in black tights covered with steel spangles." He pokes fun at his broken heart and despair, which he attributes as much to the humiliation of having to wear a pastry-chef costume as to the loss of his bewitching clown. Almost immediately afterwards he became "transported with enthusiasm" for one of his classmates, an American named Barnett, who is shown provocatively flinging his shoulders back and peeing in the garden. In reporting these infatuations—through all of which runs an intriguing exotic motif (a Russian, an American, a clown)—Gide adopts a somewhat satirical tone, designed to prevent the reader from taking them too seriously, but the tone doesn't keep them from registering as signposts.

The last and most intense of the infatuations, with a family friend, "Lionel de R . . . ," was different. It took place in 1884, when Gide was fully adolescent, making it harder for him to laugh off its sexual implications. He counters the danger by introducing, for the first time in the autobiography, the sharp distinction between sensuality and emotion. He and his cousin carried on with romantic abandon, making "lovers' trysts" (*rende\-vous d'amoureux*) and sending one another coded letters. But for all its passionate extravagance, Gide insists that the relationship had "not the slightest tinge of sensuality," mainly because Lionel was so "powerfully ugly." It is an ambiguous defense, because of course it implies had his cousin been attractive Gide might have felt differently. But he argues that an even more fundamental barrier—one in his own psychic constitution—prevented such a development: he already found himself in the grips of his dualistic ontology—"that fundamental incapacity," as he puts it, "for mixing the spirit with the senses, which is, I believe, somewhat peculiar to me, and which was soon to become one of the cardinal aversions of my life." His feelings for Lionel, in other words, were not unlike his feelings for Emmanuèle: they engaged his heart but not his desires. For his part, Lionel seemed to confirm Gide's austere distinction, at least as far as men were concerned. When Gide tried to give him a "fraternal embrace," Lionel demurred, observing solemnly: "'No, men don't kiss.'" Ineluctably, the moment sounds another warning.

Gide's account of his boyish attachments is exactly paralleled by another group of scenes that show his indifference or even hostility to women. The first of them, as we've seen, occurs at the start of the autobiography when he bit his female cousin, and his antiseptic love for Emmanuèle also falls into the same category. The other episodes concern his revulsion against prostitution, which might seem to follow from his strict religious principles but which Gide himself dissects as betraying a more fundamental disturbance.

About the time of his friendship with Lionel, for example, he became obsessed with the idea that a schoolmate, Bernard Tissaudier, was frequenting the Passage du Havre, a covered walkway behind the Lycée Condorcet, which Gide had learned from his mother was disreputable. He tried to imagine what might be involved in these encounters, but he could summon up only phantasmagoric images: "I had a vision of my poor Tissaudier being orgiastically torn to pieces by hetairae." When he implored his astonished friend to avoid the wicked street, Gide suffered another attack of his *Schaudern,* collapsing in breathless sobs. The text contrasts the hysteria of his own reaction with the ironic composure of young Bernard, who shared none of Gide's exaggerated fears.

A few pages later he describes his terror when a streetwalker actually spoke to him. He gives a revealing analysis of his excessive and disingenuous aversion. He admits that he had been fooling himself in thinking that his horror of prostitutes was inspired by his "virtue." His anxiety was misplaced, because in reality prostitution did not tempt him in the slightest. "My lack of curiosity about the other sex was absolute," he confesses; "if I could have discovered the whole mystery of womankind with a single gesture, it was a gesture I should not have made." The real issue, in other words, was not prostitution but women—not commercially tainted heterosexuality but heterosexuality *tout court.* Or, as he says elsewhere, he was driven from prostitution—the "most generally admitted solution" to a young man's sexual predicament—not by his ideals but by his "nature."

The emphasis in the leisurely narrative of Gide's first two decades may be on his ordinariness, but, as we have just seen, this dominant theme is set against a subtle countermelody hinting at his difference and pointing, ever more explicitly, to the sexual realm. Shortly before the end of the First Part he rouses himself to admit his growing doubts about the moral universalism that had guided his life to that point. "It was beginning to dawn on me," he writes, "that duty was perhaps not the same for everyone, and that possibly even God himself might loathe a uniformity to which all nature was in contradiction." He goes on, "The truth was I was intoxicated by the diversity of life now first beginning to dawn on me, and by my own proper diversity . . ." We stand before the great watershed in Gide's life: the decision to answer the call of his different nature—to seek his "own proper diversity"—in Africa, an epochal turning point in the history of modern homosexuality, comparable in some ways to the trial of Oscar Wilde two years later.

∞ GIDE'S ACCOUNT OF HIS homosexual liberation focuses on three episodes, the first in 1893–94, the second in 1895, and the last in 1897, each with a somewhat different erotic valence. He begins, however, with a series of programmatic statements that establish an ideological framework for their proper understanding. The great theme of the Second Part of his autobiography, he announces, is the discovery of joy, of "a state of happiness which I hardly imagined possible." Yet even his most emphatic proclamations are tinged with ambivalence. He speaks, for example, not simply of happiness but, in a telling phrase, of "that blinding dazzlement of happiness [*quel aveuglement de bonheur*]", where "*aveuglement*" carries the sense of "infatuation" or "delusion." In the very next sentence he refers obscurely to a recent event (dated in a footnote to the spring of 1919) that has disturbed his normal serenity—the event being a crisis in his marriage caused by his affair with a young man named Marc Allégret. Gide's happiness, we sense, will come at a distinct cost.

A second theme sounded right at the start is his doctrinaire naturalism. It has been building quietly in the First Part of the autobiography, where, for example, he remarks that "in spite of every kind of starching, dressing, pressing and folding, the natural stuff persists and remains unchanged—stiff or limp, as it was originally woven." Now he confronts the reader with an accusing question: "In the name of what God or what ideal do you forbid me to live according to my nature?" And he sets the demands of that nature against the Christian teachings that until then had guided his life and that "had caused a profound disturbance in my whole being." Lest he be accused of abdicating to his baser instincts, he insists that the decision to act on his desires was both conscious and principled—that he was following, as he puts it, "the inclinations of my mind and not of my body." But he weakens the force of this claim by admitting that his past efforts at "resistance" had only increased his "natural propensity." There is a palpable sense of finally giving way to his imperious urges.

He also takes the occasion to state again, and yet more categorically, the radical distinction he drew between love and desire, a distinction that let him undertake his voyage of liberation without, he insists, abandoning his commitment to Emmanuèle: "I had resigned myself to dissociating pleasure and love; and even thought that this divorce was desirable, that pleasure would be purer and love more perfect if the heart and senses were kept apart." Later he asserts that the idea of mixing them "almost shocked" him. Gide's attitude exactly inverted that of John Addington Symonds, for whom, we may recall, sex without sentiment was intolerable.[4]

Something of Gide's ambivalence is apparent in his explanation of how the trip to Africa came about. Even as he immodestly compares it to the pursuit of the Golden Fleece, he reveals that his own role in the decision was remarkably passive. He was on the verge accepting an invitation to join a scientific expedition to Iceland when an old school friend, Paul Laurens, persuaded him to come along on a trip to the South. "The choice he made of me as a companion decided my fate," writes Gide, suggesting, implausibly, that he might otherwise have lived out his life in full repression. Still, the decision was momentous, even if accidental. He and Laurens set off on their journey "fired by no less lofty an enthusiasm than that which thrilled the gallant youth of Greece, setting sail on the Argo." The Greek topos is significant, because it identifies Gide's odyssey with the homophile classicism of Symonds and other nineteenth-century pioneers of the Cause.

He says very little about why he found it necessary to go to Africa to realize his nature and achieve his joy. He seems to regard the need to escape his mother's watchful eye as self-evident. Doubtless he associated his venture with the long tradition of Northern Europeans (one thinks of Goethe) who have traveled to the Mediterranean for sexual release. "I fell a victim to the lure of the South," he remarks. Later he suggests—as Christopher Isherwood and Stephen Spender would as well—that difference had a peculiar erotic charm for him: "Some people fall in love with what is like them; others with what is different. I am among the latter. Strangeness solicits me as much as familiarity repels." He adds, almost as an afterthought, that the particular difference to which he was drawn in Africa was brown skin. Otherwise the text is silent about the imperial circumstances that let him fulfill his desires—and may even have shaped those desires.

4. Being only human, Gide was unable to maintain his distinction inviolate. The affair with Marc Allégret, during the writing of the autobiography, caused a crisis in his marriage precisely because the relationship with the young man was both sexual and emotional. See Jean Schlumberger, *Madeleine et André Gide* (Paris, 1956).

But the entire adventure is bathed in an orientalist mystique. Sailing across the Mediterranean, he conjured up the Dark Continent's intoxicating mixture of danger and delight: "Africa! I repeated the mysterious word over and over again; in my imagination it was big with terrors, with alluring horrors, with hopes and expectations; and throughout the hot night I turned my longing eyes towards the sultry promise of that lightning-swathed horizon."

Readers are apt to be confused by the proliferation of Arab boys in the Second Part of *Si le grain ne meurt.* There is good reason for this confusion: the boys are largely interchangeable. All of them are barely adolescent and physically small, with thin naked legs. Gide's erotic fixation bordered on pedophilia. The boys are also generally mute, so that the sexual encounters take on the character of pantomime. None of them is given any psychological individuality, not even the rudimentary individuality that Stephen Spender confers on his Hamburg boyfriend, Walter, or Christopher Isherwood on his first Berlin crush, Bubi. Instead Gide identifies them with their jobs or with objects: they are guides, porters, tambourine players, and flutists. Even their names are confusing: there are, for example, two Ali's and two Mohammed's. Gide makes a point of emphasizing the impersonality of his attraction. Commenting on the boys who played on the terrace of his hotel in Biskra, he observes, "It was not with any one of them in particular that I fell in love, but with their youth indiscriminately."

Their impersonality underlines his contention that homosexual desire was for him a purely physical urge. One could even say that had the Arab boys taken on greater psychological density they would have lost their allure. But the effect is to create a yawning gap between the European adventurer, with his intellectual and emotional complexity, and the compliant objects of his lust, who barely rise above the level of animals. For the most part Gide seems to accept this arrangement with the clearest conscience in the world. He never discusses his penchant in the self-critical manner of Christopher Isherwood.[5]

The one exception was Gide's servant Athman, but Athman is the exception that proves the rule. He differed from the other boys both physically and intellectually: he was tall and articulate. Relatively fluent in French, he served as Gide's erotic intermediary. Nothing in the text suggests that Gide had a sexual relationship with him or even found him attractive. On the contrary, because Athman was not an object of desire Gide developed a genuine friendship with the young

5. In *Homos* (Cambridge, Mass., 1995), the critic Leo Bersani advances the provocative argument that Gide's liberation of sex from psychology was his most revolutionary achievement. See pp. 113–29.

man, even attempting to bring him back to France, much to Madame Gide's horror. The moment of their parting, with Athman watching "grief-stricken" as
Gide's train left, is among the most poignant in the book. Athman, like Emmanuèle, belongs to the world of spirit and emotion, not the world of sex.

Gide's sexual initiation occurred in the Tunisian city of Sousse with "a young
brown-skinned Arab" whom he noticed outside his hotel and who was distinguished from the other boys by his greater timidity and the slenderness of his
bare legs. After the youngster volunteered to serve as his guide, the earth-shaking
event proceeded to unfold in an eerie ritual silence:

> When Ali—this was my little guide's name—led me up among the sandhills,
> in spite of the fatigue of walking in the sand, I followed him; we soon reached
> a kind of funnel or crater, the rim of which was just high enough to command
> the surrounding country and give a view of anyone coming. As soon as we got
> there, Ali flung the coat and rug down on the sloping sand; he flung himself
> down too, and, stretched on his back, with his arms spread out on each side of
> him, he looked at me and laughed.

At this point the seemingly inevitable erotic progress was interrupted by an attack
not, as one might expect, of guilt but of "curiosity," a development that mystifies
Gide himself and whose meaning has proven equally obscure to his interpreters:

> I was not such a simpleton as to misunderstand his invitation; but I did not
> answer at once. I sat down myself, not very far from him, but yet not very
> near either, and in my turn looked at him steadily and waited, feeling
> extremely curious as to what he would do next.
>
> I waited! I wonder today at my fortitude . . . But was it really curiosity
> that held me back? I don't know anymore. The secret motive of our acts—I
> mean the most decisive ones—escapes us; and not only in memory but at the
> very moment of their occurrence. Was I still hesitating on the threshold of
> what is called sin? No; my disappointment would have been too great if the
> adventure had ended with the triumph of my virtue—which I already loathed
> and despised. No; it was really curiosity that made me wait . . . And I watched
> his laughter slowly fade away, his lips close down again over his white teeth
> and an expression of sadness and disappointment cloud his charming face.
> Finally he got up:
>
> "Good-bye, then," he said.

The interlude gives Gide an opportunity to rehearse his argument against Christianity and to state again the principled character of his revolt. But it has the subtler purpose of conveying a sense of his restraint—of showing his self-possession even in the face of the most tempting erotic invitation of his life—qualities that will later distinguish him from the profligacy of Oscar Wilde and Alfred Douglas. Once his fundamental dignity has been established, the scene can continue to its blissful climax:

> But I seized the hand he held out to me and tumbled him on to the ground. In a moment he was laughing again. The complicated knots of the strings that served him for a girdle did not long trouble his impatience; he drew a little dagger from his pocket and severed the tangle with one cut. The garment fell, and flinging away his coat, he emerged naked as a god. Then he raised his slight arms for a moment to the sky and dropped laughing against me. Though his body was perhaps burning, it felt as cool and refreshing to my hands as shade. How beautiful the sand was! In the lovely splendour of that evening light, what radiance clothed my joy! . . .

Gide must be forgiven for taking refuge in atmospherics at the end. As a good dramatist, he is saving his more graphic language for the two later encounters. We can appreciate the true courage of his narrative only when it is set against the coy evasions to which he had recourse in telling the same story twenty years earlier in *The Immoralist*.

We never see Ali again, and presumably neither did Gide. Despite many temptations, moreover, Gide appears to have had no other homosexual experience during the visit of 1893–94. Instead he recounts of series of more or less failed heterosexual adventures, which serve to confirm the unambiguous character of his orientation. The episodes seem to have been arranged to document his constitutional aversion, which increased as the women became more maturely feminine. The first of them, and the only one in which he enjoyed even a partial success, was with a barely sixteen-year-old prostitute named Meriem, whose figure Gide describes as "almost childish," suggesting that her body resembled those of the pubescent boys who excited him. Even so, he succeeded with Meriem only by pretending he was making love to "little Mohammed," a tambourine player, "half-naked, . . . black and slender as a demon," whom Gide had seen earlier that same evening. As he says, rather quaintly, "If that night I was valiant with Meriem, it was because I shut my eyes and imagined I was holding Mohammed in my arms." With Meriem's older cousin En Barka he failed completely, which he attributes to her greater physical maturity and more obviously feminine beauty. Two later encounters, after he had left Africa, continued the pattern. The first was with a high-class Roman prostitute, whom Gide called "the Lady" and whose affectation he compares unfavorably with the cynicism and savagery of Meriem. The other was with an ample Swiss woman, who worked as his maid, about whom he remembers mostly the disgust he felt when he "tumbled on to her bosom between her open legs." Gide was the purest of homosexuals, untempted by women, indeed positively repulsed by the female body. In this respect he might be considered Stephen Spender's opposite among gay autobiographers.

 THE SECOND TRIP TO AFRICA, early in 1895, was conducted under the ambiguous aegis of Oscar Wilde and Lord Alfred Douglas. In his treatment of Wilde and Douglas, Gide is at pains to contrast their indiscretion and debauchery with his own reserved and altogether masculine brand of homosexuality. He speaks with pride of his embarrassment and castigates them for their shamelessness. There is no sense of solidarity with these men who shared his tastes. On the contrary, even as he made a public issue of his own homosexuality by writing his autobiography, he damns them for flouting the codes of accepted manly conduct. His apology, in other words, is conceived in the narrowest possible terms.

When Gide happened to come across Wilde's and Douglas's names on the roster of his hotel in Blida, his first instinct was to flee. He wiped out his own name, paid his bill, and headed for the railroad station. His motives remain unclear to him, but he surmises, insightfully, that some obscure feeling of self-hate—an impulse, as he puts it, to "disown" or "repudiate" himself—must have been involved. On his way to the station he decided that he was being cowardly, so, rather like Gustav von Aschenbach in another homoerotically charged situation, he ordered his luggage returned to the hotel.

The Oscar Wilde he met there was drastically changed from the man he had known earlier in Paris and Florence. Where before Wilde had displayed "the most absolute discretion," he now seemed determined to abandon all reserve. He insisted on speaking expressly, and often publicly, of his inclinations, in language whose queenly exaggerations much distressed Gide. The text reproduces (or invents) several of these utterances. Thus we hear Wilde say of Bosie, whom Gide had not yet met, "'You'll see him, and you'll tell me if it's possible to imagine a more charming divinity. I adore him; yes, I positively adore him.'" The remark offended not only Gide's sense of propriety but also his doctrinaire notion that one "adored" only women. Later, Wilde was not satisfied just to ask a procurer to show them some young Arabs but insisted on stipulating that they be "'as beautiful as bronze statues.'"

Lord Alfred's lack of restraint was even greater. Indeed, by comparison, Wilde seemed "gentle, wavering, and weak-willed." Bosie hisses and stomps his way through Gide's pages, making one scene after another. His predatoriness was unbounded. He was forever trumpeting his desires, where Gide preferred to bury his in silence. "Douglas," he complains, "returned incessantly and with disgusting obstinacy to the things I spoke of only with excessive embarrassment." When they were about to go out after dinner, Douglas remarked, "'I hope you are like me. I have a horror of women. I only like boys. As you're coming with us this evening, I think it's better to say so at once.'" "Saying so" was exactly what Gide didn't want to do. Above all, Douglas raised the specter of unmanliness, both in his own person and in the boys he chased. Gide mentions especially a young nobleman named Ali with whom Douglas became besotted but whose beauty left Gide cold precisely because of "the effeminacy of his whole appearance." The affair between Douglas and the girlish Ali so disgusted Gide that he temporarily returned to celibacy.

Yet out of these unpromising circumstances emerged the most ecstatic sexual experience of his life, the night he spent with the flute player Mohammed. For it was Wilde who took Gide to the Moorish cafe in Algiers where he saw the "marvelous adolescent" whose slim boyish figure and slender bare legs transfixed him. When Gide and Wilde left the cafe, Wilde asked, in one of the immortal lines of gay literature, "'Would you like the little musician?'" Gide of course wanted him desperately, but he is careful to preserve an image of embarrassed reluctance: "I thought my heart would fail me; and what a dreadful effort of courage it needed to answer: 'Yes,' and with what a choking voice!" At the same time he further demonizes Wilde (almost literally) by having him break out in gales of Mephistophelean laughter—"interminable, uncontrollable, insolent"—at the sight of Gide's moral collapse. "The great pleasure of the debauchee is to debauch," he intones censoriously. Yet his indignation did not prevent him from following Wilde to an apartment where he was joined by Mohammed, while Wilde retired to the next room with another boy. Inevitably one feels that, instead of blackening Wilde's character, Gide ought to show a little gratitude.

"Every time since then that I have sought after pleasure," he writes, "it is the memory of that night I have pursued." Before he begins his account he recalls the misery into which he fallen after his experience with Ali at Sousse. Save for "one delicious evening" with a young boatman on Lake Como, he had relapsed, "wretchedly," into masturbation, as his life became "a frightful desert, full of wild unanswered appeals, aimless efforts, restlessness, struggles, exhausting dreams, false excitement and abominable depression." But all that was now reduced to insignificance. "What name," he asks, "am I to give the rapture I felt as I clasped in my naked arms that perfect little body, wild, ardent, lascivious and dark?" After so many years of repression Gide experienced what can best be described as an erotic explosion: much to Mohammed's astonishment he achieved orgasm five times, and even after the boy had left he masturbated himself into exhaustion, as he "prolonged the echoes" of his bliss until dawn. "It was now that I found my normal," he proclaims; "no scruple clouded my pleasure and no remorse followed it." Most strikingly, he insists that his ecstasy was purely physical, uncontaminated by thought or emotion: "My joy was unbounded, and I cannot imagine a greater, even if love had been added." Somewhat defensively he asks, "How should there have been any question of love? How should I have allowed desire to dispose of my heart?" Again we are inclined to suspect that the his glib opposition between love and desire was made possible by the discrepancies in age, power, and imperial circumstance between him and his chosen object.

Gide ends *Si le grain ne meurt* with his engagement to Emmanuèle in 1895, but he breaks the book's chronological framework to insert a brief account of a second visit to Mohammed two years later. It is the most explicit sexual scene in the autobiography and raises further questions about both his political views and his conception of homosexuality. By then Mohammed had become addicted to absinthe, and Gide describes him as "not so much lascivious now as shameless." Gide was accompanied by his acquaintance "Daniel B.," who, much to Gide's horror, proceeded to sodomize the boy:

> Daniel seized Mohammed in his arms and carried him to the bed which was at the other end of the room. He laid him on his back on the edge of the bed, crosswise, and soon I saw nothing but two slim legs dangling on either side of Daniel, who was labouring and panting. Daniel had not even taken his cloak off. Very tall, standing there in the dim light beside the bed, with his back

turned, his face hidden by the curls of his long black hair, his cloak falling to his feet, he looked gigantic. As he was bent over the little body he was covering, he was like a huge vampire feasting on a corpse. I could have screamed with horror.

The critic Michael Lucey interprets the scene as a "colonial rape,"[6] in which the towering and still fully clothed European devours his small, naked prey. Lucey also argues that Gide, who, in contrast Daniel B., says he takes his pleasure only "face to face," here assumes the role of critic of imperialism. "Gide," writes Lucey, "is distressed because from his point of view Mohammed has accommodated himself to the European homosexual culture represented by Wilde, absinthe, impudence, and, of course, fucking."[7] I'm not sure the text will bear such a vigorous anti-imperialist reading. What seems indisputable is that Gide is here distinguishing his own restrained erotic practice from a more extravagant variety of homosexuality, much as he had earlier distanced himself from the excess and effeminacy of Wilde and Douglas. I doubt that he would have found anal intercourse any more tolerable if Daniel B.'s victim had been a fellow European. Gide's image of the ideal homosexual was profoundly conservative; it envisioned as little deviance as possible, in manner and sexual behavior, from the heterosexual standard of his class and time.

Even his own practice, modest though it was by comparison, left him feeling ambivalent. For all the brave words about the naturalness of his desires, he can't disguise his lingering doubts. Indeed, in some respects his liberation seems more like a collapse, both ethical and physical. In *The Immoralist* Michel's African journey, on which he overcomes his inhibitions, is portrayed as a return to life and health. But Gide's own experience was just the opposite. As he traveled to the South he grew sicker. The adventure with Ali at Sousse in no way improved his condition. On the contrary, his physical disintegration seems a metaphor for the moral depravity into which he had sunk.

Perhaps the clearest evidence of Gide's ambivalence is the role he assigns the Devil in his story. His recourse to this theological figure (which also plays an important role, as we'll see, in Julien Green's autobiography) reflects what I have called the French weakness for abstraction—the need to lend their narratives a metaphysical dimension. Repeatedly Gide implies that his homosexuality was a

---

6. Michael Lucey, *Gide's Bent* (New York, 1995), p. 36.
7. Ibid., p. 37.

work of the Devil. The Devil, he says, duped him into the fateful illusion that his love for Emmanuèle should not express itself carnally. Likewise, even as he blames Oscar Wilde for debauching him, he implies that Wilde was merely a frontman for Satan. "Since my adventure at Sousse," he writes, "there was not much left for the Adversary to do to complete his victory over me." We are thus not surprised to learn that, after the "folly" and "madness" of his erotic wanderings, he returned, "with . . . transports of love," to reading the Gospels. The revival of his piety kept him "from lapsing into a state of complacent hedonism and easy acquiescence."

The decision to marry Emmanuèle was perfectly consistent not only with his circumscribed conception of homosexuality but with his ambivalence as well.[8] It was prompted by the death of his mother and can best be understood as a delayed act of obedience to her. When Madame Gide died Gide faced the sudden prospect of being liberated to pursue his desires, and the prospect terrified him: "I felt dazed, like a prisoner unexpectedly set free, like a kite whose string has been suddenly cut, like a boat broken loose from its mooring, like a drifting wreck at the mercy of wind and tide." The marriage saved him from himself.

In the extraordinary final paragraph of the book Gide tries to explain his decision. He does so by invoking an abstract, Manichaean logic setting Emmanuèle's virtue in opposition to his demonic sensuality:

> A fatality led me; perhaps also the secret desire to set my nature at defiance;
> for in loving Emmanuèle, was it not virtue itself I loved? It was the marriage
> of Heaven with my insatiable Hell; but at the actual moment, my Hell was in
> abeyance; the tears of my mourning had extinguished all its fires; I was dazzled
> as by a blaze of azure and the things I refused to see had ceased to exist for me.

On one level the marriage was a delusory act, made possible only because his grief had temporarily caused him to forget his urges. But, more fundamentally, it was a necessary and self-imposed curb on those very urges, which otherwise might have driven him into the depravity of Wilde, Douglas, and Daniel B.

Despite his historic and liberating journey to Africa, Gide remained a divided man. His heroism consisted in coming to terms with his sexual condition,

8. The decision was abetted by a prenuptial consultation (unmentioned in *Si le grain ne meurt*), during which the doctor assured Gide that the marriage would result in a spontaneous release of his natural heterosexual instincts. André Gide, *Madeleine (Et nunc manet in te)*, trans. Justin O'Brien (New York, 1952), pp. 21–22.

if on carefully delimited terms, in spite of his own intense internal resistance. Even more, it consisted in the decision to tell his story long before any other gay autobiographer could summon the courage to do so. Marcel Proust famously warned him he could write anything he wanted, so long as he didn't say "I." To his everlasting credit, Gide ignored Proust's advice.

Jean Genet, ca. 1937.

Journal du voleur

NE WOULD BE HARD PUT to imagine two men less alike than André Gide and Jean Genet or two autobiographies more dissimilar than *Si le grain ne meurt* and *Journal du voleur*. Gide was the pampered only child of a well-off Parisian family, raised in bourgeois comfort to assume the role of literary mandarin. Genet was an orphan who grew up with poor foster parents in the provinces, spent time in reform school as a juvenile delinquent, and eventually became a thief and a prostitute. Likewise, though both men were homosexuals, their desires and practices could scarcely have been more different. Where Gide sought out boys for impersonal sex while maintaining his uncompromised masculine identity, the openly effeminate Genet indulged in grand romantic passions, often with straight men, by whom he hoped to be ravished.

Gide and Genet also fashioned directly contradictory sexual ideologies. Gide, as we know, viewed his homosexuality as a natural fact that not even the most strenuous moral campaign could alter. Moreover, because his proclivity belonged to a deep, probably biological, stratum of the self, society, he argued, acted unjustly in condemning it. Genet's attitude was considerably more aggressive. He spoke as if he had become a homosexual—just as he had become a thief and a prostitute—in order to overthrow the conventions of bourgeois morality. Far from being an ethically neutral datum of his constitution, homosexuality for him was in some sense a revolutionary choice. Brazenly appropriating the language of religion (language that had condemned Gide), Genet even claimed to

Jean Genet, *The Thief's Journal*, trans. Bernard Frechtman (New York, 1964). I have checked Frechtman's translation against Gallimard's 1993 reissue of *Journal du voleur*. Genet notoriously bowdlerized his own writings, removing or toning down the graphic sexual descriptions of the original in subsequent editions. Frechtman's version retains passages and language that have since been expunged.

have achieved saintliness in his perversion: he had realized a kind of perfection of evil. In terms of the current debate among students of homosexuality, Gide might be described as an arch-essentialist, Genet as an arch-constructionist. Both of them subordinated their stories to polemical abstractions, albeit radically opposed abstractions.

As texts, *Si le grain ne meurt* and *Journal du voleur* are, if anything, even more unlike than the homosexual lives they recount. Gide's autobiography is a classical narrative, lucid and economical, presenting the author's experiences chronologically from his earliest memories to the great sexual crisis and its ambiguous resolution in Gide's mid-twenties. Genet, by contrast, adopts the techniques of literary modernism: he systematically fragments his account, switching without notice from the events of the 1930s, which are his primary concern, to characters and episodes that belong to the period of composition (the late 1940s). He also interrupts the narrative with abstract meditations and lyrical flights. For the connoisseur of traditional autobiography, the deliberate confusions and windy philosophizing of *Journal du voleur* can prove annoying. His montage technique sabotages any sense of the protagonist's development—just the issue with which Gide was most concerned. Genet's literary manner inhibits our effort to read his story as a causal explanation of the person he has become—to read it as anything other than the author's free choice.

The matter of style raises the question of whether *Journal du voleur* is an autobiography at all. Critics are divided on the issue. Michael Sheringham, in a recent study of French autobiography from Rousseau to Perec, writes, "*Journal du voleur* is generally recognized to be an authentically autobiographical text, by contrast with such autobiographical fictions as *Miracle de la rose* and *Pompes funèbres.*"[9] But in his superb biography of Genet, Edmund White insists that *Journal du voleur,* like the four other prose texts Genet wrote in the 1940s, is a novel, no different from those others (save for *Querelle de Brest*) in drawing heavily on incidents from Genet's life.[10] According to White, *Journal* fictionalizes Genet's experiences in Spain, Eastern Europe, and Belgium during his twenties, just as *Notre-Dame-des-fleurs* gives a thinly disguised account of his provincial childhood and *Miracle de la rose* of his years in reform school as an adolescent. At the same time, White freely mines *Journal* for its autobiographical revelations

---

9. Michael Sheringham, *French Autobiography* (Oxford, 1993), p. 146n.

10. Edmund White, *Genet* (New York, 1993). "One must never forget that Genet was writing fiction, not autobiography" (p. xviii).

and, in a perhaps significant omission, fails to provide a sustained analysis of its fictional structure, such as he provides for the other "novels." Implicitly he seems to concede that it is somehow different from them.

Genet's own pronouncements in the book are ambiguous. Like Gide, he occasionally inserts programmatic statements, in the manner of Rousseau, that seem to affirm the text's factual reliability. But the statements are never straightforward and can even be read as asserting his creative freedom. "Let the reader therefore understand," he writes at one point, "that the facts were what I say they were [*les faits furent ce que je les dis*], but the interpretation that I give them is what I am—now." At first the sentence might seem to make a perfectly unexceptionable distinction between the empirical elements out of which the autobiographical narrative is fashioned and the interpretive pattern to which the writer, trying to make sense of his past, subordinates them. But Genet's slippery assertion that the facts are "what I say they were" casts a shadow of doubt over those "facts." The doubt is exacerbated by the preceding sentence, in which he says that his book "is not a quest of time gone by, but a work of art whose pretext-subject [*matière-prétexte*] is my former life." Later, in a footnote (a scholarly device that might seem to stamp the *Journal* as a work of nonfiction), he offers an even more ambiguous, not to say confusing, discussion of the competing claims of invention and recollection in his text:

> The reader is informed that this report on my inner life or what it suggests will be only a song of love. To be exact, my life was the preparation for erotic adventures (not play) whose meaning I now wish to discover. Alas, heroism is what seems to me most charged with amorous properties, and since there are no heroes except in our minds, they will therefore have to be created. So I have recourse to words. Those which I use, even if I attempt an explanation by means of them, will sing. Was what I wrote true? False? Only this book of love will be real. What of the facts which served as its pretext? I must be their repository. It is not they that I am restoring.

While not entirely abandoning the familiar autobiographical distinction between fact and interpretation, the passage suggests that, in the end, artistic considerations have prevailed. Or as he puts it elsewhere, "The aim of this account is to embellish my earlier adventures, in other words, to extract beauty from them." Even more scandalously, Genet sometimes hints that not art but seduction is his real purpose. "I am assembling these notes for a few young men," he confesses, though he immediately adds that, while "romantic reverie" may have been his point of departure, he has elaborated those reveries to produce a work of art and even to achieve "moral perfection"—"that saintliness which to me is still only the most beautiful word in human language." But whether the goal is art, seduction, or moral perfection, statements of this sort cannot be easily reconciled with the ideals of autobiography. We begin to worry that Genet has invoked the conventions of the genre only to undermine their authority.

Yet the conventions are there. Or at least they seem to be. Surely, we think, we have an autobiography in our hands when we read the following paragraph:

> I was born in Paris on December 19, 1910. As a ward of the *Assistance Publique,* it was impossible for me to know anything about my background. When I was twenty-one, I obtained a birth certificate. My mother's name was Gabrielle Genet. My father remains unknown. I came into the world at 22 rue d'Assas.

The impression is confirmed when we learn from Edmund White that, with a single exception, the facts recorded in the paragraph are correct. White observes, "Genet gets the address wrong": it was 89 rather than 22 rue d'Assas.[11] But even the error underscores the unmistakably autobiographical texture of the passage: one would hardly correct the address in a novel. Nevertheless, this unassailably autobiographical passage appears not, as does Gide's corresponding assertion in *Si le grain ne meurt* ("I was born on November 22nd, 1869"), at the beginning of Genet's book but, unceremoniously and arbitrarily, after some forty pages devoted to other matters. Why this deliberate flouting of the reader's expectations? Again we are apt to suspect that Genet is toying with the genre, dropping autobiographical tidbits into his fictional and philosophical brew. He is as disrespectful of bourgeois literary conventions as he is of bourgeois morality.

Still, for all its philosophical and stylistic pretensions, *Journal du voleur* is constructed out of many of the humble and familiar elements we have met in the seemingly more modest gay autobiographies already examined in this book. At its heart stands Genet's great (if unfulfilled) romance with the handsome Serbian thug Stilitano, a romance launched in the long first section of the book devoted to Genet's life as a down-and-outer in Spain and completed, a few years later,

---

11. Ibid., p. 8. There is one other minor discrepancy: Genet gives his mother's second name, Gabrielle, instead of her first name, Camille.

when he met Stilitano again, now a pimp and drug dealer, in Antwerp. The relationship with Stilitano invites comparison with the proletarian romances conducted, during the very same years, by Christopher Isherwood and Stephen
Spender, except of course that Genet was as much a member of the lumpenprolet-
ariat as Stilitano, rather than an upper-middle-class intellectual engaged in sexual
slumming. Similarly, there is a good deal of common ground between Genet
and his near contemporary Quentin Crisp, in particular their shared effeminacy,
abjection, and involvement in a sexual universe divided between masterly heterosexuals (Crisp's "toughs") and suppliant queens (Crisp's "bitches"). At the same
time Genet's erotic obsession with manly criminals, traitors, and policemen is
not all that far removed from J. R. Ackerley's no less single-minded devotion to
sailors and guardsmen. My point is that Genet, who is often compared with
Proust among writers or Sartre among philosophers, might benefit from being
viewed in the less rarefied company of his fellow gay autobiographers, with
whom he has more in common than his high-minded interpreters might be prepared to admit.

⊘ ALTHOUGH *JOURNAL DU VOLEUR* contains only a few scattered passages treating Genet's life before his twenties, those passages have attracted more critical
attention than any others in the book. They have done so because they offer the
strongest support for an existential reading of Genet's life, and in particular of
his homosexuality. In them he describes his homosexuality, like his criminality,
as a choice, through which he claims to have upset established values by transforming his vice into a virtue, indeed into an instrument of saintliness. Here we
have the most important evidence for Genet's philosophical vision of homosexuality.

The first passage addresses the moment in his youth when this revolutionary
decision was taken. Sartreans refer to it as Genet's "original choice," his *choix
originel:* "Abandoned by my family, I already felt it was natural to aggravate this
condition by a preference for boys [*par l'amour des garçons*], and this preference
by theft, and theft by crime or a complacent attitude in regard to crime. I thus
resolutely rejected a world which had rejected me." Later Genet gives a more
elaborate version of the same existential decision, transferred now from childhood to his adolescent years in the Mettray Reformatory, implying that the
"choice" was not so much a single event as an ongoing resolution that had to be
constantly renewed:

In order to weather my desolation when I withdrew more deeply into myself, I worked out, without meaning to, a rigorous discipline. The mechanism was somewhat as follows (I have used it since): to every charge brought against me, unjust though it be, from the bottom of my heart I shall answer yes. Hardly had I uttered the word—or the phrase signifying it—than I felt within me the need to become what I had been accused of being. I was sixteen years old. The reader has understood: I kept no place in my heart where the feeling of my innocence might take shelter. I owned to being the coward, traitor, thief and fairy [*pédé*] they saw in me. An accusation can be made without proof, but it will seem that in order to be found guilty I must have committed the acts which make traitors, thieves or cowards; but this was not at all the case: within myself, with a little patience, I discovered, through reflection, adequate reasons for being named these names. And it staggered me to know that I was composed of impurities. I became abject. Little by little I grew used to this state. I openly admit it. The contempt in which I was held changed to hate: I had succeeded. But what torments I suffered!

Two years later I was strong. Training of this kind—similar to spiritual exercises—was to help me set poverty up as a virtue. As for the triumph, I won it over myself alone. Even when I faced the scorn of children or men, it was I alone whom I had to conquer, since it was a matter of modifying not others but myself.

Genet's assertion loses some of its force as the passage evolves. The crucial matter is the equation of homosexuality with thievery and treason, both obviously choices rather than constitutional inevitabilities: by aligning his sexual practice with his other two "vices," Genet implicitly brings it into the realm of willed behavior. But, in fact, that alignment occurs only in the sentence "I owned to being the coward, traitor, thief and fairy they saw in me." In the very next sentence "fairies" have been removed from the roster of "traitors, thieves or cowards," and by the end of the passage "poverty" has displaced all the other markers of his abjection. We get the impression that he has difficulty sustaining the notion of homosexuality as a choice.

Critics have long suspected that these passages reflect the influence of Sartre, who met Genet in 1944 and had for some years carried on the conversations with him that led to the publication of *Saint Genet* in 1952. In other words, the critics have suggested that the existential Genet may be as much a creation as a discovery of Sartre's. Whatever the case, Sartre latched onto these very passages to argue that in them Genet rejected the constitutional interpretation of homosexuality, as advanced by Gide, Proust, and such early-twentieth-century sexologists as Havelock Ellis and Magnus Hirschfeld. Instead, according to Sartre, Genet refused to distinguish between homosexuality and crime, neither of which is a biological destiny, both of which, rather, are choices:

> He became a homosexual because he was a thief. A person is not born homosexual or normal. He becomes one or the other, according to the accidents of his history and to his own reaction to these accidents. I maintain that inversion is the effect of neither a prenatal choice nor an endocrinian malformation nor even the passive and determined result of complexes. It is an outlet that the child discovers when he is suffocating.[12]

Sartre's gloss overstates the case if it is taken to mean that Genet's homosexual *desires* were in some sense the creation of his oppositional will. Throughout *Journal du voleur* Genet speaks of his "tastes" as a given. Furthermore, many years later, in an interview for *Playboy,* he explicitly repudiated the Sartrean interpretation of his sexual orientation, over which he felt he had no more control than he did over the color of his eyes. "As for my homosexuality," he remarked, "I know nothing about it. Who knows why he is homosexual? . . . As a child I was aware of the attraction other boys exerted over me. I've never been attracted by women. It was only after having felt this attraction that I 'decided,' *chose* my homosexuality freely in the Sartrean sense of the word *choose*."[13] Apparently Genet must have said something similar to Sartre in their conversations, because, in his most arrogant fashion, Sartre dismisses Genet's contention out of hand: "He himself has informed us that, as far as he remembers, he felt his first homosexual desire—a quite innocent desire aroused by a handsome child on a bicycle—at the age of ten. He has even written that his homosexuality preceded his stealing and that the latter was merely a consequence of the former. But we cannot follow him in this."[14]

Clearly the disputed passages in *Journal du voleur* assert not that Genet chose

12. Jean-Paul Sartre, *Saint Genet*, trans. Bernard Frechtman (New York, 1963), p. 91.
13. Quoted by Edmund White, *Genet*, p. 33.
14. Sartre, *Saint Genet*, p. 91.

to be attracted to men but that he chose to embrace that attraction, whatever its source, and that he did so, at least in part, as a gesture of defiance. One could even say that he chose homosexuality as an identity—as a central defining feature of his self—and, again, that he chose it, at least in part, because of its oppositional character.

But, if Genet does not entirely reduce his desires to an exercise of will, many features of his text nonetheless lend support to Sartre's interpretation—that is, an interpretation that stresses the role of choice in Genet's sexuality and the political and philosophical meaning he attributes to the choice. The most important evidence is supplied by the many passages in *Journal du voleur* invoking homosexuality, thievery, and treason as the Holy Trinity, so to speak, of Genet's transgressive religion. By repeatedly aligning the three, even if only rhetorically, he pushes his sexuality into the domain of the will and invests it with ideological significance. A similar effect is created by his frequent association of crime with arousal. Criminals, for Genet, are almost by definition sexy. He is entranced by "the murderer's rich muscularity, . . . the violence of his sexual organ." Thus even if he didn't choose to be a homosexual, he implies that he chose to be a criminal partly for sexual reasons. Admittedly, he turned to crime, in the first instance, in order to eat. But it also excited him. As he says, "I was hot for crime [*j'ai bandé pour le crime*]." The effect of such passages is to blur the line between crime and sexuality and hence between voluntary and constitutional behavior. In sum, Sartre's claims for Genet may be exaggerated, but they reflect a real tendency in *Journal du voleur* to give his homosexuality political and philosophical meaning—to insist that it was more than just a matter of his urges.

GENET BEGINS THE PROPERLY autobiographical part of *Journal du voleur* with a sustained account (taking up about a quarter of the text) of the time he spent as a beggar and petty criminal in Spain, first in Barcelona and then on a long trek down the Mediterranean coast to Gibraltar and back. He implies that the Spanish episodes occurred over a two-year period beginning in 1932. But Edmund White shows that, while Genet may have visited Spain briefly in 1931, the adventures recounted in *Journal du voleur* took place during less than six months starting in late 1933. White interprets the distortion as the novelist's method of lending his Spanish adventures greater psychological authority: "The fictive dates give a weight, a seriousness, to the experience, which it undoubtedly possessed in Genet's imagination and memory. 'Two years' is a novelistic way of rendering the poignancy and anguish of his half year in Spain."[15] The explanation is persuasive, especially in view of Genet's tendency to treat Spain as a kind of metaphor for himself, most famously in the book's closing line, where he speaks of "the region of myself which I have called Spain."

At the start of the Spanish episodes we meet Genet living in a lice-infested hotel with an older man named Salvador. The nature of their relationship is unclear, except for its asymmetry: Salvador was a good deal more devoted to Genet than Genet to Salvador. Salvador spent most of his day begging and then shared the take with Genet, who claims to have felt an "immense" love for him, albeit only "brotherly" love. Salvador could not become a romantic object for Genet because he was timid and ugly. In describing him, Genet focuses on inadequacies—or imponderables—in the two parts of male body with which his erotic imagination was obsessed: the rump and the penis. Repulsed by Salvador's "angular buttocks," he asks, "What if, unfortunately, he were to have a magnificent tool?" "Unfortunately," because such an alluring attribute would be wasted on someone without the face, the ass, and the assertiveness Genet coveted. (The question implies that they didn't have sex together, but Genet also writes, "I had managed to love that sickly body, gray face, and ridiculously sparse beard.") We are thus not surprised that when Genet got a better offer he quickly abandoned his unprepossessing and hangdog benefactor. The brutality with which he ended the relationship is nonetheless stunning: "In order to leave him without remorse I insulted him. I was able to since he loved me to the point of devotion. He gave me a woebegone look, but it was charged with a poor wretch's hatred. I replied with the word: 'Fruit' [*Tapette*]." Perhaps, as in Rousseau's *Confessions,* we are meant to admire the candor with which Genet reports his inhumanity. But, in contrast to Rousseau, he never admits that his behavior was in fact inhumane. Nor does he appear to have felt even a trace of homosexual solidarity: here, as elsewhere, he shows no compunction about abusing, even manhandling, his "fellow" queers.

Genet left Salvador because he had fallen head-over-heals in love with the young and handsome Stilitano, whom he saw for the first time at a card game during which another beggar was killed. He describes the moment as a kind of cosmic epiphany, a Tristanesque fusion of love and death:

> Turning my eyes away from the corpse, I look up, there, gazing at it with a
> faint smile, was Stilitano. The sun was about to set. The dead man and the

15. Edmund White, *Genet,* pp. 102–3.

handsomest of humans seemed to me merged in the same golden dust amidst a throng of sailors, soldiers, hoodlums and thieves from all parts of the world. The Earth did not revolve: carrying Stilitano, it trembled about the sun. At the same moment I came to know death and love.

Possibly the rapturous exaggerations—and the slightly absurd situation—are supposed to create an ironic distance, or even give the scene a hint of comedy. But finally I don't think so. Genet presents his passion for Stilitano as a *grand amour*, worthy of being described in the highest romantic diction. From the instant he saw the "tall blond youngster," he considered himself "secretly engaged."

Their next meeting (which Genet, in his contempt for chronology, actually presents first) is recounted as a kind of seduction, though a seduction that took place entirely in Genet's head. Amidst a group of beggars playing *ronda*, Stilitano's gaze lingered on Genet, who blushed with confusion. When Stilitano explained that he was a deserter from the Foreign Legion, Genet was suddenly seized by a vision of Legionnaires being wedded and dancing, as "their pricks . . . recklessly threatened and challenged each other behind a barricade of rough denim." Stilitano had done virtually nothing to encourage this extravagant fantasy, though he made a complicated pun that Genet interpreted as promising a deep kiss. Genet was utterly undone, completely "mastered." "Stilitano smiled. I was lost."

We might contemplate the elements of his infatuation. In the first place he was smitten by Stilitano's handsome face, with its "glorious . . . blond locks," bright eyes, and thick lashes, as well as by his large, muscular body. At the same time, the beautiful young man was intriguingly exotic: he was a Serb, and, despite his coloration, may even have been a Gypsy. In other words, he boasted that mysterious strangeness—with a hint of animality—that so many other gay autobiographers have found irresistible. Also exotic and arousing was the fact that his right arm had been amputated. Above all, however, Genet was fixated on Stilitano buttocks and penis, about which the text rhapsodizes at length. Both bespoke his promise as a sodomizer.

Genet was mesmerized by Stilitano's manly saunter, which so provocatively displayed his "solemn behind," his "sober posterior." All of his charm, Genet writes, "would assemble in that spot—or rather on it—and would there accumulate and delegate its most caressing waves—and masses of lead!—to give the rump a reverberating undulation and weight." Climbing the stairs to Stilitano's room, Genet "felt the movement of his mobile buttocks" and stepped aside "out of respect." The "masses of lead" stored in those "reverberating" muscles would serve as the engine to drive his sodomizing penis.

"All [Stilitano's] brilliance, all his power, had their source between his legs. His penis, and that which completes it, the whole apparatus, was so beautiful that the only thing I can call it is a generative organ." Genet made a concentrated effort to observe the magnificent object: "What first intrigued me was what Stilitano allowed me to know of it: the mere crease, though curiously precise in the left leg, of his blue denim trousers. This detail might have haunted my dreams less had Stilitano not, at odd moments, put his left hand on it." Genet imagined—perhaps correctly—that the flirtatious Serb encouraged this "scopic" fixation.

In some respects, Genet's phallic obsession and his intense desire to be sodomized are the most revolutionary features of *Journal du voleur*. It is one thing to say, as does Gide, that you are attracted to men. It is quite another to say that you want to be screwed. At the very least the claim that homosexuality in no way compromises one's masculinity—a claim essential not only to Gide but also to John Addington Symonds and J. R. Ackerley—is put at risk. But Genet is fearless, indeed defiant, in proclaiming his desire. He writes, for example, that Stilitano's erotic power was linked to the spittle observable in his mouth, which led Genet "to imagine what his penis would be if he smeared it for my benefit with so fine a substance." In a famous passage he even promotes anal intercourse into a symbol of his identity. When the Spanish police arrested him and confiscated a tube of vaseline from his pocket, he transformed the vaseline—"which was intended to grease my prick and those of my lovers"—from "the very sign of abjection" into an icon of his sexual rebellion:

> Lying on the table, it was a banner telling the invisible legions of my triumph over the police. I was in a cell. I knew that all night long my tube of vaseline would be exposed to the scorn—the contrary of a Perpetual Adoration—of a group of strong, handsome, husky policemen. . . . Nevertheless, I was sure that this puny and most humble object would hold its own against them; by its mere presence it would be able to exasperate all the police in the world; it would draw down upon itself contempt, hatred, white and dumb rages. It would perhaps be slightly bantering—like a tragic hero amused at stirring up the wrath of the gods—indestructible, like him, faithful to my happiness, and proud. I would like to hymn it with the newest words in the French language.

But I would have also liked to fight for it, to organize massacres in its honor
and bedeck a countryside at twilight with red bunting.

The passage brings extraordinary rhetorical and literary resources—drawn from
traditional religion, classical tragedy, and warfare—to bear in its celebration of
this humble emblem of anal eroticism.

Yet Genet's phallic rhapsodies remain deeply ironic, for he never once laid
eyes on Stilitano's penis, still less enjoyed being penetrated by it. Invited home
by his "ravisher," he was "in the throes of love" as he anticipated their "first
night" together. But nothing happened. Just as he entered Stilitano's room,
breathing heavily, the narrative is suddenly broken off. We next see them living
together, even sleeping in the same narrow bed, but, as Genet admits, "This big
fellow was so exquisitely modest that never did I see him entirely." Thus Stilitano's penis remained frustratingly unavailable, and its erotic power accordingly
increased. "Unable to see it," Genet writes, "I invented the biggest and loveliest
prick in the world."

Stilitano subjected Genet to a humiliating routine calculated to intensify his
sexual disappointment. In order to enhance his allure, and above all to provoke
interested homosexuals, Stilitano took to wearing a bunch of cellulose grapes in
his pants: "Whenever some queer at the Criolla, excited by the swelling, put his
hand on Stilitano's basket, his horrified fingers would encounter this object, which
he feared might be actual balls." The gesture is one of many in the text documenting Stilitano's homophobia, which Genet not only fails to condemn but pretends
to find attractive, even arousing. Not satisfied with harassing the neighborhood
queens, Stilitano also forced Genet, kneeling reverentially, to hook the bunch of
grapes into his trousers in the morning and unhook them at night. Genet was
thus regularly brought within (worshiping) inches of the hidden phallus but had
to settle for fondling its cellulose substitute, which he lovingly cupped in his
hands and held against his cheek. The gesture angered Stilitano, who promptly
turned into an abusive husband, kicking Genet with both feet and pummeling
him with his "one fist."

The relationship between the two men was more complicated than at first
appears. In many respects Genet seemed pleased to adopt the female role, bask-
ing in the reflection of his handsome and charming "lover." But if Genet played
the wife, it was often in the manner of Lady Macbeth, urging his lazy and dimwit-
ted man on to bolder crimes. There is even a hint of role reversal. Genet's bearing

and gait grew proud, and he took to eyeing younger men. At the same time, allusions to Stilitano's cowardliness and stupidity undermine the Serb's masculine image, and his heterosexuality is also made to appear somewhat fragile. He had little to do with women—fondling them only ironically, according to Genet—and was fascinated by muscular comic-book figures, like Tarzan, who were "almost always nude or obscenely dressed." Genet, in other words, gives the impression of a certain instability in the roles adopted by the two men. The clear division of labor between male and female, ravisher and ravished, which had been his point of departure, gradually breaks down.

Stilitano deserted Genet shortly after they had left Barcelona for Cadiz. Genet waited for him at the San Fernando train station on two successive days but then decided to continue the journey alone on foot. "I forgot Stilitano," he says flatly. Sartre views Genet's muted reaction to being deserted as evidence that Stilitano was not so much a person as an idea, an abstraction, into which Genet poured all his dreams of masculine potency. A more accurate assessment would be that Stilitano was subject to the familiar process of enlargement, or "crystallization" (to use Stendhal's term), by which the beloved is transformed in the erotic imagination. But that doesn't make him any less a concrete, flesh-and-blood human being, with particular physical and psychological attributes that trigger the lover's fantasies. And, in fact, Genet's grief at his abandonment was palpable. In characteristic fashion, however, it is textually displaced. It appears first in his paean to the sunrise in Cadiz, which, he writes, he "confused . . . in some obscure way with the vanished Stilitano." It emerges more directly, after a hundred pages, in a passage that self-consciously mythologizes Stilitano into a galactic phenomenon:

> When I was deserted by Stilitano near San Fernando, my grief was even greater, my sense of poverty even deeper. . . . It was no longer even the memory of him that I carried away with me but rather the idea of a fabulous creature, the origin and pretext of all desires, terrifying and gentle, remote and close to the point of containing me, for, now being something dreamed, he had, though hard and brutal, the gaseous insubstantiality of certain nebulae, their gigantic dimensions, their brilliance in the heavens and their name as well.

The exaggerated, larger-than-life character of Genet's passion likely depended on the very sexlessness the relationship, which, in a curious way, resembles the

chaste ecstasies into which John Addington Symonds worked himself over his
adolescent choristers. But the power of Genet's imagination transforms this sordid and uneventful affair into something that begs to be compared to the great
loves of history. Stilitano will reemerge later in the text, somewhat reduced but
still an object of desire, and the narrative of *Journal du voleur* culminates in the
moment when, for the first and only time, he responded to Genet's caress.

⨀ BETWEEN THE OPENING SCENES in Spain and the reunion with Stilitano in
Antwerp, Genet recounts his travels—mostly on foot—through Central and
Eastern Europe. These travels seem to have occurred in 1936 and 1937 (after a
two-year stint in the French army, unmentioned in *Journal du voleur*), and they
took Genet through Italy, Albania, Yugoslavia, Austria, Czechoslovakia, Poland,
Germany, and Belgium. According to Edmund White, the odyssey described in
Journal condenses and rearranges Genet's actual experiences, although the text
fails to mention that at the time he was fleeing from the French military authorities after having deserted.

Genet's most important romantic relationship during his travels was with a
handsome Czech guitarist named Michaelis Andritch, whom he met in Brno. The
relationship is of interest above all because it shows Genet struggling to redefine
himself sexually. He seemed to want to appropriate some of the masculine authority he had surrendered to Stilitano. In other words, the affair with Michaelis marks
the start—at least textually—of a process of "virilization" (as it has been called
by the Sartreans), although the evidence is ambiguous. One gets the impression
that Genet may have been confused about his own desires. Certainly he makes an
effort to keep the reader confused on the issue. Nevertheless, there is a discernible
pattern whereby he gradually abandoned the feminine identity he had embraced
in Spain to take on a more assertive posture, both sexually and otherwise, in the
later episodes of the book. The relationship with Michaelis was a turning point
in this development

The picture we get of Michaelis is mixed. Perhaps the most important thing
to note about him is that he was six or seven years younger than Genet. In part,
one suspects, Genet's "virilization" was simply a practical response to the fact
that he was getting older and had to assume a more aggressive role in pursuing
the handsome young men he was attracted to. A second feature distinguishing
Michaelis from Genet's earlier loves is that Michaelis was homosexual. Actually,
Genet gives contradictory testimony on the matter. He writes that he was sur-

prised to meet in Michaelis "a homosexual whose bearing was manly" (*un pédérast aux allures viriles*). But a few pages later "Michaelis, a handsome male" is said not to like men. Conceivably the second (heterosexual) Michaelis is a different person, but I'm inclined to see in this apparent contradiction evidence of Genet's discomfort with his new "virile" identity, according to which he was now playing the Stilitano part, while Michaelis played the part of his former self. The same ambiguity is implied by his description of Michaelis as "graceful but not effeminate." And when Michaelis insisted that, as a hustler, he always took the masculine role, Genet comments, "I doubted it but pretended to believe it."

Genet assumed an authoritative manner in the relationship. He introduced Michaelis to a life of theft—the ultimate manly gesture—and basked in the admiration of the younger man. Stilitano was not entirely forgotten, but he was gradually displaced ("in my heart and against my body") by the young Czech. Most interestingly, Genet recognizes that, in the new relationship, he had internalized many features of Stilitano's character. As he expresses it, "I had been the beloved of so beautiful a bird of prey, a miscreant of the finest breed, that I could adopt a certain insolence with a charming guitarist."

The affair came to an unhappy end after the two went to Poland together and were arrested. Forced to clean the jailhouse latrines, Genet adopted a stance of disdainful resistance, in part to increase his attractiveness to Michaelis. But he lost interest in the young man when Michaelis failed to show the same contempt for the police and instead reacted with feminine compliance, smiling and joking with the guards: "'You're a coward,' I said. 'You're a son of a bitch. The cops are still too good to you. One of these days you'll really lick their boots. Maybe they'll go pay you a visit in your cell and stick their pricks up your ass!'" Inevitably one gets the feeling that the source of the problem was Genet's uneasiness with his new masculine role. Michaelis had become too much the woman to retain his allure. At the same time Genet himself was far from immune to the sexual charms of the police, who, alongside thieves and traitors, had long occupied a place of honor in his erotic imagination. (Later in the book he devotes several pages to his affair with a Marseilles cop named Bernardini.) The breakup of the relationship suggests that Genet was not yet ready to forge a novel sexual identity for himself. His years as a "girl queen" (to use Sartre's phrase) were far from over.

The principal heirs to Michaelis were the young men with whom Genet carried on romances during the composition of *Journal du voleur* in the 1940s. These contemporary figures insinuate themselves ever more frequently into the latter half of the text, creating a sense of Genet's progressive masculinization. One of them was a young German athlete and former member of the SS, Erik, whom Genet buggers in the most extended and graphic sexual scene in the book (a scene cut from later editions).[16] Far more important was Lucien Sénémaud, the "little fisherman from Le Suquet," who eventually starred in Genet's 1950 film *Un Chant d'amour*.

Although nominally heterosexual (with a girlfriend and son), Lucien submitted to a relationship with Genet that ceded all authority to the older man. Lucien was small and compact, with a pretty-boy face. Genet refers to him repeatedly as a child, and at one point even speaks of his smiling "as if he were a young wife." Physically the two enjoyed a cuddly intimacy, with Lucien very much in the feminine role, snuggling up to Genet in bed and kissing his neck. "By this sign," writes Genet, "I recognize his docility to the injunctions of the heart, the submission of his body to my mind." Significantly, there is hardly a word about Lucien's penis, the organ that had figured so centrally in Genet's earlier fantasies. He expressly associates the relationship with his own sense of masculinity. When Lucien broke into tears at the prospect of being abandoned, Genet observes, "His tears and sobs on my neck proved my virility. I was his man."

But, as with Michaelis, Genet felt ill at ease in his new role. Lucien, like Michaelis, seemed too soft, lacking the edge that would make him truly desirable. Genet yearned for a more aggressive bedmate: "At night, when Lucien has gone back to his room, I curl up fearfully under the sheets and want to feel against me the tougher, more dangerous and more tender body of a thief." Genet thus conceived of the idea of transforming Lucien into a criminal, which would have invested him with the dangerous masculine energy Genet craved. The idea prompts a fantasy of being sodomized by a large black prisoner, Sek Gorgui: "Gently, but with sure precision, his tool will enter me. It will not tremble. It will not jerk hastily like mine. That presence within me will so fill me that I shall forget to come." Suddenly we are returned from the anodyne cuddling with Lucien to the raw anal eroticism of Genet's earlier imaginings. His virilization, we sense, was an incomplete project.

The impression is confirmed by Genet's romance with a young man he calls Java, whom he also pursued during the composition of *Journal*. As in the case of

---

16. Edmund White places the affair with Erik somewhat earlier, namely, during the Occupation. Erik was killed on the Eastern Front. See *Genet*, p. 278.

his contemporary Lucien, references to Java proliferate as the text advances. If Lucien was heir to Michaelis, Java was heir to Stilitano. Like Stilitano, Java was large and bulky. He belonged to the shady world of criminals and thus enjoyed the sexual cachet that Genet missed in the meek and law-abiding Lucien. Being half-Russian, he also shared Stilitano's Slavic exoticism. Somewhat contradictorily, he was, like the Serb, a coward, although Genet pretends to have found the quality seductive (cowards for him being honorary members of the erotic elite of thieves, traitors, and police). Perhaps most important, Java possessed Stilitano's mobile and alluring rump with its sodomizing promise. Genet is quite explicit in identifying the "muscle-bound, slightly swaying walk" common to the two men. Arguably, by carrying on love affairs simultaneously with Lucien and Java, Genet was able to remain in a kind of gender limbo, playing the new manly role with Lucien while keeping up his older, effeminate ways with Java.

A good deal of confusion and ambiguity, then, surrounds the image Genet projects of his sexual identity. Earlier I stressed that he made a provocative, indeed revolutionary, issue of his femininity and his desire to be possessed. We recall that he transformed the tube of vaseline confiscated by the police into a symbol of his defiance, just as he rhapsodized at the prospect of being sodomized by Stilitano. But to the extent that he presents himself as moving toward an increasingly masculine attitude he undermines his adversarial purity. The suspicion develops that, despite his contempt for convention, he may have felt embarrassed by his effeminacy. Whenever he quotes himself in the text, he invariably speaks in same manly accents as his heterosexual interlocutors. One looks in vain for the verbal affectations of which Quentin Crisp makes such a self-conscious display in *The Naked Civil Servant*. I also find it telling that in the book's only sustained description of anal intercourse—the scene with Erik—Genet assigns himself the role of penetrator. Similarly, he seems happy to leave the impression that his masterly dominance in the relationships with Michaelis and Lucien had become the norm for him, while disguising the extent to which he remained attached to the older erotic ideal, as implied by his relationship with Java. Not even the most radical of homosexual rebels, it seems, can fully escape the heterosexual prejudices of his culture.

∞ THE EPISODES IN ANTWERP, with which *Journal du voleur* culminates and where Genet was reunited with Stilitano, exactly balance the Spanish adventures in the first half of the book, thus lending the whole a perhaps suspicious symmetry. Although more fragmented than the Spanish story, the Antwerp scenes take up nearly the same number of pages (about a quarter of the text) and achieve a similar weight and authority, qualities denied to the more fleeting accounts Genet gives of his travels in Eastern Europe or his romances with Lucien, Java, and other "contemporary" figures.

Nonetheless, there are reasons to doubt the autobiographical reliability of the experiences Genet sets in Antwerp. For one thing, he is even more casual than usual in dating these events, saying at one point that the reunion with Stilitano took place two years after their separation, at another that four or five years had elapsed. Yet more disturbing, Edmund White, who places Genet's visit to Antwerp in mid-1937, argues that the visit lasted only "a few days," and hence that the events recounted in the text—which seem to occur over several months—must involve a conflation "with later, longer visits."[17] Internal evidence also raises our suspicions. Particularly worrisome is the sheer improbability of Stilitano's showing up in Belgium. Genet offers no explanation for this coincidence, or for how the almost congenitally lazy Stilitano managed to become such an underworld success in his new environment. Equally nervous-making is the complex romantic quadrangle in which Genet and Stilitano became enmeshed, a quadrangle whose plot bears an improbable resemblance to Mozart's *Così fan tutte*. In other words, the closing episodes in Antwerp feel distinctly more fictional than the episodes in Spain with which we began. Perhaps the answer to the generic mystery posed by *Journal du voleur* is that the book starts as an autobiography but ends as a novel.

The Stilitano whom Genet met in Antwerp had grown somewhat bulkier. He had also transformed himself from a bum into a dandy. He appears to have made his money pimping and in the drug trade, and he paraded around town with his whore (and meal-ticket), Sylvia, on his arm. Yet from the moment of their meeting Genet found himself once again completely in Stilitano's thrall, as if they had never been separated. Moreover, the source of Stilitano's power over Genet remained unchanged: his rump and penis, with their still unredeemed sexual promise. "In his gait," writes Genet, "I found the same savage suppleness, more powerful, less rapid and more muscular, but just as nervous." Still visible in Stilitano's mouth was the blob of spit—to facilitate the wished-for penetration—

17. Edmund White, *Genet*, p. 127.

whose erotic significance both men slyly acknowledged: "This innocent complicity at once set up a relationship between us. All his former charms bore down on me: the power of his shoulders, the mobility of his buttocks, the hand that had perhaps been torn off in the jungle by another savage beast, and finally his member, so long denied me, buried in a dangerous darkness which was shielded from mortal odors." The Serb's mastery was only increased by his newfound criminal glory. Genet, in short, was again entirely at Stilitano's mercy.

Soon Genet had become Stilitano's regular sidekick, as they reestablished the working relationship they had enjoyed in Spain. Genet apprenticed himself as an understudy in the opium trade, at one point carrying a load of the drug across the Dutch frontier. The two saw each other daily, eating lunch in Stilitano's room and going out to dinner together while Sylvia turned tricks.

Stilitano had been something of a flirt in Spain, but he now dropped broad hints that he might, at some point, become sexually available. These hints are important, because they prepare the way for the crucial moment of erotic acknowledgement at the end, where the narrative achieves its suspiciously novelistic closure. Shortly after they met, for example, Stilitano asked Genet if he still liked men. Genet answered that of course he did. He then turned the question on Stilitano and elicited an enticingly ambiguous response:

"You like them too."
"Me?"
"Yes."
"No, but sometimes I wonder what it's like."
"It gets you hot."
"Not a bit. I said it . . . "
He laughed in embarrassment.

Genet was clearly encouraged: "If Stilitano were to add to his power over me by giving me any wild hope, he would reduce me to slavery." The thought emboldened him to make a more direct overture. "I said to him, 'You know I still have a soft spot for you, and I'd like to make love to you,'" to which the smiling Stilitano reacted not with the expected box on the ears but, almost seductively, "'We'll see about it.'" The prospect thoroughly undid Genet. "My whole being wanted to be swallowed up within him," he writes.

Before long, however, Stilitano's star began to fade. Perhaps, as a novelist,

Genet feels the need to complicate the story before arriving at his denouement. In any event, he introduces two new characters, Armand and Robert, with whom he fashions the erotic (and criminal) quadrangle of the book's closing episodes. Robert was a young man who worked at a merry-go-round and with whom Genet claims to have fallen in love. More important, Robert gradually displaced Genet in Stilitano's criminal operations and, it would seem, in his affections as well. As Genet puts it, suggestively, Robert and Stilitano "lived in comradely partnership, looking for women or neglecting them in each other's company." In other words, although nominally heterosexual, they formed the kind of homo-social bond that has distinctly queer overtones. Certainly that was Genet's own interpretation of their friendship.

When Stilitano took up with Robert, Genet turned to a new love, a Flemish criminal he calls Armand, a rich and complex figure who is more elaborately characterized than any other in the book, except Stilitano himself. Indeed, Armand is drawn with such precise and distinctive strokes that one never suspects him of being merely a novelistic device, as one does Robert.

In his mid-forties, Armand was some twenty years older than Genet. In con-trast to Stilitano, he was not handsome but massive, hirsute, and brutal. With his broken nose and large shaved head, he curiously resembled the mature Genet, although Armand was "tall and splendidly built," while Genet was short and frail. If Stilitano's erotic power over Genet rested in his buttocks and penis, Armand's was concentrated in his deep voice and hairy arms. "Armand's voice," writes Genet, "touched a spot in my throat and took my breath away." His "solid and muscular" arms were often folded in the manner of an oriental pasha, an exotic image reinforced by "a delicate tattoo representing a mosque with minaret and dome and a palm tree bent by a sandstorm." (The tattoo oddly reminded Genet both of Stilitano's desertion on the road to Cadiz and of a legionnaire he had fellated beneath the walls of a mosque while serving in the army in Morocco.) Armand's folded arms alluded to his potency: they were "signs of a lordly penis"; at the same time they also represented an "answer to all metaphysical anxieties."

We are not surprised, given his physical attributes, that the sexual relation-ship with Armand had a sadomasochistic flavor. Genet reports that, before going to bed, Armand "whipped his leather belt from the loops of his trousers and made it snap," as if he were "flogging an invisible victim." Whatever "virilization" Genet may have achieved with Michaelis was now forgotten, as he embraced the most abject passivity:

When I met him near the docks, Armand ordered me to follow him. Almost without speaking, he took me to his room. With the same apparent scorn, he subjected me to his pleasure. Dominated by his strength and age, I gave the work my utmost care. Crushed by that mass of flesh, which was devoid of the slightest spirituality, I experienced the giddiness of finally meeting the perfect brute, indifferent to my happiness.

Yet Armand was also a maternal figure for Genet, who repeatedly refers to the older man's "kindness" (*bonté*). Even Armand's desire to be fellated by Genet and others invites a maternal interpretation: the boy sucking his penis was (from a psychoanalytic point of view) analogous to the child sucking at the mother's breast. The interpretation gains support from Armand's secret femininity: he had once traveled about Europe making and selling lace-paper doilies and handkerchiefs. "The idea of my calm, hulking master doing woman's work moved me." But whether a suckling mother or a sadistic father, Armand's dominance over Genet cast Stilitano in the shadows.

Although Armand and Genet lived together in Antwerp, the older man's ardor soon waned. Genet would gladly have remained "his beloved mistress," but before long Armand was saying good night and falling asleep. In part he grew indifferent because he had taken a fancy to Robert, thus setting the stage for the partner-swapping that will create the "proper" couples at the book's end. But as the sex faded Armand became more interested in his "professional" relationship with Genet, namely, as his mentor in the chief criminal activity in which Genet was then engaged (alongside the other members of the quadrangle): rolling queers.

For the modern gay reader, the accounts of these assaults on homosexuals are the most distasteful aspect of *Journal du voleur*. They also provide important evidence about Genet's sexual politics. Without exception, the abused men are described as old and rich. In other words, Genet justifies his acts by implying that class opposition took precedence over sexual identification. Most disturbing of all, these wealthy older homosexuals are made to seem legitimate targets because of their effeminacy and sexual passivity—the very qualities that distinguished Genet's own sexuality and that he had celebrated so defiantly earlier in the book.

As a self-described immoralist, Genet no doubt prides himself on the unsentimental candor with which he reports his crimes. Nonetheless the savagery of his treatment of other homosexuals is breathtaking. Here, by way of example, is his account of perhaps the most flagrant of these attacks:

A heavy-set man asked me for a light and offered me a drink. When we left, he wanted me to go home with him, but I refused. He hesitated, then decided for the docks. I had noticed his gold watch, wedding ring and wallet. I knew he wouldn't call for help, but he looked strong. I couldn't carry the thing off except by some trick. I prepared nothing. Suddenly I thought of using the cord that Stilitano had given me. When we got to the corner of the docks, the man asked me to screw him.

"All right. Let your pants down."

I had him lower his trousers as far as his heels so that he would get tangled up in them if he tried to run.

"Spread your ass."

With both hand he did what I ordered, and I quickly tied them up, behind his back. . . .

"You old son of a bitch, you thought I was going to stick it in!" . . .

I smashed him in the face. He whimpered, though in silence. With the same dispatch as Stilitano, I opened my knife in front of him and showed him the blade. I should like to tell with greater precision what this moment meant to me. The cruelty into which I was forcing myself gave amazing power not only to my body but to my mind.

The unqualified viciousness of this scene should be placed against other moments in which Genet appears to appreciate the contradiction in his behavior, even to feel a genuine sense of identity with the most despised of homosexual deviants, the drag queen. At one point, for example, he recognizes his alter-ego in a "trembling old queer" whose rings Stilitano had stolen. On another occasion, after confronting "a snooty queen," he confesses, "My conscience grieved at having wounded and insulted those who were the wretched expression of my dearest treasure: homosexuality." But the best evidence of an incipient (if still deficient) sense of homosexual solidarity is to be found in his exuberant celebration of the Barcelona transvestites known as the Carolinas. In a scene at once funny and moving, he describes the Carolinas, in full regalia, carrying a floral tribute to a demolished street urinal, a procession he likens to a religious pilgrimage:

The faggots were perhaps thirty in number, at eight A.M., at sunrise. I saw them going by. I accompanied them from a distance. I knew that my place was in their midst, not because I was one of them, but because their shrill voices, their cries, their extravagant gestures seemed to me to have no other aim than to try to pierce the shell of the world's contempt. The Carolinas were great. They were the Daughters of Shame.

One can hardly believe that the same man who honored the Carolinas in Barcelona could have terrorized bourgeois queens in Antwerp. Perhaps I am judging him by the anachronistic standards of today's identity politics and failing to do justice to the class issue that weighed more heavily in his mind over half a century ago. Even so, his clinical and sometimes gleeful accounts of gay bashing make one wonder whether Genet wasn't simply a man without a moral compass, rather than the architect of a Nietzschean project to revaluate all values, as he liked to see himself.

Genet's decision to abandon Armand and return to Stilitano at the end of *Journal du voleur* was triggered by Stilitano's unexpectedly proposing that they rob Armand. The proposal thrilled Genet, because it meant that Stilitano had finally chosen him over the better-looking Robert. He imagined that a similar alliance had been forged by Armand and Robert. Here is where the text inadvertently echoes the finale of *Cosí fan tutte*, in which Fiordiligi is reunited with Guglielmo, Dorabella with Ferrando. Genet himself seems to feel that a musical analogy is appropriate to the situation. "I had chosen my partner in this dance," he writes.

Genet offers a tortured philosophical explanation of his decision to betray Armand, a further variation on the inverted moral reasoning he has used to justify all his actions. He argues that by abandoning Armand he would be able to savor a new and particularly exquisite vice, or, more precisely, to turn yet another established value on its head: "The idea of betraying Armand set me aglow. I feared and loved him too much not to want to deceive and betray and rob him. I sensed the anxious pleasure that goes with sacrilege." But a simpler explanation suggests itself: Genet was still infatuated with the younger and handsomer Stilitano, who, in contrast to Armand, retained his sexual mystery. In other words, the betrayal of Armand testifies not to Genet's revolutionary immorality—which seems a mere rationalization—but to the persistence of an old-fashioned and altogether conventional romantic attachment. Genet, I believe, returned to man he still loved and, above all, desired.

This interpretation is supported by the unabashed emotion and sensual excitement generated in the book's last scene, describing the reconciliation with Stilitano. Walking back to his hotel late at night, Stilitano began to reminisce about their life together in Spain. At first Genet played hard to get. After years of pining away, he apparently felt he deserved a little courting:

> "You had a big crush on me at the time."
> "What about now?"
> "Now? Do you still have it?"
> I think he wanted to be assured of my love and that I would desert Armand for him. . . .
> "Not like before." . . .
> "You don't like me as much?"
> "I don't love you."

But Genet's body betrayed him. Even as he denied being in love he felt his "pants getting hot." A moment later, as they passed under a dark railroad bridge, Stilitano moved closer and asked Genet to light a cigarette for him:

> I took one from his pocket, lit it, took a drag, and put it between his lips, in the middle. With a neat flick of his tongue, Stilitano moved it to the right corner of his mouth and, still smiling, took a step forward, threatening to burn my face if I didn't back up. My hand, which was hanging in front of me, went right to his basket. It was hard. Stilitano smiled and looked me in the eyes.

The moment is not without ambiguity, for just then Genet was reminded of an episode, a bit earlier, when Stilitano had been humiliated by getting trapped in a Palace of Mirrors, from which he had to be extricated "screaming with anger." But, with the Serb's dimwittedness and feminine vulnerability properly acknowledged, the scene is allowed to work its way to a satisfying, if brisk, romantic conclusion:

> I felt his penis beneath my lightly groping fingers.
> "You like it?"
> I didn't answer. What was the use? He knew that my swagger had just gone dead. He took his left hand from his pocket and, putting his arm around my shoulders, squeezed me against him while the cigarette guarded his mouth, protecting it from a kiss. Someone was coming along. I muttered very quickly:
> "I love you."

Admittedly, having gotten all the information he wanted about Armand's stash, Stilitano left Genet at the door of the hotel. Genet then returned to his room and went to bed alone, while Armand made love to Robert in the next room.

An undeniable melancholy hangs over the book's final tableau. We suspect Stilitano's motives and doubt that the grand love affair will ever amount to much. Nonetheless, Genet has made a strenuous effort to bring his narrative to a close with a traditional romantic gesture. He finally achieves some measure of the erotic satisfaction that has been withheld since that fateful moment, years earlier, when he first saw the golden Stilitano under the setting Spanish sun. Beneath its philosophical veneer and literary experimentation, I am suggesting, Genet's story turns out not to be so very different from that of other gay autobiographers in search of love and sex.

Julien Green at 16.

Jeunes années

ULIEN GREEN WAS BORN a decade before Genet—and into thoroughly bourgeois circumstances—so we might anticipate that his autobiography would be more conventional and repressed than Genet's. On the other hand, *Jeunes années* was written almost a quarter century after *Journal du voleur,* in the 1960s and 1970s, when the more relaxed sexual climate would seem to invite greater candor. Neither of these calculations prepares us for the yawning gap—stylistic, moral, and above all sexual—separating these two confessional works. Green seems thoroughly ashamed of his desires, even if he takes pleasure in revisiting the handsome faces he admired in his youth. His account of his homosexual experience is so fastidious that he cannot even bring himself to name the bodily organs and erotic practices celebrated with such rhapsodic abandon by Genet. The history of gay autobiography in France confounds our naive expectation that the genre should move inexorably toward self-affirmation.

If Green is in some sense Genet's opposite, *Jeunes années* represents an intriguing variation on the themes of Gide's *Si le grain ne meurt.* Like Gide, Green describes an outwardly happy Parisian childhood disturbed by a sense of isolation and inner turmoil. As the only son living at home (his much older brother had left for America in 1904), he, too, was the object of his parents' suffocating attention, although in Green's case five older sisters shared in pampering him. And, as with Gide, Green's Bible-quoting mother was a far stronger presence than his retiring

---

Jeunes années (Paris, 1984) collects into two volumes, with a new concluding section, the four volumes of autobiography Julien Green published between 1963 and 1974. In this chapter I have cited the four-volume English translation: I. *Partir avant le jour* (1963) (*The Green Paradise,* trans. Anne and Julien Green [New York, 1993]); II. *Mille chemins overts* (1964) (*The War at Sixteen,* trans. Euan Cameron [New York, 1993]); III. *Terre lointaine* (1966) (*Love in America,* trans. Euan Cameron [New York, 1994]); IV. *Jeunesse* (1974) (*Restless Youth,* trans. Euan Cameron [New York, 1996]).

father, who, like the mother, grew up in the American South and worked in Paris as the European agent for a cotton oil company.

But the most important common denominator linking Green and Gide is their shared dualism. In Green's case the opposition between spirit and flesh retains its theological character. Indeed, much to his annoyance, he is often grouped with Georges Bernanos and François Mauriac as a Catholic novelist. The crucial difference between Green and Gide is that where Gide reconfigures traditional dualism into a naturalistic antithesis between heterosexual love and homosexual lust—with a view to carving out a legitimate space for the latter— Green holds to an older doctrine that condemns all sexual desire, whether homosexual or heterosexual, as a Satanic temptation. Much of his story, accordingly, is recounted as a struggle between his wayward urges and his spiritual calling. One might argue that religion functioned to curb Green's sensuality in the way that marriage curbed Gide's. Perhaps we need to remind ourselves that Green's experience was far from unique: he is the autobiographical spokesman for all those gay men who have not followed Gide toward liberation but have carried on a lifelong battle with their desires. Green is the great memorialist of homosexual repression.

His dualism finds many outlets in the text, almost assuming the character of a structural principle. In childhood it emerged as a tendency to categorize everything in terms of purity and impurity. Later it expressed itself in the way he divides the men in his life into those with whom he was in love—invariably distinguished by their handsome faces—and those he desired, in which case his fixation was on the body. In the last years recounted in the autobiography the opposition appears as one between chaste days at home devoted to writing his *Pamphlet against the Catholics in France*—which celebrates the Inquisition and attacks modern Catholicism for its moral laxity—and squalid nights cruising near the Trocadero.

Much of the interest of *Jeunes années* stems from the moments in which Green resists his own tendentious categories—when, for example, he makes fun of his compulsive distinctions between purity and impurity, love and lust, faces and bodies, the sacred and the profane, or when, under the pressure of circumstances, the categories themselves begin to break down. Thus in the third volume he is unable to maintain the fiction that his love for the handsome Virginian named Mark was the entirely Platonic affair of his original conception. More generally, the meticulous attention he devotes to recreating the infatuations of his youth undermines the ideological structure he erects to condemn his homosexuality. Hence, despite the book's Augustinian premises, its actual effect is surprisingly sensual. It has more in common with other gay autobiographies than its doctrinal austerity would lead one to expect.

Gide seems often to be in the back of Green's mind, on the one hand as a literary model to emulate, on the other as a sexual example to be avoided. As a novelist Green retained Gide's preference for classical lucidity, and he also followed Gide in regularly publishing his journal, which recently reached its sixteenth volume and has been pronounced "the longest published diary in world literature."[18] In the 1930s Gide mounted a campaign to convince Green to embrace the pederastic ideal of *Corydon*. Pulling in the opposite direction was the Catholic philosopher Jacques Maritain, whose counsel ultimately prevailed when Green returned to the Church in 1939. In the Journals—which are largely silent about sexual matters—Gide appears as an admired and sympathetic mentor. But the portrait of him in *Jeunes années* is uniformly hostile. Green manages to make Gide seem at once cold and hysterical, with more than a hint of effeminacy. He also goes out of his way to disparage *Corydon*, whose defense of homosexuality, he says, held no interest for him "because it did not address the principal question, which was the struggle between the flesh and the spirit." He implies that Gide had failed in his effort to recast the dualistic heritage of Western civilization to accommodate homosexual desire, whereas his own vision, however pitiless, remained true to that heritage. Still, the obvious parallels between Gide's and Green's stories, as well as their similar philosophical bent, invite the suspicion that a certain anxiety of influence must have shaped the composition of *Jeunes années*. Green's experience, one might say, was what Gide's would have been had Gide been unable to talk himself out of the repressive implications of his dualistic ontology.

⟟ IN THE OPENING PAGES of the autobiography Green establishes the basic theological opposition that will organize his narrative throughout. He contrasts two early childhood experiences, the first of which he interprets as a religious epiphany, the second as an encounter with the Devil. Yet even in this stark contrast between the forces of Good and Evil, Green's language betrays a certain ambiguity.

18. Euan Cameron, review of *Pourquoi suis-je moi? Journal 1993–1996*, *Times Literary Supplement*, October 4, 1996, p. 9.

He recalls "a minute of intense delight" that occurred when he was still young enough to be sharing a room with his parents:

> There came a moment in this room when, looking up at the windowpane, I saw the dark sky and a few stars shining in it. What words can be used to express what is beyond speech? The minute was perhaps the most important one of my life and I do not know what to say about it. I was alone in the unlighted room and, my eyes raised toward the sky, I had what I can only call an outburst of love. I have loved on this earth, but never as I did in that short time, and I did not know whom I loved. Yet I knew that he was there and that, seeing me, he loved me too. How did the thought dawn on me? I do not know. I was certain that someone was there and talked to me without words. Having said this, I have said everything.

The passage is typical of *Jeunes années* in asserting a dogmatic idea in remarkably agnostic language. The posing of questions to which Green responds with some variation on "I don't know" occurs, literally, hundreds of times in the text. Similarly, the almost Wittgensteinian insistence on the unspeakableness of his experience is a constant refrain. Green's sensibility is at once apodictic and modest: he affirms his theological perspective even while confessing his incomprehension. The manner reflects the precariousness of his faith, which alternated between periods of enthusiasm, when he thought he had a vocation, and periods of alienation, when his Catholic friends like Jacques Maritain had to keep a firm watch on him lest he succumb to the seductions of Gide on the other side. At the same time, as with many mystics (one thinks especially of St. Theresa), the visionary experience is described in erotic language: it was a *ravissement* in which he felt himself loved by an imaginary male, inviting us to interpret it as a transparent sublimation.

On the very next page he tells of his first encounter with the Devil, an event he places around 1907:

> What idea did I have of the fallen angel? I do not know, but, some days, seized with an ungovernable curiosity, I suddenly opened the door of the clothes closet that was in my parents' room and, with a beating heart, called the devil. For I imagined that he lived there.
>
> Nothing happened at first. The inside of the closet was dark; the long line

of clothes, squeezed close one to another like a flattened, headless crowd, could only be seen dimly. I had to call once more; I was aware of that at least and also knew that two calls would not be enough. Three calls were necessary, were exacted. So I called a third time and the unforgettable thing happened. The clothes moved. They parted gently to allow someone to pass. I am sorry today not to have had the heart to wait instead of rushing away, howling.

One would like to find deep significance—and a certain humor—in the notion that the Devil makes his first appearance in the closet, but the metaphor of the closet is an Americanism that, as George Chauncey has shown, was never used even in America before the 1960s.[19] Nonetheless, beginning with this childhood experience, the Evil One will show up regularly in Green's text, above all as the instigator of his homosexual prowlings in the last volume. Here Green again follows the example of Gide, although Gide's Devil sometimes seems like a stage Mephistopheles, whereas Green's strikes one as the genuine item. When, in 1928, Green asked a priest in Jacques Maritain's home what the Devil looked like, the priest answered promptly, "'He is a handsome young man.'"

Green traces the origins of his bleak view of sex to two early experiences with his mother, who, he reports, always watched him closely, "having a horror of certain misbehaviors." He was particularly susceptible to her authority because she was, on the whole, such a powerful and loving figure, whose good-night kiss young Julien awaited with almost Proustian anxiety. In the first episode he was discovered masturbating by one of his sisters. Her shrieks brought his mother running into the room with a candlestick: "I appeared in the light, just as I was, not understanding what it was all about, smiling perhaps, my hands on the forbidden regions." Here, as throughout, Green reaches for the nearest circumlocution; he can hardly bring himself to describe any part of body below the neck, and the genitals are entirely unmentionable. When his mother returned she was brandishing "a long, saw-toothed knife" and crying, in English, "'I'll cut it off!'" Little Julien melted into tears, as the family cook burst out laughing.

Rather like young André Gide's visit to Dr. Brouardel, the scene is so theatrical that the cook's response seems the sole appropriate one. His mother sounds as if she were reading her lines out of a Freudian primer. Green says that he can recall the moment only because the cook kept its memory alive by regularly

19. See *Gay New York* (New York, 1994), p. 6.

grabbing a bread-knife, "in fits of gaiety," and saying (in her French accent), "'Alcotétof!'" The scene at once establishes a dire prohibition and satirizes it as preposterous.

The second episode occurred a few years later, when Green was about ten. In it we find the same impulse to circumlocution and the same theatrical excess. His mother was giving him a bath: "I lay in the warm water and, a few steps away, my mother was drying her hands with a worried air when suddenly she glanced down at a very precise part of my person. As though she were talking to herself, she murmured: 'Oh, how ugly that is!' [*Oh! que c'est donc laid!*] And she turned her head with a kind of shiver." One almost suspects Green of playing the Gidean card, invoking the stereotypical image of a mindlessly repressive mother. Elsewhere his mother is shown to be lighthearted, even risqué. She was much amused, for example, by a cartoon in the journal *Le Rire* in which Eve asks Adam for the handkerchief around his waist: "'I can't,' replied Adam, '*Le Rire* would be suppressed.' Great merriment on my mother's part. 'The French are so funny!'" But shortly before her death, in 1914, she told Julien of the hideous physical degeneration from syphilis of her handsome brother Willie. The revelation persuaded Green of the urgency of her jeremiads, which until then he had found rather exaggerated. He fully embraced her ideal of purity, which, he says, "has sometimes harmed me, sometimes protected me, and I am still indebted to . . . on many scores, for it will probably stay with me until I die." The world was divided into the pure and the impure, with virtually everything connected to the body falling into the latter category. Admittedly, Green sometimes pokes fun at his own zealous Manichaeanism. He was nonplussed, for example, when a teacher forbade him to read Zola, for the simple reason that "Pure and Impure had never mentioned Zola to me." But when it came to his body and his sexual feelings, he accepted his mother's views wholeheartedly: "I never looked at myself naked, nakedness being impure, and finally believed, in a vague way, that my entire person was one of those only to be seen dressed and never to be touched, under any circumstance."

In contrast to the rambunctious young André Gide, with his rough-housing and scientific experiments, Green had a cloistered childhood. His erotic education, and the earliest intimations of his homosexuality, occurred largely through the medium of pictures, examined first in books in the family home and then, directly, on visits to museums. Green's account of these early visual stimuli confirms the peculiar repressiveness of his upbringing—above all his habit of erasing the genitals from consciousness—and his tendency to associate sex with violence. He expressly attributes his visual education to "the enemy."

The first pictures to which he reacted were Gustave Doré's engravings for Dante's *Inferno,* whose writhing naked bodies he traced with his own pencil when he was seven. Even more devastating was Lecomte du Nouy's "The Bearers of Evil Tidings," which Green saw in the Musée de Luxembourg—the same museum where Gide claimed to be unmoved by the nude statuary. Green became obsessed with the naked figures of two black slaves killed by the indignant pharaoh. The sight of them caused a "torment of unappeased hunger." "I remember very clearly that under a kind of hallucination, I fancied that one of the great brown bodies struck down by death really lay under my very eyes, and it seemed as though my whole being, soul and flesh, threw itself on him." We should probably not make too much of the racial element in Green's obsession, because, in contrast to Gide, it did not become an *idée fixe.* Nonetheless he suggests that his life might have turned out differently had it not been for the influence of Nouy's painting.

As a young man, Green seriously considered becoming a painter himself. His own childhood drawings explored the themes of sensuality and suffering to which he responded in Doré and Nouy. He recalls one particular drawing in which naked men and women were hounded and whipped by "a cruel torturer." He became convinced that they were being tortured precisely for their nakedness. In his "frenzied attention" he both identified with and somehow possessed the figures. But, as usual, he also felt that his drawings were inspired by the Devil. Revealingly, the drawings that so excited and terrified him had no genitals. They were the first manifestation of a lifelong aversion to "the shameful parts" of the body.

The sculptures in the Louvre, to which he was taken by his unsuspecting mother, completed his erotic education. His heart beat fiercely as he walked among the marble statues. He also experienced the precise physical sensation that always marks sexual arousal in the autobiography: a "burning feeling throughout the front part of my body." Nude statuary would continue to exert a powerful erotic pull well into his adulthood, notably in the form of a bronze Narcissus in Naples after the First World War and a plaster copy of Praxiteles' Hermes in the vestibule of Cabell Hall at the University of Virginia. Green's sexuality was both wildly expansive and strangely contained: he worked himself into a kind of delirium over his drawings and statues, even as he effaced or averted his eyes from their sexual organs. He also notes that his extravagant voyeurism never led him "to make dangerous gestures that might have enlightened me regarding myself." This is his prim and obfuscatory way of saying that it didn't lead to masturbation, which, after the experience with the bread knife, seems to have played only a minor role in his early life. His was an eroticism of the eye and the imagination, the exact opposite of André Gide's sexual materialism.

Green gives a detailed account of the temptations to which he was subjected at school. He divides his schoolmates into two categories: those he calls "angels of purity" and those who "seemed the incarnation of evil." In all his experiences he insists on his complete innocence, indeed on his inability even to comprehend the vile acts to which his wicked playmates invited him. His melancholy picture of schoolboy sex recalls the equally grim accounts of John Addington Symonds and J. R. Ackerley.

The first of the "bad boys" was a young Jew named Bernstein, in whose handsome insolence the mature author again sees the handiwork of the Devil. "One day," he reports, "when we were in the classroom waiting for the teacher, [Bernstein] stood near the professor's desk and, with a smile on his lips and sparkling eyes, he ripped his trousers open and exposed himself to us." As with his drawings, Green claims barely to have glanced at the boy's penis (which, as usual, he can't bring himself to name), focusing instead on his "diabolical" grimace. Later Bernstein propositioned Green, who, as always in such situations, failed to understand what was being suggested, although, illogically, he responded by calling Bernstein a "'Dirty Jew'" and got into a fight with him. When Green was thirteen, Bernstein took his hand and tried to drag him "behind the clumps of lilacs or some other spot." By then Bernstein (like the reader) had grown exasperated with Green's protestations of incomprehension and accused him of merely pretending to ignorance. But Green sticks to his guns: "I had literally no idea of what he wanted to do. A moment later, I had forgotten all about it."

Several other boys fall into the same depraved category. Sometimes Green mistakenly thought he had found an angel, only to suffer a painful disillusionment. One such was a young scout named Muselli, who "had the prettiest face imaginable, with great dark eyes and an angelic expression that attracted me to him." Green fell in love with the boy, not only on account of his looks but also "because he corresponded to the peculiar idea I had of purity." What a shock, then, when, on a hike, the angelic Muselli uttered "the coarsest words it has ever been given to me to hear, an artless invitation to pleasure of which I did not understand a syllable, but which remained forever in my memory." We might wonder how Green so easily committed to memory words that made no sense to him. In any event, he promptly moved Muselli from Column A to Column B. "'Impure,' I thought, 'he's impure!'" The experience would be repeated in the War with an American ambulance driver, from whose angelic mouth spewed an uninterrupted stream of profanity.

A gang of four bad boys reintroduced Green to masturbation and even succeeded in seducing him on a train. He begins to describe the experience—as one of the boys stretched a hand toward him—but quickly retreats into a huffy evasion: "I need not enter into details concerning what happened, the triteness of which had something about it that was both gloomy and mechanical." The episode lasted only three or four minutes and, again somewhat illogically, Green pretends to have forgotten it completely. He even denies that he had any sense of doing something wrong.

At the opposite end of the emotional spectrum were his disembodied romantic attachments. Chief among these was a blue-eyed adolescent, Frédéric, for whom, at fifteen, Green conceived "a passion as pure as it was violent." After a year and a half of watching the boy "with a thumping heart," Green still couldn't summon the courage to speak. But, in a gesture that would be unthinkable in an American context, his classmates explained the situation to Frédéric, who, "out of pure generosity," asked the astonished Julien to see him home from school. "It was plain that he had been told everything, and I felt myself dying with shameful joy." Green insists that he entertained no sexual hope, or even desire:

> What more did I want? I do not know. I did not have what are termed evil
> desires for anyone, and not for him any more than for another. Had I been able
> to tell him I loved him, I think a great load would have been lifted from me,
> but it would have been necessary to make me understand that I was in love, a
> fact of which I was completely ignorant. He knew it, I did not. All the boys in
> my class understood, and I was the only one not to see what was the matter.
> However that may be, he restored peace in me, out of sheer kindness of heart.

None of Green's professions of innocence is quite believable. Here, as elsewhere, we sense his determination to shape his account according to certain abstract principles, above all the separation of his experience into antithetical categories of spirit and flesh and his doctrinaire commitment to the notion that he understood nothing.

One of Green's school friends fitted into neither of his fixed categories: a boy named Philippe, who was homosexual like Green himself. The two had a brief sexual relationship, which is described in Green's typically hazy fashion but seems to have consisted of mutual masturbation. (Presumably Green is describing an orgasm when he speaks of "a terrifying joy that left me mute and trembling.") Convinced that they had damned themselves, he dragged the skeptical Philippe off to confession—an act of zealotry that, to his credit, Green relates as high comedy. Like his seduction by the four bad boys on the train, the episode makes it hard to credit his claim to sexual ignorance. But Philippe's real importance is that he became Green's confidant in matters of the heart (such as the Frédéric affair) and remained such into old age. In other words, he became what in American parlance would be called a "sister." But Green doesn't let the friendship with Philippe disturb the brittle certainties of his narrative. He continues to divide the world into angels and devils and to present himself as utterly uncomprehending.

The first volume of Green's autobiography culminates in the account of his conversion to Roman Catholicism when he was fifteen. To the secular reader, the conversion seems an obvious attempt to cope with his emerging homosexuality. It gave him a powerful set of intellectual and institutional weapons with which to combat his desires. It also held out the prospect, in the idea that he might have a vocation, of permanently removing him from the temptations that were becoming ever harder to ignore. The conversion occurred after his experiences with Bernstein, Muselli, and the gang of four, and while he was in the throes of his passion for Frédéric. It was also contemporaneous with being pursued by the last and most aggressive of the bad boys, Roger, who plied him with naughty books and took him on a tour of a neighborhood where hustlers hung out. The fiction of his innocence was clearly wearing thin, and Roman Catholicism provided him with an elaborate ritual of avoidance, a means of containing his impossible sexuality. As he says at one point, "I felt that the Church was erecting itself around me, like an invisible fortress that sheltered me from the world."

Because Green remained a Catholic, we can hardly expect him to embrace this demythologized reading of his conversion. Nonetheless his account supports such a reading by focusing on the way his religious instruction—with a Jesuit named Father Crété—intersected with his sexual and romantic concerns. Father Crété sensed that, despite his spectacular piety (Green devoured religious books and went to mass daily), he was highly vulnerable to temptation. Hence the priest's urging that he become a Benedictine monk, which would have established a *cordon sanitaire* between Green and the world of the flesh. Rather conventionally, Father Crété believed the problem was women, and Green wonders what the good father would have thought had he known the truth. But, against all plausibility, Green continues to insist that he remained ignorant of the untoward nature of his feelings.

Green would arrive at their conferences, his "heart wrung with sadness because of Frédéric," but Father Crété's inspired words soon caused "a far more mysterious love to blaze up again and tear me from this earth." The sublimation would hold until the next morning, when he again saw Frédéric in the *lycée* and his "heart turned heavy as stone." He blames the failure of communication less on himself than on Father Crété, because the priest never asked about homosexuality. The closest Father Crété came was to remark, one day, "'Just think, in *lycées* there are boys who do not even respect one another,'" a remark that, typically, Green pretends to have found entirely opaque: "Boys who respected one another . . . I imagined well-bred boys exchanging low bows, and others, mere louts, doing nothing of the kind." If Father Crété had posed a direct question—about Frédéric or Roger or any of the others—Green insists he would have answered "with complete honesty." Perhaps, but when he masturbated he studiously avoided Father Crété and sought out an anonymous confessor in another church—a stratagem that will be familiar to many a wayward Catholic—suggesting that he was less naive than he likes to pretend. Nevertheless, Catholicism served him well as a defense mechanism. Repeatedly in the course of his youth Green would return to the Church—to daily mass and regular confession—in an effort to bring his truculent desires under control, most notably after his grand romantic adventure in America.

GREEN SPENT THE TWO YEARS before his departure for the University of Virginia in the fall of 1919 as an ambulance driver, first for the American Field Service in the Argonne forest and then for the American Red Cross north of Venice, after which he served as an officer-cadet in the French Army during the post-War occupation of the Rhineland. His experiences in the military are the subject of the second volume of the autobiography. The War was in no sense an erotic watershed for him, as it was for J. R. Ackerley. He never got close to the fighting in the Argonne, and the Italian front was entirely quiet during his stay. Essentially he continued in the pattern he had established at school, dividing the men with whom he served into the pure and the impure, and maintaining, as best he could, his increasingly threadbare self-image as an innocent. The only new element was the peculiar exotic attraction exercised by the foreigners he met. As with Gide and Genet, national difference had a distinct sexual charm for Green. Rather too conveniently, however, the foreigners seemed to replicate the categories he had developed for classifying his schoolmates in France.

The enigmatic Americans are best represented by the son of a Presbyterian minister, Jack, who was a fellow ambulance driver in the Veneto. From the first Green experienced a baffling contradiction between Jack's angelic face and the filth that emerged from his mouth. Green "resolved" the contradiction, ingeniously, by obsessing about Jack while the young man was asleep (and hence silenced). But then a new contradiction emerged: despite his best efforts, Green found himself growing conscious of the sleeping angel's "long sinuous body." He takes the opportunity to restate the categorical opposition he drew between the face and the body, especially the genitals: "For me, humanity's shame consisted in those parts of the body immediately beneath the stomach, and I tried to pretend they did not exist, yet the beauty of a human face overwhelmed me." Nonetheless his imagination seemed to be slipping south, rebelling against his own high-minded distinction. Under these uncomfortable circumstances he had recourse to his familiar incomprehension. He insists that he "did not begin to understand" the meaning of the "chaste yet burning desire" he felt for his sleeping American.

The ignorance defense suffered a serious blow when Green became privy to two homosexual incidents among the men with whom he was stationed. In the first another driver confided in Green his intense feelings for his bunkmate, but Green didn't take the matter seriously, he claims, because both men were so ugly. He could not so easily deny the sexual nature of the second incident. At dinner one evening a "splendidly built" American, Jeffries, told of how he had indulged a request from an older Frenchman known as the Count. Green, as usual, is vague and censorious about the particulars, but one can reasonably deduce that the young man let himself be fellated:

> I heard [Jeffries] giving precise and revolting details, accompanied by laughs
> of mockery and embarrassment, of a story which horrified me, but which I nev-
> ertheless listened to very attentively. The evening before, yielding to the
> Count's pressing entreaties, he had given him what he wanted so badly. In this

way I learned how *that* was sometimes done and I immediately conceived a violent and extreme disgust for the act.

The Count was put on trial for his offense, and at the trial Green heard the disgusting act rehearsed by the prosecutor, in whose fury the mature author claims to detect an envious lust. The experience apparently penetrated Green's innocence, for it led him to undertake the first sexual initiative of his life. The day after the trial he found himself alone in an ambulance with Jeffries and, emboldened by the Devil, pressed himself "ever so slightly" against the strapping American, who, however, pushed him away. It was a modest beginning, but a beginning nevertheless.

The most important of the Americans was a sailor from New York, Ted Delano, whom Green met not at the front but in Paris, where Ted was courting one of his cousins and lived for a time in the Green home. Ted was to remain a presence—and a significant point of reference—in Green's life for some years after the War. He fell unambiguously into the "bad boy" tradition, and more than any other individual he came to represent the purely bodily attraction against which Green set the idealized figures with whom he fell in love, above all the young Virginian Mark, his central preoccupation in the third volume. Green's reaction to Ted was violently physical. Whenever he was in the sailor's presence he experienced the tell-tale symptoms of arousal that he had known since he first gazed at Lecomte du Nouy's "The Bearers of Evil Tidings": a burning sensation, a sudden tightening of his insides, an ache of "unbearable desire" through "the whole front part of my body." He struggled to keep himself from glancing at Ted's muscular neck and tough, stocky body, "indecently" clad in a tight sailor's uniform. But just as significant—or so Green contends—the minute Ted was out of sight he ceased to torment. Unlike J. R. Ackerley's sailors, in other words, he never became an obsession. In effect, Green's reaction fitted only too neatly into the ideological scheme by which he separated the flesh from the spirit. Ted had no existence in his mind, whereas the men he loved—like the *lycéen* Frédéric or, later, Mark—haunted his imagination day and night, even when separated from him by thousands of miles. He remained in the grips of a powerful metaphysical binarism.

Green made his first trip to Italy in the summer of 1916, while still in school, when he spent a month in Genoa with his sister Eleanor. Italy immediately established itself as a separate mental zone, where he was temporarily released from

his Catholicism. Like Gide, he associated the South with a kind of vestigial pa-
ganism and the suspension of inhibitions, although, in contrast to Gide, it symbolized for him not liberation but corruption. As nearly always happens when
Green recounts his sins, he can't entirely insulate himself from the text's sensual
incitements.

The Genoa trip exposed him to two particular provocations: Boccaccio's *De-*
cameron and the erotic engravings of Giulio Romano. The *Decameron* was the
first "wicked book" he had chanced on, and the blood rushed to his face every
time he came across the word "voluptuousness," even though he insists, after his
fashion, he "had no idea what was meant by voluptuousness." Visual images, as
usual, made an even stronger impression. Hence the delight mingled with horror
he felt contemplating the engravings of Romano, which "celebrated physical love
with a care and attention to minute detail that staggered" Green. He was inspired
to undertake an obscene drawing himself, though he did not, he assures us, abandon himself "to excesses of a physical nature" (i.e., masturbation). Back in France
he suffered paroxysms of guilty revulsion and recommitted himself to his "salvation."

While he was stationed for five months in the Veneto during the War, he did
not once go to church. This second Italian visit became the occasion for two
significant erotic developments: the discovery of his narcissism and his sole brush
with heterosexuality. One day in his room in Maestre he had "a sudden urge" to
look at himself naked in the mirror, something he had never done before. As if
making up for past neglect, he not only looked but actually embraced himself: "A
strange delight flowed through me as I observed that I was slim and well-built,
but the sensation only lasted for a second, for a sudden irresistible force threw
me forward and most of my body was now pressed against the mirror." The
moment reminded him of the statues that had so affected him in the Louvre years
before. Although he says nothing about his genitals, for once at least he doesn't
expressly disparage them. Still, the lesson he drew from kissing his image was
mixed: "I vaguely perceived that the flesh was not something to be despised, but
that instead it possessed some sort of divine protection that forbade desire."

In Genoa, on another visit to his sister, he took it into his head to do with
his brother-in-law's secretary, Lola, "what Boccaccio's characters did." The project seems to have been a purely literary inspiration, which Green plays mainly
for laughs. Just as he was telling Lola he wanted to see her undressed, they were
interrupted by the brother-in-law. Green was relieved and promptly returned to

his room, where he fell into a deep sleep, although he adds, unpersuasively, "It seems evident to me now that if I had had my way with Lola, I would probably have been a different person." On the rare occasions when heterosexual opportunities again presented themselves, he invariably gave up the chase with suspicious ease. Once he sold a signet ring to pay for a prostitute, but he ended up spending the money on a ticket to the theater and a few books. By his own admission, the notion that he was interested in women "remained purely cerebral." His heterosexual efforts did not measure up to even the modest standards set by Gide in North Africa. He was, if anything, more exclusively homosexual than his great predecessor.

Green visited Italy again on his way to America. At the Museo Nazionale in Naples he had another of his disturbing confrontations with the male nude. In this instance it was a room filled with Pompeian bronze figures, and a statue of Narcissus in particular. Delighted yet terrified, he paced around the bronze, his anxiety contained only by the happy fact that "the male attributes were reduced to the minimum and were no more than a very stylized and idealized image of a part of the body that horrified me." The Devil again put in an appearance, disguised now as a warden who sounds uncannily like the Mephistophelean character in Thomas Mann's *Death in Venice:* "Of all the encounters I have ever had on this earth, my meeting with this man was certainly the most sinister. . . . He greeted me and asked what the *signorino* thought of the statue. *Bellissima, no?"* For a mere trifle the Satanic warden arranged to have a copy of "the infernal statue" shipped to Green in America, where it haunted him throughout his stay. He concludes the episode with a by-now familiar refrain: had it not been for this menacing encounter, he writes, "the course of my life might have been different."

During his occupation duty in the Rhineland Green had a mysterious relationship with a figure he refers to only as "the fair-haired cadet." The cadet was also a member of the French army, but, because they were isolated, with two older officers, in the German village of Oberlinxweiler, a somewhat exotic aura hangs about the affair. Green's account is even more obscure and unforthcoming than usual, making it hard to interpret. Nonetheless, it is by far the longest episode in the second volume, suggesting its importance for him. Arguably its murkiness is meant to convey his own incomprehension at the time. It is set against his more or less contemporaneous encounter with the provocative sailor Ted, creating the impression that the cadet belonged to the opposing category of ethereal, Platonic loves represented later by the Virginian Mark. At the same time there is an unmistakable physical current in the relationship: the story turns on the question of whether Green would sleep in the same room, indeed in the same bed, with the cadet—a classic homosexual predicament that will recur at the end of the Mark episode—and it culminates in a frankly erotic wrestling match, yet another familiar trope in gay autobiographies. In its confusion, ambivalence, and evasiveness it is the archetypal Greenian experience.

The shadowy older officers seem to have inherited the Satanic role. Enchanted by the young cadet, they praised his looks to Green and even conspired to get the two into the sack together. At first Green was indifferent: when he was offered a room with the cadet, he said he preferred to sleep alone. The disappointed cadet "turned away sharply," and the following day the officer who had made the proposal swore at Green "in an incredibly coarse way." But the notion must have festered in his unconscious, because a little later, when he found himself lodged in the same room with the cadet, he had what he calls the "strangest" experience of his youth: "Having turned off the light, I stood barefoot and motionless in the darkness, and I suddenly felt tempted to jump into the cadet's bed. I had no idea where this urge came from and, no doubt, that was why I did not give way to it." Later on he attributed the idea to the Devil.

In another suggestive episode he and the cadet were together with two women. At one level the scene functions to confirm the nominal heterosexuality of the cadet, who was supposedly "sick with desire" for another man's wife. But, as often happens in such pairings, the real energy is homosexual—or at least homosocial. "Who were these women and what on earth was I doing there?" Green asks. "I don't know the answers to these questions, but the fact is that I was in a room lit only by the light of the moon, talking to one of the girls while my friend was kissing the other. What a strange scene." Green was clearly pretending, and he implies that the same may have been true of the cadet. When Green saw him later in Paris and disingenuously proposed that they "have some fun" with women, the cadet called his bluff, replying with a melancholy smile, "'I preferred you the way you were in Germany.'"

As tensions built up on both sides, the relationship turned hostile. But the cadet's growing anger made him only more attractive to Green, who, as we recall, had associated arousal with violence since childhood. "I don't know who began the quarrel," he writes, "but I do remember that my friend looked even more handsome than usual, for he was one of those boys whose beauty is only revealed gradually." Matters came to head in their wrestling match, whose eroticism Green makes no effort to hide:

> His steely body tossed and turned against mine and he tried to punch me in the face, but I had no difficulty pinning both of his arms and in a sort of ecstasy I realized I could do whatever I wanted with him. I slowly pushed him backwards, and we both lost our balance and fell down together, he with his back to the ground in such a way that his harder fall rather cushioned mine, and I found myself stretched bodily on top of him.

The episode made such a powerful impression on Green that he later reproduced variations on it in his novel *Moira* and his play *Sud*. It was as close as he came to a sexual encounter until he stepped onto the streets of Paris one night after his three years in the American South. During his stint in Germany he had ceased practicing his religion. But when he got back to France he subjected himself once again to a renewed burst of piety, as if he were making amends for his transgressions, however ambiguous, with the handsome blond cadet.

GREEN ACCEPTED AN INVITATION from his maternal uncle Walter Hartridge to attend the University of Virginia in the fall of 1919. His decision to go to the American South was overdetermined. In the first instance he was returning to the ancestral home about which his mother had spoken with such melancholy pride throughout his childhood. At some deep psychological level it may even have been a return to the womb, so intimately was the South associated with his mother's memory. There was also an affinity between the defeated Confederacy and Green's sense of himself as an outsider—and ultimately as a homosexual. He would eventually devote more than a dozen of his books to the South, particularly during the Civil War era, and in his play *Sud* the sexual connection is made explicit. At a metaphorical level, finally, the South became for him a kind of imaginary Greece, populated by living embodiments of the statues he had admired in the Louvre. Green first drew this association when he went to the American Embassy in Paris to get his passport and there encountered a sentry whose "perfect features . . . reminded one of the curly-headed gods of Greek art." At the University he would discover that the classical world had an ambiguous reputation.

The three years in America represented a watershed in Green's life, and his account of them in the third volume forms the most compelling segment of the autobiography. These were the years in which he lost his innocence, although not his virginity. The discovery of his sexual identity was a complex process in which personal relationships intersected richly with intellectual influences. The most important of the former was his chaste romance with the young man he calls Mark S. Completing for Green's attention was a large roster of intensely physical creatures, heirs to the randy *lycéens* and the sailor Ted Delano, who raised Green's long-standing opposition between the spirit and the flesh, love and desire, to a yet more excruciating pitch. Intellectually the task of enlightenment was assumed by the great turn-of-the-century European sexologists, above all Havelock Ellis, who play a more prominent role in Green's story than they do in any other autobiography examined in this book. The antinomies that had bedeviled Green were not overcome—they never would be—but the young man who sailed home to France in 1922 was a dramatically changed person. It was only a matter of time before he made a no less dramatic change in his life.

The notion that the American South was somehow a reincarnation of ancient Greece found architectural expression in Thomas Jefferson's beautiful university buildings. It was also implied by the large plaster cast of Praxiteles' Hermes, which disturbed Green whenever he passed it in Cabell Hall. In a perverse way even the bronze Narcissus, sent by the demonic warden in Naples and ensconced in his aunt's home in Savannah, contributed to the fanciful equation. But above all Green's imaginary construction was inspired by the abundance of exquisitely handsome young Southern gentlemen he met on the campus: "It was as if the inhabitants of Mount Olympus (wearing jackets) were living among us. . . . The curly-haired gods of a vanished world dwelt here beneath the trees and porticos of the University." As with John Addington Symonds and so many other modern homosexuals, the classical world became for Green a significant resource for imagining his erotic identity.

The classical connection, in all its ambiguity, was made explicit by Green's Latin teacher. Coming to a passage in Virgil about frolicking shepherds, Mr. Fitzhugh delivered a brief speech, every syllable of which Green claims to have remembered: "'Gentlemen, it seems pointless for me to disguise the meaning of this passage: we are dealing here with the shame of Antiquity, by which I mean boy-love.'" It was a moment of blinding self-revelation: "I realized that the strange passion of which Virgil spoke resided also in me. . . . I bore the shame of Antiquity." We might wonder why the teacher's remark effected such a sudden illumination when his own concrete experiences—whether with the bad boys in school, or Philippe, or Jeffries, or the blond cadet—had left him entirely in the dark. But Green insists on his epiphany. He also reveals that he remained under a curious misapprehension: he convinced himself that he alone among living mortals suffered from the shame of Antiquity. "Between me and these generations that had disappeared over twenty centuries ago there was this extraordinary link," he concluded. "Whatever it was that had drawn me to Frédéric at the *lycée* was nothing else than this same passion which no one had spoken of for two thousand years and which had disappeared from the face of the earth." Enlightenment brought new error in its wake. One wonders if anyone's progress toward self-knowledge was ever more tortuous.

In general Catholicism loosened its grip on Green during his American sojourn. But following the Virgil episode it enjoyed one of its periodic revivals, as Green took to rising at six in the morning in order to attend daily mass. Still, the Church no longer provided the sure protection it had when he returned to it after his adventures in Italy and Germany. On the contrary, temptation now reared its ugly head even within the sacred walls: at mass he found himself unable to keep his eyes off a dark-haired boy a few pews away. His mind drifted from his prayers, and he received communion "with a troubled conscience."

Green's long account of his infatuation with his fellow undergraduate Mark S. is the most remarkable achievement of the autobiography. He conveys a vivid impression of the sort of crazed infatuation (to which repressed homosexuals are peculiarly vulnerable) that manages to sustain itself for years on sheer hope, without any evidence that the passion is reciprocated, without even speaking to the beloved, indeed without a clear idea of one's own motives. The infatuation sprang instantly to life when, after the first Christmas break, the young man rushed past him on campus. Green experienced a feeling that he claims was unknown to him until then, though it resembled what he had earlier felt for Frédéric. "Because of someone I had seen for only three or four seconds, I was now enslaved," he declares. But, in contrast to the situation with Frédéric, Green was able to give the feeling a name: without any hesitation he called it love. One suspects that his exposure to Virgil in Latin class may have been the source of this sudden conceptual clarity.

From the start Green was fixated on Mark's face, and his face alone. Over and over the text celebrates the young man's rosy cheeks, his sparkling black eyes, and his full red lips. Mark seems to have had no existence for Green below the neck. He was heir to the tradition of bodiless angels who inspired a spiritual passion that Green insists had nothing to do with desire. One might say that Green exactly inverts Gide's formula: where, in his encounter with Mohammed, Gide speaks of desire without love, Green speaks here of love without desire. Its only somatic effect was "a feeling of pain in the middle of my chest," which, presumably, he distinguished categorically from the burning sensation along the front of his body that signaled arousal. When he tried to imagine what he wanted to do with the young man, he pictured them embracing one another, perhaps kissing chastely. But the centerpiece of his fantasy remained a purely verbal event: he would tell Mark that he loved him. Because "this violent, all-embracing love" was so pure, he felt no need to mention it in confession.

Green contrived opportunities to pass Mark in the galleries and corridors of the University. He virtually set up camp on the lawn outside the young man's room, hanging about for hours on end in the hope of catching a glimpse of him, at one point even stealing up and planting a kiss on his door. Eventually Green took to discussing his obsession with a confidant, who sensibly urged him to speak to the boy. So great was his passion, and so fierce were his inhibitions, that he was able to sustain the "relationship" on an entirely imaginary plane for more than two years. Not even John Addington Symonds—who courted his first chorister, Willie, a year before attempting a kiss—managed this kind of discipline.

Green finally worked up the courage to introduce himself, though not until the spring of 1922, leaving only a few short months before his departure for France at the end of the academic year. He knocked on Mark's door and was cordially received. The opening exchange sounds rather improbable ("'I've been wanting to see you for a long time.' 'You shouldn't have waited so long.'"), but soon they were meeting daily for extended conversations, either in Mark's room or on spring walks about the campus. To his delight, Green discovered that Mark was much like himself: he too was a puritan, appalled by the debauchery of their fellow students. Before long Mark's remarkable indulgence for his company as well as their shared prejudices gave rise to the hopeful fantasy that the shy young man just might entertain similar romantic feelings, despite the unwelcome news that he had once loved a hometown girl who died. At first the idea strikes the reader as a classic example of homosexual self-delusion, but Mark's enormous tolerance for their vapid discussions and his willingness to sit still while Green gazed on him with "a look of adoration" make us wonder if it was so far-fetched after all. Green endlessly mulled over whether he should declare himself but concluded that he preferred to stay in doubt rather than risk disappointment.

The story has an epilogue: after Green's return to Paris, Mark came to visit in the summer of 1923. Green's account of the visit focuses on two incidents. The first seems to contradict his oft-repeated disclaimers about wanting Mark sexually. On a trip to Rouen there was an ambiguous replay of Green's experience with the blond cadet when they were faced with the prospect of sleeping in the same bed: "Mark undressed and I averted my gaze. A moment later, we were lying next to each other in the darkness. Some time went by. He then told me not to be surprised at what he was about to do, jumped out of bed, switched on the light, threw his pillow and a few cushions on the floor, and then lay down on his improvised bed." Green tells the story again in the last volume of the autobiography, where he insists that he wanted nothing more than to spend the night innocently at Mark's side. But we get the unmistakable impression that his shopworn distinctions were on the verge of collapse. In an unusual moment of lucidity he admits that his wish to touch Mark's rosy cheeks and mahogany hair probably disguised "secret, consuming yearnings."

In the second incident (also recounted in both the third and fourth volumes) he almost made the declaration from which he had shrunk in Virginia. They were walking along the Seine toward the Pont-Royal:

"There's something very important I want to say to you, Mark."
"Very well, I'm listening."
But the simple words stuck in my throat and I was unable to articulate them. A minute or two later, on the other side of the bridge, I told Mark: "I'm sorry, I can't."
He squeezed my arm lightly and said: "I understand very well."
Yet again, I had considered the risk of losing his affection forever too great a risk.

In the fourth volume Green gives the exchange a more optimistic spin, interpreting Mark's response to mean that he had understood the situation from the moment Green knocked on his door at the University. Later, however, he concludes that Mark's sexual anxieties related not to homosexuality but to syphilis. In any event, Green remains defiantly proud of a relationship that, because it was unfulfilled, was entirely compatible with his religious convictions. "Throughout the sadness of my student life," he concludes, "it shines like a ray of sunshine through

the lowering clouds. No man would dare reproach me for it." Despite its profound repression, Green's American romance registers as one of the great loves
in the gay autobiographical tradition.

Set opposite the chaste infatuation with Mark were a large number of sexually tempting creatures—stunning undergraduates, handsome adolescent cousins, and provocative strangers glimpsed on the street. They were not categorically different from their forebears at the *lycée* or in the military, but in America
they seemed to proliferate with alarming abandon. Green also found it ever
harder to ignore the intense physical response these men caused—"a tightening
of the intestines as if someone had punched me in the stomach." Repeatedly the
text sets up an explicit contrast between the carnal figures and the disembodied
Mark. But it also gives a sense of Green's growing, if reluctant, awareness that
the two realms were not in fact unrelated to one another. A kind of dialectical or
antiphonal pattern emerges. The siren figures also had their part to play in the
drama of his emerging sexual identity.

A sailor Green saw during his first summer vacation, which he spent with
relatives in Georgia, best represents the increasing power these figures exercised
on his imagination. No words were exchanged. Rather, the sailor existed as pure
body, a nude statue come to life: "When he crossed the space lit by the nearest
street-lamp, he looked as though he might have been a silver statue, and so tightly
was his spotless uniform moulded to his body that it was as if he were naked."
At the same time Green dimly sensed the connection between his raw sexual
response and the "secret" love that he had learned about in Latin class and that
had found its modern expression in his devotion to Mark. He also explicitly
linked the Savannah sailor not only to his obvious predecessor, Ted Delano, but
also to the naked slaves in Lecomte du Nouy's "The Bearers of Evil Tidings."
The latter association was telling, because when Green tried to imagine what he
wanted to do with the sailor or his various replicas, obscurely sadomasochistic
images would occur to him—"unknown pleasures where sweetness mingled
with ferocity."

Alongside the ethereal Mark and the erotic figures like the Georgia sailor,
Green's Southern universe contained a third category of men who played a role
in his sentimental education: a group of "sisters," heirs to his Parisian friend
Philippe. The portrait of them is hardly flattering. Invariably they are described
as ugly and affected. They were thus light-years removed from either the handsome, salubrious Mark or the beguiling if dangerous sailor-types. As was the case

for J. R. Ackerley, the queer world struck Green as both unerotic and dissolute. One searches the pages of *Jeunes années* in vain for even the faintest hint of homosexual solidarity.

The most prominent of these sisterly figures was an unattractive and sharp-tongued boy with the doubtlessly significant name of Nick (the Devil continued his work in Virginia). Nick shocked Green with lurid accounts of watching his boyfriend take baths. But his central function was to introduce Green to the homosexual classics, notably, Edward Carpenter's *Love's Coming of Age* and John Addington Symonds's two homophile pamphlets. Even more important were the writings of Havelock Ellis. The crucial feature of Ellis's books—which explains the profound influence they exercised not just on Green but on so many of his generation—was that they described sexual acts without euphemism. They thus shattered his pretension to sexual ignorance, which had served him so long as a defense mechanism. The books, he writes, spoke "a painful and precise truth that avoided all hypocrisy and substituted allusions with facts that were so crude I stood up in amazement." Not surprisingly, Green's reaction to this sort of candor was ambivalent, because it put an end to romanticism. "Where were Romeo and Juliet?" he asks forlornly. But the brutal empirical reality was not to be gainsaid. "They were facts, no more, no less. Discuss them as one might, they remained where they were, like objects, like mountains, foolish perhaps, but real."

Naturally, the volume of Ellis's *Studies on the Psychology of Sex* that made the deepest impression was the one treating homosexuality, *Sexual Inversion*. As with most readers of this work, Green responded less to Ellis's conceptual ruminations than to the case histories at the book's end. Green read them with intense resistance, but he could not fail to see how closely they described his own inchoate desires. They demolished the illusion that he was the sole modern inheritor of the shame of the Antiquity.

In spite of the categorical distinction he had established between the spirit and the flesh, he could not separate the thoughts inspired by Ellis's case histories from his feelings for Mark. The book unleashed a "maelstrom of fantastical dreams in which Mark's face kept reappearing." He fought to keep the two realms hermetically sealed, but by the time of his departure for France in summer 1922 the task had become Herculean. The disparate components of his American experience—the spiritual love for Mark, the cravings he felt for the various god-like physical specimens, and the sisterly ministrations that introduced him to the writings of Ellis—were threatening to converge. And while Green would never

achieve a fully coherent identity, the old dispensation, in which the separate
strands of his existence were kept isolated from one another, had reached the end
of its useful life.

⊘ AFTER THE EMOTIONAL EXUBERANCE and high drama of the Green's years in
the South, the last volume of the autobiography comes as a letdown. In part the
deflation stems from the almost mechanical inevitability with which Green took
to the Parisian streets less than a year after his return. But above all it reflects his
unremittingly dreary portrait of the sexual regimen he adopted. His story contains not even a glimmer of the elation with which gay autobiographers have
traditionally recounted their first homosexual experiences. And because he remains maddeningly vague about everything associated with the body, his escapades also make for dull reading. J. R. Ackerley (who was a little older than
Green and writing at just about the same time) had a similarly disabused attitude
toward his sexual life, but Ackerley gives an unforgettably precise and vivid description of his grueling labors. Green's talent is for retailing the strategies and
illusions of erotic denial; he is an uncongenial guide to the mysteries of fulfillment.

Inexplicably, after dinner one night in March 1923, he put away his book and
announced to his family, "'I'm going out.'" He confidently assigns responsibility
for his decision not to the irresistible power of instinct but to the Devil: "I must
have been guided," he insists, "for the fact remains in my memory that I was
going straight to where I would have the best chance of meeting someone." The
someone he met, beneath the lamplights near the Trocadero, was about as far
removed as imaginable from the Greek gods of his dreams. The man was in fact
"startlingly ugly," yet Green nonetheless succumbed, as he says, "like an animal
snared by a hunter."

He immediately sank into a routine. His days were spent studying and writing, but every night, after dinner, he would return to the Trocadero (or another
well-known cruising area) in order to repeat some trivial variation on that first
experience. This became the pattern of his life for the next decade and a half—
until his definitive return to Catholicism in 1939. He would take his pleasure
quickly and then, repulsed, flee home, "unable to rest until I had washed, rubbed
and soaped myself not once but ten times in our bathroom." He gives the impression that he never met anyone young and attractive like himself, or anyone he
might have been interested in seeing more than once. All of his pick-ups re-

minded him of characters out of Hieronymus Bosch. Indeed, he came to think of his sexual predations not as the road to hell but as hell itself. "At the deepest level of reality," he laments, "voluptuous sensuality was nothing more than the punishment that is to come, as far as we can know it in this world."

Green suffered periodic revolts against his vicious regime. In a mood of blackest despair he would revive the practice of attending daily mass. He was especially drawn to a neighboring convent chapel, where the White Sisters, symbols of purity, venerated the Blessed Sacrament. As the nuns sang the liturgy, he felt himself transported to a gothic past where he was "sheltered from the modern world." During 1924 his studious mornings were devoted to writing his first published work, the pamphlet in which he attacked modern Catholicism for its moral flabbiness and called for a return to the rigors of the Counterreformation. He was fully aware of the bizarre contradiction into which he had fallen. The pamphlet, he knew, was really an attack on himself. "'This is to do with you,'" he told himself. "'Shame on you who preach to others and behave disreputably in the streets.'"

Toward the end of 1924, at a literary salon attended by François Mauriac and Anna de Noailles, Green met a young man whose handsome face immediately captured his heart. The account is sketchy, but "Robert" (the journalist Robert de Saint-James) seems to have moved into Green's home and become his "companion." Green compares his feelings for Robert to those he had earlier entertained for Mark: he was in love but felt no desire. In other words, the relationship did not begin in sexual attraction and then subside into friendship (a common enough experience, familiar to us in the loves of Goldsworthy Lowes Dickinson). Rather, it appears to have been asexual from the start and to have made no dent in Green's nightly forays. Several years later the two had a heart-to-heart in which they confessed their common sexual practices. The confession led to a thoroughly modern agreement to carry on as before, but candidly: "Our love was secure as long as we maintained a respect for the truth between ourselves, and we promised never to conceal anything from each other, a promise that was kept to the letter." Among the disappointments of Green's last volume is his failure say anything about the relationship beyond this liberal cliché.

The concluding section Green added to the two-volume edition of the autobiography in 1984 centers on a trip he and Robert took to Hamburg and Berlin in the summer of 1929—as it happens, at just the moment when Stephen Spender and Christopher Isherwood were arriving in those two German cities to undertake the liberating adventures described in *World within World* and *Christopher and His Kind*. In Hamburg, like Spender, Green discovered a universe of beautiful sun-bleached youths, a kind of Aryan paradise. And in Berlin, like Isherwood, Green debauched himself in the city's homosexual underworld. But where Isherwood's account is memorably circumstantial, Green, typically, falls back on censorious generalizations. He was relieved to escape from "the deafening gaiety" of Berlin to "the true Germany" of Weimar, Goethe's city of poetry and culture. Coming at the end of Green's long story, the opposition between fleshly Berlin and spiritual Weimar is in fact the last version of the inveterate dualism through which he has interpreted his experience from the start. God and Devil, love and desire, face and body, Weimar and Berlin—the recurrent dyads are all symbols of his chronic inability to find peace with his sexuality. By comparison the divisions that troubled André Gide's life seem almost reasonable.

The most arresting feature of *Jeunes années* is Green's profound revulsion from his own desires. The autobiography abounds with examples of erotically charged situations but refuses to take pleasure in any of them. Much of the interest in his story lies in the rituals of avoidance, the mental gymnastics, with which he tries to cope with his contradictory impulses. As we will see, a similar complex—of intense desire contradicted by no less intense aversion—also provides the central drama in Andrew Tobias's *The Best Little Boy in the World*. But the American text is unencumbered by the theological abstractions with which Green tries to explain his predicament. Instead, in common with the English autobiographers we have already examined, Tobias treats his hang-ups, like his desires, as purely human phenomena, neither more nor less mysterious than anything else in life. Tobias's account, in other words, is innocent of the philosophical impulse that links Green to Gide and Genet in a shared intellectual tradition. However different the doctrines to which the three French autobiographers are addicted, they remain, in their various ways, prisoners of abstraction.

5

TWO AMERICAN DIARISTS

Jeb Alexander

and

Donald Vining

∞ COMPARED TO THE FRENCH and British, Americans came late to gay autobiography. I have been able to discover none published before the 1970s, half a century after André Gide's *Si le grain ne meurt.* In the last decade or so, as if to make up for previous neglect, gay autobiographies have flooded the American market. Some of them, like Greg Louganis's *Breaking the Surface,* have even becoming best-sellers. The vast majority of the recent books tell the same story: they are coming-out narratives, accounts of escape from the closet, set against the background of the Gay Liberation movement. Arguably they represent a homosexual variation on one of the most venerable autobiographical topoi, from St. Augustine to Malcolm X: the transformation of the old man into the new. In the next chapter I will consider three representative specimens of the genre, Andrew Tobias's *The Best Little Boy in the World* (published pseudonymously in 1973), Martin Duberman's *Cures* (1991), and Paul Monette's *Becoming a Man* (1992), all of which offer particularly rich explorations of the closet and its agonies.

But what can we say about the self-representation of gay Americans before the recent autobiographical torrent? In particular how did gay Americans who came of age in the first half of the twentieth century register their life experience? The men I have in mind were rough contemporaries of the British and French autobiographers who have been our primary concern up to now—the generation of J. R. Ackerley (b. 1896), Julien Green (b. 1900), Christopher Isherwood (b. 1904), Quentin Crisp (b. 1908), Stephen Spender (b. 1909), and Jean Genet (b. 1910). One would like to have access the stories of these Americans, not just for their own sake but also for the light they might shed on the coming-out narratives of more recent vintage.

In the absence of gay autobiographies from the first half of the century, I have turned to an alternative source, namely, diaries. Admittedly this choice introduces a certain methodological strain, because diaries are not written with the same interpretive intent or architectural control as autobiographies. If handled with care, however, diaries can be read as proto-autobiographies. Even the most circumstantial diarist occasionally steps back from his quotidian account to reflect on the larger meaning of his life. Moreover diaries themselves often serve as the autobiographer's raw material: *Christopher and His Kind* is closely based on (and often quotes from) Isherwood's diaries of the 1930s, just as Martin Duberman's diary supplies *Cures* with its most memorable episodes. The recourse to diaries may violate the generic purity of my study, but I regard it as a legitimate way to stretch the chronological boundaries of the American story, much as the unpublished memoirs of John Addington Symonds and Goldsworthy Lowes Dickinson allowed me to add several decades the British story.

I turned up four diaries that seemed suitable candidates for analysis. The two I finally excluded were those of the novelist Glenway Wescott (1901–1987) and the composer Ned Rorem (1923–). The disadvantage of Rorem's *Paris Diary* and *New York Diary*—which caused a sensation when they appeared in the mid-1960s—is that they begin too late and were published too soon. Rorem's earliest entry dates from 1951, thus giving us no purchase on the first half of the century, and the account of his sexual life is much less full and candid than that in diaries written earlier but published later. Indeed, Rorem often falls back on the strategies of disguise perfected by Christopher Isherwood, decades before, in *Lions and Shadows*. Glenway Wescott's journals from 1937 to 1955, released three years after his death under the title *Continual Lessons,* are a more useful document for my purposes, both because of their sexual frankness and because their main theme is the writer's block Wescott suffered when he tried to turn his homosexual experience into fiction. But Wescott's journals begin when he was already in his late thirties and had been in a settled (if complex) relationship for nearly two decades. They thus give no account of his homosexual coming of age, the subject that lies at the heart of the classic gay autobiographies.

By contrast, the diaries of Jeb Alexander[1] (1899–1965) and Donald Vining (1917–1998) offer both the historical reach and the detailed attention to formative sexual experiences I was looking for. Jeb Alexander, who spent his adult life as a government clerk in Washington, D.C., kept a diary from 1912 until within a year of his death. In 1993 his niece Ina Russell (to whom the fifty hand-written volumes had been entrusted) transcribed and published a selection of the diary from the years 1918 to 1945. Donald Vining, who grew up in Pennsylvania and moved to New York City in 1942, kept a diary, on a daily basis, from 1933. In 1979 Vining himself began publishing condensed versions of the text under the title *A Gay Diary*. The fifth volume, which carries the story down to 1982, appeared in 1993. In my analysis I have focused on Vining's account of his life before 1950, when he turned thirty-three.

Jeb Alexander and Donald Vining invite comparison because, while their lives were in many respects similar, they reacted to their homosexual circumstances so differently. Neither man can be considered an artist or intellectual in the accomplished sense of the other figures examined in this book. Rather, both worked as bureaucrats—Alexander in the federal government, Vining, from 1950, in the Development Office of Columbia University. But both thought of themselves as destined for a literary career, and Vining, who labored hard to realize his ambition, actually succeeded in publishing a number of stories and one-act plays. In keeping with their

1. "Jeb Alexander" is a pseudonym given to the author by the diaries' editor, his niece Ina Russell.

imagined identity, both devoted themselves assiduously to culture—to classical music, playgoing, high-brow reading, and European travel. Significantly, many of their friends regarded them as snobs. In an important sense, moreover, the diaries themselves vindicate both men's literary aspirations: they are works of phenomenal diligence, vigorously and even eloquently written. At their best they are insightful, funny, and often affecting. Thus, despite their humble careers and relative obscurity, Alexander and Vining are not so far removed from the more celebrated gay autobiographers as first seems to be the case.

There are also striking parallels in Alexander's and Vining's lives as homosexuals. Some of these parallels might appear relatively trivial, such as the fact that they both met most of their sexual partners through cruising—Alexander in Lafayette Square (directly across from the White House), Vining in Central Park—or that both lived or worked for a number of years in Y.M.C.A.'s, which in Washington and New York, as elsewhere, were havens for gay men. More important, they had to deal with similar experiences of oppression, in the form of police surveillance and arrest, and they were involved in similar efforts to negotiate the burden of secrecy. In their twenties they became enmeshed in a circle of gay friends whose lives provide the diaries with some of their most colorful vignettes. These friends gave them a sense of community and contributed to Alexander's and Vining's evolving gay identity, but they were also a source of tension, not only because they introduced romantic strains but also because their behavior sometimes threatened the compromise between visibility and circumspection both men favored. Finally, both men's lives came to focus on a central love affair, and the diaries are much preoccupied with establishing the boundaries between the categories of lover and sexual partner, or lover and friend.

Despite these similarities, Alexander and Vining give radically opposite accounts of their experience. Jeb Alexander's diary narrates a descent into loneliness, despair, and drunken inertia, while Donald Vining's moves in the direction of ever greater assurance, contentment, and activity. On the surface there seems to have been little obvious difference in their circumstances. To be sure, Alexander was nearly two decades older than Vining, and Washington's gay subculture in the 1920s was not as robust as New York's in the 1940s. Yet George Chauncey has argued, in *Gay New York,* that American society grew more homophobic during precisely the years when Vining flourished—from which one might deduce that Alexander actually enjoyed an environmental advantage.[2] Apparently the same circumstances that defeated Alexander only spurred Vining on to greater combativeness. Unhelpful as it might seem, we are thrown back on the mysteries of character. Indeed, Alexander was a man of such fecklessness that he might well have been undone by life even if he had not been a homosexual. The important point is that Alexander's and Vining's diaries

2. In the 1930s, according to Chauncey, "a powerful campaign to render gay men and lesbians invisible—to exclude them from the public sphere—quickly gained momentum. . . . Never before had gay life been subject to such extensive legal regulation." *Gay New York* (New York, 1994), pp. 331, 356.

show us, in often riveting detail, two very different responses to the situation in which American homosexuals found themselves in the years before the first stirrings of Gay Liberation.

In what follows I have attempted to construct (and analyze) the autobiographies that Jeb Alexander and Donald Vining might have written had they converted their diaries into life narratives before midcentury. As will be evident, I am persuaded that they would have told dramatically dissimilar stories, again confirming my thesis of the great variety of modern gay experience as reflected in the autobiographical record. Yet, different as they are from one another, Alexander's and Vining's stories are even further removed from the coming-out narratives that have dominated American gay autobiography in the past three decades. They belong to a vanished sexual and political dispensation.

Jeb Alexander and C. C. Dasham in Atlantic City, July 24, 1927.

Jeb and Dash

HE JEB ALEXANDER WE MEET in the published diary had just graduated from high school and was about to leave for college. The earliest entries reveal certain distinctive—and enduring—features of his personality, notably his timorousness and uncertain hold on reality. Homosexuality is never mentioned or even alluded to, but we sense that it had already established itself as a kind of subtext in the author's mind.

Alexander was a terrified young man. An unspecified anxiety made him cling to the familiar artifacts and routines of his middle-class home in suburban Washington and to dread any change in his "quiet life." He was particularly fearful of going off to college and the burden of initiative it would entail. Yet his situation at home was anything but happy. His parents, especially his stepmother, assailed him for his passivity and sloth. For both parent and child, his indolence not only threatened failure in the world but, more fundamentally, impugned his manliness. It betrayed an inner femininity. As his stepmother said, "'Jeb can remain a sissy all his life.'" He reacted to these assaults by withdrawing into silent agony. He also suffered from a horror of conspicuousness—of being noticed or spoken of. Overhearing his parents complain about his tendency to run off to the movies, he wails, "Oh, why can't they stop talking about me." The desire to be invisible, which would so profoundly shape his life as a homosexual, was already a fixture of his psychic constitution even as a teenager.

Jeb and Dash: A Diary of Gay Life, 1918–1945, ed. Ina Russell (Boston, 1993). In publishing her edition Ina Russell concentrated on Alexander's homosexual life and above all its central romantic episode, his love affair with C. C. Dasham. To protect their anonymity (and that of their relatives), she has given most of the figures in the book, including the author, pseudonyms. She also eliminated all entries from 1912 to 1917 and after 1945, the former because they contained "nothing new" (p. 4), the latter because Alexander had fallen into the drunken and dispirited routine of his final two decades; in a late entry he himself refers to "the nothingness of the last eighteen years" (p. 4).

As if to compensate for his defeats, real and imagined, Alexander escaped into fantasy. At first these fantasies were not erotic—at least he records none—although they would become such in time. Rather, he dreamed of literary fame. Donald Vining also hoped to become a writer, but Vining always aimed at realistic targets—a marketable short story or radio play. By contrast, Alexander's imaginings were from the start grandiose. "At the Library of Congress today," he reports, "I read James Joyce's *A Portrait of the Artist as Young Man*. I am going to write a novel some day based on my own life from earliest youth in the manner of *A Portrait*." Instead of taking concrete steps toward actually writing or training himself as a writer, he preferred to daydream of hobnobbing with his literary brethren: "Had I only with me James Joyce in 1900 and Robert Louis Stevenson in 1868, the two of them also eighteen years old, what kindred fellows should we be!" He was aware of his own weakness. "I am a headless dreamer," he confesses, "a drifter, oblivious of the gathering clouds of tomorrow." The combination of anxious inertia and exaggerated visions of glory hardly prepared him to deal effectively with his sexual predicament. On the contrary, it was formula for disaster.

Alexander attended Washington and Lee University, in Lexington, Virginia, during the same years that Julien Green was an undergraduate at the University of Virginia, just a few miles to the east in Charlottesville. Although he was an indifferent student and left without a degree, the years at college were as much of a watershed in his erotic life as they were in Green's. As with Green, moreover, the decisive events occurred largely in his imagination. His "Mark" was a fellow undergraduate from Mississippi, C. C. Dasham ("Dash"), whose appearance on the horizon, like Mark's, seemed to him almost a divine intervention. When, on October 28, 1918, Alexander first caught sight of the "pale-eyed freshman," he recorded, "The boy looked like a god, thrillingly beautiful." It was the most fateful moment of Alexander's life, although whether it represented his great good fortune or the beginnings of a catastrophe is open to debate.

During the two and a half years Alexander and Dasham spent as undergraduates together, they were never more than casual acquaintances. But Alexander quickly became obsessed with Dash, on whom he projected his fantasies of escape: "O, I know I am shy and weak, but I believe that with Dasham I would be godlike, and he would be godlike with me. . . . I imagine us on the high seas; I imagine us shipwrecked and cast adrift to lost islands. Everyday I live a joyous life with him, if only in my imagination." Crucial to maintaining the fiction was not only Dash's physical beauty but also his supposed wholesomeness and unsullied innocence. The fiction anticipated Alexander's later aversion to the queer world, whose effeminacy and decadence appalled him. It was of course an impossible fantasy, because it assumed that Dash was a perfect specimen of American manhood, a rugged individual naturally at home in the wilderness, and hence an unlikely figure to reciprocate Alexander's passion. Yet even at nineteen he did not shrink from calling his feelings "love," though he gave them no specific sexual content: "I dreamed of a cabin on a mountain spur above pines and rocks and white flecked rapids, together with my love in the wild beauty of Night." We are not surprised to learn that Walt Whitman profoundly influenced his ideal of male comradeship. Throughout his life he turned to the "Calamus" section of *Leaves of Grass* to restore his faith.

By the time of his twenty-first birthday, almost two years later, the pressure to acknowledge the sexual nature of his attraction had grown overwhelming. Still, very much like Julien Green in the relationship with Mark, he resisted the idea, because it threatened to destroy the manly image on which his romance depended: "As much as I long for him, I am fearful of the slightest response, fearful that it will pull him from his pedestal, afraid that a touch of earth will destroy the celestial vision." A few months later, with a little help from Havelock Ellis—who, we recall, played a similar role in Julien Green's erotic education—he admitted that he had been fooling himself: "This diary of mine is a tissue of posturing. My real thoughts on such matters as sex are not admitted even to myself. I *will* be frank. I am madly in love with C. C. Dasham. 'Sexual inversion,' Havelock Ellis calls it." He recognized, moreover, that Dash was not the first such object. There had been numerous high-school classmates about whom he had dreamed of similar "visionary adventures, shipwrecks, desert isles, and the like." But the moment of truth did not liberate him from his escapist fantasies. Instead of setting about the practical business of realizing his desires, he elaborated those fantasies with greater abandon. "Sweet boys!" he exclaims. "I love them all. Could we but dance together, vine-crowned, intoxicated, and joyously on the windy hills over the green grass beneath a cloud-tufted sky." As with his predecessor John Addington Symonds, a tendency to literary inflation substituted for action.

I should not give the impression that Alexander's college years were as chaste as Julien Green's. He knew just what was happening, for example, when another undergraduate made a pass at him, though he was repulsed by the fellow's ob-

viousness and effeminacy. More important, in his last year at Washington and
Lee he actually had several sexual encounters with twin brothers, Tommy and
Malcolm Brisbane. Rather surprisingly, he felt no pangs of guilt. But he was mys-
tified by the uncanniness of the arrangement, in which the brothers seemed to
him interchangeable: "One twin and I engaged in lovemaking, with the other
watching, though not dispassionately. Then the other twin had his turn." The
uncertainty of knowing which twin he held in his arms made the experience seem
unreal. He could not invest it with the psychological weight of his purely invented relationship with Dash. "Love is a curious thing," he reflects. "I genuinely
love the twins, yet if I never saw them again I wouldn't think a thing of it." On
one of their last outings he virtually ignored Tommy and Malcolm as he grew
infatuated with a fifteen-year-old boy they met who suddenly became the object
of his Whitmanesque reverie. Imaginary lovers, it seems, were always preferable
to real ones.

We could write Alexander off as a hopeless fantasist were it not for the inconvenient fact that he was apparently right about C. C. Dasham. The evidence
in the diary is inconclusive, but it strongly suggests that Dasham was involved
in a homosexual relationship during his undergraduate years. Dash was always
in the company of young Harry Agneau, the son of a local judge. Then in the
spring of 1921 Dasham and Agneau were mysteriously expelled from school. A
classmate reported the scandal to Alexander: "'It's Dasham and Agneau. They
weren't proper gents—or maybe you know that already.'" Less than two months
later Henry Agneau killed himself.

In spite of the jealousy he had felt toward Agneau, Alexander was devas-
tated. He barricaded himself in his room, paced back and forth "like a caged
felon" and wondered, "What is to become of me?" He was convinced that he
would never see Dasham again. On the one hand the separation seemed to deliver
him from a deadly fixation, but on the other he was unwilling the believe that
feelings so intense should come to nothing. "Perhaps he was for me only a dream,
a part of an obsession that threatens to ruin my life," he muses. "But how could
such a passion rule a human soul if there were no meaning to it, if this were the
end?" As we know, he was to meet Dash again, in Washington, five years later.
The greatest imponderable of Alexander's story is what might have become of
him had that chance re-encounter not taken place. The meeting led to a brief
romance, from whose failure he was unable to recover. Might he have coped

more successfully with his fate had C. C. Dasham never re-entered his life? It is not always a good thing when our dreams are realized.

ALEXANDER RETURNED TO Washington permanently in mid-1922 and moved into the Y.M.C.A. at 1736 G Street, N.W. He worked less than a year in one of his father's grocery stores before taking a job as a Government Editorial Clerk. Thereafter he remained in the same office, copyediting official documents and feeling increasingly caught in a rut, until he retired. Throughout the diary he bemoans the monotony of his labors and the philistinism of his colleagues.

During the first half of the 1920s he fell into a regular habit of cruising in Lafayette Square. In contrast to Julien Green's nightly forays to the Trocadero, Alexander's early sexual adventures were undertaken with high romantic hopes. In other words, he did not follow Green in compulsively distinguishing between a world of pure emotion and one of promiscuous bodies. Admittedly, he soon became disenchanted, and after a few years he seems to have largely given up cruising. But at the start he went to Lafayette Square with the same hopes he entertained at college.

His first outing occurred while he was still in school, during the summer of 1920. It was precipitated, one August evening, when he saw two young men in the park "furtively engaged in mutual masturbation under cover of the dimness." Four days later he returned and got picked up. His account combines his characteristic romantic extravagance with a nice attention to detail, including an awareness of danger. It also reveals his preoccupation with social status. The man's outfit, cultural achievements, and place in the world seem as important as his physical charms:

> I have at last found a friend, a lovable, handsome fellow, a realization of the friend I have dreamed of during all those lonely nights while I walked alone through the streets. Above all, our friendship is mutual. It has burst into full blossom like a glowing, beautiful flower. It happened like this: I went to Lafayette Square and found a seat in the deep shade of the big beech. It is the best bench in the park. A youth sat down beside me, a youth in a green suit with a blue dotted tie. He has beautiful eyes and sensuous lips. He wants to become a diplomat, but is devoted to music. Earlier tonight he had been singing at the Episcopalian Church, and is taking vocal lessons. His name is Randall Hare.

We strolled down to the Ellipse, where we sat affectionately together on a dim bench. Later we came to rest in the moon-misted lawns near the Monument. With an excess of nervous caution I gazed about, watching for some prowling figures. "We are safe," Randall whispered. And he was right. Nothing disturbed us as we lay in each other's arms, my love and I, while the moon beamed from a spacious sky and the cool night breezes rustled our hair. The black trees stood like sentinels against the silvery grass. Afterward, we lay close together and gazed at the stars above, becoming fast friends, exchanging confidences. Ah, happiness!

The illusion lasted just over two weeks before he discovered that Randall didn't view the relationship in the same light. "'Did you think that when I wasn't with you I was *singing*? If I wanted a clinging vine I'd find—a woman.'"

The diary records occasional successes, but on the whole cruising proved an unhappy experience. Sometimes he suffered the unavoidable disappointment of misjudging his quarry. But the real problem was that his passivity made him inept at the game. In 1923, when he set out for Lafayette Square virtually every night, he reports he had gone four months without meeting anyone. He compares himself unfavorably with the intrepid Randall Hare, whom he often saw on the prowl and who on one occasion even tried to give him some pointers: "As usual I let such lads as I found attractive slip through my fingers. Randall Hare was sitting between *two* soldiers. He never fails to get something. He sees what he wants, and takes it. If I only had Randall's easy assurance and powerful abilities!"

His inhibitions were not entirely groundless. Lafayette Square was patrolled by plain-clothes men. The diary rails against them with uncharacteristic vehemence: "It is such a hideous feeling to be under the surveillance of the police, to be spied upon, followed, sneered at, by such filthy swine." He even articulates what sounds like the beginnings of an ideological critique, complaining of the futility and the injustice of the practice. The surveillance, he charges, accomplished nothing but to turn homosexuals "into miserable, furtive, persecuted creatures." One cop, whom Alexander dubbed "the Sneak," became a particular object of his fear and loathing. Typically, however, his outrage got mixed up with his snobbery: "Why in God's name would human society want its morals to be watched over by a creature with a soiled hat and a cheap coat?" He hated the Sneak for his bad taste, just as he admired Randall Hare (at least in part) for his green suit and blue dotted tie.

Almost as terrifying as the prospect of arrest was the thought of being noticed. He never picked up a man in uniform because its meaning, he feared,
would be transparent to all; it would be like marching before a brass band. Not
just in Lafayette Square but anywhere in public, he was certain that people saw
right through him: "I was seized with that hideous feeling that every person
I passed was inwardly mocking me, saying, *There goes a fairy,* or something
worse." His terror of visibility reduced him to silent paralysis. The only way to
avoid detection was to remain inert and say nothing.

Alexander became convinced that he was living under a double burden. The
first was naturally his homosexuality, which he regarded as congenital. In the
diary the notion of the "curse" or, sometimes, the "cloud" of homosexuality becomes a constant refrain. Reading *Sons and Lovers,* for example, he rages against
Fate for leaving him indifferent to women: "Oh, why, *why* must I suffer under
such a curse? Why can't I escape it, overcome it? As well ask why the canary
doesn't calmly fly away from the cage." But what rendered his situation unbearable—and set him apart from someone like Randall Hare—was his morbid self-
consciousness, which not only made the burden of contempt more crushing but
robbed him of the initiative to find his way in the queer world. It was bad enough
to be a homosexual, but to be a fainthearted homosexual was truly intolerable.
In these early years the diary often gives way to bouts of self-pity, in which he
represents himself as a great romantic soul trapped in an utterly inadequate
vessel.

In the mid-1920s Alexander was rescued from his solipsism and perhaps incipient madness by a group homosexual friends. At the core of the circle were a
half-dozen young men, most of them also residents at the G Street Y.M.C.A.
Much of the pleasure and pathos of the diary comes from following the intertwined lives of this little community, whose membership remained surprisingly
constant over the years. Alexander's sense of identity evolved as he measured
himself against the qualities he admired or (more often) disliked in these friends.
Alongside the love affair with Dash—who was very much a member of the
circle—the friendships were the defining experience of his life. Yet, for all the
support his friends gave him, he never felt completely at ease in their society.

The first of the friends turned out also to be the best. Max Stone was only
eighteen (six years younger than Alexander) when they met in an art class at
George Washington University. Max eventually became a painter, and no doubt
their shared devotion to culture provided the friendship with its basic cement.

Although Max was handsome, Alexander never felt attracted to him, so the relationship was not complicated by sexual tensions. Rather, it had from the start a genuinely intellectual character. A typical diary entry reads, "We went back to my room and had one of our long, intimate, comradely conversations about love and friendship among homosexual and other people, about the joys of reading and owning books, and other subjects." Through Max's conversation Alexander began to emerge from his isolation. Just as important, the younger man worked hard at helping him overcome his debilitating self-consciousness. After someone had made a homophobic remark in an elevator, Max urged, "'Struggle, boy, against that morbid state of mind that you feel coming on.'" Alexander experienced a new confidence, he boasted, as he sought to follow Max's mantra, "'You must be brazen.'"

A very different friendship evolved with a tall, gangling German, Hans Vermehren. In this case sex was a factor at the beginning. On one occasion, in fact, Hans did him "an enormous injury," resulting in a trip to the hospital and obliging him to give up alcohol, coffee, "and all sexual excitement or indulgence." Although Alexander was flattered by Hans's attentions—like Max's homilies, they boosted his self-confidence—the sexual relationship was fairly one-sided. Indeed, despite his charm and conviviality, Hans came to define an obsession with sex that Alexander increasingly viewed as a defect of the homosexual world. Still, when Hans was arrested on a morals charge, Alexander was as outraged as were the other members of the circle; the episode underlined their sense of solidarity in the face of oppression. And he recognized that he was losing "a dear friend" when Hans decided to return to Germany in 1931. Perhaps the most poignant moment in the diary comes, fourteen years later, when Alexander saw the first pictures of the concentration camps and realized, tears streaming down his cheeks, that Hans must have been among their victims.

About two other friends, Isador Pearson and Junior Whorley, he had more mixed feelings. Both men were effeminate, often flamboyantly so, and even went in for drag. They could also be extremely boisterous. In private and with enough liquor, Alexander sometimes unbent sufficiently to enjoy their antics. The diary recreates several parties at which Isador and Junior pranced about in costume and did imitations of Queen Victoria and Whistler's mother. It also contains a priceless account of a fishing expedition with Isador and one of Alexander's cigar-chomping uncles (who later mused, "'That Isador was an odd one'"). But any public encounter with Isador or Junior was a source of deep mortification. Alexander would look to escape as quickly as possible, thanking God that, for all his burdens, at least he had been spared effeminacy: "Homosexuality may be curse enough . . . but it is a double curse when one has effeminate ways of walking, talking, or acting." Somewhat improbably, Isador got married in 1942, although he remained a member of the circle of friends. Alexander showed no surprise at this turn of events, which suggests just how different their world was from our own. It was also a remarkably tiny world. Alexander's first trick, the predatory Randall Hare, eventually became one of its familiars. He too married, and, in an ironic twist of fate, Alexander found himself chaperoning Randall's wife and their two children on a European trip in the first weeks of the Second World War, when Randall, a successful diplomat, was called away to London.

The circle of friends provided Alexander with a haven in a heartless world. But it also served as a constant reminder of the ways in which he was still a loner, unwilling to embrace the manners and concerns that gave the homosexual subculture its distinctive character. The diary never tires of denouncing his friends' obsession with sexual intrigue, gossip, and display. "All that queer stuff— it makes me sick to think of it," he rants. His friends may have eased his loneliness, but they did not cure him of dreaming of an ideal comrade who would be manly, discreet, and edifying.

CꙨ AS HE GREW MORE DISAPPOINTED with the meager results of his cruising, and as he resisted full integration into the society of his friends, Alexander tried to solve his problem by way of a familiar retreat into fantasy. In fact, the diary suggests that he came close to developing into a full-fledged delusionary. He invented an imaginary lover, whom he called Vincent Eric Orville. His "dream boy" was the most complete realization of the Whitmanesque companion that had occupied his mind since college. Vincent Eric combined the happy-go-lucky insouciance of the class cut-up with a more deliberate rebellion against convention and authority. There was perhaps nothing necessarily pathological in such a fabrication; in a sense it was just a garden variety masturbation fantasy. But Alexander elaborated his creation in obsessive detail and accompanied him on extended adventures: "I know what he thinks, does, is; all his opinions, his life history, and scores of times have I lived, entirely in my imagination, through our meeting in Washington and the days following it." In effect Vincent Eric became more real to him than the people he saw and worked with every day.

The love affair with C. C. Dasham took place in the shadow of this hallucinatory romance. Alexander himself seems to have been aware of the connection. When Dash entered his life, Vincent Eric was promptly dismissed, only to be resurrected as the affair floundered. From the start, in other words, Dash was burdened with living up to the impossible expectations created by his imaginary predecessor.

The diary entry for December 19, 1926, records, "C. C. Dasham, the idol of my college days, is domiciled in this building. . . . He has still that beautifully molded mouth and chin. . . . He still has an indescribable air of boyishness about him." It goes on to insist, unpersuasively, that, though his charms were undiminished, Dash no longer exercised his old magic: "The moment I saw him I knew I did not love him." Before long, however, Alexander found his undergraduate infatuation reviving. By March they were close enough to reminisce about their experiences at Washington and Lee. The diary does not make clear just how frankly they discussed Harry Agneau's suicide. Dash is recorded as observing, "'I received a mean letter from Judge Agneau, with a cruel implication that I should feel responsible.'" But Dash preferred to dwell on more agreeable subjects. His cheerfulness and discretion were among the qualities that most endeared him to Alexander, just as they distinguished him from the denizens of the queer world.

Dash seems to have initiated the sexual relationship. The diary is characteristically reticent. We learn only that on July 15, 1927, Dash came to his room to see his new camera and stayed the night. The next day's entry is slightly more forthcoming: "O, that look in his eyes as he pressed me hard, that look of wistful, yearning tenderness—I shall never forget." The romance flourished during the summer and autumn, when they went on several trips together (including one to Atlantic City, where the photograph at the front of this chapter was taken). They seem to have kept the relationship secret from their mutual friends in the Y.M.C.A.

Perhaps we should be more astonished that the affair occurred at all than that it failed to last. For Alexander, with his overactive imagination, it must have validated his wildest fantasies. The boy he had loved but hardly known in college had suddenly dropped into his bed. Small wonder that he invested the relationship with an almost mystical significance and reacted so poorly when it collapsed. We can only infer Dash's feelings, but there is every reason to think that he took the matter much less seriously from the start. In the diary he emerges as pragmatic, affable, and not a bit intellectual. Pictures suggest that they were no better matched physically than temperamentally: Dash was a more attractive man.

The first sign of trouble came when they visited Niagara Falls in September 1927. Alexander overslept and missed the train to Toronto. Dash complained the next day, "'I *hate* your eternal dawdling and chronic oversleeping. You' *jus' shif'less!*'" As a lover Alexander was an exasperating combination of the ineffectual and the domineering. He was a chronic ditherer—always behind, never getting anything accomplished—yet he made increasingly fierce emotional demands.

By the beginning of 1928 Dash had decided that he wanted out. As a New Year's resolution he imposed a "Touch Me Not" policy, though he hoped to remain friends. Perhaps he had simply lost interest. Alexander blamed the change of heart on Dash's growing conviction that homosexual relations were "'unnatural.'" But nothing about Dash suggests that he was particularly moralistic. Rather, one imagines he was reaching for an excuse to extricate himself from an uncomfortable situation. Above all he was growing weary of Alexander's inquisitorial suspicions about his fidelity. When Alexander demanded to know whether he had slept with anyone else, Dash responded angrily, "'The answer is no, but it's none of your *damn* business.'"

Alexander suspected virtually everyone of coveting his "Dashie-boy." He appears to have been right in the case of Randall Hare, who added Dash to his list of conquests. What is striking about Alexander's behavior, however, is not his rather conventional sexual jealousy but his deeper fear that Dash was being robbed of his innocence by their affected and sex-crazed friends. Over and over the diary rails against the corruption of his manliness, simplicity, and natural virtue. One seriously doubts that Dash ever was such an innocent, just as one doubts that their friends were scheming to drag him down into a "whirlpool" of homosexual excess. Alexander remained firmly in the grips of the imaginary construction he had been nursing since college. Although he was involved in a love affair with a man, he acted as if it somehow had nothing to do with "homosexuality." The friends who in reality were the best allies against his crippling self-absorption were thus transformed into the enemies of his happiness.

The affair did not end abruptly with Dash's New Year's resolution. In fact, it enjoyed something of a renaissance in the summer of 1928, when Alexander offered the irresistible bribe of a trip to Europe. But its moment had passed. The wrangling soon began again, Alexander protesting his eternal love, while Dash, more firmly now, insisted that the sex was over. Dash seems to have been serious about wanting to remain friendly. Even after they had abandoned the Y.M.C.A., the two continued to see each other for breakfast or to attend concerts or movies. For a while in the late 1930s they actually lived in the same building (though in different apartments), where hearing Dash's footsteps overhead gave Alexander a sense of "warmth and companionship."

But while Dash moved on with his life, Alexander was unable to let go of the affair. For years he dreamed of its revival and lived off its memory. "I feel as if I'm frozen in time," he moans, "left behind somewhere while the world goes on, stuck in the summer and fall of 1927." When he and Dash occasionally got together for an evening, the pleasure of recollecting past adventures (such as their trip to Europe) was followed by miserable brooding about their vanished sexual relationship, which could no longer be mentioned. Gradually even these occasions came to an end. By the early 1940s he was complaining that Dash no longer called except to borrow money. The melancholy satisfaction of dwelling on his former romance gave way to a sense of emotional deadness. If he no longer thought of Dash so often, it was because he no longer thought about much of anything.

⬭ THE FINAL YEARS OF THE DIARY are almost unbearably sad. We get the sense of a life simply shutting down. He was bored to numbness by his job, where he never advanced beyond the position he had taken in 1923, and where he grew increasingly delinquent. Almost every night he would sit for hours in his neighborhood bar, drinking himself into oblivion. He saw his old friends less and less often. Instead he withdrew to his cluttered room amidst collections of books, phonograph records, stamps, mugs, and wine labels. His sex life also came to a virtual halt, though he sometimes woke to find one or more disreputable characters in his bed. He could seldom recall how they had met. Dash, on one of his rare visits, delivered a stern warning: "'Jeb, you are devoting your life to drink and carousing, and your office eventually will find they can get on without you.'" The words left him "feeling unhappy, insecure, and trapped."

The diary records his growing sense of isolation. Even more pathetically, it also records his almost yearly resolve to launch his much delayed literary career. The mystery is that this "shiftless" and defeated man somehow mustered the discipline to carry on with his diary. Night after night, standing at his bureau in his pajamas, he produced a narrative of his increasingly eventless life.

In some respects the diary was a ritual of avoidance. Rather than setting to work on the stories and novels he felt sure would make him famous, he would revert to keeping his journal. A typical entry from the later years records, "I lay there telling myself that I should simply begin my career as a literary artist. I did get up and put on my bathrobe. But instead of starting something original in the way of letters, I have been puttering around and writing in my diary." The diary was easier: it required no great constructive powers and, because it remained a private document, it did not bring the risk of failure.

Reading the diary also became a kind of substitute for living. As the years went by, he would spend more time consulting past entries, revisiting the blissful moments of his youth: the first view of Dash at Washington and Lee, the night of love with Randall Hare on the lawn beneath the Monument, above all the summer and fall of 1927, when the impossible dream of his great romance miraculously came true. Or he would escape entirely from the homosexual world, which had proved such a disappointment, by rereading the accounts of his earliest years, which, despite their sorrows, were untainted by the preoccupation that had ruined everything since: "Tonight I got out my diary of 1918 and read of summer days at the bank, of evenings under the moon of Rock Creek Park. What an innocent boy I was, before this accursed obsession took hold of me and clouded my life."

Yet, paradoxically, the diary was also a means of giving expression to the homosexual identity that he otherwise found so distasteful. As several of the entries make clear, he wrote with an imaginary reader half in mind and seems to have taken it for granted that someday the diary would be published.[3] But it had to be the right reader. He was appalled by the idea the diary might fall into the hands of someone—obviously heterosexual—who would see in it only a record of pathology: "It occurred to me today with something of a shock how horrible it would be for this diary of mine to be pawed over and read unsympathetically after I am dead, by those incapable of understanding, who would be filled with disgust and astonishment and think of me as a poor demented wretch, a neurotic or a madman who was better off dead."

3. In her Introduction Ina Russell notes the careful arrangement Alexander made in his will for the disposition of the diary, clearly implying his hope that it would eventually see the light of print.

The one thing worse than such a hostile audience would be for the diary never to be read at all. But the reader had to be somebody who would understand, somebody to whom he could entrust his "innermost soul"—"somebody," as he says, "who is like me." I would suggest that, as in the case of John Addington Symonds before him, Alexander wrote for an imagined audience of future homosexuals. To be sure, they were to be of the manly variety, purified of the affectations he found so hateful in his friends; the element of internalized homophobia in the text cannot be denied. But there is at least an implicit note of protest, even a hint of solidarity, in his vision of an unborn readership that would understand. Perhaps we have here a reason for his mysterious dedication to the diary, even as his life came to a stop. If only unconsciously, he must have felt that his tale of woe might be a link to a brighter future for his kind.

Donald Vining, typing his diary, in the Men's Residence Club, New York City, 1947.

A Gay Diary

"THE REHEARSAL OF 'Let Us Be Gay' was worth all the others we've had so far." Thus recorded eighteen-year-old Donald Vining, devoted amateur actor, in his diary on May 22, 1936. It is the first occurrence of the word "gay" in the text, and the editor (also Donald Vining, writing nearly half a century later) takes the opportunity to comment: "The title of this volume is meant to have this old as well as the new meaning." The new meaning would not make its appearance for another decade, toward the end of World War II. But the old meaning provides the key to the diary's tone throughout: again and again it tells a story of perseverance, of triumph over adversity, of making the most of the hand one is dealt in life. Above all, *A Gay Diary* tells a story of happiness.

The eudaemonistic motif is sounded most brightly every New Year, when Vining likes to sum up the year's events and give them a grade. Jeb Alexander often does the same thing, but in Alexander's diary these annual reckonings become the occasion to rehearse his misery, increasingly so as he grew older. Alexander's entry for January 1, 1935, is entirely representative: "Alone in my room. Last night's was the quietest New Year's Eve I have spent in years. There I sat, an invalid, waiting for 1934 to make haste and die. It was a cruel year. I tried so hard to be happy and yet blow after blow rained on my head from a pitiless Fate." Donald Vining's recapitulations sound just the opposite note. Their almost vulgar exuberance puts one in mind of Horatio Alger or Norman Vincent Peale. As 1939 came to a close, for example, he writes, "No days of the year can be counted on to give me such joy as a diarist as do the first and the last. I relish the

---

Donald Vining, *A Gay Diary, 1933–1946* (New York, 1979); *A Gay Diary: Volume Two, 1946–1954* (New York, 1980). Like Ina Russell in her edition of Jeb Alexander's diary, Vining has not wished to out anyone unwillingly and often uses pseudonyms in the published diary.

summary. It always makes me realize how much better off I am than when the year began and gives me a happy, satisfied feeling." He then proceeds to list the twelve "happiest moments of the year," ranging from the loss of his virginity to the first time he heard Dorothy Maynor sing "Depuis le jour." Vining, one might say, was a natural Benthamite, hoarding his pleasures. Even when genuinely disagreeable things happened to him, he always managed to find a silver lining. Thus at the end of 1943, during which he was arrested for cruising in Central Park and rolled by one of his tricks, the summary is as upbeat as ever: "In bold print it looks as tho I've gone thru quite a bit of sordid experience this past year, but none of it was as sordid as it seems on the face of it. It has been a wonderful year that has jammed my head and heart with material that I shall certainly use in my future writing and living."

Inevitably one wonders what might have been the source of this seemingly bottomless fund of optimism and gumption, which contrasts so starkly with Jeb Alexander's defeated passivity. The first thing likely to attract our attention is Vining's family situation. When the diary begins in January 1933 he was a high-school senior living alone with his mother in Bloomsburg, Pennsylvania. His father had departed westward in search of employment years earlier. It was the middle of the Depression, and, much to his regret, poverty forced Vining to delay his education. Except for an underfunded semester at Carnegie Tech (today Carnegie-Mellon) in 1934–1935, he continued to live at home, working at odd jobs, for three years after graduating from high school. These circumstances hardly sound like a formula for bliss, but in Vining's response to them we get the first indications of his peculiar resilience.

In certain ways, the relationship with his mother had elements of the suffocating intimacy that Freudians, especially American Freudians like Irving Bieber, came to view as a primary cause of homosexuality. When he went away to the Yale Drama School in 1939, for example, his mother moved to New Haven with him for the two years. The diary also reports that she sometimes urged her charms on him: "Mother came in to wake me and it was like old times as she lay beside me and we cuddled close to one another." But Vining took a knowing and ironic attitude toward such experiences: "If some of these amateur psychoanalysts could see our behavior they'd immediately shout 'Oedipus complex!'" His lighthearted dismissal of the psychoanalysts is typical. Unlike Martin Duberman, who was emotionally crippled by therapists, Vining seems never to have considered himself neurotic or looked to be "cured" of his problem.

The diary gives the impression that the order of authority between mother and son had been reversed. Even as a teenager, Vining played the adult, while his mother played the child. He was forever cleaning up her messes, making order where she left chaos. He lectured her, usually in vain, on the need to curb her extravagance. With an absent father and a spendthrift mother, he was virtually forced to take charge. Developing a sense of mastery was the price of survival. Later he would bring the same can-do spirit to the challenges posed by his homosexuality.

One other, and spectacularly interesting, fact about his mother no doubt contributed to his sexual poise: she was a lesbian. The diary doesn't say so expressly until 1941, but Vining was evidently aware of the fact even in high school. He nowhere speaks about what thoughts the discovery prompted. But surely it must have eased his burden: sexual deviance was not the alien phenomenon it was for Jeb Alexander but something present in the heart of his family. In the early years his mother sometimes expressed disapproval of his homosexuality, but eventually they developed a sense of queer camaraderie. When the family cat took an interest in a visiting male, the diary reports, "I thought we'd split our sides at the thought that even our cat was perverted." The implicit permission he got from this most intimate figure in his young life was, I suspect, of incalculable importance. It stands in sharp contrast to Jeb Alexander's experience with the members of *his* family. One of the most mortifying scenes in Alexander's diary recounts a visit to the Y.M.C.A. by his brother Henry in 1924: "Tonight Henry provided me with a cruel reminder of the world's attitude toward us unfortunates who live in this half-world of thwarted desire and unreturned love, of jeers and whispered comments and meaning glances, of eternal seeking and never finding. He stopped by and, sitting on my bed chatting, he blurted out, 'There was a fellow down in the lobby ought t'have been taken out and frailed hell out off— *a damn fairy!*'" Vining might seem to have had the more dysfunctional family, but in fact its idiosyncrasies probably worked to his advantage. It obliged him to take responsibility for himself, even as it softened the blow of his differentness.

Another paradoxical advantage came from the very real economic hardship he faced during the Depression. Throughout the 1930s the diary suggests that he was troubled more by his precarious finances than by his wayward desires. He worried constantly that he would be forced to drop out of college because he couldn't afford the tuition. He was sometimes so poor he went hungry, leaving him weak and dejected. Jeb Alexander, while hardly well off, never had to over-

come such adversity. We might reasonably conclude that being poor gave Vining a sense of perspective about his sexual difficulties. Whatever suffering they
caused him, he knew that worse things could happen to a person. "There is nothing quite so demoralizing," he observes glumly, "as lack of work and lack of
income." Just as important, he did not allow poverty to defeat him; by scrimping
and borrowing he managed to get through college and launch himself in the
world. The experience no doubt contributed to the sense of resolve that is such
a striking feature of the diary. Having triumphed over "real" misfortune, he was
not about to be done in by mere prejudice.

⌒ DURING THE YEARS BEFORE he went off to college in 1937, Vining seems to
have been preoccupied with two high-school classmates. The diary entries are
fairly sketchy, but we get a sense of him sorting through the confusion caused by
his physical attraction to the one boy and his more sisterly feelings for the other.
Nothing concrete came of either relationship, but the teenage Vining went about
pursuing his desires with business-like determination. From the start he was a
pragmatist in matters of the heart, calculating his chances and planning his attack.
Moreover, if things didn't work out, although he might weep a bit, he was quick
to recover from his disappointment.

Even the earliest references to homosexuality in the diary are strikingly
matter-of-fact. "The opposite sex holds no physical attraction for me," he records
in 1933. We look in vain for evidence of self-contempt; there is nothing remotely
resembling Jeb Alexander's wailings about "the curse." Rather, the tone is circumstantial, dispassionate. When he found out that most of Shakespeare's sonnets were written to a boy, he immediately reported the discovery to his mother
and a skeptical teacher. Apparently he was unembarrassed by the conclusion they
might draw from his interest in the matter. He also developed a talent for converting whatever he heard to constructive homosexual uses. After a radio psychologist had pronounced love the finest thing in the world, Vining adapted the
idea to his own situation: "As he said it, something in my brain clicked and at
once I decided never to feel furtive in my love affairs hereafter. Perhaps my lust
for those of my own sex is something to be ashamed of, perhaps not, but at any
rate my love for them is not." Similarly, he seems to have been blessed with a
preternatural ability to resist the standard homophobic fare of the day. A case in
point was his Hygiene instructor: "Lux talked about the biological and physio-
logical factors of sex and discussed menstruation and homosexuality. I resented

and yet was amused by his repeated references to homosexuality as 'disgusting.'"
Psychological speaking, we are light-years removed from the cringing agony to
which Jeb Alexander succumbed in the face of prejudice.

Vining attended college from 1937 to 1941, the first two years at West Chester State Teachers College, the second two at the Yale Drama School. Even at
West Chester State he spent most of his time performing with a student theatrical
company. Although his devotion to acting was fervent, we are bound to wonder
whether an unconscious sexual instinct didn't draw him to this particular environment. Here again we encounter one of those contingent realities—seemingly a
matter of happenstance—that set his life apart from Jeb Alexander's. Naturally
he got to know several other gay men in the theatrical communities of West
Chester and New Haven. But even more important for his emerging identity was
the pervasive sexual tolerance of theater people, at least by contrast with society
at large. Among his fellow actors he made a number of straight friends, of both
sexes, with whom he was able to talk about his homosexuality and who reacted
calmly to the news. Figures of this sort are entirely absent from Jeb Alexander's
diary. Whether by luck or intuition, Vining had found his way into a world that
strengthened his already well-developed self-confidence.

At West Chester State he continued to struggle with the difference between
"love" and "lust." As had happened in high school, he soon met a boy—clearly
another homosexual—with whom he felt an intense kinship but who left him
cold sexually. The diary shows him working through his contradictory feelings
in a typically analytic, guilt-free manner:

> I could wish that when I fall in love I should want to see my loved one as
> eagerly as I want to see Bob at night; I could wish that the reunion should be
> as deeply satisfying as it is when I meet him mornings and I could wish that
> we'd be as compatible as he and I. And yet surely I can't be in love with him. I
> don't want the ultimate of him physically. He is so thin and at present not of
> the best complexion. His hair (and lovely hair gets me) is nondescript. It is not
> lust, decidedly, but I fear it *is* love. Love without the physical side. The love of
> friendship.

Eventually Bob developed into a confidant, with whom Vining could discuss his
infatuations. But the opposition between sex and friendship remained a concern
for years. In the late 1940s he would elaborate an almost philosophical distinction
between the two.

Not long after arriving at West Chester he met the first great love of his life, Charles Taylor, who was also an amateur actor. Although Charles sometimes sent ambiguous signals, he was apparently straight. Thus we might fear that Vining was about to launch one of those pathetically impossible romances that fill the early pages of so many gay autobiographies. But in fact he wasted no time on imaginary shipwrecks or escapes to desert islands. Instead he put his mind to work, in his usual pragmatic way, figuring out how to improve his chances. The diary reveals a calculating seducer, who grew annoyed when circumstances conspired to frustrate him: "I'm so furious I could throw things. I had Charles so near my grasp that I *know* I could have gotten him, and people clustered around us. Then, when I intended to play my cards on the way home, Don Eastburn and Don MacLaren walked up the street with us. . . . Damn it. Damn it. Damn it." But if Vining was calculating, he was also prudent. The next day Charles no longer seemed ripe for the plucking, and Vining adjusted smoothly to the altered situation: "He was out of his mood of last night and not open to seduction so I behaved sensibly." The combination of initiative and reasonable caution may not have worked with Charles, but eventually it proved a recipe for success.

Vining was a devout empiricist in sexual matters. He kept his eyes and ears trained for tell-tale evidence. One evening, Charles said that he wouldn't mind meeting "'a strange person'" in an alley, and then corrected himself—"'a strange girl, I mean'"; Vining astutely pounced on the remark: "His use of person the first time is too habituary a dodge with me for it to slip unnoticed." He also took note that Charles seemed to be obsessed with homosexuality—he was forever declaring this or that acquaintance "perverted"—and, not unreasonably, Vining interpreted the obsession as a sign of interest. When Charles revealed that once he had actually given in to the importuning of two perverts, Vining, practical as always, immediately began thinking of how to turn the revelation to his advantage. "If he lay with others just to oblige, maybe he'd do the same for me," he reasoned. "I'll ask him for that for a birthday present if we're still here June 20th." As it happens, Charles confounded his plans by unexpectedly marrying one of their fellow actors. Vining allowed himself a brief moment of depression, after which, characteristically, he bounced right back. As the newlyweds left on their honeymoon he felt "a little low," but the very next entry reports, "This day has been wonderful from first to last." The entire episode was carried off in typical Vining style: he went after his prey using his wits and industry, but when things didn't pan out he cut his emotional losses. The contrast with Jeb Alexander's inertia and overinvestment in the affair with Dash could hardly be more pointed.

During his years at West Chester, Vining also developed a conscious, if not fully consistent, policy of self-revelation. It might be described as "modified hang-out." In most situations, and with most persons, he was entirely closeted. "I do not truly want to be known as a 'fairy,'" he writes, "except by certain enlightened people." The exception was important. Not only for the enlightened few but for those he might possibly attract as lovers (like Charles Taylor) he found ways to signal the truth about himself. Thus on a number of occasions the diary refers to his "self-satirizing," his "joking," or his "silliness." What exactly was involved is not specified, but the implication is that he developed a habit of joshing about his tendencies, maybe even pretending to be effeminate. Such, at least, is suggested by the following entry: "Charles said that just last night, after they dropped me off, he and Friedman and Barbour were discussing me and decided that I hadn't any homosexual traits and that all my joking about myself was just joking."

Vining seems to have felt ambivalent about the behavior. On the one hand, he recognized that it was demeaning. It was an instance of what Paul Monette would later criticize as the "clown" persona behind which homosexuals sometimes hid. On the other hand, it served as a tool for advancing his sexual interests. Just before leaving West Chester for Yale, he decided to review the "policy." He talked it over with another theatrical friend, Reds, to whom he had felt attracted:

> Reds gave me much advice which I really think I shall take. I seriously discussed with him the problem of setting up my defense mechanism of joking if I went to Yale. He said that he, at least, would probably have been angry at my advances had I not taken everything so lightly and been such a self-satirizer, whereas as it was he didn't mind so much, was distinctly flattered, and tho't the whole business as funny as I did for a while. He said he thinks I should not worry about public opinion if I feel I'm right, that I have as much right to love my own sex and make advances as any fellow has to like girls.

Reds was a classic example of the sort of enlightened heterosexual Vining met in the theatrical world, and no doubt his words (the likes of which Jeb Alexander never heard) gave Vining a psychological boost. But the passage is interesting mainly for the way it documents how he used his joking as a technique of seduction. It also shows him as a complete pragmatist, weighing his options, thinking about how best to get what he wanted in the future.

When Vining's sexual initiation finally took place, during his first semester at Yale, it did not follow the script he had been rehearsing in his head for so long. Instead of being the seducer he was the seduced, an irony he fully appreciated. The boy—a fellow drama student—wasn't even someone he particularly cared for. But Vining did not hold back just because the situation failed to match his theoretical preconceptions. He was always ready to adapt to changed circumstances. He was also always ready to learn. Indeed, his account of the seduction sounds as if he were taking notes—storing away lessons for his own use in the future:

> When we got up in D's room, D soon flopped onto his cot and I sat in the chair over in the corner. Soon D beckoned and said, "Come sit over here by me. I can't hear you." I laughed at the ruse and went over. D's next move in what would seem to be a well-routined technique was to reach up, take my glasses off, and put them on the desk beside the bed. Then he pulled my head down onto his chest. The boy . . . seduced me with a polish that could only have come from long experience.

Vining claimed to be pleased with his adventure. In the diary he evaluates it with his customary enthusiasm. "The experience did wonders for me," he writes; "I feel as tho I grew two inches taller today." But, in fact, it had not been a complete success. He discovered, to his chagrin, that he was rather inhibited sexually. He felt uncomfortable with anything more adventuresome than kissing and fondling. When, the next week, D went "much further," Vining managed not to protest, but he didn't enjoy it. He had the same reaction with second boy a few months later: "Again it was unsatisfactory for me when it went beyond a passionate embrace. I was too tight, tense, and inhibited." The problem would bedevil him for years. Even after he had had sex with hundreds of different men, he was still complaining about his "psychological block." Despite his almost congenital optimism, apparently he had internalized some of the bad feelings about homosexuality he pretended to despise. The decision to go to New York was taken, at least in part, with a view to addressing these residual doubts. "I must resolve my inner sexual problem," he declares, "and find out for myself if I can really find genuine satisfaction in thoroughgoing homosexuality." His erotic difficulties suggest that my portrait of him as Jeb Alexander's opposite mustn't be overstated:

for all his resilience, he was not immune to the repressive ideas abroad in his society. He would have been inhuman if he were.

⟳ DURING THE YEAR AFTER HE LEFT Yale Vining lived in New Jersey and took a job at the Fort Dix post exchange, where he sold supplies (including condoms) to the soldiers who came pouring through the base after America's entry into the Second World War. Sexually it was an uneventful year, a kind of latency period in which he girded his loins before plunging into the gay life with abandon. The job gave him time to work on his writing, which was always his first concern. It also allowed him to take voyeuristic pleasure in the countless attractive young men he waited on in the PX. But he was frustrated that he seemed unable to follow up on the sexual beginning he had made at Yale.

The only adventure reported in the diary was decidedly unpleasant. Hitch-hiking home from Fort Dix one day, he let himself be picked up by "a big fat businessman." As had happened with the two boys at Yale, he again found himself sexually inhibited: "It was worse than the others because I couldn't bring myself to even kiss or caress the man as I had Bart and Joe, who had real attractions." But, in typical fashion, he turned the disaster to profit: he pumped his seducer for information and learned that the fellow had sometimes managed to get as many as three soldiers into his car and give them blow jobs. Once again we have a sense of Vining taking notes on his experience, providing himself with a sexual education by whatever means he could.

The most revealing episode of the year occurred when he registered for the draft. He had long been a pacifist and was determined not to fight in the War, even though, as a liberal and philo-Semite, he fretted that Jews were being perse-cuted by the Nazis. He hoped to be exempted as a conscientious objector, but, failing that, he was always ready to plead homosexuality. The diary never sug-gests that he found the military ban unfair. Rather, his whole strategy in life was based on the principle of accommodation, of carving out a satisfactory existence for himself under adverse conditions. Psychologically, he was disinclined to ask fundamental questions about those conditions. His natural tendency was to take advantage of the Army's rules rather than to protest them.

So, instead of an agonizing confrontation, the visit to the draft board is made to seem almost agreeable, even faintly comic. The diary describes the inter-viewing psychiatrist as "marvelously tolerant, taking the whole thing easily and calmly, without shock and without condescension." After a few delicate questions, he marked Vining's papers "'Sui generistic "H" overt.'" The classification officers objected because, they said, Vining showed no "outward signs," no "psycho-neurosis." But the enlightened doctor stuck to his guns, though he agreed to substitute a blunt "homosexual" for the discreet "H" in his original diagnosis. For his part, Vining pronounced himself entirely satisfied with the outcome; he worried only that the news might cause his mother embarrassment if it got known about town.

He had to deal with a more painful situation when the reason for his exemption was leaked at Fort Dix. A vulgar sergeant "made ribald jokes, saying that when they'd told me to urinate in the bottle I'd started to squat." Despite the hurt, Vining didn't allow himself to be goaded. He neither retaliated nor collapsed in misery but rode out the unpleasantness with a show of nonchalance. It was the classic accommodationist tactic. "I can see these next three weeks are going to be no picnic," he remarks stoically, "but I'll face the issue without retrenching."

In September 1942, a month after his visit to the draft board, Vining moved to New York City. Except for one year (1944) in Los Angeles—where he worked as a janitor for Paramount and checked out the movie industry—New York became his permanent home. He stayed briefly at the Sloane House Y.M.C.A. before taking a room in the Men's Residence Club on 56th Street (itself a former Y.M.C.A.), where he lived for years. In the Residence Club's pool, showers, and steam room he met many of the casual tricks and potential lovers who populate the diary's entries. During the 1940s he supported himself mainly as a desk clerk at Sloane House and, later, in an office job with the Philippine Desiccated Coconut Corporation.

Once he got to New York, Vining entered with surprising ease into the city's homosexual life. The diary gives a richly circumstantial account of his many escapades, and, as the years pass, it becomes increasingly preoccupied with the sexual and emotional complexities attending his search for a lover. Naturally, it also tells us a great deal about the nonerotic aspects of his life. He continued to labor away writing stories and plays, which occasionally found publishers but more often were rejected (he took his defeats philosophically, resolving to do better). He was forever organizing amateur theatricals or salons for aspiring writers. He also became a systematic consumer of New York's cultural offerings, especially the opera, Broadway plays and musicals, and the Metropolitan Museum. Still, the diary's main interest, after 1942, is with his sexual and romantic life.

The account of his cruising is particularly full and unapologetic. It contrasts strikingly with Jeb Alexander's desultory experience in the early 1920s. Vining took up cruising in earnest during his year in Los Angeles, where he visited Pershing Square with religious regularity on Saturday nights. In New York it came to occupy even more of his time, at least during the warm months, which sometimes found him in Central Park several evenings a week.

He approached the task in his familiar enterprising spirit. The most impressive thing about his outings is that he virtually never went home empty-handed. Perhaps he was a more attractive man than Jeb Alexander (who, we recall, once languished for four months without a pickup in Lafayette Square), but the crucial difference was that he suffered from none of Alexander's self-consciousness. In fact, he enjoyed the intrigue and drama of the pursuit almost as much as the sex that followed.

Vining had reasonably specific ideas of what he was looking for in a trick, but he was always flexible, adjusting to the market, and never locked himself into the rigid "Ideal Friend" syndrome that made J. R. Ackerley's sexual hunting such a nightmare. He liked tall, muscular men (he was himself six feet and weighed just over 150 pounds), preferably with hairy chests and large genitals (again, like himself, as he discreetly reveals at one point). Effeminacy was a turn-off, as it was for Jeb Alexander, but, in contrast to Alexander, he wasn't obsessive about the matter. In some respects he was a firm sexual materialist: he appreciated a skilled erotic technician and worked conscientiously to make himself a better lover. But even among his one-night stands he looked for human warmth, affection, and qualities of mind—the ability to talk intelligently, cultural interests, a sense of humor. In other words, he didn't make a sharp distinction between his tricks and his serious loves. Rather, his promiscuity was informed by a gentle romanticism.

As in his pursuit of Charles Taylor at West Chester State, Vining's aggressiveness was tempered by caution. He was alert to the danger of being rolled by his pickups. In reality this occurred very seldom, but when it did, he responded courageously: he fought back and usually succeeded in routing his tormentor. Nor was he intimidated by the threat of being exposed as a queer: after an attack he would promptly call the police. Like a good empiricist, he also learned from his mistakes. When a Los Angeles trick, Dick Wilson, asked to see his glasses and then proceeded to steal his watch and wallet, Vining blamed himself for ignoring the "obvious signs of nefarious intentions." A year later a New York pickup made the same request: "It was Dick Wilson's routine but this time I wasn't to be caught off guard." Even in the moment of passion he kept his wits about him.

The other danger he faced was being arrested. It happened to him three times in the 1940s, and he always reacted the same way: he made a great show of his self-possession. When, in 1943, he and several others were rounded up while sitting on a park bench and jailed overnight, he refused to panic: "It was a travesty on justice and the working of the police department," he writes, "but instead of arousing my indignation as a citizen (not to mention victim), it sort of amused me." In effect, he responded just as he had to registering for the draft, namely, by working hard to minimize the trauma. Jeb Alexander, we recall, behaved very differently: he lashed out against the police surveillance to which he was subject in Lafayette Square. In a sense, Alexander's response was more "correct" by modern political standards. But under the historical circumstances Vining's conciliatory attitude was better gauged to save emotional toil. It was a measure of his pragmatism.

The most serious arrest occurred in 1949, when detectives caught him groping a fellow in Central Park. Again, he maintained his poise: "The handcuffs mortified the others but somehow that didn't bother me. My self-respect and self-love are so unassailable that it takes a great deal to make me feel humbled or disgraced." He was taken aback, however, when the judge—who, in contrast to the "nice" detectives, was "a stinker"—sentenced him to fifteen days in the workhouse on Riker's Island. At first he was appalled by the criminal homosexuals, many of them Black transvestites, with whom he was housed. It was, in effect, the universe of Jean Genet. But Vining quickly transformed himself into a sociological observer, studying the prison culture and gathering "material" for his fiction. In fact, he entered into the inmates' world with something approaching delight. "Joined a group listening to Gloria's reminiscences of her days in vaudeville," he writes toward the end of his stay. "I laughed so much I was rolling on the ground. . . . Supposedly anti-social me was having the time of his life." Today we might be inclined to fault him for his relentlessly benign view of what was, objectively, an odious system of oppression. But it was entirely consistent with his accommodationist approach to the homosexual predicament under the *ancien régime,* an approach he had adopted while still in high school, and one that served his interests rather better than the impotent protests of Jeb Alexander. He simply refused to be defeated by the less-than-ideal historical conditions in which he found himself. Rather, he looked for ways to make the best of those conditions and to protect himself against the psychological damage that would result from dwelling on his suffering.

◯ VINING HAD CONCEIVED OF THE IDEA of finding a permanent mate well before he got to New York. Like many gay men, he drew a direct analogy between his wants and those of heterosexuals: "I desire a lover to live with just as normal people desire wives or husbands, and I intend to settle down with a lover someday." The matter-of-factness and determination are altogether typical. Eventually he found such a mate, although the relationship had to endure considerable storm and stress in the early years and required many compromises before it evolved into a lifelong partnership. Vining succeeded where Jeb Alexander failed because he brought to the effort his familiar combination of energy and practicality—rolling with the punches, trimming his idealistic sails. But, perhaps just as important, he also had the advantage of two serious trial runs before he finally met Mr. Right. Jeb Alexander, by contrast, undertook his affair with Dash as a romantic novice and paid the price for his inexperience.

Vining launched his first significant relationship barely a month after arriving in New York. It began, humbly enough, in the shower room of the Men's Club: "Took a shower when I got home and fell head over heels in love with an adonis in the opposite shower. Such perfect proportions, such handsome head. He got a hard-on and cast many a glance my way but I was timid and then an old man came in for a shower and spoiled it all." His timidity lasted exactly one day. The affair with Fred Naylor (as Adonis was called) rested on a firm foundation of sexual compatibility. For the first time in his life, and much to his relief, Vining was able to overcome his inhibitions: "It was what I always wanted it to be and what it never has been before. The things that have always been repulsive to me before, lush kisses and soul kissing, didn't bother me a bit and every moment was pleasurable." Unfortunately, good sex was not enough to ensure a successful romance. Fred had no intention of giving up his diversions—Vining calls him "a professional courtesan"—and, even worse, he felt ambivalent about his homosexuality. For a while Vining hoped to triumph over circumstances, but, as with Charles Taylor years before, his sense of self-preservation told him when to withdraw his investment. Within three months of their meeting he ventured out to a bar and picked up a sailor. As usual, he quickly recovered his equipoise.

A longer and more serious relationship began in 1945, after Vining returned to New York from Los Angeles. With Dick Bennett, unlike Fred Naylor, the romantic attachment seems to have been mutual: for a couple of months Vining and Dick actually lived together in the same room in the Men's Club. This time sex was the problem. Dick was interested in anal intercourse ("browning"), with a dash of sadomasochism, both of which were beyond Vining's erotic range. But because he was deeply in love—and because of his basic flexibility—he made a valiant effort to adjust. "I was more than anxious to try things on Dick's terms," he declares bravely. Try as he might, however, the only effect was to make him impotent. Vining worked earnestly to salvage the relationship. He encouraged Dick to have outside affairs, so long as they remained casual. He also sought advice from his friends, and on one occasion he and Dick even discussed their difficulties with Vining's mother. But, always the realist, he prepared stoically for the inevitable end: "Our future lies in different directions. What Dick's may be, I have no idea. I suppose all this is like the year on crutches, the days in jail, the years of debt and penury—very good for my art in the long run but hell to live thru." When Dick finally gave up on the affair, Vining shed a few bitter tears, but he was soon back in the sexual mill. There were a number of other suitors waiting, and he promptly treated himself to a brief fling in the which the sex was more to his liking.

We might expect that the next relationship, which ultimately proved enduring, would achieve a synthesis of the sexual rapport Vining enjoyed with Fred Naylor and the emotional satisfactions of the affair with Dick Bennett. But nothing of the sort happened. Instead, the romance with "Ken Jefferson" (whose real name, we learn in the fifth volume of *A Gay Diary*, was Richmond Purinton) followed its own idiosyncratic path. From the start it had a very different character from its two predecessors, and it underwent a complex, sometimes painful, evolution over the course of three years before settling into its definitive form at the very end of the 1940s.

The two men met, in the spring of 1946, in the basement steam room of the Men's Residence Club. Ken was a former master sergeant, living off his retirement. He was older than Vining, though how much older (twelve years) wasn't revealed until late 1947. Unlike the affairs with Fred Naylor and Dick Bennett, the new romance got off to a slow start. They spent a month talking and socializing, and their first session in bed, when it finally occurred, was limited to necking.

The beginning was emblematic. Though they immensely enjoyed one another's company and shared many tastes and opinions, they rather quickly found that their sexual needs diverged radically. Ken's genuine erotic interest in Vining did not last more than a few months. The diary is soon complaining that they might go weeks without having sex, and within two years it had stopped completely. By the end of the summer, moreover, they both began pursuing other opportunities. Ken did so on principle, declaring his commitment to "complete freedom and casualness" in libidinal life. Vining felt differently. His desire for Ken had only increased, and, while his pickups were nearly always better technicians, they left him unsatisfied emotionally. As he says after one of his outings, "There is no substitute for Ken, tho almost anybody is superior sexually."

Over the next two years Vining wrestled with his predicament. On the one side was his erotic idealism—the belief that he should not settle for a relationship that, however companionable, was essentially sexless. In this mood he would declare himself ready to give up on Ken and take his chances with somebody new. Or, in his tough-minded way, he would set limits on how long he was prepared to wait for things to change.

On the other side was his natural flexibility and his ingrained habit of pragmatic adaptation. Like a good Burkean conservative, he prided himself on the modesty of his expectations. "Much of my happiness," he writes, "stems from my not demanding so much from life as other people do." Realistically he knew that desire, especially homosexual desire, waned. Which meant that all long-standing relationships had to make accommodations for sexual variety. "If this is the best any of us can hope for, and it certainly seems to be, what use in tossing Ken over and looking for someone else?" he asks himself. "In one year, or two, or five, or seven, it would come to the same thing." The only difference with Ken, according to this line of reasoning, was that the sex had ended rather sooner than usual.

As the relationship entered its third year the pragmatic argument seemed to carry the day. Vining's utilitarian calculus increasingly persuaded him that the sustained satisfactions of companionship outweighed the fleeting pleasure of sex. "Sex lasts an hour or so every now and then," he asserts. "Compatibility as companions affects hours out of every day." Jeremy Bentham could not have put it better. Though they still relished each other's company and were often physically affectionate, they had withdrawn into separate erotic worlds. Ken picked up tricks in the Men's Club or at gay parties, while Vining cruised. "That hasn't made me happy," he concludes soberly, "since I often lust for him intensely, but I have learned to put up with it and count it no great loss if our happiness is bought at that price."

The relationship had to withstand a final crisis when Vining went to Europe for four months in the summer of 1949. While he was abroad, Ken began an affair with one of Vining's close friends, Jim Boothe, a young man Vining had met in 1945 when they both worked as desk clerks at Sloane House. Vining was so hurt and angry that he immediately resolved to make a complete break with friend and lover alike. Although he had reconciled himself to Ken's having sex with other people, the idea of his having sex with a friend apparently violated some deep structural prohibition in Vining's psyche, a prohibition resembling the incest taboo. In other words, he was not chiefly motivated by fear that Jim Boothe might replace him in Ken's affections. Rather, his violent reaction grew out of a more fundamental conviction that sex and friendship belonged to hermetically sealed realms. The rigidity with which he embraced the notion seems odd in a man generally so given to compromise.

Over the years friendship had become one of Vining's most cherished values. The diary—unconsciously amending Freud—expressly places it alongside love and work among the supreme goods. Not all of his friends were gay: both at school and in the amateur literary groups he organized he counted several straight men and women among his intimates. But, in the 1940s at least, his closest bonds were with a handful of homosexual contemporaries, whose lives and views are extensively recounted in the diary. One of these friends, George Worrell, he had known since childhood, and another, Joe Heil, was the second boy with whom he had had sex at Yale. The newer ones, like Jim Boothe, were men he got to know at work or in the Men's Residence Club.

I can't pretend to understand the unconscious logic by which sex and friendship became antithetical principles in Vining's mind. The diary is mute on the question, as if it were simply a self-evident truth. But he held to it with remarkable consistency. After Joe Heil moved to New York and became a friend, for example, Vining was dismayed by Joe's frequent proposals that they renew their fling. Similarly, he was bitterly unhappy when George Worrell violated the taboo by taking an interest in Dick Bennett during their romance.

Ken's affair with Jim Boothe brought into focus a more general sense of ambivalence about his friends that Vining had been nursing for some time. Increasingly he saw those friends falling victim to what he derisively called "the gay world." The phrase denoted many of the same things Jeb Alexander had in mind when he complained that his Dashie-boy was being corrupted by "all that queer stuff." The gay world meant an exaggerated preoccupation with appearance and display, whether in clothes or furnishings, and a corresponding neglect of serious intellectual and cultural matters. It also meant devoting too much time to drunken socializing and not enough to building a serious career (such as Vining himself was trying to do with his writing). Above all, it meant a "neurotic" obsession with sexual intrigue and a constitutional inability to maintain stable relationships. At the height of his anger over Ken's betrayal, Vining contemplated ridding himself not only of the two immediate culprits but of his whole gay acquaintanceship.

Eventually his pragmatic instincts reasserted themselves, as one knew they would. To be sure, Jim Boothe's banishment was permanent: Vining never spoke to him again. But toward Ken he relented. The ice was broken when Ken wrote him a solicitous letter during his imprisonment on Riker's Island in early November 1949. Within a month the relationship was back on its old footing. Vining concluded, in his level-headed way, that the satisfactions of their well-honed companionship outweighed a single treachery: "Our common fund of memory, our almost perfect acquaintance with each other's tastes and peccadilloes make our social intercourse so much easier and smoother than it would be with someone else." As for the lack of sex, he had already reconciled himself to that a year earlier. "'I don't say things are the way I'd like them,'" he admitted to his friend George Worrell. "'It isn't just a matter of what you want but of what you can get.'" The remark perfectly captures Vining's philosophy of life.

As the decade ended on New Year's Eve 1949, Vining was able to produce another of his familiar blithe summaries: "It was a mighty good year all around." True, he had spent two weeks in jail, and his faith in friendship had been gravely wounded. But those setbacks counted for little against the happy fact that he and Ken had managed to finish the year as close as they began it. They were still together, over three decades later, when the fifth volume of *A Gay Diary* ends in 1982.

☾ AS EARLY AS 1941 Vining conceived the idea of writing a book about homosexuality. The project evolved through different formats in his mind, but more and more he came to imagine it as an autobiographical novel. By the late 1940s the novel had become his main preoccupation, and in 1951 he managed to complete a manuscript and send it to a literary agent. Two years later the manuscript had been rejected by fourteen publishers.

In the diary—which served as a kind of archive for the novel—Vining often speaks about the message he intended the book to convey. First and foremost it was to refute the notion that homosexuals were doomed to unhappiness. He objected strenuously to the novels that had been published on the subject because they always ended in tragedy. Even Gore Vidal's *The City and the Pillar,* although superior to most, perpetuated this dire view of the homosexual's lot. "I must try to be more truthful," he comments after finishing the Vidal in 1948. Of another (unnamed) novel he writes dismissively, "More 'sensitive' boys, another suicide finale when the relationship is discovered. Such poppycock. How did such a stereotype ever get in circulation when it's so false and silly?"

His own novel, therefore, would have a happy ending. To be sure, the crisis in his relationship with Ken momentarily shook his confidence; work on the novel came to grief as he began to doubt that two men could manage to live together on a lasting basis. But he never gave up on the idea that his book would preach a fundamentally uplifting gospel. It would show that, with intelligence and initiative, a gay man could fashion a perfectly satisfying existence for himself. "Mine is no plea for sympathy, for myself or others," he writes, "but is much more an attempt to guide flounderers in their search for happy adjustment to homosexual life." The great enemy of such a happy adjustment was the self-defeating tendency of homosexuals to feel sorry for themselves. Hence his novel would contradict the image of homosexuals as victims. "I will ridicule any self-pity that creeps into my book," he announces.

The novel, in short, was to illustrate the pragmatic philosophy of adaptation that Vining believed explained his own sexual and romantic success. As I hope my analysis of his diary has made clear, there was much truth in this self-portrait. Time and again his wiliness and resilience enabled him to survive misfortune and get what he wanted—or at least to make the most of what he was given. But we should not ignore the significant element of illusion in the story he told himself about his life. It was an entirely functional illusion, a useful private mythology, but it resulted in a distorted picture of his society, one that consistently understated the real burdens under which homosexuals lived. It also resulted in a certain harshness in his judgment of other homosexuals and an inability to appreciate that the pathology of their lives—what Vining criticizes as "the gay world"—might have its source in something beside a failure of will.

Occasionally, in his campaign against self-pity, he even acted as if the obstacles homosexuals faced were more invented than real. The notion is implicit in his surprisingly light-hearted accounts of registering for the draft and his imprisonment on Riker's Island. It is fully evident in his negative reaction to James Barr's novel *Quatrefoil,* which he read in 1950: "It perpetuates the myth of social antagonism to homosexuality, which is nonsense. We are neither hounded nor ostracized these days, but tolerated beyond our deserts." The judgment could have been issued by a right-wing zealot.

One can readily imagine what the young Donald Vining would have made of Jeb Alexander's diary. In Alexander's life Vining would have seen a textbook illustration of the price a homosexual paid for failing to bring mind and will to bear on his situation. Instead of figuring out how to realize his desires, Alexander abandoned himself to extravagant fantasies; instead of prudently negotiating the hazards of cruising, he flailed away impotently at his oppressors; instead of taking sensible advantage of his big romantic chance, he made inflexible demands and then collapsed in despair when the relationship failed. He was, in sum, the archetypal homosexual victim, against which Vining would doubtless present himself as a happy counter-example.

The judgment is in some ways persuasive. Alexander was indeed maddeningly impracticable, even self-destructive. But we are also bound to feel that so categorical an estimate is too simple. It fails to reckon with the real damage that prejudice—never mind oppression—can effect on a nature not blessed with the psychological reserves or experiential advantages Vining enjoyed. Admittedly, Jeb Alexander might have made a mess of things even if he had been straight. But I can't escape the lingering suspicion that the burden of homosexuality pushed him over the edge—that it transformed what would have been a fragile and precarious life into a catastrophic one. Donald Vining's fierce—and thoroughly American—ideal of self-reliance was a useful fiction for his own purposes. But it is an unreliable guide to understanding the Jeb Alexanders of the world.

6

THE CLOSET AND ITS DISCONTENTS

Andrew Tobias, Martin Duberman, and Paul Monette

∽ AMERICAN GAY AUTOBIOGRAPHIES began to appear in the 1970s, with Andrew Tobias's *The Best Little Boy in the World* (1973) one of the first. In the past decade the original trickle has become a flood. We now have scores, perhaps hundreds, of autobiographies by gay men and lesbians from all walks of life—gay athletes, gay soldiers, gay ministers, gay politicians, even gay talk-show hosts. The proliferation of the genre obviously reflects the great transformation of gay life since the first stirrings of liberation at the end of the 1960s. The autobiographies are themselves testimony to that transformation. They chart the process by which American gays have moved from a despised and largely invisible minority toward not just acceptance but a growing sense of moral authority and political empowerment.

I have read many, though by no means all, of these books, and I have been struck by the remarkable similarity of the stories they tell. The vast majority of them are conversion narratives. They begin with an account of the oppressions—social and psychological—endured by the closeted "old man," and they describe the writer's inexorable progress, through moments of crisis, toward self-acceptance and the announcement—more or less public—of his new identity. Often the autobiography is itself a central step in the process, the ultimate coming-out gesture. As frequently happens in conversion narratives, the story of the bad old order is usually the more memorable part of these accounts, which lose some of their tension and pathos as the moment of liberation approaches. One reason for the considerable success of the three autobiographies I examine in this chapter is that they concentrate on the years of repression and unhappiness, ending just as the way out is discovered, and thus spare their authors the dramatically unenviable task of portraying the new dispensation in any great detail. Yet even in Andrew Tobias, Martin Duberman, and Paul Monette the happy conclusion is less persuasive than the miserable beginning. Paradoxically, the conversion narratives are often rescued from the structural boredom built into the form by the catastrophe of AIDS, which introduces a new darkness into what threatens to become an unrelieved story of enlightenment. Of the three autobiographies considered here, Paul Monette's takes greatest literary advantage (if one can put it that way) of the AIDS tragedy, for, though his autobiography ends with an ecstatic romance, he writes under the assumption that the reader already knows the harrowing story of his lover's death, as told in the memoir *Borrowed Time,* which appeared in 1988, four years before *Becoming a Man.*

We can appreciate the distinctive profile of these American gay auto-

biographies if we set them against the very different accounts produced
by the figures—British, French, and even American (in the cases of Jeb
Alexander and Donald Vining)—already examined in this book. I would
not suggest that the burden of secrecy is absent from the earlier texts. On
the contrary, it exists as a kind of unstated background reality in all of
them. Occasionally it even comes to the fore: one thinks, for example, of
Christopher Isherwood's painful encounter with a British customs official
at Harwich when, in 1934, Isherwood tried to bring his lover, Heinz Neddermeyer, into the country (although *Christopher and His Kind*, written in
California in the 1970s, itself belongs, at least in part, to the American
coming-out tradition). But in general the story of oppression remains at
the margins of the earlier books; it is a central organizing principle in none
of them. Some of the older autobiographers, notably J. R. Ackerley and
Julien Green, explicitly deny that social pressure or fear of embarrassment
has played any role in their lives; they attribute their troubles either to
personal idiosyncrasy (Ackerley's search for the Ideal Friend) or to some
abstract conundrum (Green's metaphysical tug-of-war between God and
Satan), never to a failure of self-acceptance based on the homophobic prejudices of their culture. We may choose to see them as victims of false
consciousness, but the fact remains that they simply do not interpret their
experience in terms of the closet categories implicit in virtually all the recent American autobiographies. Most striking in this regard are the two
American diarists discussed in the previous chapter. Donald Vining, we

recall, expressly attacks the idea that he and other gay men have been unduly put upon, and he views his life as a story of success and happiness. Jeb Alexander tells a much more doleful tale and is more inclined to lash out against prejudice, but even Alexander insists that he is unhappy mainly because of the "curse" of homosexuality—his biological fate—not because he is oppressed. Neither man thinks the central problem of his life is the fact of living in the closet, which is the basic assumption of all the recent American autobiographies. Our first inclination may be to assume that Tobias, Duberman, Monette, et al. have finally got the story right. But perhaps we should be alert to an ideological impulse at work in their accounts—a determination to construct a narrative of oppression and liberation, even if it means painting a blacker picture of the past (and a rosier one of the present) than is warranted.

We might wonder why American gay autobiographers of the last three decades have become so addicted to the coming-out story. What explains why this particular version of a homosexual life is now the only one we tell ourselves? Most obviously coming out seems to be a reaction against the unique oppression American gays suffered in the 1950s, which scholars have pronounced the most homophobic decade in our history. The interpretation is strongly supported by the autobiographers themselves: Tobias, Monette, and especially Duberman portray the Fifties as an era of psychiatric conversion fantasies, political witchhunts, and blanket denial, against which they eventually summoned the courage to rebel. But, of course,

they did not rebel alone: coming out was part of a movement, Gay Liberation, which itself was but one component of the identity politics that came
to dominate American life in the 1960s and 1970s: by proclaiming their
sexual orientation the essence of their selfhood, gays were merely following in the footsteps of Blacks and women who had made similar claims for
race and gender. At a more speculative level, I am inclined to see in the
coming-out stories a paradoxical or up-side-down version of America's
Protestant heritage, a psychic puritanism, if you will, that has little tolerance for ambiguity or hypocrisy and wants the conscience to be utterly
clear, unitary, and at peace with itself. Europeans, by contrast, seem able
to live with a good deal more psychological dissonance. Certainly that is
the inference one would draw from the French and British autobiographers, who don't agonize over their sexual secret with anything like the
same intensity. In fact, some of them (J. R. Ackerley and Julien Green
come immediately to mind) pretend to be indifferent to public opinion.

I have decided to focus on the closet autobiographies of Andrew Tobias (1947–), Martin Duberman (1930–), and Paul Monette (1945–1995)
for a number of reasons, personal as well intellectual. In the most general
sense I have chosen them as representative spokesmen of the recent American tradition. At the same time all three, but especially Duberman and
Monette, impress me is offering unusually rich and finely observed versions of the closet experience: theirs are thus more inviting targets for
analysis than any of the other coming-out autobiographies I have read.

Perhaps I am saying no more than that, like most of the writers I have considered in this book, they are intellectuals: Tobias is a nationally syndicated financial adviser, Duberman is a professional historian and sometime playwright, and Monette was a novelist and poet. Their books thus have something of the complexity of argument and texture that distinguishes the British and French works we have examined.

I have also been drawn to Tobias, Duberman, and Monette because their autobiographies exhibit similarities and differences that beg for comparison. The most immediate similarity is chronological: all three books focus on a closeted life in the 1950s and 1960s, and they end with a coming-out experience in the early 1970s. Tobias and Monette were roughly the same age in those years: both tell stories that stretch from childhood to their mid-twenties. But, significantly, they were very different ages when they chose to record the unhappy tale of their first two and half decades: Tobias, at twenty-five, recounts a drama he is still in the middle of, and his book ends in an appropriately unsettled fashion, without benefit of the ideological hindsight or accumulated wisdom to which Monette had access when he wrote his version of those same decades nearly twenty years later. On the other hand, Monette's and Duberman's narratives are virtually contemporaneous—*Cures* appeared in 1991, *Becoming a Man* in 1992—but Duberman was by then in his early sixties, almost a generation older than Monette, and hence his account of the 1950s and 1960s relates not his childhood and adolescence but the experiences of a man in his twenties, thirties, and early forties.

There are also interesting differences of tone and focus among the three books. Tobias, by far the youngest author, writes a book that, depending on your point of view, might be considered charmingly unselfconscious or annoyingly sophomoric. He has two great themes. The first is the physical toll repression has taken on him: he describes himself as a person whose body has shut down because of the impossible desires that inhabit it. The most memorable (and funniest) scenes in *The Best Little Boy in the World* record his much delayed and excruciating efforts to bring his body back to life: to learn how to fart, how to masturbate, and, finally, how to have gay sex, which, even when he throws himself into the effort, turns out to be incredibly difficult. The second theme is telling the truth about his sexuality—"coming out" as an intellectual process—above all to his parents. The chief irony of his story is that he proves better at declaring his sexuality than at performing it, although by publishing his autobiography under a pseudonym ("John Reid") he acknowledges that even the truth-telling remains incomplete.

Martin Duberman, as both the oldest and the most scholarly of the three autobiographers, is more sober and analytical. To a greater extent than Tobias or Monette, he is concerned with representing his experience as the product of a distinct moment in American history, the homophobic

1950s and 1960s. Accordingly, his account focuses on the ideological and institutional mechanisms through which the work of repression was done, above all the American psychiatric profession. *Cures* is an appropriate (and appropriately ironic) title for his book, because at its center lies an account of the years of psychoanalytic therapy devoted to the Quixotic goal of changing him into a heterosexual. His various analysts figure more prominently in the book than any of his lovers or sexual partners. Or, better put, his romantic and erotic adventures are shown becoming grist for the psychoanalytic mill, through which they are sabotaged and disfigured. Moreover, just as his version of the closet stresses the cultural and political forces at work shaping his unhappy life, his conception of the way out is also cultural and political: the book moves inexorably toward identity politics—toward affiliation with his fellow sufferers in an increasingly collective and public gesture of resistance.

Perhaps because, unlike Martin Duberman, Paul Monette was not obliged to do battle with American psychiatry, or perhaps because he brought the sensibility of a novelist to his task, he felt freer to explore the psychology of the closet. Certainly the distinguishing feature of *Becoming a Man* is its withering analysis of the many disguises Monette assumed in his years of denial. One false identity follows another until he finally musters the courage to accept the true self hidden behind the masks. Monette is the least postmodern of authors: he never doubts that his straight—or asexual—selves were impersonations, while his gay self is the real thing.

He has an equally old-fashioned—some would say unexamined—idea of the way out of the closet: it lies not, as with Duberman, through politics but through romance. To be sure, *Becoming a Man* expresses political opinions: it contains a running attack on the enemies of his tribe, above all the Catholic Church, and a call for homosexuals to declare themselves. But the central movement of the narrative is toward love, toward finding the partner in whose embrace Monette can shed his false selves and fully inhabit his sexual and emotional identity as a gay man.

Tobias, Duberman, and Monette, then, give us three different versions of the closet. Tobias's focus is on the body and the mysterious tension between speaking and being homosexual. Duberman draws our attention to the cultural work of repression and points toward a political solution. Monette is the psychological analyst of the closeted life who looks for a way out in romance.

Andrew Tobias, in high school, ca. 1963.

The Best Little Boy in the World

I FIRST READ "JOHN REID'S" *The Best Little Boy in the World* sometime in the 1970s. My copy of the book is the third printing, dated 1979, of the Ballantine paperback, although I'm inclined to place my original reading somewhat earlier. By the end of the 1970s the book's author was widely known, within the gay community, to be Andrew Tobias, whose career as a financial adviser was just beginning to take off: he had been a contributing editor to *New York Magazine* from 1972 to 1977, when he moved to *Esquire,* and the most famous of his financial best-sellers, *The Only Investment Guide You'll Ever Need,* appeared a year later. I duly recorded on the title page of my copy that the book's author was really Andrew Tobias, and I further noted that he had disguised his college experience (from 1964 to 1968) by transferring it from Harvard to Yale—thereby creating the textual (but false) coincidence of spending three years in the same university as Paul Monette, who was a Yale undergraduate from 1963 to 1967. (Adding to the Yale connection was the fact that Martin Duberman also got his B. A. there, in 1952, and then taught in the Yale History Department from 1957 to 1962. Finally, I myself was at Yale from 1958 to 1962 and even took a course with Duberman—a matter I will return to in the next section.)

I remember reading *The Best Little Boy in the World* with great enthusiasm and recommending it to others. My enthusiasm did not stem from self-recognition: I had no trouble "learning" how to have gay sex, and I had long been out to my family and friends, although not to my straight professional colleagues (which awaited a piece I published in the Fall/Winter issue of *Salmagundi,* in 1982–83). I am sure I admired the author's willingness to expose his vulnerability and to make a public issue of his right to be a gay man. Mostly, however, I recall finding the book funny and moving, above all in the way it showed how sexual repression could lodge itself in the body, leaving Tobias incapable of doing anything with the men he so passionately desired other than stage imaginary wrestling matches. I even suspect that reading *The Best Little Boy in the World* planted the seed of the present study: of all gay autobiographies, it is the only one I assumed from the start would be included among those I would examine.

My enthusiasm was hardly unique. I don't know how many printings of the first (1973) and second (1976) editions were ordered by the original publisher, G. P. Putnam's Sons, but the Ballantine paperback of 1977 was reprinted fifteen times, and in 1993 Ballantine issued a trade version, which as of 1997 was in its sixth printing. *The Best Little Boy in the World* may well be the most read of all gay autobiographies. Among gay men of a certain age, it enjoys almost iconic status.

Rereading the book after nearly two decades has proved a disappointment. Even back in the 1970s I recognized that it was somewhat slapdash: Tobias admits that he wrote it in a matter of weeks during the summer of 1972. Moreover the end of the book had always been a letdown. In effect Tobias runs out of life, and in the last third he gives up on autobiography and produces instead a guided tour of gay culture in Boston and New York circa 1970. The Afterword to the second edition of 1976 concedes that many readers had found the latter half of the book wanting.

Now, however, the book's defects seem to me far graver. They afflict not just the weak ending but the strong beginning as well. In the most general sense I no longer find the book's tone amusing. Rather it strikes me as jokey and exaggerated—italics and CAPITALIZATIONS proliferate annoyingly, while phrases Tobias takes to be funny ("for crying out loud") seem merely grating. On reflection I recognize that the bothersome tone reflects Tobias's notion of how to reach the imagined audience at whom the book was directed. *The Best Little Boy in the World* was written not for gays (though surely they have been its main readers) but for straights. Somehow I had ignored or repressed this fact, though Tobias himself is quite forthright about it. He often addresses the straight reader directly in the text. Describing a chaste night spent in bed with a much desired college roommate, for example, he asks, "Can you imagine sleeping like that—with Ali MacGraw, if you prefer—and not being able to touch?"

The jokey tone, in other words, is a way of ingratiating himself with a hostile audience. Tobias knows that an amused straight reader will more likely give his story a sympathetic hearing. In a way, his strategy is no different from André

Gide's in *Si le grain ne meurt:* he is writing a work of polemic, aimed at disabusing heterosexual readers of their prejudices, so he does everything he can to endear himself to those readers. But the matter goes deeper. He also wants to suggest that the style is the man: he talks like one of the guys in order to imply that he himself is straight in every respect but the (narrow) matter of sexual desire. His humor is of the jock variety, as far removed as imaginable from the arch queenery of Quentin Crisp, and it seeks to convey the message that homosexuality has nothing to do with effeminacy. Here again his strategy resembles Gide's, who, we recall, drew a sharp contrast between his own virile pederasty and the effeminate inversion of Oscar Wilde.

The book betrays other prejudices as well. It is often misogynistic. In an effort to depict the agony of heterosexual dating, Tobias resorts to cartoonish exaggerations of his dates' unappealing bodies and overactive libidos. Likewise, his decision to use a pen name no longer seems entirely innocent. In the 1976 Afterword he pleads the wish to spare his parents "pain and embarrassment," which is certainly defensible. But why, one wonders, does he remain anonymous in the new trade edition of 1993? In a brief Afterword he alludes to the AIDS epidemic ("I'm fine. A lot of my friends are not.") but is silent about his continued unwillingness to assume responsibility for the book. Inevitably we suspect that he fears endangering his successful career as a financial writer. A certain vulgar commercialism, we are now apt to notice, is already evident in the original text: at one point he defends homosexuality as a sensible way to save money on "pediatricians, orthodontists, [and] gynecologists." The author of *The Best Little Boy in the World* is too transparently the same man as the author of *The Only Investment Guide You'll Ever Need.*[1]

I have countered my disappointment on rereading Tobias with two sorts of considerations. The first is the historian's familiar caution against "presentism": judging the past by the standards of today. *The Best Little Boy in the World* is now a quarter century old, and we should not expect it to mirror the more enlightened views of a Martin Duberman or a Paul Monette writing in the 1990s, never mind the cutting edge of Queer Theory. Indeed, the real interest of the book lies precisely in its historical character: its awkward mixture of the progressive and the retrograde obviously appealed to a wide audience of gay men at a

1. In March 1995, two years after the last edition of the book, Tobias took public responsibility for it. He did so in an interview/article in *OUT* magazine. The piece reports that he first came out publicly in December 1992, at a Renaissance Weekend (made famous of course by the Clintons).

certain moment. The second consideration has been to remind myself that the book should be judged as a piece of propaganda—as a kind of strategic misrepresentation whose chief goal was to confound the more virulent forms of homophobia. Tobias's immediate target was the psychiatrist David Reuben, whose *Everything You've Always Wanted to Know about Sex but Were Afraid to Ask* had already sold eight million copies when Tobias was writing and whose "putrid chapter" on homosexuality announced that gay sex was invariably devoid of sentiment, being only the rudest sort of physical coupling. Tobias answered Reuben, cleverly, by presenting his own case as something like the opposite: his emotions were, if anything, overstimulated while his body remained inert. My more general point is that the terms of debate were very different a quarter century ago from what they are today. Hoping to rout the David Reubens of the world, Tobias reasonably sought to narrow the field of battle and avoid offending potential allies. He apparently decided that playing the straight gay man and sometimes throwing the less presentable members of the tribe overboard were the unavoidable price of polemical success.

⌒⌒ TOBIAS'S RELATIONSHIP WITH HIS parents is the central preoccupation of *The Best Little Boy in the World*. The book ends with his coming out to them—an event that is anticipated and even rehearsed throughout the book—and it begins with his effort to recreate the peculiar family atmosphere of his childhood. Officially he insists that his mother and father were good and loving, as well as profoundly devoted to his own happiness. But the concrete experiences he recalls leave a very different impression: over and over his parents are exposed as morally rigid and sexually repressive. He never blames them for his problems—to do so would be "ridiculous," he insists, "because they have to rank among the world's best parents." Still, the book shows them creating expectations that left him tied in emotional knots and alienated from his body long before the issue of homosexuality reared its ugly head at adolescence. One of his running jokes is to refer to his parents as "the Supreme Court," an implicit acknowledgement of their remoteness and authoritarianism.

Along with an older brother (who, in another running joke, is always called "Goliath"), he grew up in Manhattan, the weekends being spent at the family's colonial home in Brewster (really Bedford Village), New York. The Tobiases might be considered an affluent version of the typical sitcom family of the 1950s, although Tobias himself, in contrast to Martin Duberman, seems unaware of the distinct historical flavor of his experience. By repeatedly assuring him that he was "the best little boy in the world," his parents aimed to inculcate two virtues: goodness and ambition. But he soon found that the two did not sit well together: the more he achieved—athletically, scholastically—the less he liked himself, because his achievement reflected not virtue but egoism. "Deep down," he recalls, "I knew I wasn't 'good' at all—just selfish, just out for myself. I was a phony, and I knew it."

The conviction of his badness—and the fear that he would be found out— set the psychological stage for his disastrous response to his homosexuality. Even more influential was his parents' hysterically negative attitude toward the body, especially toward any manifestation of sexuality. Again, they seem almost a parody of Fifties denial: the subject was simply beyond mention. "In *my* family," he writes, "one of the things we *never* talked about was that thing down there. Never. . . . This was a Bad Area. This was an area the Best Little Boy in the World used for one thing, in private, and one thing only." His anxiety increased when he found he had a slight physical defect, a varicocele, on his scrotum, a matter he hid from his parents until it was discovered, to his mortification, by the family doctor.

The repression affected him not merely in the penis, as one might expect, but in the anus as well. He never explores the meaning of this connection, in which a Freudian will be inclined to detect homoerotically linked erogenous zones. He simply knew that the two were equally prohibited: "I would no sooner have fooled around with my Bad Area than I would have stuck my finger up my Other Bad Area." Perhaps the book's most spectacular revelation, delivered in the opening sentence, is that he didn't learn to fart until he was eighteen years old. "I . . . never farted," he explains, "because I knew it was a bad thing to do." Within the family his anal retentiveness earned him moral points at the expense of his brother, who was forever stinking up the car on the trips to and from Brewster. Significantly, eighteen was also the age at which Tobias first learned to masturbate. He knew about the practice, in a vague way, from the talk of other boys at school and camp, but so pervasive was the genital blackout that he never figured out what to do. Moreover, he couldn't ask anyone about it without risking humiliation. "Can you imagine the ridicule if I admitted that masturbation hadn't happened to me yet?" he asks. "WHAT ARE YOU, ANYWAY, SOME KIND

OF HO-MO?" His only sexual experience in these years was a single wet dream at thirteen, and that experience was hideously compromised by its inspiration. "My wet dream," he reveals, "was about Tommy Roth."

The knowledge that he was a homosexual came to him in a sudden and awful moment at the age of eleven (two years before Tommy Roth appeared on his horizon). At a party, he overheard his father and a guest talking about the infamous Kinsey statistic: "'I've read that, too; but ten percent just couldn't be right. There couldn't be that many people with homosexual tendencies. . . .'" (The incident must have occurred in 1958 or 1959, a decade after Kinsey's Male volume had appeared.) Tobias's recognition was immediate and unambiguous: "I *knew,* I'm not sure how, but I *knew* I was in the 10 percent." Moreover, the knowledge launched the main project of his life for the next decade: keeping his "Big Secret" inviolable. "I had found out about myself," he writes, "but no one else would ever find out as long as I lived. That stigma and keeping it a secret were the fundamental core of my mind, from which all other thoughts and actions flowed." He poured huge amounts of psychic energy and no little ingenuity into the task. One of his defenses was to remain as ignorant as possible about homosexuality: if he knew too much, he reasoned, he risked looking or acting like a homosexual. Another was to throw himself even more compulsively into academic and athletic pursuits. A third was to avoid psychiatry: "I . . . would no more have considered talking to a psychiatrist than one of the ten most wanted criminals would consider stopping to get directions from a cop." It was his most sensible decision, sparing him the therapeutic agony that blighted Martin Duberman's life in these same years.

But what exactly did he understand about himself when he concluded he was a homosexual—something so shameful that keeping it secret became his chief object in life for ten years? Here we come up against an interesting contradiction in his account. Clearly he associated the word with his feelings for several of his male contemporaries, of whom Tommy Roth was the foremost example. Yet what he wanted to do with Tommy and the others was extraordinarily anodyne. It had no connection with genitals and didn't even contemplate kissing. It approached the physical only in the antiseptic wish to wrestle. In short, it was a desire less for possession than for identification:

> Oh, what I would have given to be Tommy's real best fiend. God, how I
> wanted to be *like* him, to do the same mischievous, self-assured things he did,

to have muscles and blond hair and a smile like his. Nothing in our relationship would be disgusting, nothing unmentionable. Just to be like the Hardy Boys, two blood brothers, two cowboys . . . that's it: two cowboys.

The imagined relationship, in other words, was fully in keeping with the sexual repression that had blanketed his entire young life.

At the same time, "homosexuality" had acquired another connotation in his mind, although he doesn't explain how he came by it. In this second sense it meant effeminacy. Here was the identity that Tobias truly feared, far more than any concrete sexual acts he was unable even to imagine. Because his horror of effeminacy was so great, he sometimes told himself, contradictorily, that he was not a homosexual after all. There was simply no connection between what he felt for Tommy Roth and any kind of visible unmanliness, though, mysteriously, the same term seemed to be used for both things:

> Those people I saw in the streets with their pocketbooks and their swish and their pink hair—they disgusted me at least as much as they disgusted everyone else, probably more. I would sooner have slept with a girl, God forbid, than with one of those horrible people. Do you understand? I wasn't a homosexual; I just desperately wanted to be cowboys with Chip or with Tommy.

Denouncing queers, he reports shamefully, became one of the ways he maintained his cover. When a man offered to give him a blow job at the Museum of Natural History, he turned the incident to his advantage at camp the next summer. "I related my genuine disgust," he reports. "I heaped all the worst invectives I could on that perverted *thing*, to establish my own normality—and I even managed to deduce from the subsequent conversation what the hell a blow job *was*." Apparently he didn't consider his behavior hypocritical, for the simple reason that he drew a watertight distinction between his own innocuous (if fierce) desires and such perverse acts. And yet at some level of his mind he must have known that the two were linked. Otherwise the Herculean effort to maintain his Big Secret—the task that absorbed his every waking hour from ages eleven to twenty-one—makes no sense.

 DURING HIS FOUR YEARS at college, from 1964 to 1968, Tobias's basic predicament remained unchanged, although a number of complications were introduced, and he became increasingly depressed about his life. His goal was the same: to

find another visibly normal male to whom he could attach himself in a relationship that would be emotionally intense but physically innocent. Yet the budding
financial analyst grew more and more aware that his project was statistically
flawed, even contradictory. On the one hand he knew, "in a theoretical, mathe-
matical sort of way," that he could not be the only "straight-looking, athletic
young man in search of someone to be cowboys with." On the other, because all
the candidates must be engaged in the same cover-up as himself, they could never
hope to find each other. In any case, he reasoned, "Even if one in ten boys really
did have 'tendencies,' who was going to risk everything on a one-in-ten chance?"

Among the complications introduced by college was his first sustained infatuation, with the roommate, Hank, of his sophomore through senior years. Beside
lasting longer, it differed from his earlier attachments in that it now included the
need to declare his love. But, even though he desperately wanted to tell Hank of
his feelings, the idea that the confession might elicit a response remained intolerable. "I didn't want him to love me back," he asserts. "That would probably have
ruined it. (Well, that would have made him queer, you see, and who wants to be
cowboys with a queer?)"

Another difficulty that intensified at college was the question of what do
about women. Dating was an integral component of the deception he felt obliged
to practice. In college in the 1960s, dating meant performing sexually, or at least
conveying the impression to one's fellow students that one performed. In Tobias's
case the anxiety was heightened because he went on double dates with Hank and
had to worry that, by the chain of confidences among girlfriends, the news of his
inadequacy would find its way back to the one man whom he most wanted to
convince of his normalness.

The treatment of women in *The Best Little Girl in the World* is the book's
greatest embarrassment and where it most shows its age. In one respect Tobias's
purpose is unexceptionable: he wants to create a visceral sense of the awfulness
of pretending to desires that one doesn't feel—pretending, moreover, not just
verbally but physically. The embarrassment stems from his implication that what
he pretended to feel about women would have been entirely acceptable if only
those feelings had been genuine rather than feigned. He never suggests that the
treatment of women as sexual (or not-so-sexual) objects was inherently objec-
tionable or that it might be in any way related to the oppression of homosexuals.
In effect, his notions about gender were no different from those of a typical
straight man of his day.

The pattern had established itself already in high school. Of one of his dates he writes, "She had a four-inch chin. . . . When she walked through doors, she had to turn her head sideways so her hand would reach the door knob before her chin hit the door." Another girl was "weighed down by two of the most enormous, terrifying boobs I could imagine"; on their outing she revealed herself to be a slut: "She pried open my mouth with her crowbar tongue and stuck it in." The first thing he did when he got to college was to subscribe to *Playboy* and hang each month's centerfold over his bed. Still, his recital of the contortions he went through in order to keep up the facade of heterosexual potency is often touching and hilarious. On one drunken summer night in Spain with Hank, he carefully steered his woman to a vacant room in their hotel and then begged off on grounds of exhaustion. When he and Hank met the next morning, they had their usual exchange: "Hank: 'How was it?' 'Good,' I said." For all the agony it caused him at the time, the episode ended up serving his purposes: "Hank had virtual proof, short of being an eyewitness, that I screwed girls." Back at school he milked the story for every last ounce of heterosexual credit.

A final complication at college arose from a fellow student, Jon Martin, who was not only effeminate—"lisping" and "shrieking"—but openly homosexual. Even worse, he preached the liberationist doctrine that was just then beginning to emerge in certain enlightened corners of American culture: "He talked constantly of 'closet cases' and 'closet queens.' He believed in liberating the world. He thought it was sick and hypocritical to hide one's true sexual preferences." Jon Martin would have caused Tobias little grief had he not been a close friend of a straight young man, Brook, whom Tobias not only admired but eventually fell in love with. Much as he had done with the fellow who tried to pick him up in the Museum of Natural History, Tobias reacted by never missing a chance to denounce Jon Martin. His hatred was perfectly genuine, moreover, for Martin threatened the entire apparatus of normal masculinity that Tobias was laboring to keep in place.

Tobias made it to the end of his undergraduate career with his fundamental defenses intact. He even managed to maintain them throughout the following year (1968–69), when he took a job with IBM in New York, "sublimating my sexual energy into my work, as usual." But the effort, he found, was becoming unbearable. His suffering was always more psychological than physical: much as he regretted not being able to realize his cowboy fantasies, the sexual denial was nothing compared to the burden of eternal vigilance. Increasingly he felt a profound need to tell someone about "the single most important thing in my life that I thought about for hours each day."

The amazing thing about Tobias's story is that he reached the decision to declare himself a gay man before he had had even one homosexual experience. In this respect his life represents the most radical version—indeed almost a caricature—of the coming-out ideology that now dominates the American gay community. Martin Duberman and Paul Monette—both vigorous adepts of coming out—had numerous homosexual encounters over many years (accompanied with varying degrees of guilt) before they concluded that, for their own happiness and that of their kind, the closet had to be abandoned. But, uniquely among gay autobiographers I have read, Tobias launched his exit from the closet while still a virgin. In fact he had already become a practiced truth-teller before he turned his attention to bringing his body up to speed with his mind.

The breakthrough occurred the summer after his first year in New York. The text of *The Best Little Boy in the World* contains not a single date—a measure of Tobias's unhistorical imagination—but we can deduce that he came out in 1969, which was also the summer of the Stonewall riots. He never mentions Stonewall. In part his silence merely reflects that fact that when he was writing, in 1972, Stonewall had not yet come to be viewed as a symbolic watershed, the gay equivalent of the fall of the Bastille. But his silence also betrays his political naivete, in particular his failure to recognize that he was living in the midst of a sea change that no doubt influenced his own life. In particular we are apt to suspect that the hateful teachings of Jon Martin may well have insinuated themselves into his mind and nudged him, however unconsciously, toward his great change of heart. But in the text he presents it as an entirely individual matter: at a certain point he simply found he could no longer bear the lie.

Although the distinctive feature of Tobias's experience was the decision to speak before he acted, his first confession was complicated by desire. He came out to his old college friend Brook, to whom, by the summer of 1969, he had transferred the cowboy fantasies previously lavished on his roommate Hank. In other words, Tobias was, after his peculiar fashion, in love with Brook, so that telling him the truth was at some level an invitation to start a relationship. (One also wonders about the role played by Brook's friendliness with Jon Martin, but Tobias says nothing of that connection.) After three drinks, "and more stammering and prefacing and blushing that I care to remember," he told Brook that he liked boys rather than girls: "I told him because after eleven years of silence,

I could stand loneliness no longer, I could stand pretending no longer, and I wanted to tell someone that I loved him." As he surely must have known, Tobias had chosen the ideal confessor. Brook was the very embodiment of enlightened sympathy, as would befit a friend of Jon Martin's. More than enlightened, he had himself tried sleeping with men, in order "to find some physical expression for the emotional 'love' he felt for other guys." Although the experience had not proved to his liking, that did not keep him from throwing himself into the project of unleashing Tobias's repressed sensuality—hugging him, giving him back rubs, lying on top him, even wrestling with him. It sounds almost like the complete realization of Tobias's fondest erotic imaginings, but, because it was done without arousal (at least on Brook's part), Tobias properly cherished it as the sign of acceptance and affection Brook intended. After fantasizing "thousands of times" of telling someone he was a homosexual, he finally had a person to talk with: "I was luxuriating in *honesty* for the first time in my life. And relaxing my defenses. Creakingly, haltingly at first, and not without second thoughts, yet letting my guard down all the same." At that point in his history, talking about his sexuality seemed vastly more important than doing anything about it.

Over the course of the next year Tobias developed into an expert practitioner of the art of coming out. He proceeded to tell virtually all of his straight friends. And while none of them responded with quite the enthusiasm of Brook, they all greeted the news sympathetically. In fact, we begin to wonder why Tobias had invested so much agony, over so many years, in maintaining his deceit when the reaction to his story was unfailingly benign. But when he set up his defenses in the late 1950s, the policy of secrecy was far from irrational: American homophobia was then in full bloom, and his automatic decision to hide his desires made perfect sense. The uniformly tolerant reception he got a decade later testifies to a profound shift in attitudes that was just beginning to take place among people of a certain age, class, and education—to wit, Tobias's own contemporaries at certain elite universities and in certain cities. But, characteristically, he is oblivious to this epochal change: he treats his good fortune as evidence not of a historical transformation but of the happy accident that he had such decent friends.

Tobias learned to savor the pleasures of telling his story. For one thing, he enjoyed the surprise it always elicited. But most of all he enjoyed learning that his long deception had been successful: "It was confirmation that my masquerade had been convincing and that my masculinity remained, more or less, intact." In other words, his coming out had a reactionary subtext: even as he confessed to

loving men he carefully distanced himself from all those manifestations of effeminacy that had been his main reason for taking to the closet in the first place.
Thus, when he gave his "sales pitch for homosexuality" to his brother, he aimed
at disabusing Goliath of his stereotyped ideas about "hairdressers, interior de-
signers, and sadistic concentration camp managers." Similarly, among the joys of
his new candor he reckoned the permission it gave him to subject men to the same
erotic objectification that heterosexuals subjected women to: "How refreshing to
walk down the street with a straight friend and, while he was nudging and leering
about the approaching girl, nudge and leer back about the approaching girl's
date!" As with André Gide before him, his coming out was conceived in the
narrowest possible terms. It left many of his heterosexual credentials—and his
claims to heterosexual privilege—in place.

The closest thing to disapproval he heard from those he told was the occasional suggestion that, if he felt bad about being gay, he might consider seeing a
psychiatrist. But Tobias had always entertained a vigorous skepticism regarding
therapy. He was a natural essentialist: he understood instinctively that nothing
was going to alter how he felt. "I knew for sure," he informs us, "that I was not
changeable. Hypnosis, Freudian psychoanalysis, shock treatments, or just 'the
right girl' were not going to work in my case." Beside his innate essentialism, a
healthy self-regard kept him from becoming a sucker for the "cure." As he says,
"I had grown rather attached to myself over the years, screwball though I was."
Martin Duberman could have used some of his robust narcissism. Tobias also
makes the subtler, almost philosophical, point that homosexuality was so integral
to his sense of self that without it he would no longer be the same individual: "A
me that liked girls rather than boys wouldn't be me at all." Thus when someone
asked if he would take a pill to become straight, his answer was unambiguous:
"That would make me an entirely different person. *That would be like killing
myself.*" His response whenever anyone proposed psychiatry was to turn the
tables on his straight interlocutor: would his friend consider seeing a shrink in
order to become a homosexual? He felt no differently, he insisted, about becoming a heterosexual.

Coming out to his friends was one thing. Coming out to his parents was
quite another. The project haunted his imagination, as he tried to picture how
they might respond to the news. On a weekend in the summer of 1970 he went
down to Brewster resolved to tell them, rehearsing his "sales technique" as he
drove. Even though he knew, in a general way, that his parents would react "rela-

tively well," he still fretted endlessly. He imagined his father seized by "fleeting images of unthinkable sexual perversions" and the memory of "swishy types who had occasionally approached him in his youth." Nor did he relish the idea of destroying his reputation as the best little boy in the world. "Was I ready to live without their thinking I was perfect?" he asks. Apparently not, because by the time he arrived in Brewster his resolution had evaporated: "I decided that telling them was almost certain to make them unhappy, and I doubted whether the new closeness and honesty in our relationship would be sufficient compensation for the hurt." Two years later, in the midst of writing his autobiography, he was once more on the verge. But again he delayed. Ultimately the revelation takes place offstage, as it were: the book ends with a chapter that reads in its entirety: "I told them. They said so far as they were concerned, I was still the best little boy in the world." It is an effective, if laconic, resolution of the story's central drama.

⊙ HAVING SPENT THE BETTER PART of a year telling his story to his friends, Tobias began, with their encouragement, to take some tentative steps toward actually becoming the homosexual he had announced himself to be. Among his book's enduring attractions is its account of just how difficult he found that task. Of course, Tobias was not the first gay autobiographer to confess his problems in having sex with another man. J. R. Ackerley, for example, acknowledged that anything beyond embraces and caresses appalled him, and even with a much desired partner he was likely to suffer from premature ejaculation and impotence. I have suggested that a similar squeamishness may have influenced Stephen Spender to give up on homosexuality, at least officially, in the mid-1930s. And clearly André Gide had a very narrow sexual palette, which excluded any practice that might compromise his masculinity or sense of decorum. But no gay autobiographer I've read experienced more trouble with sex than Tobias. Certainly none has given a more vivid account of the agonizing process by which he tried to bring his desires into line with the expectations of the men he pursued.

Ironically, his first adventure turned out to be his best, but only because at the time he was blissfully ignorant that the encounter was so innocent. As he recognized later, he had managed to have "sex without *doing* anything." On the basis of an ad in the Personals, he made a date with a hustler, who, to his delight, turned out to be the complete embodiment of his cowboy fantasies: masculine, rugged, and handsome. The "sex" too was of the cowboy variety he had always dreamed of: they hugged, rolled about, wrestled, and felt each other's muscles.

Tobias makes a point of recording exactly what they didn't do: "We weren't kissing (cowboys don't kiss!); we weren't putting our cocks, God forbid, in each other's mouths, or anywhere else, though we were touching places I had never touched or been touched before." They carried on for hours in this fashion, never reaching orgasm, because, Tobias asserts somewhat improbably, he was unaware that that was what generally happened when people had sex. Only later did he figure out how little, by prevailing gay standards, had taken place: "We were doing everything I wanted to do. And not feeling that there were other things Dick wanted to do, I wasn't self-conscious about just wrestling around."

In the summer of 1970 Tobias moved to Boston, where his college chums Hank and Brook—now his main confidants in sexual matters—were in residence. Through Hank he met a gay friend who tried to introduce him to oral sex. Tobias didn't like it at all. Erotically he was no further along than when he had declined a blow job in the Museum of Natural History years earlier: "The more he sucked, the more upset I became, partly at the picture of the situation in general, and that I could be party to such a thing; more specifically because I couldn't come." He now realized that his experience with the New York hustler had been anomalous: if he wanted to be a gay man he would be expected to do things (and have things done to him) that he found repulsive. In spite of all his brave talk, his body remained in thrall to the closet's repressions. He was not even normal, it seems, in his abnormality.

The full dimensions of his predicament were revealed that same summer when he picked up his first trick in a gay bar. Now it was no longer just a matter of a blow job but the complete standard repertory of gay sex: "He wanted to kiss (germs!); he wanted to put our respective things in our respective mouths. . . ; and he even tried to, well, rob me of my virginity. This last was not only disgusting to think about, but was also, judging from what little progress he was able to make before I resisted, likely to be excruciating." The nervously jokey language itself testifies to Tobias's continuing unease about gay eroticism, even as it serves, like so much of the book's writing, to co-opt straight readers by implying that he shares their distaste.

Still, Tobias was unhappy about his inhibitions. "God damn it!" he exclaims, "Why can't I be like everyone else and like to do those things?" His reaction was very different from J. R. Ackerley's, who was unembarrassed by his limited desires. Tobias took it for granted that he needed to work on his sexual skills. His determination to do better reflects a typically American devotion to self-improvement, as well as a certain conformism ("What are people going to think of me?" he asks at one point). He declines, in the book, to describe "every tiny step" of his progress toward "normal, uninhibited sex," but he does give a general report. "If the road to good sex extends from Lisbon to Leningrad," he concludes, "I am at the time of this writing lost somewhere in the Pyrenees, but hopeful." In the Afterword to the 1976 edition he updates the metaphor: "I am slogging through snowdrifts in the Italian Alps. Substantially further along, in other words, but still a little off course."

The first summer in Boston was devoted to working on his sexual problem. He made nightly forays to Boston's best known gay bar, Sporters, and on weekends he sometimes traveled to Provincetown. (Paul Monette also moved to the Boston area in 1970, and Sporters was Monette's bar of choice as well, so the two may conceivably have met.) By fall, rather predictably, he had tired of one-night stands and began looking for a lover. From the start this was a rather academic enterprise: he was inspired more by the *idea* of a lover—and the wish to show him off—than by deep longing. Indeed, Tobias is the least romantic of gay autobiographers—at the opposite end of the spectrum from a self-confessed "love junkie" like Monette. Moreover, he is fully aware of the emotional deficit under which he labored. Like John Stuart Mill, he grew up convinced that he had been "born without feelings." Or, more accurately, his only feelings were for himself: he was "coldly analytical, calculatingly self-centered." Naturally he wants to believe that his adventures in gay love have uncovered a hidden vein of sentiment. But, again like John Stuart Mill, his emotional transformation is not very convincing. In his early relationships, at least, he remained profoundly self-absorbed. The romances, accordingly, seem curiously weightless, and we never take the interest in them we do in the account of his decade in the closet or his sexual travails.

The most serious of the relationships was with a Southerner, Chris, who was a student at the Harvard Business School. Although they didn't live together, they considered themselves lovers for eight months, from September 1970 to April 1971. Tobias admits that the affair was never fully reciprocal, with Chris more involved than himself. At the same time, Tobias was still far from out of the sexual woods; by his own reckoning, as we know, he had barely reached the Pyrenees. So the relationship was hampered by erotic incompatibility. In effect, he remained stuck in his adolescent wrestling fantasies. Having sex with Chris essentially meant shutting his eyes and concentrating on those fantasies. Chris had to satisfy himself as best he could, without disturbing Tobias's concentration. Tobias captures his attitude in a nicely self-critical formulation: "Go ahead and come when I come, that's okay by me; only don't make too much noise or move around too much, or you will make me lose my train of thought, and *I* won't be able to come. And if it's all the same to you, try not to get it on me." In only one respect did they achieve genuine intimacy: despite his embarrassment, Tobias eventually managed to tell Chris about the content of his "lurid" cowboy scenario. Doing so represented a major opening-up, even though it didn't improve their sex life. More than anything else, it marked a shift of the relationship from romance to friendship.

Tobias defines lovers as "two gay men who spend most of their time together and who are supposed to feel guilty if they have sex with someone else." As the formula implies, the threat of infidelity is virtually built into the conception. Because sex with Chris was not very satisfying for either party, they soon decided, "as some gay lovers do," to venture out on their own "every so often." They established two rules: you always had to confess, at least after the fact, and you never had sex with a common friend. There is something drearily familiar about their decision (we may recall that Donald Vining adopted a similar policy). Above all, it appears to have been taken without much thought, although we shouldn't expect two men in their early twenties, and with limited experience, to behave like seasoned philosophers of love. The tension between intimacy and the desire for variety is an ancient issue, and a particularly vexed one for homosexuals. But Tobias has nothing interesting to say about it—in contrast, for example, to Martin Duberman, for whom it becomes a subject of serious reflection.

As we fully expect, Tobias managed to break both of the rules in a matter of months, sleeping with Chris's best friend around Christmastime. By then, in any case, the sexual relationship had largely run out of gas, though they continued to talk often on the phone. The end came (as we also fully expect) when Chris's friend revealed the infidelity. Tobias labors to salvage what he can from the wreckage: he insists that, though a sexual failure, the relationship was an emotional success. Better yet, he argues that he still loves Chris. "There is no 'right guy' or 'right girl' out there waiting to be discovered," he philosophizes, "there is only the hard work of building and investing in a relationship—and I have invested in Chris." He resolves the issue with a pop psychologist's banality—clothed in the language of finance.

After the breakup in April of 1971, the last year of the narrative sinks into a complicated and utterly forgettable account of partner-swapping—a game of musical beds so intricate that Tobias himself can't describe it without resorting to the language of farce. Other gay autobiographers (and novelists) have told this story better, although all of them, we should remind ourselves, had the advantage of much more experience. When Tobias decided to write his book, in summer 1972, barely two years had elapsed since he made his date with the New York hustler, and his first sustained romance was but one year behind him. The other gay autobiographers treated in this book were near twice his age (or more) when they took pen in hand. Had Tobias waited until his forties, no doubt he too would have had more insightful things to say about the dilemma of love and sexual adventure.

Despite its callowness and unfinished quality, *The Best Little Boy in the World* retains its place in the history of gay autobiography because of its uniquely grim account of the closet. No other autobiographer describes such a massive blackout of desire, and none tells a more rending story of the determination to repress every conceivable evidence of his sexual identity. By comparison Martin Duberman and Paul Monette—mighty sufferers in their own way—seem practically sybarites. So intense was the denial that its residues survived in his body even after he had made his revolutionary decision to come out. Indeed, among the indelible ironies of his story is the gap between his newly honed confessional skills and his recalcitrant flesh: once he had made his breakthrough with Brook in the summer of 1969, he was telling virtually anyone who would listen that he was gay, yet even the most rudimentary sexual acts remained a torture for him. Long after we have forgotten his misadventures with Chris and the other bedmates who proliferate in the final section of the book, we remember the frightened teenager, always on guard against letting his disguise slip and dreaming furtively of wrestling with Tommy Roth, just as we remember his strenuous but hapless efforts to force his reluctant body to endure the hardships of gay sex.

Martin Duberman, ca. 1967.

Photograph by Sean Kernan.

Cures

ARTIN DUBERMAN IS the only figure in this book whom I know personally. Although it has been a fairly distant acquaintance, I have been paying attention to him for nearly four decades now, ever since I took his seminar on American history as a sophomore or junior at Yale. I am also intensely aware that my feelings about him are ambivalent. Our lives and concerns have overlapped in complicated ways. We are both scholars, indeed professional historians, both gay men who have written on sexual issues, both liberals. But we have been curiously out of sync in the way our thought and practice have evolved on these very matters. In the interests of candor, therefore, I want to begin with a brief account of our association and our divergence. Doing so is itself an implicit tribute to Duberman, who has long argued that academics need to be more honest about the hidden motives of their work.

The seminar I took with Duberman contributed, significantly I believe, to my decision to go to graduate school and become a scholar. He was an effective and genial teacher, cheerfully disabusing my classmates of their Republican prejudices, and he became a kind of model for my own emerging professional identity. I recall his gently criticizing me when I wrote a dull senior essay (on the Venezuelan boundary controversy) and sharing his own convictions and doubts about the scholarly life. He attractively combined intellectual seriousness with a certain ironic distance from his work: even as his first book, a biography of Charles Francis Adams, was published to much acclaim in 1961, he told me that he still thought seriously of giving up scholarship for art, in particular for playwriting.

I was not aware that we were in a similar sexual predicament, though dealing with it very differently. As we will see, Duberman was then spending his weekends in New York's gay bars and baths, while devoting hours during the week to a punitive regimen of psychoanalytic therapy aimed at curing him of homosexuality. I was engaged in a much simpler exercise in denial and self-transformation: after a number of homosexual experiences in high school, I had become a serious Roman Catholic, attended mass every day, and had virtually eliminated sex—even the thought of sex—from my life. I don't know whether Duberman had an inkling that my religiosity and intellectual ambition were elaborate defense mechanisms, but I certainly had no suspicions about him. He seemed unambiguously masculine and confident: I particularly recall the stir he caused among envious undergraduates when he came into the dining hall one day with a beautiful date. Yet I also recall a boozy evening spent, with the other students from the seminar, playing the piano and singing in his Silliman College faculty suite, an experience that impressed me as curiously intimate.

A new phase in our relationship began almost a decade later when I published my own first book in 1969. The book was a defense of Freudian radicalism—the theoretical union of Marx and Freud in figures like Wilhelm Reich and Herbert Marcuse—and very much a product of the late 1960s cultural moment. Duberman, too, had moved leftward during the decade, becoming an articulate defender of the civil rights movement and of student radicals, so that, politically at least, we were still on the same wavelength. My book was reviewed in *The New York Times* by one of his closest friends, and, through the complicated grapevine of gay academics, we soon learned of our respective personal situations: our shared secret was now out, and we made arrangements to get together, at his New York apartment, probably in 1970.

I can vaguely remember the meeting but not a word of the conversation. I don't know, for example, whether we talked about our time at Yale. Nor am I confident that I got a clear picture of just how different had been our adjustment to homosexuality. After three years of marriage, I had divorced and moved to San Francisco with a lover in 1967. I found the change not only gratifying but remarkably easy—it had been managed without any thought of seeing an analyst—and I was comfortably out to my family and close friends. As we learn from *Cures*, however, Duberman remained stuck where he had been a decade before: having a lot of gay sex, mostly with hustlers, but still subjecting himself to the brutalities of psychotherapy.[2] In terms of attitudes toward homosexuality,

---

2. Depending on the exact date of my visit (which I can no longer ascertain), the statement may not be entirely accurate: Duberman's third and final analysis ended in the fall of 1970.

one might say that by 1970 I was considerably to his left: though closeted in my public and professional demeanor, I was practicing my sexuality without guilt and delighted to be living in America's gay Mecca.

The situation changed dramatically within two years, by which time Duberman had not only abandoned therapy but declared himself a homosexual in print, in his book *Black Mountain*. In effect, he had outflanked me and begun the evolution that would lead to his becoming one of the country's most prominent gay academics, the author of several books and collections on gay history and the founder and director of the City University's Center for Lesbian and Gay Studies. To be sure, there was no sudden break. I wrote praising him for coming out in the pages of *Black Mountain,* and a few years later he produced a generous blurb for my book on modern sexology. But a subtle parting of the ways had nonetheless occurred. Accurately or not, I increasingly felt he disapproved of my failure to follow his example and declare myself publicly or become involved in the struggle for gay liberation. In other words, I had the sense that he saw me as part of the problem: I was one of those professionally established figures, with an emerging intellectual reputation, who by staying invisible inadvertently conspired to maintain the system of oppression. Today I am inclined to think he was right, but at the time I was acutely conscious of the temptation to self-promotion—to a kind of public narcissism—that coming out entailed. Indeed, I thought Duberman himself rather too given to parading his psyche.

Behind our particular differences about coming out and involvement in the emergent gay movement lay a more general difference in our attitude toward scholarship, teaching, and, ultimately, politics. At Stanford in the 1970s I found the life of a professor very much to my liking. I admired my colleagues' achievements, had no serious doubts about the value of scholarly writing or the traditional forms of pedagogy, and entered with gusto into the rituals of the university world. Duberman's experience, especially at Princeton in the 1960s, had been just the opposite. He squabbled with his colleagues and the administration, published essays denouncing traditional teaching as intellectually empty and psychologically dishonest, and, as revealed in *Cures,* felt ever more alienated from his own scholarship. In retrospect I think I may have grown too comfortable in my privileged situation, and certainly as the 1970s advanced I was involved in a kind of reaction against my own (relatively modest) Sixties radicalism, writing articles for *The New Republic* critical of Michel Foucault, popular culture, and even the gay rights movement. In 1979, after I had complimented Duberman for an attack on Masters' and Johnson's reactionary book about homosexuality, he responded that he had been incommunicado because of his sharp disagreement with my recent views. Clearly we had ended up in very different places, not merely with regard to homosexuality but in our entire orientation toward the academy and toward political involvement.

Except for a brief exchange in 1995 and a dinner in 1997, we have been out of touch since the late 1970s. In the meantime the gap between us has probably narrowed, if only because I have curbed my move to the right and adopted a stance on coming out close to Duberman's own. Indeed, by making our shared sexual destiny the subject of this book, I am in a sense following his lead, however belatedly. But I remain aware that my interpretation of *Cures* can never be fully isolated from the history of our interaction and disagreement in the 1960s and 1970s. In writing about his intimate account of those years, I worry that I may sometimes be guilty of refighting our ancient battles, implicitly defending my own very different experience of homosexuality as well as the no less different intellectual and political choices that experience led me to make.

⁓ *CURES* IS MAINLY THE STORY of Duberman's suffering, but, much more than either Andrew Tobias or Paul Monette, he describes that suffering as the product of larger cultural forces. The chief agents of his oppression were the three psychoanalysts with whom he was in therapy over much of the period from 1955 to 1970. Yet, even as he brings his three witchdoctors to hatefully vivid life, he characterizes them as mere mouthpieces for the American psychiatric establishment, which in turn he sees as a vehicle for enforcing the repressive ideas about sex and gender that dominated American society in the 1950s and early 1960s. In this fashion his autobiography becomes a kind of cultural history.

He begins his account not with the sexual traumas of childhood and adolescence—the usual fare of gay autobiographies—but with a visit, just before he turned eighteen, to a fortune teller at the Calgary Stampede. It is a clever choice, for it allows him to present the fortune teller as a precursor of his therapists. Like the doctors, she was a bogus authority to whom he irrationally succumbed because of his abject unhappiness and intense desire to change. The woman invited him to write down the one question that most preyed on his mind. "I wrote on the piece of paper, 'Will I always be a homosexual?'" He knew intellectually that fortune tellers were "a pack of thieves and liars" spouting "prepackaged mumbo-jumbo," just as the skeptic within him always entertained doubts about the mumbo-jumbo of psychoanalysis. Yet he took seriously her assurance that his "particular trouble" could be fixed, if he just wanted it enough. When she then urged that he abandon his old life and join her gypsy troop, Duberman momentarily felt tempted, even though he recognized the absurdity of the idea. Both the demand that he give up homosexuality and the promise that he could be cured of his wayward desires if he submitted to the right authority would become staples of his analytic experience in the succeeding decades. The book's opening scene at once reveals his vulnerability and establishes a critical perspective on the therapeutic dogma to which he fell victim.

Beginning the autobiography when he was almost eighteen contributes to his argument against psychoanalysis in another, yet subtler, way. It sabotages any effort to give his condition a Freudian reading by virtually ignoring the formative influences that, according to analytic theory, were the invariable causes of homosexuality: an absent or indifferent father and a "binding" or seductive mother. Where parents figure prominently in the autobiographies of Paul Monette and Andrew Tobias, Duberman's mother and especially his father are reduced to mere shadows. They come to our attention mainly when his therapists try to convert them into the familiar villains of the analytic narrative, while Duberman himself resists these caricatures by offering more innocent (and vastly more plausible) interpretations. His last analyst, adopting the theory with mad consistency, even demanded that he end all relations with his supposedly castrating mother. One suspects that in telling his story Duberman has intentionally chosen not to cooperate with the Freudian indictment by removing most of the evidence with which the case might be mounted.

The irony is that what little we learn about his mother and father seems to conform to the analytic stereotype, even if it won't bear the heavy etiological burden his doctors were determined to impose on it. His father, a Russian Jew, emigrated to the United States in 1913, married his second-generation Austrian-American wife a decade later, and was nearly forty when Duberman was born in 1930. Both parents were "hell-bent" on assimilation, so he grew up in a family where Judaism and Jewish culture were at best nominally observed. The absence of any sort of Jewish identity is an intriguing feature of Duberman's story. It was facilitated by the accident of his blond good looks (he was, in his own words, "the beautiful, blond God/baby") and perhaps actively cultivated by the ambitious young scholar: he describes himself (accurately, in my recollection) as "Anglo-Saxon in appearance and manner." One wonders about the connection between his repressed ethnicity and the paralyzing trouble he experienced with his sexuality: perhaps his aversion to the first form of difference fed into his horror of the second. Certainly one source of alienation between father and son was the father's obvious foreignness, though Duberman himself insists that the more important matter was his father's "indifference," toward not only his children but also his wife, with whom he had long since fallen out of love. The father's only real passion was his dress manufacturing company, whose considerable success provided young Martin and his older sister with a comfortable Manhattan childhood.

If his father was indifferent—psychologically absent, according to analytic theory—the other side of the coin was his mother's neediness. Duberman describes her as a talented woman frustrated by the lack of opportunity to express that talent—the generic fate of so many women of her generation. As a result she had become a "termagant, nagging and voluble." There is more than a hint in the book that she found some outlet for her frustration, as well as her romantic disappointment, by overinvesting in her young son. "A beautiful infant," he writes, "I was my mother's adored favorite, pampered and perambulated." In other words, although not necessarily "binding" or "castrating," she established a compensating intimacy that might appear to support the classic Freudian interpretation.

The treatment of his parents points to a more general difficulty for the reader of Duberman's autobiography. No matter how convincing we may find his argument that he was profoundly damaged by the foolish certainties of American psychoanalysis, we never escape the suspicion that he was nonetheless a man very much in need of psychiatric help. One can hardly say so without falling into the viciously circular logic by which analysis held him in its thrall: according to his doctors, his unhappiness proved that homosexuality could never bring fulfillment and that conversion to heterosexuality was his only hope, whereas, in Duberman's own view, he was miserable precisely because psychoanalysis (and through it the culture at large) had filled his mind with repressive falsehoods. But why, we are apt to wonder, was he so susceptible to the self-loathing doctrine of analysis? After all, other gay men managed to survive the homophobia of mid-century America without nearly so much grief: we may recall Donald Vining's indefatigable resiliency or even, for that matter, Andrew Tobias's admittedly painful but ultimately less destructive reaction. One imagines that Duberman would have tied himself in knots about his homosexuality even if he had never met a psychoanalyst. Or perhaps, more helpfully, we might say that his neurotic terror made him the perfect candidate for analysis, and, while analysis clearly aggravated his condition, a more tolerant therapeutic practice—Freud's own, for example—might well have helped him.

Because he begins with the fortune teller episode, which is followed by his departure for Yale in the fall of 1948, we learn about his early sexual experiences—just as we learn about his parents—only fleetingly and, as it were, retrospectively. Nonetheless, what he reveals is stunningly unambiguous: his homosexual desires were strong and clear, and he even managed to give them limited expression. "As far back as I could remember," he writes, "I had been attracted erotically only to men, and my masturbation fantasies had always focused exclusively on them." He had a preteen crush on a boy with whom he slept in a common bed at camp, and, nearing puberty, he invented a game called "fussing," which involved going into a closet with another boy "and body-rub[bing] ourselves into pleasure." At the same time he had equally unambiguous evidence of his indifference to women. As a heterosexual, he did not even measure up to the humble standards set by André Gide. In contrast to Andrew Tobias, moreover, he risked serious embarrassment by putting himself to the test. With some friends he went to a Florida whorehouse, where, following instructions, he got on top of his prostitute and "rubbed up and down against her body," only to find that his "cock stayed resolutely limp." He had the same experience with his high-school girlfriend after the senior prom. "Again, I couldn't get it up," he reports. Later in life, when, at the urging of his analysts, he courted various women, his reaction was no different: he felt not so much as a tinge of heterosexual interest. In other words, when Duberman entered on the psychoanalytic project to suppress his homosexuality and become a heterosexual, he knew, on the basis of concrete experience, just how great were the odds against him. After all, many gay men find that they can function sexually with women, even if their desires (and often their fantasies) remain homosexual. For them the idea of converting to heterosexuality is grounded in at least some measure of erotic success, however tenuous. By contrast, Duberman's utterly failed heterosexual adventures make his resolution to be "cured" all the more astonishing: he faced not just the usual hurdle of suppressing his homosexuality but the even more daunting one of creating heterosexual desire, as it were, out of whole cloth.

His four years as a Yale undergraduate are treated almost as cursorily as his childhood and adolescence: he devotes fewer than six pages to them (in contrast to Paul Monette, in whose slightly shorter book the Yale years take up some seventy pages). He was, by his own admission, in a state of radical denial. Although he had called himself "a homosexual" when he posed his fateful question to the fortune teller, he now rejected the designation. In order to avoid any experience that might force him to embrace the dread label, he tried to avoid sex entirely. But when a fellow undergraduate casually warned him to stay away from the New Haven Green because it was "'a hangout for fairies,'" he got drunk and ventured to the Green that very night. The account of his experience is revealing:

> I saw a very fat, middle-aged black man sitting quietly on a bench. I sat down on the empty bench opposite him. After a minute or two, he started whistling softly, tantalizingly in my direction. Fueled by liquor, I got up, reeled my way over, and stood boldly in front of him. He started playing with my cock, then took it out of my pants. Wildly excited, I started to fondle him.

Duberman steadfastly refused to draw the obvious conclusion from this episode. It corroborated, but in reverse, what he should have learned from his heterosexual experiments with the Florida prostitute and his high school girl friend: just as attractive women left him indifferent, he was "wildly excited" by even the most unalluring of men. He did not suffer, as did Andrew Tobias, from the sort of restricted sexual tastes that might have lent a certain plausibility to his denial—in Tobias's case the claim that he wasn't really a homosexual but just wanted to wrestle and play cowboys. On the contrary, the evidence of Duberman's intensely and unambiguously homosexual orientation was overwhelming. Once again, the conversion project, to which he would devote much of the next two decades, is made to seem ludicrously delusional, and thus all the more extraordinary.

∞ THE CONTINUOUS NARRATIVE OF Duberman's autobiography begins only when he arrived at Harvard to pursue his graduate studies in 1952. The move to Cambridge brought an immediate change, although he gives no explanation as to why. Within a few months he started going to gay bars, in particular to Boston's staid Napoleon Club. On his very first trip to the Napoleon he got picked up by a fellow graduate student, "Ray,"[3] who not only became a lifelong friend but introduced him to a circle of gay acquaintants, almost all of them also graduate students. This development, he insists, marked a great advance in his life,

---

3. In a Note at the beginning of *Cures*, Duberman says he has often used pseudonyms, "as indicated by quotation marks on the first presentation." I have followed his practice.

bringing him "from individual isolation to collective secrecy"; it represented a "quantum leap in happiness from private to shared anguish." We may recall the salutary role of gay friendships in the lives of Jeb Alexander and Donald Vining. But Duberman's friends seem to have offered him surprisingly little protection against his demons. Ray in particular turned out to be nearly as vulnerable to the psychoanalytic pitch as Duberman himself and became a therapeutic codependent. In other words, his gay friendships failed to serve as a bulwark against the homophobic depredations of his psychoanalysts—or of society at large—and may even have weakened his defenses. Apparently he was bound and determined to suffer.

The Napoleon Club also introduced him to romance. His first affair, which lasted only a few months, was with a former Yale classmate from a Brahmin family. Although they called themselves lovers, Duberman never felt as strongly attached as his partner. Indeed, the relationship fell apart, he argues, because his fragile ego could not bear up under the adoration. But no less important was its grave sexual inequity. He was "deeply bound" by conventional notions of manliness and refused to do anything the culture had judged feminine: "Giving blow jobs and getting fucked were innately passive, female activities; getting blow jobs and giving fucks were active and male. . . . I was somebody who got blow jobs and gave fucks." It was hardly a formula for romantic success. As so often happens in *Cures*, Duberman sees himself victimized by his mindless adherence "to the cultural script then dominant."

His next relationship, which began in 1953, only a few months after the breakup of the first, was a different matter altogether. This time Duberman fell genuinely in love, and he doesn't appear to have suffered from the sexual inhibitions that undermined the first affair, at least not to the same degree. Most important, the relationship lasted much longer: it had not yet fully run its course when he left Cambridge to take a position at Yale in 1957. He implies that had it survived, his life might have turned out very differently: he could well have been spared falling into the clutches of the therapists, who left him such an emotional cripple. The relationship, we are made to feel, was the great missed turning-point of his life.

"Larry" differed from Duberman's first boyfriend in another way, which set an ominous precedent for the future. He came from a working-class Irish family and held a clerk's job in Filene's department story. Virtually alone among American gay autobiographers, Duberman became addicted to the British habit of falling in love with poor young men, many of them straight (Larry was an exception). He is aware of the lineage: the text refers to the pattern in the romantic lives of E. M. Forster and J. R. Ackerley, though not those of Christopher Isherwood or Stephen Spender. The parallel is uncannily precise: like his British forebears, he went in for men who were unambiguously masculine and unintellectual (but not, he insists, unintelligent). Larry, for example, was "muscular and compact in build, low-keyed, intense, essentially nonverbal." One can hardly avoid speculating about the meaning of his sexual tastes. They suggest an unconscious Anglophilia, the erotic consequence perhaps of the assimilationist impulse he had inherited from his parents and led him to cultivate an "Anglo-Saxon" persona. Significantly, none of the men he pursued appears to have been Jewish: on the contrary, they were typically white Protestants (Larry again excepted), often from the provinces, with the kind of athletic bodies and jock personalities familiar to us from Andrew Tobias's cowboy fantasies, but with the important addition of class difference. Once again, we might be inclined to wonder about the hidden ethnic rationale of Duberman's infatuations—the extent to which they engaged some deep-seated aversion to his Jewish origins and served to affirm, unconsciously, his fragile Anglo-American identity by sexual incorporation.

Why did the relationship with Larry fail? Duberman's explanation is a maddening combination of plausible social analysis and self-serving excuses. The immediate cause was the temptation to infidelity. They managed to resist for two years, but by 1955 sexual boredom had begun to take its toll, and both of them, but especially Duberman, started having outside adventures. The story is familiar, indeed banally so. What distinguishes Duberman's account is his characteristic stress on the role of social forces in the collapse of the affair. In the most general sense he sees them falling victim to Americans' unexamined notions about constancy, above all the preposterous idea that true desire was eternal: "We . . . had to cope . . . with the then-current cultural nostrum that when two partners were *really* meant for each other, neither sexual arousal nor emotional commitment ever flagged; health was defined as the absence of desire for more than one person, or at least the need to act on the desire." This monolithic consensus left no conceptual space for making "some needed distinctions between emotional and sexual fidelity," distinctions that might have helped them negotiate the dangerous terrain between the erotic tedium of monogamy and the destructive vortex of promiscuity. Of course, as he admits, heterosexual couples in "the conformist Fifties" faced the same dilemma, but they did so with institutional advantages unavailable to gay men: not only marriage and children but the cultural celebration of heterosexual faithfulness and the corresponding shame associated with its failure. Gays, by contrast, were hobbled with the same inherently utopian ideal yet enjoyed none of the supports that, despite unavoidable infractions, held the creaky system in place. His reasoning is persuasive, even if it betrays more than a hint of special pleading and fails to account for the many gay men, like Donald Vining, who succeeded in balancing, albeit precariously, the conflicting claims of intimacy and adventure, even in the Ozzie and Harriet years.

The troubles he suffered with Larry were doubly fateful, because they inspired Duberman to seek out his first analyst, "Dr. Weintraub." He had become convinced that his infidelity represented not a failure of will or character—or perhaps emotional incompatibility—but a structural flaw that doomed all homosexual relationships. Genuine and sustained intimacy between gay men now seemed to him impossible, and, because intimacy was what the culture told him he most wanted, he drew the seemingly inescapable conclusion that his only hope lay in becoming a heterosexual. Such was the reasoning that brought him to Dr. Weintraub's consulting room, where, naturally, he found the doctor prepared to support his glum assessment with the full homophobic arsenal of American psychoanalysis at midcentury.

Duberman recognizes that a number of factors conspired to make him particularly vulnerable to the siren call of analysis. He lived in the part of the country, the East, where analysis flourished. His home town, New York, was in fact America's psychoanalytic capital. In the 1950s, furthermore, analysis was enjoying its great moment of authority in this country: the turn inward perfectly suited "a culture that had grown apolitical and conservative." Most crucial of all, Duberman was a Jew and an intellectual, and American psychoanalysis was not only dominated by Jews but served as a principal avenue by which they achieved professional stature and intellectual distinction. When Jews, especially East Coast Jews of means, had a problem, they almost automatically thought of taking it to an analyst, who came to be regarded as a kind of secular rabbi. Moreover, in the post-War years, homosexuality carried a unique political stigma for Jews, many of whom were under the impression that the Nazis had been a gang of homosexual sadists. As a Jewish intellectual, uncomfortable with his desires and failing in his first important relationship, Duberman's decision to seek out Dr. Weintraub was culturally overdetermined. His fate reminds me of how much luckier I was to be a gentile who endured the 1950s in the intellectual wasteland of San Diego, California, where Jews were nearly as invisible as gays, and where nobody (at least nobody one knew) went to an analyst. We could hardly have failed to have very different experiences of homosexuality.

Weintraub was the most humorless and apodictic of Duberman's therapists. He seems almost a parody of the homophobic American Freudian, issuing orders and pronouncements with categorical assurance. He immediately told Duberman that the fundamental matter in his case was the conflict between his "neurotic homosexual 'acting-out'" and his "underlying healthy impulse toward a heterosexual union." At first Weintraub simply advised him to give up the relationship with Larry, but soon enough the advice became an ultimatum: either abandon Larry or abandon therapy. A long struggle ensued, in which Duberman alternated between the "attraction, tenderness, [and] wonderfully passionate sex" he and Larry still enjoyed and his growing conviction that Weintraub's diagnosis was correct. Following the doctor's orders, he eventually broke off the affair, only to relapse into its pleasures. He then tried to reconstitute it, but stripped of its former romantic aspirations. Although he decided, after less than a year, to end the therapy, by then Weintraub had poisoned the well. The ironic consequence was that, with homosexual love now authoritatively discredited, Duberman felt liberated to pursue his wandering desires without restraint. "Being certified as 'sick' hobbled my confidence but liberated my libido," he remarks. To his credit, he sees that he may even have been complicit in Weintraub's diagnosis. One is reminded of Freud's dictum that every illness has its secondary gain. "In breaking away from Larry," Duberman confesses, "I was *using* the insistence of orthodox psychiatry that I was incapacitated for love to justify some unorthodox and overdue sexual adventuring that the culture would sanction only for those lost souls unable to partake of the *real* satisfactions of monogamy." But the adventuring brought him little enjoyment beyond the release of sexual tension. On the contrary, he remained consumed by guilt. After one encounter, although the sex had been good, he recorded in his diary: "'My revulsion is working overtime. All sorts of resolutions. Eager for work—never going to waste time bar-hopping again, etc. No satisfaction there anyway. All set for a return to analysis; must have a wife and family, only possible things that matter.'"

     ∞ WITHIN WEEKS OF ARRIVING at Yale, as an instructor in American history, in the fall of 1957, Duberman had become so depressed that he once again went into therapy. He felt bereft of his circle of gay friends and saddened by the effective end of the affair with Larry. But almost as important—and characteristic of Duberman—was his anxious awareness of living in a "fiercely homophobic time." He mentions in particular the Newton Arvin scandal, which resulted in two young faculty members at Smith College being cashiered. More or less contemporaneously, an acquaintance at Yale was also fired because of a homosexual incident. Thus, despite an intense desire for "sex and companionship," Duberman committed himself to celibacy. Before long, however, he adopted a less draconian (if schizophrenic) policy: in New Haven he took "the veil," while on weekends he became a regular at New York's bar and bath scene.

His new therapist, "Dr. Albert Igen," a professor of psychiatry at the Yale Medical School, assumed a more prominent place in Duberman's life than Dr. Weintraub ever had. For one thing, the analysis with Igen lasted much longer: five years, or the full duration of Duberman's tenure at Yale. Moreover, because (with one relatively brief exception) Duberman developed no sustained homosexual relationships in those five years, Igen was without serious rival for his emotional attention. Dr. Weintraub had been up against Larry, but Igen's competition consisted mainly of "several mini-affairs and an occasional one-night stand." The analyst became, in effect, Duberman's significant other, the figure whose approval he craved more than anyone else's. It was the transference with a vengeance.

Where Weintraub had been peremptory, Igen was "low-keyed and compassionate." He did not assault Duberman with brusque orders to end his homosexual activities or offer utopian promises about the certainty of conversion. But the substance, if not the manner, of what he said was identical: Duberman needed to devote himself systematically to the task of changing his sexual orientation, an enterprise whose success depended above all on how much he wanted it to happen. If anything, the message was all the more pernicious for being delivered in such reasonable tones. Weintraub's arrogance had inspired resistance, whereas Igen's "mournful" sympathy left him defenseless. But Duberman's main point is that, whether pompous or humane, both therapists gave him the same bad advice. Both urged him on an impossible and ultimately self-destructive path.

Duberman is eager to show that Igen, like Weintraub, spoke not just with his own voice but with the institutional prestige of American medicine. Indeed, all three of his analysts, he insists, echoed "the consensus within the American psychiatric establishment," and thus their assessment of him registered as nothing less than "the culture's verdict" that he was a defective human being. "Psychotherapists," he charges, "were functioning as cultural police rather than as physicians or scientists." He supports this argument by citing examples of popular attitudes, as reflected in the movies and the press. But above all he invokes the malign authority of the three best-known psychoanalytic studies of homosexuality published in the 1950s and 1960s: the evil trio of Edmund Bergler's *Homosexuality: Disease or Way of Life?* (1956), Irving Bieber's *Homosexuality: A Psychoanalytic Study of Male Homosexuals* (1962), and Charles Socarides's *The Overt Homosexual* (1968). All three uttered the same clichéd nonsense about binding mothers and absent fathers, just as they advertised the near universal efficacy of the analytic "cure." Duberman has no trouble dismantling their fake scientific pretensions, such as Bergler's ludicrous claim to have converted 99 percent of his homosexual patients to heterosexuality. But he is mainly interested in showing the extent of their authority, as measured by the reverence and frequency with which they were cited or the honors that were bestowed on them. Interestingly, he doesn't argue that he was personally affected by reading any of their books, although at one point he admits that he wrote Bergler asking for help. Indeed, with the ambiguous exception of Bergler, he doesn't expressly claim to have read them at all. But in a way that is just his point. He sees himself as the archetypal victim of social pressures that reached him through a rich and often invisible nexus of influences. His private therapists were only the most direct purveyors of the culture's judgment that homosexuality was inescapably pathological. Weintraub and Igen were local stand-ins for Bergler, Bieber, and Socarides, who in turn served as flacks for the dominant social and sexual regime. Once again, Duberman is writing cultural history as much as autobiography.

Through most of his five years on the Yale faculty, while working feverishly to turn his dissertation into a book, he remained stuck in his divided life: austere weeks in New Haven, where he fell more and more under Dr. Igen's sway, alternated with indulgent weekends of largely impersonal sex in New York, from which he returned with a fresh supply of guilty memories to feed the analytic maw. Only three episodes disturbed this pattern, and in each of them Igen served as a malignant interpretive guide. In mid-1958 Duberman began a ten-month affair with a young man, "Billy," whom he met on Fire Island. In most respects it represented a downmarket version of his earlier affair with Larry: it started with wild attraction and talk of life-long commitment but soon degenerated into routine and experiments with outside partners, a development that, as before, Duberman interpreted as proof of his (and indeed any homosexual's) constitutional unfitness for intimacy. Dr. Igen's contributed to the debacle by telling Duberman that he had no genuine interest in Billy—because, of course, homosexual desires were always psychic mirages—but was merely trying to make up for the closeness he had never enjoyed with his father.

In the wake of the failed affair with Billy, and at Igen's urging, Duberman then turned his attention to the other side of the psychoanalytic recipe—unleashing his suppressed heterosexuality—and made a serious effort to establish a relationship with a woman. His chosen object, "Nancy," was a Yale graduate student in American literature. For two years, no less, they "danced around" the possibility of becoming lovers. (Nancy, I suspect, was the attractive date I saw Duberman bring into the Silliman College dining hall.) As when he had visited the Florida whorehouse in high school, he was not afraid to put himself on the line. "I tried hard to coax the desire into being," he writes. "We would have a few drinks of an evening in my apartment, turn on music and dance, kiss gently on the lips, and wait expectantly for my body to go into hormonal overdrive— which it never did." Igen, naturally, was ready with a prefabricated psychoanalytic explanation for his failure: if the underlying problem with Billy had been Duberman's distant father, the relationship with Nancy was sabotaged by lingering terrors of his castrating mother. "'Is it any wonder you have had difficulty ever since in entrusting yourself to a female?'" the doctor asked. "'You're chronically angry at women and refuse to get it up for them. To enter a vagina is for you to risk being swallowed alive.'" Homophobia clearly drove American Freudians, like Igen, to bizarre intellectual contortions, which helps explain why so many gay men of Duberman's generation have turned to biological explanations of homosexuality with a palpable sense of relief. Igen managed to top even his fanciful notion of a man-eating vagina when, in 1961, Duberman came down with a case of penile herpes and was forced to give up all sex for over a year. The disease, Igen confidently announced, was only incidentally the result of a virus. Its real cause was the protest emerging from Duberman's firmly heterosexual unconscious, which had risen in rebellion against his homosexual acting-out by fashioning an organic impediment. "Wondrously intricate in its workings," Duberman comments with justified sarcasm, "my unconscious had come up with a brilliant solution. It had created . . . an unarguable physical obstacle to sexual activity." Igen's reasoning was a kind of *reductio ad absurdum* of the psychoanalytic style.

The analytic explanation of his desires now seems to us so absurd, and the promise of a cure so cruelly fraudulent, that we are apt to wonder how a man of Duberman's intelligence of education could have been such a dupe. For the most part, he views his surrender as evidence of the overwhelming power of social convention: individual intelligence and sophistication, he suggests, count for little against the uncontroverted authority of public opinion. Objectively, his analysts' ideas may have been as insane as those of the Calgary fortune teller, but the force of prejudice transformed them into wisdom.

Yet even in the 1950s, some part of him resisted his doctors' (and society's) verdict. He quotes a diary entry from mid-1959 to show that his capitulation was never complete: "'I haven't as yet really resolved in my mind whether I want to make the 'grand effort' or, instead, give up the analysis. . . . If I once decided that I was unwilling—perhaps unable—to give up my drives and go through the prolonged agony necessary for a 'conversion,' then I would be forced to accept my present condition and make the best of it.'" The very fact that "conversion" appeared in quotation marks implies a certain healthy skepticism. In the next sentence, to be sure, he disavowed his "rebellious thoughts" and reaffirmed "'the inadequacies of homosexual life.'" Nevertheless, he sees in his doubts, faint as they were, the earliest glimmerings of the revolution that would eventually stand of the psychoanalytic diagnosis on its head.

Just as he interprets his misery as a social phenomenon—the result of historical pressures beyond his control—he suggests that his occasional moments of resistance reflected not individual insight but his unconscious absorption of a counter-discourse just then beginning to be articulated. Accordingly, the text balances its survey of the homophobic teachings of Bergler, Bieber, and Socarides with a consideration of such adversarial voices as Evelyn Hooker, Thomas Szasz, and Franklin Kameny, who already in the 1950s were beginning to challenge the pathological interpretation of homosexuality. Duberman's account here leans heavily on the work of scholars like John D'Emilio and Ronald Bayer, because, by his own admission, he knew nothing of these oppositional figures at the time. At most, he implies, their message reached him through a kind of cultural osmosis. The claim may not be very persuasive, but it is consistent with his treatment of the psychoanalytic homophobes (Bergler, Bieber, and Socarides), whose influence, we recall, he attributes less to his actual reading of them than to their cultural resonance. Throughout *Cures,* in other words, Duberman's strategy is to present himself as a kind of *tabula rasa* on which historical forces—mostly malign but sometimes beneficent—left their impressions. His story, in contrast to

Andrew Tobias's, is told not as a personal odyssey but as the representative saga of his generation of gay men.

⚭ IN 1962 DUBERMAN TOOK A JOB at Princeton, where he served on the History faculty for almost a decade. Naturally, the move ended his analysis with Dr. Igen. Perhaps because he was still in the midst of his medically enforced celibacy—and hence under less psychological pressure—he treated himself to a three-year vacation from therapy. But he made up for this analytic holiday by throwing himself into his scholarly work with punitive intensity. He was enormously prolific, and his rise through Princeton's academic hierarchy was accordingly rapid. He received tenure after only three years and in 1967 became one of the youngest full professors in the history of the social sciences at the University.

Duberman's attitude toward his intellectual accomplishments is ambivalent. Much of the time he argues that his powers of mind and his productivity were the only things counterbalancing his sense of worthlessness as a homosexual. In this mood he is not beyond crowing about his publications and the awards they garnered. Indeed, some have found *Cures* insufferably arrogant and self-promoting, and even a friendly reader might complain that Duberman is excessively fond of quoting his own prose. But he makes the plausible case that his intelligence, even as it was befuddled by his psychoanalytic gurus, nurtured the seed of his future emancipation. More immediately, his academic success gave him a "base of self-esteem," without which, he speculates, he might well have been "obliterate[d]" by his feelings of sexual failure. Scholarly work had already become his fragile ego's main defense while he was still a graduate student. "How could a 'sick' young man like me," he asked himself hopefully, "be functioning with as much clarity and insight as my Harvard professors assured me I was?"

But almost as often he speaks of his scholarship as a desperate and mechanical ritual of avoidance, an enterprise to which he felt no real commitment and from which he extracted no real satisfaction. More than anything else, he toiled at his writing to keep his demons at bay. Its great attraction was that it took his mind off his problems, if only temporarily. Typically he adopts the language of alienated labor in describing it. He felt "chained" to his desk, "dutifully churning out" prose in "a routine as motorized as the road." At one point he even suggests, somewhat fancifully, that his indifference to sadomasochism might be explained by his addiction to work: "I'm not seriously tempted by S/M," he explains, "because I do my own self-flagellation—I write." In effect, he treats his scholarship as a kind of self-protective fraud: it represented a huge investment of time and energy in an activity that meant little to him but that eased his pain. Without saying so expressly, he implies that that time and energy should have been invested in the one matter about which he truly cared, even though the whole point of *Cures* is to show how history conspired against such honest self-exploration. Not surprisingly, he never settled comfortably into his identity as a professor but continued to imagine alternative careers, some of which he would eventually realize. "For a while," he admits, "I thought the answer for me might be to chuck it all—Princeton, academia, personal achievement, the purported life of the mind."

He exempts one element of his scholarship from this indictment. In his early publications—his biographies of Charles Francis Adams and James Russell Lowell, as well as a collection of essays on the Abolitionists—he was truly engrossed by the involvement of all these figures in the antislavery movement. For a change he found himself writing not merely to avoid his troubles or shore up his ego but with a genuine sense of emotional identification. Yet even here there were ironies and contradictions. In defending the antislavery activists, he was taking issue with a tradition of scholarship that interpreted their politics as the irrational displacement of personal insecurities. Against this psychologizing, he insisted that, far from being "fanatics," the Abolitionists had reacted to objective evil with fully appropriate political means. (I can still recall Duberman advancing this argument when I was his student at Yale.) The irony, of course, was that even as he mounted his scholarly critique of psychological reductionism, he allowed himself to be victimized by the very same tendentious reasoning on the part his analysts. He applauded the antislavery intellectuals for their fight on behalf of the oppressed "yet never drew (at least not consciously) what later would seem the obvious analogy of the need to struggle on behalf of my own liberation." In other words, even in this rare instance where his scholarly labor was not alienated, it remained, by his own lights, oddly incoherent and unselfconscious.

One of Duberman's alternative careers, in which he became increasingly involved while at Princeton, was protest politics, especially the civil rights movement. In general, he contrasts the authenticity of his political writings with the phoniness of his scholarship. Beyond its objective value as a contribution to desirable social change, his "work in the movement" had the added advantage of enhancing his sense of self-worth and thus serving as a counterweight to the destructive influence of therapy.

In reality, however, the same contradictions that bedeviled his scholarship also bedeviled his politics. The most obvious tension, as he recognizes, was between his political optimism and his psychological pessimism. "It was easier," he concedes, "to harangue the country about changing its ways than to change my own," although one could well argue that, in so far as he bought into the psychoanalytic fantasy of becoming a heterosexual, his psychological and political views were fully congruent—and equally utopian. He also wants to believe that in defending black separatism, he was laying the structural foundation for his later commitment to the gay movement. But he is unable to sustain this agreeable image of political continuity. Set against it is the recurrent lament that his fight on behalf of blacks, like his later sympathy for women, involved a displacement of resentment that should properly have been expended on behalf of homosexuals. "Always," he complains at one point, "I was instantly alive to every protest movement but my own." As I've noted, the central theme of *Cures* is that he could not begin to fight his personal battle until historical conditions had changed. But this conviction doesn't keep him from taking a sometimes jaundiced view of his actual political commitments. Though less severely, they also, he implies, suffered from the false consciousness that marred his scholarship. One often feels that he is too hard on himself—that he doesn't take sufficient pride in his real achievements as an intellectual, just as he is too quick to judge his activism by the constricted standards of today's identity politics. His besetting weakness is less arrogance than self-betrayal.

⟍ WHILE AT PRINCETON DUBERMAN also launched his second alternative career, namely, as a playwright. He somehow managed to find time, even while keeping up his punishing academic routine, to write a historical dramatization of American race relations. As the topic suggests, his playwriting was closely linked to his politics, and both were conceived as avenues of escape from the prison-house of scholarship. The play, *In White America*, opened in October 1963 and enjoyed a remarkable success: it ran for more than 500 performances and won the Vernon Rice/Drama Desk Award as the year's best Off-Broadway production. None of Duberman's other plays, several of which were produced in the late 60s and early 70s and represented his first tentative efforts to make a public exit from the closet, ever approached his original triumph.

In retrospect, Duberman is almost as suspicious of his playwriting as he is of his political activism—or, for that matter, of his scholarship. It, too, he implies, was a psychic dodge, another Band-Aid on the open wound of his sexual disability. Exactly like his prize-winning books and his involvement in the civil rights movement, it served to counter his feelings of worthlessness. If only momentarily, the success of *In White America* gave him a sense that he "was really in pretty good shape, not the badly damaged, disfigured human being my disapproved sexuality had implied." None of his achievements, it seems, was psychologically innocent: whatever he accomplished was motivated, at least in part, by the tortured emotional logic of his sexual secret.

In 1964, with a view to advancing his career as a dramatist—and perhaps even receiving a call, like Christopher Isherwood, from Hollywood—Duberman moved to New York, from which he commuted to Princeton, where he dutifully continued to meet his academic responsibilities. The inspiration for the move was as much sexual and professional, because by the mid-1960s he had settled into a new phase of his gay life. Having given up on intimacy and, for all his youthful looks, anxiously approaching middle age, he abandoned the usual bars and baths and began to seek out hustlers. It was, he convinced himself, the logical fulfillment of his well-honed critique of the repressive (and heterosexual) ideal of monogamy. Paying for sex eliminated the awkward preliminaries as well as the phony aspirations to romance, and of course it was surefire way to avoid erotic boredom, which, he had become persuaded, was the unavoidable fate of all sustained relationships.

Such, at least, was the theory. The practice turned out to be quite different. Duberman imported all his frustrated romantic hopes into his pursuit of this *ne plus ultra* of impersonal sex: he compulsively turned his purchases into grand affairs of the heart, laboring to transform them from desperately poor and often manipulative young straight men, selling their bodies to pay the rent, into fully committed homosexual lovers. The most extended of these relationships was with a twenty-three-year-old carpenter, who was also married and a father. Duberman is only too aware that he was caught in the grip of stereotypical fantasies about class and masculinity: "Jim" was a former high-school football star from a New Jersey working-class family, "the buried and bereft American male desperate to have his distant dad hold him in his arms at night." In effect, Duberman became the young man's "good" father and therapist as well, listening patiently to his troubles and trying to help sort them out. Here we get a clear sense of his still ambivalent feelings about psychoanalysis: despite his eagerness to expose its wrongheaded conception of homosexuality, he offers a thoroughly Freudian reading of his infatuation with hustlers like Jim. He admits, in effect, that his motive was the very one Dr. Igen had identified in the earlier relationship with Billy (the young man he had met on Fire Island in 1958 and courted for ten months): he was playing daddy, creating a father-son bond that repaired the deficiencies of his own childhood experience. At the deepest psychological level the hustlers were really his younger self, toward whom he now assumed a loving parental role.

After abasing himself for a year with Jim—swallowing the young-man's "self-protective lies" and rescuing him, "with checkbook in hand," from various disasters—Duberman was more than ready to return to therapy. Thus began, in 1965, the last and most traumatic of his psychoanalytic adventures, the final attempt, as it were, to straighten himself out. From an intellectual perspective, his third analyst, "Karl," brought nothing new to the argument. In every particular, he advanced the same views Duberman had already heard from Weintraub and Igen or read in the publications of Bergler, Bieber, and Socarides: homosexuality was a psychological chimera caused by binding mothers and distant fathers, and the goal of analysis was to reconfigure, by way of the transference, those defective bonds so as to liberate the patient's heterosexual desire. With unqualified Bieberite assurance, Karl reported that, of his recent homosexual patients, "all, without exception, had succeeded in making heterosexual adjustments."

Yet, even though it looks like the same old story, Duberman's account of his therapeutic encounter with Karl is vastly more gripping than his accounts of the two earlier episodes. It absorbs almost a quarter of his text and is easily the book's most memorable achievement. The obvious source of its literary success is that the analysis took the form of group therapy, so that we are introduced to a half-dozen characters whose idiosyncrasies add a welcome variety to the normally claustrophobic self-centeredness of autobiography. Duberman exploits his unusually detailed diary to recreate the group's often contentious debates, just as he draws on his skill as a dramatist to stage exciting, even bloody, confrontations among its members. His three most impressive "creations" are an attractive young swinger, "Judy," whom Karl repeatedly urged on Duberman as a suitable mate; a homosexual "convert," "Dick," whom Duberman was supposed to emulate but who turned out to be a sexual bust in his manufactured marriage; and a vicious homophobe, "Stan," who accused both Dick and Duberman of wanting to suck his cock, thereby prompting a fist-fight. As Duberman rightly says, the group sessions make for "good theater" and hence for irresistible reading.

His theatrical talents are also on display in the overall structure he gives to the story of Karl and the group. It is organized as a morality tale, in which the supremely self-confident therapist is eventually exposed as a charlatan. Karl's comeuppance initiates the long-awaited downfall of the psychoanalytic empire, a kind of Freudian *Götterdämmerung* that liberates our suffering hero, like the Rhine Gold, from the mythological prison in which he has been held captive for well over a decade. Actually the story's inspiration is less Wagner than Goethe: Karl is the Devil to Duberman's Faust. He is described as "a vivid, electric, physical presence—a short, wiry, energetic man in his late forties, exuding confidence and certitude, with piercing eyes and a trim Van Dyke beard that gave him a Mephistophelean look." Foreign-born (presumably German or Austrian), he radiated "a fiery conviction that proved difficult to resist." He is far and away the book's most vivid character, as Duberman records great stretches of his vapid, arrogant theorizing, all the better to hang himself with in the end. It is a deeply satisfying story.

Karl's main line of attack was to undo the faulty Oedipal ties that, according to the theory, were the source of the problem. He began with a brutal assault on Duberman's "'unhealthily symbiotic' relationship" with his mother, now a widow. Even though Duberman saw her but seldom—their contact often limited to a weekly phone call—Karl ordered him to cut her out of his life altogether. When Duberman defended his mother as "'really a very good woman,'" understandably embittered by her disappointments—a loveless marriage, no outlet for her talents—Karl pounced on the phrase as confirming his pathogenic interpretation: "'What would cause you to defend your mother so vigorously as 'a good woman' other than guilt?—which in turn, of course, is a mask for incestuous wishes you never worked through as a child.'" Duberman's skepticism began to be aroused, and it only increased when Karl demanded that he tape-record their weekly phone conversations. What Duberman heard, listening to the tapes, was not the binding castrator of Freudian theory but a justifiably unhappy victim of America's prevailing misogyny. The experience prompted his first act of analytic defiance. "No," he concluded, "I was not going to put this woman out of my life, as Karl insisted. I stopped making the tape recordings."

Having failed in his attack on the maternal side of the Oedipal pathology, Karl next turned his attention to the other half of the equation, Duberman's failed relationship with his now-dead father. With his usual sublime confidence, he spelled out the analytic logic by which Duberman's unresolved paternal complex had brought him not only to homosexuality but to his ill-fated obsession with hustlers: "'Because your father was so distant, you cannot believe to this day that an adult male could care about you—and indeed that's the main reason you pursue males sexually, and especially unavailable males like hustlers: it's a way of belatedly trying to get your father's love while simultaneously confirming that you can't.'" As often happens in *Cures,* the diagnosis contained a grain of psychological truth embedded in a mass of ideological prejudice. Duberman himself admits that his consistent preference for butch male prostitutes to whom he could play daddy begged for psychoanalytic explanation. But Karl leapt from this discrete insight to the categorical assumption that Duberman's sexual attraction to men—which was unambiguous and long predated his addiction to hustlers— was equally pathological. And, of course, Karl never even considered the possibility that Duberman's "endemic unhappiness reflected not on the inherent nature of homosexuality, but on the persecutions leveled against homosexuals by a hostile, intolerant heterosexual majority."

The answer to Duberman's unfulfilled paternal needs, and therewith the release of his frozen heterosexuality, lay, naturally, in the transference. If Duberman forged a proper emotional tie with a father figure who truly cared for him, he could then correctly work through the relationship and come out at the other end a bona fide heterosexual. He managed to persuade himself that Karl was a legitimate candidate for the task: "He, an older man, *did* care about me." Karl proposed that they solidify the healing bond, and thus set the magical transformation in motion, by teaching a university seminar together. The idea was that Duberman would be in charge of the historical issues (the course was to treat American protest movements), while Karl would supervise the seminar's group dynamics. The proposition fitted well with Duberman's long-standing belief that college teaching was riddled with posturing and game-playing and needed to be subjected to a ruthless psychological critique. When Princeton balked at authorizing a course in which Duberman's therapist would be hired as a coteacher—initiating a fight that led eventually to his quitting Princeton for the City University—the seminar was given at Hunter College in 1969.

Ironically, rather than solidifying their emotional bond, the course revealed Karl's grandiose pretensions and desperate insecurities. Unwilling to confine himself to his facilitator's role, he was soon issuing opaque pronouncements about educational philosophy and intervening aggressively in the seminar's substantive discussions with information that Duberman knew to be false. It was the familiar story of the emperor's new clothes: rather than a sovereign dispenser of psychological wisdom, Karl exposed himself as an ignorant academic wannabe. The experience could hardly fail to damage his analytic authority, and, although Duberman didn't break off the analysis for another year, the seeds of doubt had been firmly planted. For once, Duberman's much-maligned professional skills as a scholar had performed a useful psychological service.

In the last year of therapy with Karl, Duberman found himself increasingly emboldened to voice his doubts about the psychoanalytic line. His disenchantment was nourished by the discovery that Dick's heterosexual "conversion" was a sham: what Dick felt for his wife, it turned out, was a pale imitation, not just erotically but emotionally, of what Duberman had felt for Larry back in the 1950s. To his own surprise, Duberman heard himself accusing the other members of the group of being "hung up on an old-fashioned view of homosexuality." Typically, however, he takes no personal credit for his rebellion: as is his habit, he sees himself as the unwitting mouthpiece for broader historical forces at work in the culture. "Some of gay liberation's new views were percolating inside me," he infers.

When the end finally came, in late 1970, it was Karl who abandoned Duberman, rather than the other way around. Karl suddenly announced that he was marrying another member of the group, "Helen," and, from their honeymoon in Costa Rica, he wrote enigmatically that an obscure complaint obliged him to spend his "'last remaining days'" in a tropical climate. Duberman never saw him again. Only years later, in a reunion with Helen, did he learn the full scope of Karl's perfidy. Apparently the great critic of Duberman's "acting-out" had been having an affair with Helen all the while she was in group therapy, and Helen was only the latest in a long line patients with whom he had had sex. In Costa Rica, bitter about his failed ambitions as a writer (a major source of his hostility to Duberman), he had taken to drink, promiscuity, and spousal abuse—"the whole heterosexual nine yards," as Duberman puts it. By then, of course, Karl's influence over Duberman had long since collapsed. But, in reporting the downfall of his nemesis, he indulges in a well-earned, almost gleeful, display of revenge, and the reader—certainly the gay reader—is hardly less pleased. Karl's undoing, we are made to feel, marks the symbolic end of the homophobic regime of American psychoanalysis. We stand on the threshold of a new ideological era.

ALAS, THE BIRTH-PANGS OF THE new era were prolonged and agonizing. Duberman would not begin to find his way out of the woods, intellectually or emotionally, for another two years. Even as he released his pent-up anger toward Karl, he remained addicted to the therapeutic ideal, though no longer in its psychoanalytic guise, and he proceeded to join a series of counter-cultural self-help groups, always with some notion of fixing his problem. First came Anthos, the East Coast branch of Esalen, where he absorbed a lot of nonsense about self-actualization and tried (unsuccessfully, as always) to ignite his heterosexual fires in an erotic "marathon" with a couple of obliging women. Next he went in for yoga with "Swami Satchadananda," followed in turn by the martial art of Aikido. If Paul Monette was a "love junkie," Duberman would have to be called a "therapy junkie." He knows his weakness, and the account of his alternative therapeutic experiments is appropriately self-mocking.

Much more serious—and the real reason he remained so unhappy—was his inability to extract himself from the sexual cul-de-sac in which he had landed: his romantic obsession with hustlers. In the year after the analysis with Karl came to an end, he began the most destructive of these affairs. "Danny" was a virtual retread of Jim: in his early twenties, athletic, straight, and working-class. He was even more threatening and exploitative than his predecessor: he had been a drug dealer, and he cultivated Duberman mainly with a eye to launching a career as an actor. The particular irony is that Duberman, himself the victim of so much psychoanalytic foolishness about "curing" his desires, entertained fond hopes of converting Danny into a homosexual. His old friend Ray, stepping into the gap left by Karl's departure and assuming the role of ersatz-psychoanalyst, pointed out that the doomed affair represented a transparent effort to appropriate Danny's masculinity: "'You've invested Danny with all the magical endowments of the stereotypic male—the vigorous, boisterous roustabout, the All-American hellraiser stud—a persona you have long coveted for yourself and had hoped to incorporate by taking him hostage.'" Duberman could hardly disagree: a fixation on American manliness runs like a red thread through his erotic history. But he nonetheless submitted to more than a year of abuse before he mustered the strength, late in 1972, to break off the relationship. By that time, significantly, he had taken his first steps toward coming out publicly. The real solution to his ills, he was discovering at last, lay not in therapy but in politics.

"And then came Stonewall." Duberman's portentous sentence introduces his account of the epochal uprising against police harassment, on June 27, 1969, by the patrons (many of them drag queens) of a Greenwich Village bar, the Stonewall Inn. We fully expect the event, whose historian he would ultimately become, to mark a fundamental watershed in his life, all the more so when we learn that the Stonewall Inn was his own neighborhood watering hole—his "bar of choice"—which he visited at least once a week. But Duberman was not present that crucial evening, and he concedes that, had he known about it, he would have been unlikely to join the protesters. When, within weeks, the Gay Liberation Front had formed and embraced all his favorite New Left issues—with the significant addition of homosexual emancipation—Duberman took no interest.

His aversion, indeed outright hostility, to the nascent movement persisted for nearly three years. On the anniversary of the Stonewall riot, which was celebrated with New York's first Gay Pride parade, Duberman stayed away, exercising his usual (ironic) defense mechanism: "I remained in my apartment, barricaded in books, deeply immersed in finishing my history of the cultural revolutionaries of Black Mountain College." The next year, 1971, he at least deigned to attend the parade, viewing it from the sidewalk, but he contemptuously dismissed it in his diary as "'cripples on yet another march to the faith healing shrine.'" At some level, he insists, he was absorbing the new message, but the self-immolating dogma he had learned from years of therapy remained deeply entrenched in his psyche. "'What it seems to come down to,'" he confided to his diary, "'is that I've internalized for so long the social definition of homosexuality as pathology and curse that I'm unable to embrace a different view, though I'd desperately like to.'" He also deluded himself with the notion that self-acceptance was in some way a "copout," the psychological counterpart of the laissez-faire politics he so despised. Thus, in a familiar pattern, did his ideological convictions sabotage his emotional needs.

The astonishing thing about Duberman's coming out, in 1972, is that it was at once so sudden and so public. He began planning his declaration well before he had resolved the doubts about his own pathology and indeed while he was still enmeshed in the final throes of his destructive relationship with Danny. On paper, at least, he moved from self-hate to self-advertising with no time in between for self-acceptance, the *via media* in which many of us (certainly I myself) had settled by the late 1960s or early 1970s, leading mostly closeted but highly satisfying lives as gay men. In contrast to Andrew Tobias, who in these very years was busy telling his story to anyone who would listen but never for a moment thought of taking a public stand, Duberman decided to announce his homosexuality to the world, although, at the time, he could not have honestly told even his closest friend that he felt proud and happy to be gay.

The actual announcement might seem relatively innocuous, but Duberman fought with his publishers and agonized over it for months. It took the form of a single, parenthetical, even apologetic sentence in the nearly five hundred pages of *Black Mountain*. Speaking of the College's effective dismissal of its theater director, Bob Wunch, after his arrest on a homosexual charge, Duberman wrote, "'It's hard to think well of a place that would cooperate as fully as Black Mountain did in an individual's self-destruction. . . . But perhaps I exaggerate—a function of my own indignation as a homosexual, a potential victim.'" He followed up with a similar confession in a *New York Times* essay treating recent gay liberation writings, an essay that contained the all-important phrase "'we homosexuals.'" From our present vantage point these two gestures may look tame enough, but they caused a scholarly earthquake at the time. Reviewers of *Black Mountain* attacked Duberman for his self-indulgence, and I have heard speculation that the sentence cost him a Pulitzer. Although I remain uncomfortable with the gap between his private agony and his public affirmation, I have come to appreciate the undeniable courage of his act, which, in its way, was comparable to André Gide's willingness to say "I" in the pages of *Si le grain ne meurt* a half-century earlier, even as Marcel Proust urged discretion.

Duberman's own view, of course, is that his public declaration, rather than putting the cart before the horse, was the very act that enabled him to set his life on a healthy course the following year. His is an extreme variant on the central proposition informing all coming-out stories: that the ability to speak one's identity is the *sine qua non* of homosexual liberation. Accordingly, *Cures* ends with a consideration of two developments in 1973 that Duberman takes to mark his escape from the old regime of isolation and self-betrayal. The first was what he calls "affiliating": his move to join several gay political organizations, of which the Gay Academic Union turned out to be the most important. The high point came in November 1973 when he delivered the keynote address at a well-attended GAU conference on "The Universities and the Gay Experience." Calling the speech a "rite of passage," he began, significantly, by comparing it to his bar mitzvah, thus allowing his long-suppressed Jewish identity to surface, at least rhetorically, at the same moment in which he asserted the need for gay men and women to come out of the closet. Perhaps even more important, he also started a relationship with a filmmaker whom he describes as "deeply sweet and affectionate, a scrawny, manic mix of absolute mush and magnate imperialism, undersized and over thirty." The relationship was not easy, and we don't have much confidence that it will endure. Nonetheless, as Duberman himself notes, it marked "a promising departure in every way from my pattern of infatuation with borderline young hoods," a pattern that had made him miserable for the better part of a decade. At last he had settled on a reasonable erotic choice: a gay man, an artist/intellectual like himself, someone closer to his own age, and emphatically not (in Ray's words) "the All-American hellraiser stud" he had pursued in vain for so many years. He was finally waking from his long nightmare.

◯◯ THE PARADOX OF *CURES* is that it is a conversion narrative about liberating oneself from the tyrannical idea of conversion. One might even call it a deconversion narrative. The thought of changing anything so deeply ingrained as one's sexual orientation, it tells us, must be abandoned as not merely hopeless but, worse, self-annihilating. The particular villains in Duberman's case, as we know, were Freud's American acolytes, who, contemptuous of the overwhelming evidence before their eyes, blithely preached their crazed gospel of transformation. Adding to the unhappy irony of Duberman's experience is that no thinker could have been more helpful to him than Sigmund Freud himself. I am thinking not just of the Freud who famously wrote the mother of an American homosexual, "Homosexuality is assuredly no advantage, but it is nothing to be ashamed of, no vice, no degradation. . . . Many highly respectable individuals of ancient and modern times have been homosexual, several of the greatest men among them. . . . It is a great injustice to persecute homosexuality as a crime—and a cruelty, too."[4] Even more fundamental was Freud the unsparing critic of conversion, the thinker who believed that the human psyche is deeply resistant to change and that emotional maturity lies in accepting that we are not going to be born again into new and better selves. Nothing would seem more foreign to Freud's deeply humane pessimism than the facile and sadistic doctrine of heterosexual conversion propounded in his name by Duberman's *bêtes noires*, Bergler, Bieber, and Socarides. But perhaps I am again guilty of telling my story rather than Duberman's. For my recovery from my own (much milder) case of conversion fever—the Roman Catholic asceticism of my undergraduate days when I was Duberman's student at Yale—dates from the moment, in my senior year, when I began to read Freud and found there the great psychological realist who dismisses not just the "illusion" of religion but also its secular variation, the danger-

4. In *Letters of Sigmund Freud* (April 9, 1935), ed. Ernst L. Freud, trans. Tania and James Stern (New York, 1960), p. 423.

ously seductive promise that "we shall all be changed." Some years would pass, and I would make many hurtful mistakes, before I drew the logical consequence of Freud's wisdom for my sexual life. But I credit him with having saved me from the truly mad project of self-refashioning that made Martin Duberman such an unhappy man for so long.

Paul Monette, photographed by his lover Roger Horwitz in the mid-1970s.

Becoming a Man

WHEN PAUL MONETTE published his autobiography, *Becoming a Man*—for which he won the 1992 National Book Award for nonfiction—he was generally thought of as a gay novelist, arguably among the three most prominent of his generation. By "gay novelist" I mean not a novelist who happens to be gay, or even one (like Gore Vidal) who deals with homosexuality in some of his work, but a writer whose fiction consistently, even exclusively, addresses gay issues. In Monette's case the label was not entirely accurate, at least as far as "novelist" is concerned. He had indeed authored six novels, all of them treating gay themes, but he began his career as a poet and returned to poetry in the late 1980s with *Love Alone: 18 Elegies for Rog*. More important, his single greatest success—and, in the view of many, still his masterpiece—was his 1988 AIDS memoir, *Borrowed Time*, recounting the death of his lover. Less well known, he had, after his move to Hollywood in 1977, written a number of screenplays and "novelizations"—the bastard genre that recirculates successful movies as airport paperbacks.

The two writers with whom Monette invites comparison are Edmund White (b. 1940) and Andrew Holleran (b. 1943). Holleran's first novel, *Dancer from the Dance,* was published the same year (1978) as Monette's (*Taking Care of Mrs. Carroll*). It remains the most evocative portrait of the gay erotic extravaganza of the 1970s and, like many first novels, has an unmistakably autobiographical feel. Holleran was never able to follow up on the book's promise: his two subsequent novels, *Nights in Aruba* (1983) and *The Beauty of Men* (1996), emerged with painful slowness and little of their predecessor's sexual allure. But, like Monette, Holleran found his voice in the 1980s in nonfiction: as a monthly columnist for *Christopher Street* magazine chronicling "the Plague" in a series of often autobiographical essays subsequently collected in *Ground Zero*, which, like *Borrowed*

Time, appeared in 1988 and shares with Monette's memoir a high place of honor in the literary record of AIDS.

The parallel with Edmund White is rather different but no less suggestive. White is most admired for his autobiographical sequence *A Boy's Own Story* (1982) and *The Beautiful Room Is Empty* (1988), whose coming-out narrative is in many ways the "fictional" counterpart of *Becoming a Man* and which, under a more capacious definition of "autobiography" than the one I have relied on, would fit nicely into the present chapter. Like Monette and Holleran, White too has turned to nonfiction, first (with Charles Silverstein) in *The Joy of Gay Sex* (1977), a kind of user's manual for the sexual revolution of the 1970s, followed by *States of Desire* (1980), a travelogue through America's gay playgrounds on the eve of AIDS, which exhibits something of the prelapsarian euphoria of Holleran's *Dancer from the Dance.* More recently, as we know from chapter 4, he has published a magisterial biography of Jean Genet, a book, I am persuaded, that at some level represented his escape from America's AIDS catastrophe. In 1983 he began living part-time in France, where he labored at the research and writing of *Genet* (1993) during precisely the years when Holleran and Monette were making the AIDS epidemic the main subject of their writing.

These comparisons may suggest the extent to which AIDS was at once Monette's personal tragedy and his literary salvation. Monette himself died of the disease in 1995, preceded by not only his lover, Roger Horwitz, but also Horwitz's successor, Stephen Kolzac, as well as many friends. Yet the disease gave Monette his great subject, which he embraced with polemical zeal. Without AIDS, which galvanized his creative energies, he would probably have remained a middlebrow novelist of minor repute rather than what he in fact became: one of the major public voices, alongside Larry Kramer, through which the gay community expressed its pain and outrage.

Although the story told in *Becoming a Man*'s ends in 1974—on the evening Monette met Roger Horwitz—the shadow of AIDS hangs over the book. Monette assumes, no doubt rightly, that his readers will be familiar with *Borrowed Time,* to which *Becoming a Man* is a kind of prequel. But he also makes the connection explicit. He introduces himself as "forty-six now and dying by inches" and, on the same page, recalls the funeral of Stephen Kolzak. Later, when he relates his childhood fascination with *Lassie,* the narrative suddenly flashes forward to a 1990 meeting of the Radical Faeries, who gather near a ranch where the television show was filmed, and some of whom, he observes, have catheters on their chests—"for the plague has ravaged the tribe." AIDS lurks in the background throughout, fueling his anger and countering the book's express movement from the death of the closet to the life of coming out with an ironic reminder that life also turns out to mean death.

Monette's version of the closet is, in a way, more extreme than either Andrew Tobias's or Martin Duberman's. For Tobias the closet meant above all that his body had shut down: he could neither fart nor masturbate, and most of his energy went into translating his illicit desires into acceptably benign disguises, like wrestling. Duberman's closet was a world of suffering and self-contempt, from which he tried to rescue himself through the psychoanalytic fantasy of conversion. But for Monette the closet was more (or, rather, less) than somatic anesthesia or permanent unhappiness: it was a world of nonbeing. "Nothingness" is the idea to which he returns again and again to convey an impression of his life before coming out. His was a "story where nothing happens," indeed "no story at all," only a "blank page." For twenty-five years, he writes, he "accepted the fact that nothing had ever happened to me and nothing ever would. That's how the closet feels, once you've made your nest in it and learned to call it home." Sometimes he varies the image, substituting death for nothingness: the closet was a "coffin world" in which he was "a ghost," or it was a windowless "prison." But the variations retain the central idea: he was less in pain (like Duberman) than simply absent. In literary terms, the chief difference between Duberman and Monette is that, where Duberman has written a book of arguments, deploying his sober prose to mount a well-reasoned critique of the homophobic regime, Monette's is a book of metaphors, whose vividness and wit conjure up a more visceral, though less systematic, impression of that same regime.

In this existential void Monette's life took the form of impersonations, a strategy he refers to as "'de-selfing.'" He became an actor, a ventriloquist, playing various roles whose immediate function was to enable him "to pass for straight." Thus the book's second most prominent image, after nothingness, is that of the theater: he was not so much in the closet as on stage, performing the different scripts he wrote to substitute for his dangerous inner emptiness. Some of his roles were serious—pretending to be an intellectual or an artist, for example—but more often they were comic, such as playing the clown, the courtier, or the witty charmer (which inspires another of his running metaphors, that of his "doggy life," according to which he was forever wagging his tail in an effort to please).

Comedy in fact serves an important, if elusive, function in Monette's self-presentation. On the one hand, as just noted, he associates it with the despised theatrical posturing of his closeted existence. On the other, *Becoming a Man* is itself an often funny book, though its comedy resembles neither the slapstick jokiness of *The Best Little Boy in the World* nor the stand-up routine of one-liners favored by Quentin Crisp in *The Naked Civil Servant*. Rather, Monette's way of skewering his own and society's homophobia is a kind of Voltairean overstatement. At the same time he also links comedy to effeminacy: his early clowning implied a failure to embrace the manly sobriety of his peers, just as the text's wicked jabs imply that the young clown has grown into a bitchy queen. The association is extremely subtle, however: set against Quentin Crisp's flamboyance, Monette seems almost conventionally masculine, yet he is far less intent than either Andrew Tobias or Martin Duberman on maintaining an impeccably butch image. I never met Paul Monette, but from the antic manner of his text I picture him as someone who, while he could easily pass for straight, was unembarrassed by the exaggerations of gesture and speech that our culture reads as borderline effeminate.

The ambiguous status of comedy in the book points to a more fundamental tension, perhaps even a contradiction, in his account. The basic conceit of *Becoming a Man* is its opposition between the performative world of the closet and the authentic world of coming out, where he was able to find his true self in the arms of "the laughing man." All of his earlier identities were false—"constructed," we might now say—while his identity as a gay man who falls in love with another gay man was unambiguously real—or "essential." In an early aside, Monette actually introduces the theoretical controversy between essentialists and constructionists, the former holding that homosexual identity is a natural, transhistorical phenomenon, the latter that it has emerged only in the past century as a creation of specific social and ideological conditions. He says that his own sympathies lie with the essentialists—logically so, because essentialism fits better with a story that sets the artificial (and largely comic) impersonations of his first twenty-nine years against the genuine and romantic gay self that emerged from beneath those impersonations when he met Roger Horwitz.

But the text gives us reason to suspect that the "real" gay romance of the book's conclusion is, at some level, yet another performance, stylized and culturally contingent. Monette himself insists that it must be real, if only because he can think of no possible source for his image of "two men in love and laughing," an image he carried about in his head for years, though he had "never read it in any book or seen it in any movie." In fact, however, he had learned it, with the necessary gender shifts, precisely from the movies, above all from the B-romances that filled his youthful imagination and supply his text with a running set of analogies. In this regard *Becoming a Man* resembles an earlier gay autobiography, Arnie Kantrowitz's *Under the Rainbow* (1977), whose title alludes to its sustained comparison between the author's story and *The Wizard of Oz*: Kantrowitz's black-and-white life in the closet, like Dorothy's in Kansas, gives way to the technicolor world of coming out, a veritable Emerald City of sexual and emotional satisfactions. Monette himself recognizes the connection: "I am a child of Hollywood," he writes, "full of B-plots and Bette Davis lines." Or even more exactly: "Somewhere deep inside the closet of lies, I clung to a misty-eyed Hollywood ending: Bette Davis waiting to meet Paul Henreid in *Now Voyager*." His eventual migration to Hollywood and his part-time career as a screenwriter—a bit like Duberman's move to New York and flirtation with Broadway—thus seems entirely appropriate. In a sense, Monette lived his life as a movie, and while his final role, as a gay love junkie, was undoubtedly his best, it cannot be categorically separated from his earlier assumptions. Perhaps the same point can be made, more abstractly, by saying that the distinction he draws between an actorly and an authentic self won't bear too close inspection: self-dramatization was as intrinsic to his make-up as any other quality of character. The text of *Becoming a Man* displays an unabashedly performative sensibility. Indeed, the book's effectiveness depends very much on its theatrical exaggerations.

In ideological terms Monette's autobiography differs from both the completely apolitical narrative of Andrew Tobias in *The Best Little Boy in the World* and Martin Duberman's rich embedding of his story in America's cultural history during the 1950s and 1960s in *Cures*. On the rare occasions when Monette summons the malign public voices of his youth, he invokes not Duberman's psychoanalytic trio of Bergler, Bieber, and Socarides but Roy Cohn, J. Edgar Hoover, and, most revealingly, Cardinal Spellman. He attacks Cohn, Hoover, and Spellman as self-hating homosexuals who launched an antigay pogrom whose logical consequence was the AIDS epidemic, which, like ACT UP, he tends to view as a heterosexual plot and regularly compares to the Holocaust. The tactic is risky, because it depends on stereotyped, indeed homophobic, images of his persecutors as "closeted mama's boys" and "sick queens." Similarly, the Holocaust analogy, also drawn by Larry Kramer, blunts a number of complex questions about intention and moral gravity.

The most striking feature of Monette's political stance is his anticlericalism, which is directed above all at the Catholic Church, headed by its "Nazi Popes." He admits his "prejudice" in the matter, but the ferocity of his hatred is nonetheless startling:

> A new Inquisition is in full cry, led by the rabid dog in brocade, Cardinal Ratzinger of the Curia, the malevolent divine who laid down the law that loving gay was a matter of "intrinsic evil." In the decade of the AIDS calamity I've come to see the church of the Polish pope as a sort of Greenwich Mean of moral rot—thus in my small way returning the compliment of Sturmführer Ratzinger. Hardly a week goes by that we don't hear from the pope's minions in the colonies—O'Connor in New York, Mahony in L.A.—spewing their misogyny and homophobia, delirious with triumph that sex finally equals death.

For autobiographical reasons, I happen to have a high tolerance for this sort of rant, but other readers find that it seriously disfigures Monette's work in *Becoming a Man* and *Borrowed Time* as well as in his later fiction. Doubtless it overstates the Church's role in fostering homophobia, ignoring, for example, the resolutely secular (and vestigially Jewish) prejudices of the American psychoanalytic community, at whose doorstep Martin Duberman of course lays the largest share of the blame. I am inclined to indulge it, however, as the modern gay counterpart of Voltaire's unfair but liberating attack on *l'infâme:* characteristically exaggerated, perhaps imprudent, but emotionally justified. Still, Monette's running image of a homophobic world run by Catholic clerics, assisted from time to time by "wacko fundamentalists" and "rat-brain politicians," represents a fairly thin piece of historical analysis. Despite its political *obiter dicta, Becoming a Man* is thus closer in spirit to the strictly personal narrative of *The Best Little Boy in the World* than to Martin Duberman's effort to write autobiography as cultural history.

∞ MONETTE SPENT THE FIRST eighteen years of his life, before he went off to Yale in 1963, within a classic nuclear family in the mill town of Andover, Massachusetts, ten miles northwest of Salem, "where," he comments pointedly, "they burned a half-century of witches, mostly gay and lesbian." His young father, a returning World War Two veteran, drove a truck for the local coal company but soon rose to an office job, so that during Monette's school years the family became distinctly middle-class. He was an only child until the birth of his brother, Bobby, when he was six—a critical turning point, as we'll see, in his supposedly eventless childhood. Despite his "blue-collar" roots, he complains that he came to be seen as a kind of effete aristocrat, despised by the working-class bad boys, whose vulgar masculinity aroused him. At the start, in other words, he fell into the English pattern of class-coded homoeroticism, but, in contrast to Martin Duberman, it was just a childhood phase and left no discernible trace on his adult sexual life. Compared with either Tobias or Duberman—fellow Manhattan sophisticates—Monette's origins were decidedly provincial, even impoverished.

Monette insists that his sense of existential emptiness—of the "nothingness" of his life—antedated the first stirrings of sexual desire. It was his permanent state of mind as far back as he can remember. Psychologically speaking, he was in the closet even before he had anything specific to hide, as if he had some premonition of his future differentness and anesthetized himself in advance. He acknowledges that in insisting on so negative an account of his childhood he is "fighting against the evidence." He will credit neither his mother's recollections of a happy boyhood nor the heartwarming family anecdotes and the scrapbook of smiling photos. When he is shown pictures of his laughing younger self, his only response is, "Not me." He regards his success in school and the admiration it won him as equally bogus: his straight A's and his teacher's comment "*Paul is perfect*" correspond to no recollection of his ever taking pleasure in his achievement or recognition. "Me against the evidence yet again," he concedes. If anything, he views his successes as an ironic measure of his alienation, very much as Martin Duberman views his prize-winning books.

Inevitably the reader begins to suspect that Monette's empty childhood is an ideological construct, dictated by the Manichaean categories of the coming-out narrative, which allows no light to penetrate the darkness of the closet. In *Cures* Duberman admits to just such an ideological weakness: "I sometimes think I retrospectively exaggerate my unhappiness in the pre-Stonewall years—perhaps in order to exaggerate, to the same degree, the liberating aspects of post-Stonewall." As with Duberman, I find I can't read Monette's account of his youth without a constant sense of autobiographical resistance: his unqualified assertion "That's how the closet feels" simply does not correspond to my own recollection, which is of a childhood and adolescence filled with varied and often gratifying experiences, albeit darkened by the burden of a dangerous secret. I keep wanting to object, "True, the closet was no picnic, but it did not reduce the rest of my life to a desert of nothingness: it did not blot out the pride of academic success, the joy of music-making, the pleasure of friendship." His repeated admission that he is fighting the evidence leads me to doubt that his childhood was in reality so unlike mine—or, less presumptuously, to surmise that he has unconsciously re-fashioned a past better suited to his adult convictions. Conceivably, of course, he might respond that I have lightened the portrait of my own youth in order to justify my failure to come out sooner than I did.

Life with his mother and father may have been empty, but it was hardly oppressive. On the contrary, he draws an attractive picture of both his parents. He is especially eager to discredit the psychoanalytic etiology, which traces ho-mosexuality to a dysfunctional family complex. "Possessive mother? Absent fa-ther? Not especially. I thought they were both quite nice, and beautiful as movie stars. If anyone was distant, I was." He calls his parents "decent" and "brave" and admits to having been "fearfully proud" of his father in particular. Under-standably, they were not thrilled by his early flirtation with "genderfuck"—prancing about in his mother's heels and cutting paper dolls—but such pressure as they applied was inconsistent and "half-hearted." A few years later they showed a similar restraint when they discovered his pornography collection. He reaches a firmly anti-Freudian conclusion: "My family didn't make me queer." He also notes that their social circumstances (and perhaps their Episcopalian reli-gion) inoculated him against the therapeutic virus to which Martin Duberman succumbed: psychiatry was "out of the question . . . for the working class in a country town."

His parents showed their bravery above all in the uncomplaining selfless-ness with which they accepted the burden of raising their second son, who was born with spina bifida, never learned to walk, and suffered life-threatening ill-nesses throughout his childhood. Monette's own reaction to his "'crippled'" brother's birth was traumatic, even in a life where nothing was supposed to hap-pen. "This was the week I became invisible," he writes. He explains that he felt responsible for his brother's disability because his mother had fallen while walk-ing him to school when she was pregnant. But the explanation is unconvincing, because he didn't know of her pregnancy at the time; indeed, as a six-year-old he probably knew nothing at all about pregnancy, and, by his own account, he made the connection between her fall and his brother's condition only thirty years later.

The actual relation between Bobby's paralysis and his own psychic trauma was more devious. For one thing, it appears to have dated not, as he claims, from his brother's birth but from the moment, a few years later, when he first experienced homosexual desire. The channel through which the unhappy connection was forged, ironically, was the admiration he felt for his parents: already burdened with a son crippled in body, they were threatened, he now feared, with one crippled in spirit: "There had already been enough damage to our family, more than enough of the pain of being different. The last thing they needed was something weird from me." At a deeper level, this sentiment transformed itself into the conviction that Bobby was being punished for Monette's own sins. The sole way to ease his guilt was to become bodiless, "because the body was too upsetting to think about, let alone play with." His agony only increased as he came to appreciate the full measure of his brother's courage and humanity. One almost has the sense that Monette was victimized by the very goodness of his family: his brave parents and his heroic brother left him unable to accept his imperfect self. His family may not have made him queer, but it unwittingly conspired to push him deeper into the closet.

Both the notion of his bodilessness and the idea that nothing ever happened to him are contradicted by the account of his sexual initiation at the hands of a lower-class schoolmate named Kite. "I was nine and half," he begins, "when everything changed." His seducer was a "ruffian, . . . famous for picking fights and for a mouth like a sewer."[5] The seduction is related in Monette's inimitable manner, at once sexy and comic, which captures the excitement of the moment even as its deflationary language eliminates the bathetic self-consciousness that usually ruins such scenes:

> Kite was taking a leak in the bushes. His eyes locked on mine, that superior patient smile again, and I was lost. The stream dribbled to drops, and he shook it, but didn't put it back in his pants. Ducked instead through the broken window of the toolshed. I followed, shedding my A's like a chrysalis. He yanked my pants down, and we rubbed our two hard weenies together. Neither of us any bigger than the first joint of my little finger, hairless and nothing to shoot. But I was hooked on pleasure from that day on.

5. Kite bears an uncanny resemblance to the similarly named Count Kai, the disheveled boy who courts little Hanno Buddenbrook "with a fiery, aggressive masculinity impossible to resist" in Thomas Mann's novel, *Buddenbrooks*, trans. H. T. Lowe-Porter (New York, 1964), p. 421.

The episode introduces us to perhaps the most amusing character in *Becoming a Man,* not the ruffian Kite but Monette's "weenie," whose adventures and "thoughts" assume a life of their own in the course of the book. Soon promoted from his "weenie" to his "dick," the perky organ makes a much more congenial companion than Martin Duberman's droopy "cock" or Stilitano's massive "prick"—"the biggest and loveliest prick in the world"—before which Jean Genet worshiped. Although it would fail him briefly during his high-school years at Andover Academy, throughout most of Monette's odyssey his dick, reliably stiff, served as a compass of his true feelings, a signpost of his essential self, buried under the layers of play-acting. Sometimes he tried to discipline the unruly member. He writes of one guilty adventure in his early twenties: "I punished my dick by refusing to touch it, trying to starve it to death, so revolted was I by the moral chaos it had brought me to." But generally he treats it as a font of practical wisdom. During his long years in the closet, he observes, "all I would have to go on was my dick."

The arrangement with Kite continued for several months, transforming the putatively bodiless nine-year-old into a full-time sybarite. It marked one of those right-angled conversions that shouldn't occur in his storyless life. The pair soon expanded their erotic repertory, and the affair culminated in a treehouse rendezvous during a Lawrentian storm:

> We stripped naked and wrestled on the plank floor, rain coming in on us, roof
> tarpaper flapping above us like a sail. I think that was the day we discovered
> sixty-nine, though here I am probably editing memory shamelessly. Surely
> we'd contorted ourselves to double-suck before, in the pup tents of summer or
> somebody's barn. Yet here in the tree, in our animal coupling, it was the two
> of us who seemed to generate the rising wind and rain. . . . Eventually we
> stopped—still too young to come, even in the whirlwind.

In this, as in his other descriptions of sex with Kite, the text contributes subtly to advance Monette's essentialist viewpoint. The boys invented almost the full panoply of gay eroticism without the help of any script, and, though barely a word was spoken, we get the impression of the untutored efflorescence of a full-fledged sexual relationship. He may not have felt in love with Kite, but he won't dismiss the experience, as might a straight man, as a mechanical substitute for heterosexual play. Even as a child he knew that it revealed his future identity: "Nine is not too young to feel the tribal call," he insists.

The idyll came to a sudden end when his mother caught them with their flies unzipped in Monette's bedroom. "'What're you boys doing?'" she asked. He gave a one-word answer, "'Nothing,'" which he repeated the next day when she posed the question again. The word is meant to resonate with the book's central theme of the closet's nonbeing. But in fact his mother's inquisition—the most "indelible" moment of his first two decades—marked another "sea-change" in his young life: he gave up Kite and resolved never to do anything similar again, conscious not only that "something very bad had happened" but also, as I've noted, that his parents already had enough grief in their lives. He refuses to demonize his mother's role in the episode. She was merely a victim of the era's repressive consensus, worried less about "homosex" than about "sex itself." It was "the last straw" in a long series of "disappointments and humiliations" that had overwhelmed her.

⚭ AFTER THE ADVENTURE WITH Kite there is a hiatus in the autobiography until Monette arrived at middle school (seventh and eighth grades), where, on the threshold of puberty, he fashioned the first of his disguises, the courtier: "I became a comedian and a charmer, breathlessly smart and witty, the Noel Coward of the junior division." The immediate inspiration was his horror at being identified with a "meek, nervous" boy named Austin Singer, who was beaten up by one of their thuggish classmates and forced to swallow a glob of spit off the ground ("'Lick it, homo'"). Monette never spoke to Austin again. "The cold truth I took from the scene of Austin Singer's humiliation was this: *At least I could still pass.*"

The logic of the courtier role was that it excused him from "the hetero rites of passage"—the roughhousing and the raunchy talk among pubescent boys—even as it provided him with a substitute gratification. He played the courtier only to his female classmates (toward the boys he adopted an attitude of terminal niceness), especially the most desirable of them, like the bombshell Cilla Fitzgerald, whose witty confidant he became. The arrangement let him participate vicariously in their teenage sexual rituals. The mature author takes an uncompromisingly severe view of his performance: "I should have been finding a boy of my own instead of talking to Cilla Fitzgerald about which one of her many suitors for the Junior Prom she ought to accept. That was the most sinister aspect of my courtier's self-denial: the sizing up of straight men for a mating dance I had no part in." Years afterward he discovered that the charade had been in vain: Bobby told him of being set upon one day by a gang of toughs who announced, "'His brother's a queer.'" Apparently his classmates in the late-1950s had little trouble decoding the effeminacy implicit in his "eunuch charm": to them he seemed less a sexless clown than a "budding queen." He may not have been as obvious as Austin Singer, but he never fully succeeded in passing.

Nor was his life really as sexless as his courtier role implied. He did in fact find a boy of his own, a worthy successor to Kite. A year younger than Monette, Richie had yet to reach puberty, but the sex they indulged in was a good deal more advanced (if still not fully grown-up), and it was no longer conducted in silence. Just as important, because Monette was physically the more mature, he enjoyed a kind of masculine privilege he hadn't with Kite:

> We took turns lying on the floor, the one on top poking his dick between the bottom one's legs and getting some friction going. That and a lot of sucking. I think I was probably old enough to shoot, if I'd only known how, but Richie was still a few paces behind, not quite to the border of adolescence. Thus he was fascinated by the wispy bush of hair that had started in my crotch, as well as by the veiny straight-up member I was sporting, three times the size of his, in my thirteenth summer. . . . Richie would grill me about the glandular changes of the previous year, all the while squeezing and milking me, studying the pre-cum as it drooled out. "Lookit all your juice," he'd murmur in awe, so that a weird rooster pride warred with the awkwardness I felt, leaking this substance that had no name.

They carried on in this fashion throughout the next school year. Monette felt the same "animal hunger" he had with Kite, but there was an important difference: he wanted to kiss Richie and was "aware of feeling tender as well as carnal," a sentiment that Richie—though Monette speaks of him as "a fellow queer"—didn't reciprocate. The affair ended not in discovery, as with Kite, but in betrayal: Richie joined two other boys under the school bleachers to taunt Monette with calls of "'Homo.'" The episode led him to renew the vow of chastity he had taken after being caught with Kite, motivated now not just by the wish to spare his family but by a self-protective determination never again to risk such a humiliating disappointment. "To avoid the sudden cut of a boy like Richie," he writes, "I would remain barren for the next ten years, unseducible and impassive, defying anyone to prove that Paul Monette was queer." Thus began his interregnum of repression, which corresponds almost exactly to Andrew Tobias's ascetic decade (after overhearing the infamous Kinsey statistic) and which is a recurrent feature of the American coming-out autobiography. Not for the first time, however, Monette exaggerates the purity of his abstention, for his "barren" years would be regularly punctuated with sexual encounters, however brief and guilty. He was never able to maintain the level of denial achieved by Tobias.

∞ ON THE BASIS OF HIS maligned record of A's, Monette spent his high-school years as a day student at Phillips Academy in Andover, which, along with Phillips Exeter, was the most prominent training ground for the sons of the Eastern establishment on their way to the Ivy League, above all Harvard and Yale. At Andover his life came nearest to approximating the "nothingness" he categorically associates with the closet. Even his courtier impersonation, with its subliminal queenliness, had to be abandoned in this all-male world. His feelings of inadequacy were as much social as sexual, and his account of the Andover years is informed by a sense of class resentment that carried over into Yale. "Andover ground me beneath the heel of its Bass Weejuns," he whines.

The most striking feature of his portrait of Andover is the contrast he draws between his "gray" self and the "golden Adonises" who filled his masturbatory fantasies with "a Parthenon frieze of heroic male flesh parading to the showers after practice." He constructs Andover as a kind of junior-league Greece, a comic variant on the ancient civilization he would evoke so memorably in *Borrowed Time* when describing his pilgrimage in search of tribal origins with his dying lover. The portrait echoes the ersatz-Greek paradise discovered by Julien Green at the University of Virginia in the 1920s, and its intellectual roots lie as far back as John Addington Symonds's homoerotic phil-Hellenism, testifying to the remarkable continuity of Greece as a talisman in the modern homosexual imagination.

The satirical tone of Monette's Grecian fantasy is already evident in the account of his first successful effort at masturbating to orgasm. He had been trying on a daily basis for two years, but to no avail—a failure he overinterprets as resulting from the guilt he felt after being discovered with Kite. He made his breakthrough in the farcical role of a would-be scholar of antiquity:

> It happened at my desk one winter Sunday night; I was stroking my meat
> when I should have been studying Alexander's march through Asia Minor.

Maybe I was pricked by one of the naked marble gods who decorated the text. In any case I finally went too far, and my long-muted instrument reared and shot. Ropes of foam splashed across the coast of Asia Minor like a tidal wave.

The nightly masturbation ritual into which he quickly fell was curiously sexless. He would contemplate his parade of Andover Adonises (with the help of a cache of muscle-boy pornography), but he never imagined doing anything with them. Like Martin Duberman with his straight hustlers, he wanted not to possess them but to become them—with their "roaring self-assurance and aching good health." As with Andrew Tobias, the repression went so deep that it stifled desire: he could no longer even picture having sex with a male, in spite of the "acrobatics" he had practiced with Kite and Richie—an imaginative resource unavailable to Tobias. Every night he would summon the naked images "but without the least desire to fuck with them," mired in a grim routine of jacking off while viewing his inert pantheon of statues.

Even at Andover homosexuality remained on the periphery of his consciousness, though in radically negative and distorted forms. One of these was his fear and hatred of the teachers thought to be homosexual, such as the French master, with his "little coterie of Apollos" who just happened to be the same boys that populated Monette's nightly masturbation routine. Another cautionary tale was supplied by his Classics teacher, who was dismissed after he "went too far" while giving backrubs to some of his seniors. Monette never entirely escaped an imaginary identification with these sad figures: even while writing his autobiography he still had nightmares of becoming "the graying head of an English department in a second-rate boys' school," a fate he was spared, he believes, only by his decision to come out.

The other sick manifestation of his repressed homosexuality was his friendship with two other day students, Francis and Gene, whom he recognized, at some level of his mind, as sissies. Their association took the form of "infantile parody and silly in-jokes," which, however, carefully avoided any mention of sex. The three boys lived in isolated closets or, as Monette puts it, in "adjoining tombs, . . . eunuchs even among our own." He now judges the failure to communicate with his fellow queers to be the greatest evil of his time in prep school, worse than the sexlessness. Here he articulates the central precept of the modern American tradition: speaking the truth is even more important than acting on it.

When he imagines what he would most like to change in his life, he thinks not of a grand romance with one of his Andover Olympians but of breaking through the wall of silence that separated him from his two fellow sufferers: "I wish I could have shared the state of being loveless with Francis and Gene, instead of that patter of improvised camp so ignorant of its heritage, from Oscar Wilde to Joan Crawford."

As the last remark implies, a good deal of Monette's time at Andover went into creating what he later recognized as the lineaments of a gay sensibility. The movies were the chief vehicle of this self-fashioning. They did for him much of what opera did in the homoerotic schooling of Wayne Koestenbaum, whose book *The Queen's Throat* (1993), in its idiosyncratic, stream-of-consciousness way, is also a gay autobiography. Monette's particular obsession was Elizabeth Taylor, whose life and career he memorialized in a scrapbook begun during his freshman year. He doesn't understand how he came by this identification—"a kind of *emotional* drag"—in which we sense the mysterious workings of the cultural system. Somehow he had developed into a full-blown movie queen in the isolated outpost of Andover, unaware of the men out there in cities "who could quote whole Bette Davis scenes to one another, shrieking with laughter." Culturally speaking, he had become a homosexual in spite of himself—"gay in every respect," he writes, "except my dick."

During the summers Monette worked at a local grocery story and soda fountain, where two figures, in their different ways, contributed to his homosexual mis-education. The first was a sixty-year-old customer, a portrait painter, who enticed him home and gave him a blow job. Although he came, he felt none of the excitement he had with Kite and Richie; instead he thought only of the man's "desperate, mauling need" and the hideous prospect that he himself might turn into "the ravenous creature who did me in the attic." The second was his employer's "flaming son" Alex, who bleached his hair, waltzed about the store with pompons, and planned to become a beautician. Alex proved a curiously soothing companion, both because there was no sexual interest (on either side) and, more important, because his extravagant effeminacy made Monette himself seem a paragon of manliness by contrast. At the same time, he felt a secret envy of Alex, aware that the young man had come to peace with himself. Monette discovered that the culture made room for blatant deviancy of Alex's variety, but it cut no slack for someone like himself unwilling to give up his pretensions to normal

masculinity. Just about to head off to Yale, he found himself dreading the prospect of having to fit in as "one of the guys," while Alex's life stood before him
"utterly free to happen, changeable as the color of his hair."

⌘ IF THE ANDOVER YEARS were the emptiest of Monette's youth—the period in
which he most completely realized the closet's blank nothingness—the four
years that followed at Yale brought a sudden transformation: a chameleon sequence of bogus identities, a riot of fake selves. At Andover he had been both
invisible and preternaturally silent, but at Yale he erupted into preening volubility. Each academic year he assumed a new role, shouting and gesticulating his
lines, only to abandon it abruptly when the next season opened. The summers,
in their turn, were devoted to a series of disappointing sexual experiments, from
which he returned to his impersonations with a vengeance. Monette's account of
the Yale years offers a striking demonstration of how his psychic emptiness left
his public self almost infinitely malleable.

He began, in 1963, by trying to play the same part Andrew Tobias had taken
on during Tobias's own first year at college: the cowboy. Monette adopted this
improbable identity from his freshman roommates, two "frontier rugged" Cali-
fornians, a rock climber and a tennis player, with whom, also like Tobias, he
promptly fell in love. So disembodied was his attachment, however, that they
were not even allowed to join "the Olympian frieze" of his masturbation fantasies. Instead, he apprenticed himself in the role of sycophantic mimic, "as spell-
bound and singleminded as Eve Harrington studying Margo Channing." He
became their abject imitator—in dress, language, interests, and prejudices. As
he recognizes, the sycophant was the courtier *redivivus,* but modified to suit his
changed circumstances. Sometimes the imitation was innocuous enough, as when
Monette, a son of Massachusetts, pretended to share their Western contempt for
the overbred East. But it could also be masochistic: as had Tobias, he affected
their rabid homophobia, never missing an opportunity to sneer at the imagined
sexual deviance of their bachelor professors.

Another obligatory feature of his sycophant's role was dating and the sexual
bragging it entailed. Here again his experience exactly mirrored Andrew Tobias's. It is a typical stage in the American coming-out autobiography, one invariably remembered with pain and embarrassment. For his roommates' consumption, Monette invented stories of his heterosexual conquests, "cobbling details
here and there from other men's boasting." Also like Tobias, he shamelessly put

a series of young women through the wringer in order to maintain his cover. Once more his courtier skills were called upon, as he frantically dispensed charm and wit in order to deflect any erotic expectations. "Every minute of a date felt like a lie," he recalls, "but if you didn't date you couldn't be one of the guys."

By the end of the year his roommates were growing tired of his "doggy charm," but one of them nonetheless dragged him along to spend the summer at the family home in Marin County. There Monette fell in with the mother of another classmate and had the first inkling of a possible way out of his sexual predicament. Lois Bronner was the disaffected wife of a philistine businessman, the "chatelaine" of a Napa Valley estate, on whose luxurious grounds she proceeded to court her young visitor. All their talk was of poetry (thus anticipating the identity Monette would assume in his sophomore year), but he quickly figured out that she was offering him a romance of sorts, though a romance (to his great relief) with the sex part left out. It planted in his mind the idea that he might be able to find a relatively painless escape from his quandary by becoming "a gigolo whose dick was not required." His motives, he admits, were crassly economic: marriage to a wealthy matron who didn't require his sexual ministrations was not just a way to hide his shameful secret; even more, it was a ticket to affluence and the good life. Andrew Tobias, apparently, was not unique in his commercial mentality. To be sure, Monette dreaded homosexuality mainly for psychological reasons, but he fretted about its economic disadvantages as well. Put another way, he was interested not just in "becoming a man" but in "becoming a rich man" too. Of my three American autobiographers Martin Duberman alone seems to have been indifferent to such worldly concerns. We romanticize when we imagine closeted homosexuals suffering only in the heart; sometimes they also worried about suffering in the pocketbook.

Monette began his sophomore year by taking up the disguise most suited to his temperament, a kind of meta-disguise: he became an actor. Here he followed unwittingly in the footsteps of Donald Vining, who, we may recall, had been a Yale drama student just over two decades earlier. Risking the contempt of his "straight-arrow" roommates, Monette joined the undergraduate theatrical society, the Yale Dramat, fully aware that it was a hangout for fairies. He was enticed there by same inverted logic that had led him to befriend flaming Alex back in Andover: the "nelly antics" of the other actors reassured him that his own masculine camouflage was still firmly in place.

Joining the Dramat was only one aspect of a larger makeover he undertook:

he abandon his cowboy persona in order to throw in his lot with "the artsy crowd." Increasingly he presented himself as "the poet," an identity he considers every bit as phony as the courtier and sycophant that preceded it. His dismissive attitude toward poetry corresponds exactly to Martin Duberman's attitude toward scholarship, and it results in the same uncomfortable self-denigration. Monette is not engaged here in the familiar exercise in modesty by which the mature artist belittles his juvenilia, often quoting them to prove how bad they were. Aesthetic merit is beside the point. Rather, he abuses his younger poetic self because he considers it just another impersonation that helped him avoid facing up to the sexual truth. "Poetry," he declares, "served as a sort of intellectual wallpaper to brighten up the closet."

After his sophomore year he took a job in a resort hotel in northern New Hampshire. His experiment that summer was to let himself be seduced by one of the waiters, a former New Orleans drag star, bald and fortyish, who might be considered the successor to the portrait painter who "did" him a few years before when he was working in the Andover soda fountain. Monette approached the encounter as a kind of "test." Just as with the painter, his trusty "dick"—"which," he jokes, "apparently had a thing of its own for Southern Gothic"—was once again at attention, after its prep-school amnesia. But the test was inconclusive: for all his desperation "to connect with a man" and despite the ready cooperation of his organ, he found the experience "disgusting and shameful." In retrospect, he is appalled by the contempt, even hatred, he felt for his seducer. As a former drag queen, the waiter, Monette reminds us, belonged the heroic crowd that would launch the Stonewall rebellion.

In his junior year he worked a tortured variation on the poetic identity he had begun to craft as a sophomore. The agent of his new impersonation was an architecture student, Cody Williams, his roommate in Jonathan Edwards College. A self-absorbed drunk—and easily the most disagreeable character in the autobiography—Cody lacked the discipline that might have justified his grandiose artistic ambitions and the scorn he felt for his fellow undergraduates. Although he was unambiguously straight, Monette not only fell for him but concocted a bizarre fantasy of their sharing a life together—a "seduction by soul-merger"—in which "the poet" would be loved by "the architect." Somehow the higher laws of Art would overcome the inconvenient and mundane obstacle of desire. Better yet, he imagined that the spiritual bond between artists might one day magically transform itself into its bodily equivalent.

Much of Monette's time and energy during his junior year was invested in this doomed enterprise. To facilitate the desired soul-merger, he tried to make himself into Cody's double, mimicking "his every word and gesture," just as he had earlier mimicked the language and manners of his California roommates. The only difference was that his new role called for fake world-weariness rather than fake philistinism. For his efforts he was rewarded with the same abusive surliness Cody lavished on his ever-present girlfriend. The "relationship" ended, mercifully, on a drunken spree to New York, where, with Cody passed out in his arms before the Seagram's Building, Monette heard himself whispering, "'*Change me, change me.*'" Whether he hoped to be changed into straight man or a self-accepting homosexual is not clear, and, indeed, it may not have been clear to Monette himself at the time. The only certainty is that he was swearing off the kind of one-sided, delusional romance he had conducted for the better part of a year with Cody. "I would never hold another man who wouldn't hold me back," he pledged to himself.

After his junior year Monette's summer experiment took the form of a trip to Europe, a classic exercise in erotic self-discovery, for straights as well as gays. He had an intellectual cover in the form of traveling fellowship to study Tennyson's letters with a view to writing his senior honors thesis (under Harold Bloom) on *In Memoriam*. But he undertook the trip with a clear-eyed awareness of its sexual purpose. "Mostly," he confesses, "I determined to meet a man and get laid once and for all."

Emboldened by a performance of Noel Coward's *Song at Twilight*, in which in the wheelchair-bound Coward ends sobbing over a letter from a man he had loved long ago, Monette wasted little time picking up a former American sailor in Trafalgar Square and proceeding to his "first fuck." Although several years had elapsed since his amateur sessions with Kite and Richie, he responded like a seasoned veteran. Once again there is a subtle essentialist message implicit in the account of his falling instantaneously and rapturously into the time-honored practices of gay sex:

We lay down side by side, and the moment he grazed my thigh I was on him like a rash. Kissing for the first time, so hungry I frightened myself. Then he licked his way down my body and gave me head while I gripped his hair and groaned, exorcising a thousand lonely nights of pulling my pud for Cody and the like. Patiently he maneuvered us into sixty-nine. . . . He was very big, and he snarled and roared softly when I sucked him, teaching me in an instant what an animal a man could be. When he came in my mouth, it was like a tidal surge in a sea cave, so forceful that the cum streamed out of my nose. When I bucked and shot myself, hearing him greedily drink and swallow, I knew I had tasted life at last—and wouldn't end up sobbing in a wheelchair after all.

You might think that so satisfactory an experience would have settled matters once and for all: Monette had finally done it and enjoyed it, so why did he not proceeded to become a practicing homosexual (even if a closeted one), instead of devoting several more years of his life to a regime of monastic denial? His answer is that the night of ecstasy was followed by an early-morning reprise in which the sailor screwed him. Not only was the pain "excruciating," but it triggered an anxiety attack about his manliness and caused him to flee the premises, "hating myself," as he puts it, "for acceding to the *woman's* role, when what I had been so desperate for was proving I was a man." The notion that kissing, embracing, and fellating were an unmitigated delight and posed no threat to his masculine identity while getting screwed brought on a "tidal wave" of guilt seems mechanical and contrived. One suspects that Monette has produced an over-schematized version of his "deflowering," where anal intercourse is made to carry a heavier burden than it can plausibly tolerate.[6]

He reacted to the debacle by retreating to his well-established artist persona, now not "the poet" but "the novelist." He set out for the South of France, following an on-the-road script in which he accumulated adventures that, with a bit of tweaking, he believed would become his first novel. As he quips, "I was furiously reinventing myself as Novelist, to obliterate the memory of being a sex toy." He devoted his days to filling notebooks with a factitious narrative of his coming of age. The story's main inspiration was a brief and largely make-believe romance he conducted with an American girl he met in Nice. In its "final shot" he contrived to appear holding her in his arms before a caravan of French soldiers, "puffing with pride as I stroked her hair, winking back and returning their salutes, a man among men." He was still profoundly invested in his heterosexual masquerade, and one doubts that he would have been ready to abandon it even if his London sailor had treated him more gently.

6. A tiny slip betrays his exaggeration. In a clause I elided from the description of his night of love he speaks of sixty-nine as "a position I hadn't even conceptualized before, so stunted was my erotic imagination." But, as readers will remember, he had earlier described his and Kite's contorting themselves into "double-suck."

In his senior year, ever resourceful, Monette managed to create yet another disguise to keep the truth at bay. Actually two disguises, though they were closely related. In the first he parlayed his poet-identity into the role of arts impresario, a sort of campus Sol Hurok, feverishly masterminding undergraduate literary life and orchestrating visits by cultural luminaries. His whirling-dervish performance in this role opened the door to the other invented self that now absorbed him: that of blood brother. He was elected a member of one of Yale's notorious secret societies, Elihu, and threw himself into its hokey fellowship and manufactured intimacy. A particular irony is that he seized on Elihu's ritual of Thursday night "autobiographies," in which the brothers shared their hidden stories, not to tell his real secret but to concoct a fictitious account of his life as a suicidal depressive. Monette's impersonations didn't have to be upbeat; any identity, so long as it was simulated, would do. In truth, he never contemplated suicide, "having," as he says, "chosen instead a living death, the inchmeal route of the closet." But the other initiates devoured his tale, and he quickly became "the resident expert on melancholy."

The emotional focus of his blood-brother role was another Elihu senior, a handsome and, by all evidence, truly admirable young man, Bill Hilgendorf, with whom Monette became absorbed. In contrast to the California jocks and Cody Williams, Bill Hilgendorf wasn't someone he desired. We are dealing here not with another repressed crush but with something more perverse: an entirely literary projection, the one serious offshoot of his otherwise sham interest in Tennyson. In Monette's imagination Bill and his girlfriend, Star Black, figured as Lancelot and Guinevere, while Monette himself played "the Laureate," inventing an idealized future in which the couple became President and First Lady. Yet even as he fell into this most self-extinguishing of fantasies, he also convinced himself that he should tell Bill the truth about his sexuality. Somehow the revelation was deferred until after graduation, when Bill left to spend two years in China, where he was killed in a mountain accident that summer. Naturally the tragedy got mixed up with Monette's feelings about his crippled brother: once again he had the sense that the wrong man had been punished. The upshot of Bill Hilgendorf's death and the unwritten coming-out letter was to give Monette yet another excuse not to tell his story. His college career thus ended on a high pitch of synthetic emotion that left him no nearer self-acceptance than he had been as an entering freshman. It also ended with an understandable sense of mental exhaustion after four years of nonstop play-acting.

☯ MONETTE'S LONG ACCOUNT OF HIS time as an undergraduate is the most successful part of the autobiography, because it so vividly illustrates his central
theme of the closet's desperate fakery. The rest of the story doesn't maintain the
same manic tension. We are even apt to grow impatient at the snail's pace of his
progress over the seven years between his graduation in 1967 and the serendipi-
tous meeting with Roger Horwitz in 1974, especially when we remind ourselves
that the Gay Liberation movement was then taking off and other men his age or
younger (such as Andrew Tobias) were so far ahead of him. Nor is the last third
of the narrative as well-controlled as the earlier sections. One suspects that Monette was feeling the pressure of his disease and rushing himself to finish.

After graduation, with all his props suddenly removed, he lapsed into a psychic hangover that, in its inertness, resembled his years at Andover. Unable to
sever the tie with Yale, he took a job teaching freshman English, a position arranged by his professors with the idea that he might go to graduate school. He
accepted it mainly to avoid the draft, for he had no calling as a teacher and actively despised the work. Along with his progressive-minded friends, he had become a noisy critic of the Vietnam War, but his outrage over the war was as
counterfeit as were his views on literature. In reality he was a man without political convictions, for which his self-absorption left no mental space.

He rented a shoreline cottage outside New Haven, where he moped over
his stalled novel and failed to take advantage of the one sexual opportunity that
presented itself when a man cruised him on the beach. He also reverted to his old
habit of robotic masturbation, assisted by a growing stash of furtively-purchased
"stroke" magazines. He complains that even his pornography collection was
wretchedly tame: photos of decorously posed athletes, unaroused. The only salutary development was the beginning of his lifelong friendship with Bill Hilgendorf's bereft girlfriend, Star, in comforting whom he enjoyed a momentary escape from his oppressive fixation on self.

After his season of masturbating at the beach, and still scampering to avoid
the draft, he began a four-year stint working in prep-schools, as if "inspired" by
his nightmare of being fated to imitate the pathetic life of his bachelor teachers
at Andover. Throughout these years his sexuality was on hold, stuck in the neut-
ered position he had adopted after graduating. Such homosexual experiences as
he had were fleeting, except for one longer episode that was positively destructive. Both erotically and emotionally he was marching—or limping—in place,
even as the world about him began to change.

His first job was not even at the "second-rate boys' school" of his dark imaginings: "Sutton Hill," in Connecticut, was more like a reformatory for the delinquent and underachieving sons of Eastern businessmen. There he spent the two-
years (1968–1970) that encompassed the Stonewall uprising, about which he read
not a word. Although he roused himself from the lethargy of his post-graduation
blues to become something of a campus figure, he was soon performing for yet
another audience: the school's bad boys, who gathered in his room every night
for bull sessions with their long-haired and garrulous young teacher. Eventually
the inevitable happened: one of the more manipulative boys saw his chance to
escape from the school (and return to his girlfriend in New Jersey) by seducing
Monette and getting thrown out. The affair made him miserable for a year, not
because he was in love or guiltily excited by the sex—which was silent and
largely one-way—but because he felt ashamed about violating his trust as a
teacher and, even more, because he recognized that the boy was merely using
him. When he finally managed to break it off, he outmaneuvered his tormentor
by taking the story to the school authorities, who, eager to avoid a scandal, expelled the kid and let Monette depart quietly at the end of the academic year. The
entire episode registered as another bad homosexual experience and sent him yet
deeper into the closet. Even as sex it had been no better than masturbating to
pornography, just a lot more dangerous. So once again he renewed his vow of
celibacy, but coming from a twenty-four-year-old in 1970 it no longer sounds as
plausible as it did of in the mouth of the nine-year-old caught with his pants
unzipped in the mid-1950s.

Much to his surprise he got hired to teach poetry at "Canton Academy," a
coeducational prep school south of Boston (presumably Milton Academy), where
he was on the faculty six years. He taught full-time only for the first two years,
after which, somewhat improbably, he launched a career as an interior decorator.
At Canton he kept his defenses up, at least to begin with, playing the unworldly
"renegade poet" for the benefit of the female students and faculty wives, while
steering clear of the boys so as to avoid any repetition of the Sutton Hill im-
broglio.

Although was not as chaste as he had resolved to be, he spent much of his
time cultivating a series of vaguely unhealthy relationships with women, most of
them older than himself and engaged in a subtle form of fag-haggery. Whether
the wives of colleagues or decorator clients, they poured their disappointments
into his sympathetic ear. More in tune with the shifting cultural winds than Mo-

nette himself, they also gave him implicit permission to come out. But he danced away skittishly from every invitation. The unhealthy part was that they sometimes fell in love with him, most agonizingly in the case of his partner in the decorator business.

During his second year at Canton, in spite of his resolution, he let himself get emotionally involved with one of his male students, an aspiring poet. In a way it was just another version of his chronic "'de-selfing,'" with Monette wishing he could assume the identity of his young straight admirer. But it was also the first serious romantic attachment he had permitted himself since Cody Williams at Yale six years earlier. Before long he was so consumed by the infatuation that he thought of little else. The cocoon in which he had wrapped himself for over half a decade had suddenly and mysteriously frayed, and the prospect terrified him. Convinced that he was on the verge of "the final smashup," he took an unprecedented step: he put himself into therapy.

🙰 IN THE SUMMER OF 1972 Monette moved to Cambridge. The move signaled the end of his long period of psychic inertia and launched him on a frantic search for his sexual and emotional identity. The two years leading up to the epochal dinner party of September 3, 1974, were overstuffed with erotic experiments, and his account of them is exhausting in its proliferation of characters and baroque relationships. Reduced to its essentials, the narrative is taken up with three interrelated stories: his therapy, his ever more common gay experiences, and what he calls his "time with women."

The therapy began in what sounds like an exact repetition of Martin Duberman's ordeal with *his* analysts: the main issue on the table was the project of changing Monette into a heterosexual. But by 1972 the cultural ground was shifting momentously: just a year later the American Psychiatric Association would delete homosexuality from its *Diagnostic and Statistical Manual of Mental Disorders*. Moreover, his therapist, Dr. Cantwell, was a man in his mid-twenties and thus no longer wedded to the old orthodoxy. We are not altogether surprised, then, that Monette's therapy took a very different course from Martin Duberman's

The opening gambit was significant. After Monette revealed he was depressed about being a homosexual, Cantwell asked, "'What do you want?'" To which Monette answered, "'That's easy—I'd like to be straight.'" Instead of delivering a lecture on conversion theory, Cantwell merely nodded and said, "'So let's work on that.'" Monette interpreted the exchange to mean that the doctor approved of the venture and implicitly promised it would succeed. "I walked out of that first session convinced I was a new man already," he recalls. So sure was he that he could change, and so exhilarated at the prospect, that he immediately abandoned his habit of secrecy and began announcing himself, even to virtual strangers, as a homosexual in therapy to get fixed. In this oddly distorted way, the therapy became the occasion of his coming out, at least intellectually: he confessed his desires, even as he prepared to obliterate them.

At the start Dr. Cantwell seemed to play the unreconstructed Bieberite, encouraging Monette in his new-found pursuit of women. And whenever he slipped back into his old habits—admiring men on the street or even going off to have sex with them—Cantwell told him, just as Karl had told Duberman, that it signaled a wish to identify with, rather than possess, the object. Or at least that was what Monette heard. In reality he himself did almost all the talking, while Cantwell, in classic Freudian style, mainly listened. When the doctor did begin to intervene more actively, he surprised Monette by suggesting that his compulsive need to please explained why he was ashamed of his homosexuality, just as his propensity for self-dramatization was the source of his increasingly mad heterosexual exploits. In marked contrast to Duberman's analysts, in other words, Cantwell became a truth-sayer. Apparently he had meant it, at their first session, when he asked Monette what he wanted. By the end of the therapy Cantwell was even wondering why Monette didn't seriously go after several of the men he was attracted to. It is almost as if Cantwell were making amends for all the wrongs committed by his psychoanalytic predecessors.

The last chapter of *Becoming a Man* is devoted chiefly to the women Monette bedded, loved, and, in some cases, set up house with in his effort to become a heterosexual. He offers a circumstantial account of six of these affairs and admits that there were others as well, including one with his friend Star Black, with whom he "gave it the old college try." The affairs followed each other rapidly and sometimes even overlapped, so that they quickly blur in the reader's mind. As Monette jokes, his "round-robin of musical beds" came to resemble "a French farce."

The autobiographer's feelings about this heterosexual experiment are divided. One the one hand he views it as the final and most preposterous installment in a career of role-playing that began with the middle-school courtier, a career entirely geared to appearances—to looking like a man. Rereading the diary account of his tortuous straight adventures, he asks himself, *"Girl, when are you gonna get real and find yourself some dick?"* On the other hand he wants to credit it as a significant psychological watershed: for the first time sex was linked to affection, thus opening him up to genuine intimacy and ultimately to the true solution with Roger.

His straight romances were transparently an extension of the fag-hag relationships he had cultivated during the two preceding years and that can be traced back further through Star, his California matron Lois Bronner, and even the teenage prom queen Cilla Fitzgerald. No doubt contradictorily, he was trying to add sex to a well-practiced psychological routine. All his women knew he was in therapy to convert from homosexuality, for he talked about it incessantly. His "heterosexualizing marathon" was in fact profoundly narcissistic. He was forever checking himself out in the mirror, real or imaginary, to see how he looked with a woman on his arm or in his bed.

What about the sex? If we compare his performance with Martin Duberman's he gets high marks. At least physiologically, he had reasonable grounds to think he could make it as a heterosexual. But from the start there was an unmistakable sense of strain: everything was carefully managed, never rapturous, as with his London sailor. His "dick" had been a lively performer in all the homosexual adventures he had allowed it, no matter how juvenile (Kite), distasteful (his drag queen waiter), or alienated (his Sutton Hill student). Now he worried about impotence, which in fact gradually overtook him. Such success as he enjoyed, moreover, was again narcissistic, and thus implicitly also homoerotic. Of one episode, he writes, characteristically, "She told me I had a beautiful dick, which got a blip of a rise from it."

The "bareliness" of the sex is important, because Marjorie Garber has made a half-hearted attempt to claim Monette for the bisexuals, or at least as a failed convert to bisexuality.[7] She can do so only against his will. After hooking up with Roger he abandoned women categorically, and he insists that he has "never quite understood the double Janus face of bi." Although he tries, he says, "not to be gayer-than-thou about bi," like Martin Duberman and probably most gay men of his generation, he considers it yet another dodge, a way of camouflaging one's real desires under a more socially acceptable and psychologically attractive image of ambivalence.

7. In *Vice Versa: Bisexuality and the Eroticism of Everyday Life* (New York, 1995), pp. 364–68. Garber's parallel case for Stephen Spender, mentioned in chapter 2, is more persuasive.

Paradoxically, the experiment in heterosexuality went hand in hand with his gay outings, which increased rapidly after 1972. He continued to moon over (and visit) his former Canton Academy student, now a Yale undergraduate. But he was no longer satisfied with disembodied crushes. He also picked up men off the street and became a regular cruiser at Sporters, his "bar of choice," as it was Andrew Tobias's. Most bizarrely, he had affairs with his girlfriends' boyfriends, at one point finding himself in the sack with both his then-current inamorata and her supposedly heterosexual (and supposedly former) mate. In effect he got caught up in the tail-end of free-love scene of the late 1960s. The intricate sexual ballet, with its self-important candor and breezy flouting of convention, has a distinct period flavor. It also provides a sordid backdrop for the austere and, in a way, deeply conservative moment when Monette called a halt to the erotic circus and began his great romance with Roger Horwitz, at once ecstatic, heartfelt, and, at least in theory, monogamous.

     A COMBINATION OF FACTORS brought Monette to the point where he was ready to seize on the chance meeting with Roger to begin his life as a gay man in earnest. The most obvious was his growing awareness of the sexual failure of his conversion project. Toward the end the women themselves, especially Star, were urging him to recognize its hopelessness and begin looking instead for "the laughing man" of his dreams. He got the same message, as we've seen, from his therapist. But just as important was the emptiness of the one-night stands with the men he picked up in bars or on the banks of the Charles. The women furnished luxurious emotion but anemic sex, the men just the opposite: hot sex but conditioned on remaining strangers. He didn't need to be a dialectician to figure out that what he wanted was a synthesis of the two, an intimacy uniting the sense of connection he got from women with the excitement only men could provide.

As 1974 advanced, he become ever more invested in his search for "the one right man." He had to work his way through a false candidate in the person of a forty-five-year-old New York novelist, whom Monette describes as "the most fully evolved gay man I'd ever met." "Harold" was also rich and thus appealed to Monette's dream of life in the fast lane, as well as his "burning wish to be taken care of." But, for all its material and psychological attractions, the relationship was a sexual dud. Clearly, Harold was not the laughing man, and Monette is embarrassed that he let the affair drag on as long as it did.

In the summer of 1974 two developments set the stage for the story's denouement. Even as more of his nights were devoted to tricks, he spent his days on a pilgrimage to Concord, reading Thoreau, with whom he identified in a curiously ambivalent way. Thoreau's withdrawal from the false busyness of the world in order to find himself became a model for Monette's own effort to stop acting and start living according to his inner truth. Yet he also knew that the retreat to Walden Pond was itself a kind of closeting: Thoreau too should have been searching for a man, a search he had "clearly ducked" by "letting the woodcutter get away with a mouthful of philosophy instead of a kiss."

The other event was a trip to Georgia with the poet Sandy McClatchy. In Monette's mind, it began as a replay of his situation with Harold: he tried to persuade himself that McClatchy could be the one right man. "All the way down in the car," he remembers, "I told my self to go with it, not to be afraid. I was beginning to worry that I didn't know how to have sex with someone I *liked*." Much to his relief (we sense), it didn't happen. But the visit still turned out to be a "watershed": they talked openly and easily about being gay and what that implied for their literary careers. For once he could think of writing as something other than an impersonation, a more elevated version of playing the courtier. Their conversations also implanted the idea that gayness was not just a sexual orientation: it was also a "sensibility," with implications for the whole of life, including authorship.

In the course of *Becoming a Man* Monette has dropped so many hints about his love project that we are in danger of feeling manipulated by the final scene. True, he admits that love is not for everyone and might even be considered reactionary: a mimicking of "bourgeois marriage" and thus inescapably "straight-identified." He also admits his own weakness for Hollywood-inspired "romantic mush." Yet for all our resistance, the scene of his first meeting with Roger is nonetheless affecting. When they finally left the Beacon Hill dinner party arranged by Richard Howard, "the laugh that erupted between us," he writes, "was unlike anything I'd ever felt." He keeps his sense of humor: he records not only the sexual explosion of their night of bliss but also his comic volubility, "frantically talking in between kisses, trying to fill in every detail, as if now were the only chance I might get to tell him who I was."

Roger was a thirty-two-year-old lawyer, still uncomfortable with his own sexuality, in fact "up to his tits in therapy" with a view to going straight. He was no match for Monette's devouring eagerness: right from the start it was to be "the great love of our lives," the project that would erase a quarter century of loneliness and sham sociability. But he can't pretend that the legacy of the closet simply vanished. Although he had become "a new man," he would "shut down" whenever, as he evasively puts it, "things got tough." The phrase alludes to the infidelities that would blemish even his grand romance. The residue of the closet thus became an excuse for his failure to honor the monogamous ideal of his Hollywood script. "Long after I thought I'd mastered putting *love* and *fuck* in the same sentence," he explains defensively, "the wild oats I hadn't sowed at twenty came back to mock me." *Borrowed Time* is obsessed with the idea that, directly or indirectly, those infidelities were the source of the virus from which Roger died.

So the specter of death haunts his recollection of even their first night together. But he won't give up his belief that the meeting with Roger was the beginning of his "real life." The closet narrative permits no other ending. "From that moment on the brink of summer's end," he concludes, "no one would ever tell me again that men like me couldn't love."

⌒ THE GREAT PROBLEM WITH coming-out autobiographies, as of all conversion stories, is separating their psychic truth and political effectiveness from their formulaic, even oppressive, predictability. In Monette's case the difficulty is especially severe, because he draws such an extreme contrast between the old order and the new: phoniness versus authenticity, nothingness versus life. If he had taken the second opposition—his master conceit—literally, he would have been unable to write his book, for a story in which nothing happens can't be told. So he must contradict himself: his closeted years turn out to be full of watersheds—his brother's traumatic birth, his affairs with Kite and Richie, his silent closing-down at Andover, his irruption into noisy activity at Yale, his "time with women." The conceit also leads to a kind of self-abuse: he is unfair to his own achievement when everything in his past is reduced to undifferentiated fakery. We can agree with his harsh judgment of the middle-school courtier, the freshman cowboy, and the heterosexual lover. But the industry and intelligence that brought him from his working-class origins to Andover and Yale do not deserve the same contempt. Most important, his learning to love and then create works of art requires a fairer assessment: after all, he did become a poet and novelist as well as a truly distinguished memoirist, and the years of closeted admiration and practice were integral to that success. The same criticism can be leveled at Martin Duberman's dismissive estimate of his scholarship.

By implication, Monette's story is also unfair to other homosexual lives. I have resisted the extreme dichotomies of the coming-out narrative as an adequate representation of my own experience and that of many other gay men I have known. It also delegitimizes the lives of Monette's autobiographical forebears—lives whose extraordinary differences, satisfactions, and, to be sure, miseries I have charted in this book. With the possible exception of Christopher Isherwood, these forebears do not tell coming-out stories. To imply that their lives were therefore nothing but self-hatred is both unhistorical and inaccurate. Monette doesn't expressly make such a charge. Like most gay autobiographers, he is innocent of the tradition in which he writes. He reserves his hostility for contemporary gays who remain silent—the "shit-eating bachelor Republican[s]" whom he loathes as much as any Roman Catholic cardinal. But the implication is nonetheless there. Coming out of the closet, we are made to feel, is the only legitimate homosexual story.

While we might complain that the coming-out narrative is provincial and even subtly totalitarian, we should also acknowledge its enormous political virtue. Told not just by autobiographers but by millions of gay men and women, it is the story that has transformed our world. Increasingly, moreover, it is the story we all tell, even those of us who dragged their feet at the start. Andrew Tobias, Martin Duberman, Paul Monette, and the dozens of recent gay autobiographers for whom they are representative voices thus deserve to be honored for their part in changing our lives.

Samuel Delany, 1964.

Richard Rodriguez, early 1980s.

Epilogue

ALL FOURTEEN OF THE autobiographers examined in this book are white men, and only one of them is a Jew. I had originally hoped to find autobiographies written by minority intellectuals and artists, with a view to measuring the significance of race or ethnicity for the way gay men narrate their lives. But I have uncovered no texts comparable to Andrew Tobias's *The Best Little Boy in the World*, Martin Duberman's *Cures*, or Paul Monette's *Becoming a Man*—that is, texts focused on the development of the author's homosexual experience and identity. To be sure, the recent explosion of gay autobiographies has included books written by African Americans and Latinos: the actor Gordon Heath's *Deep Are the Roots* (1992), the choreographer Alvin Ailey's *Revelations* (1995), the drag queen Ru Paul's *Let It All Hang Out* (1995), former Army Sergeant José Zuniga's *Soldier of the Year* (1994), and skating champion Rudy Galindo's *Icebreaker* (1997). But these are essentially professional stories. They are concerned mainly with the author's achievements—as actor, choreographer, entertainer, skater— or, in the case of José Zuniga, with the struggle against prejudice. Except for Zuniga, the sexual issue is kept very much in the background, and even in Zuniga's book it is subordinated to his fight with the military when he decided to come out publicly at the 1993 march on Washington. Nor are any of the books much preoccupied with race or ethnicity or how it might be related to the author's experience as a gay man. Still, even these highly assimilated and relatively unselfconscious minority autobiographies hint at distinct ethnic and racial patterns, and I will return to them in a moment.

The two most interesting ethnic texts, from the viewpoint of my study, are Richard Rodriguez's *Hunger of Memory* (1982) and Samuel Delany's *The Motion of Light in Water* (1988). Neither of them is a gay autobiography in the obvious sense of the books by Tobias, Duberman, and Monette. But their differences from the accounts written by their white contemporaries, and their even more radical differences from one another, are precisely what make them so intriguing. Delany (b. 1942) and Rodriguez (b. 1944) are close in age to Monette (b. 1945) and Tobias (b. 1947) and just over a decade younger than Duberman (b. 1930). Their autobiographies, moreover, center on the same years treated by Tobias, Duberman, and Monette—from the 1950s through the early 1970s. And, most important from my perspective, both men are clearly intellectuals. Samuel Delany is among the most admired and prolific of what is called the new-wave of science fiction writers; his work is distinguished by its philosophical seriousness and its concern with alternative gender and sexual identities. Richard Rodriguez, trained at U.C. Berkeley in Renaissance studies, is an essayist whose two best-selling books have established him as "the most recognizable Latino gay man in contemporary literature"[1]; in more recent years he has appeared as a television "essayist" on the MacNeil/Lehrer NewsHour. Their memoirs, accordingly, boast the complexity and nuance that invite comparison with the other works treated in this study.

⌒ THE SUBTITLE OF SAMUEL DELANY's *The Motion of Light in Water,* "Sex and Science Fiction Writing in the East Village, 1957–1965," accurately reflects the book's central concern: it is the story of Delany's literary beginnings, set against the background of his sexual adventures. The most important relationship in the book is with the poet Marilyn Hacker, whom Delany married in 1961. It was an unusual marriage: Hacker was aware of Delany's homosexuality and indeed kept fully informed about his escapades, in which she eventually became a participant of sorts. The relationship was a rocky one, but not for sexual reasons: they had intercourse regularly and uneventfully—twice a week, in fact—but fought bitterly over literary and social matters: Hacker suffered from a severe writing block, while Delany was shamelessly productive, and she also resented the fact that their mutual friends preferred the company of her good-looking and personable husband.

Even this brief account should suggest how different Delany's story is from the coming-out narratives of Tobias, Duberman, and Monette. Delany was astonishingly comfortable with his sexuality. In exactly the years when Tobias, Duberman, and Monette were wracked by guilt and putting themselves through the most extreme tortures of repression and conversion, Delany was blithely

1. David Román, "Latino Literature," in *The Gay and Lesbian Literary Heritage,* ed. Claude J. Summers (New York, 1995), p. 437.

turning tricks in subway johns, participating in orgies at the docks, marveling at massed bodies at the bathes, and, not least important, reporting on these and other activities to his always interested wife. Nor did he keep his homosexuality a secret from his friends in the East Village. In effect, he didn't have to come out of the closet because he was never really in it. One begins to wonder whether his remarkable sexual composure had anything to do with his being a black man.

I am inclined to think it did, but the issue is complicated by Delany's racial ambiguity. Not only was he so light-skinned that four out of five people he met mistook him for white, but, after his childhood in Harlem, he led a white man's life: he attended the virtually all-white Bronx High School of Science, and the great majority of his friends and sexual partners, including Marilyn Hacker, were also white. Moreover he adopts a postmodern skepticism about identity, racial as well as sexual, insisting that it is largely constructed and thus always subject to change. The ambiguity is reflected in a set of questions that are repeated several times in the text and become a kind of mantra:

"A black man . . . ?
A gay man . . . ?
A writer . . . ?"

I don't want to overstate Delany's guiltlessness. Set against Tobias, Duberman, and Monette, he seems a paragon of self-confidence, but he had his own doubts. In the text he refuses to call himself bisexual—because, while men excited him at a distance, he could function sexually with women only when in actual physical contact with their bodies—yet he admits that he embraced the bisexual label at the time of his marriage, and, of course, the very fact that he got married implies a certain ambivalence. He also admits his reluctance to identify with the "irrepressibly effeminate" organist, Herman, at his father's funeral parlor, although he remarks that effeminate men like Herman had an established, if not fully acceptable, place in black society, and he explains blacks' greater tolerance for homosexuality as an ironic consequence of white racism. "Because we had less to begin with," he reasons, "in the end we had less to lose." He also went into group therapy briefly because of an irrational fear of traveling on the subway, and we are allowed to suspect that his deeper problem was the unease he felt about his sexual and romantic life. At first the group sessions promised to replicate Martin Duberman's unhappy experience with Karl just a year or two later; Delany's group even included a man, Hank, whom Delany assumed was going to play the role of official homophobe, in the manner of Duberman's "Stan." But after remaining anxiously silent about the issue at the start, Delany soon announced that he was a homosexual and had no problems "in the area of sexual functioning," though he worried about jeopardizing his marriage. Instead of the feared confrontation, the tension quickly dissipated. Even Hank, it turned out, was only an imagined homophobe; in reality he was quite indifferent to Delany's sexuality. The psychiatric encounter thus remains a minor episode in Delany's story: it betrays a certain discomfort, but nothing even remotely like Duberman's epic self-hatred, and it makes only a slight dent in the book's general portrait of a happy homosexual.

In an important sense Delany's sexual position is best described as "beyond gay." Although he never denies that his own desires are unambiguously queer, he is even more fundamentally an orgiast or a proponent of "polymorphous perversity," in the sense of Herbert Marcuse and Norman O. Brown. *The Motion of Light in Water* celebrates multiple encounters, with loving accounts of his nightlong adventures at the docks or in the baths. In the book's most sustained ideological discussion, he argues that the baths in particular marked a revolutionary break with the isolated and usually guilty homosexual style of the 1950s. They announced "that there was a population—not of individual homosexuals, some of whom one now and then encountered, or that those encounters could be human and fulfilling in their way—not of hundreds, not of thousands, but rather of millions of gay men, and that history had, actively and already, created for us whole galleries of institutions, good and bad, to accommodate our sex." In the same spirit he declares his hope "that once the AIDS crisis is brought under control, the West will see a sexual revolution to make a laughingstock of any social movement that till now has borne the name." Significantly, the book culminates in a graphic account of the three-way sexual and romantic relationship he and Marilyn Hacker established, over the course of several months, with a straight hustler. Delany pronounces it "one of the happiest times in my life" and insists that Marilyn fully shared in their common bliss. More than a gay autobiographer, then, Delany is a sexual revolutionary in the style of certain left-wing intellectuals of the 1960s.

⌒ ONE WOULD BE HARD-PRESSED to imagine a sensibility further removed from Samuel Delany's than Richard Rodriguez's, though both are gay men, literary intellectuals, and almost exact contemporaries. Perhaps one might argue that they share a similar racial or ethnic ambivalence. Physically and culturally, as we have seen, Delany could pass for white, even if he never fails to identify himself as black. Rodriguez, by contrast, is strongly marked by his Indian coloration and features, but his racial looks embarrass him, and he blames them for his sexual inhibitions. More important, *Hunger of Memory* is ultimately a defense of his assimilation into the Anglo culture taught him by the Irish nuns in his Sacramento parochial school, though he is also obsessed with the loss of family intimacy that this cultural "whitening" entailed. Rodriguez has become the Mexican-American writer that Chicano intellectuals love to hate, because of his critique of bilingual education and affirmative action and his hostility of what he regards as the naive sentimentality of multiculturalism. He is often called a "Coconut," the Latino counterpart of an "Oreo": brown on the outside but white inside. Not surprisingly, he has been embraced by right-wingers, like George Will, for what they see as his "brave" celebration of Americanization. So, although Rodriguez and Delany might appear to suffer from a common ethnic or racial marginality, they stand at opposite ends of the political spectrum: Rodriguez has come to be identified with the neo-conservative right, while Delany is an old-time lefty.

If *The Motion of Light in Water* is not a coming-out autobiography because Delany was never in the closet, *Hunger of Memory* is not a coming-out autobiography because Rodriguez doesn't so much as mention his homosexuality. Even worse, he sometimes pretends to be heterosexual. Of his undergraduate years, for example, he writes: "At Stanford . . . I began to have something like a conventional sex life. I don't think, however, that I really believed that the women I knew found me physically appealing." One suspects these sentences have been carefully crafted to allow Rodriguez to defend himself against a charge of lying: technically, he asserts only that his sex life was "something like" conventional, and the second sentence, one might argue, doesn't necessarily identify the implicit partners of the first sentence. Admittedly, he may have been performing as a heterosexual while at Stanford, but we don't know, for says nothing further about it, and the important point surely is that the passage conveys the clear impression that he is straight.

How, then, is *Hunger of Memory* a gay autobiography? Only in a tortured and ultimately dishonest way. The text is filled with passages that seem to promise a sexual revelation but then collapse into something different. At first the procedure appears to resemble Christopher Isherwood's peekaboo technique in *Lions and Shadows* (written of course a half century earlier), but in fact it is very different. Where Isherwood wickedly invites knowledgeable readers—the co-gnoscenti—to take his queer meaning, Rodriguez engages in a kind of shame-faced teasing. He can't quite bring himself to repress all evidence of his proclivit-ies—as if unconsciously they find their way into the text—but he seems determined to maintain what politicians call "deniability." We are left to infer that he feels profoundly embarrassed about being gay.

The author of the memoir reveals that he lives in San Francisco and goes to Sunday brunch with well-off friends (of unspecified sex) as well as to the gym, where he has buffed the fat out of his once overweight and shapeless body. About a quarter way through the book, we come to a hushed announcement. "What I am about to say to you has taken me more than twenty years to admit," he begins. "For years I never spoke to anyone about it. Never mentioned a thing to my family or my teachers or classmates. From a very early age, I understood enough . . . to keep what I knew repressed, hidden beneath layers of embarrassment." This is manifestly the language with which one launches a sexual confession, and Rodriguez, who is intensely aware of verbal effects, knows exactly what he is doing. But it is only a tease, for his great secret turns out to be not homosexuality but the recognition that his academic success has alienated him from his immi-grant family. Now, one needn't deny that Rodriguez felt a genuine sense of loss as he became assimilated to American culture: that, indeed, is his great theme in *Hunger of Memory*. But the very passage in which he displays his ethnic candor also flirts with sexual false advertising.

Throughout the book his honesty about race often serves as a screen for dishonesty about sex. Thus he writes that during adolescence he became an as-cetic because of his racial shame: "I denied myself a sensational life. The normal, extraordinary, animal excitement of feeling my body alive—riding shirtless on a bicycle in the warm wind created by furious self-propelled motion—the sensa-tions that first had excited in me a sense of my maleness, I denied. I was too ashamed of my body. I wanted to forget that I had a body because I had a brown body." At one level this confession may be perfectly truthful, but it serves, almost too cleverly, to relieve him of the need to confess that he also felt ashamed be-cause he had a queer body. In the same vein are his repeatedly-expressed fears about "effeminacy," which turns out to mean not unmanly affectation but his excessive talkativeness in an ethnic culture where men are generally silent. Later on "effeminacy" denotes his attachment to literature and to writing. Again, we have the sense of coming right to the brink of a sexual revelation only to have it dissolve into something more innocuous.

In 1990 Rodriguez published an essay, "Late Victorians" (subsequently incorporated into his second book, *Days of Obligation*), which is his only sustained discussion of homosexuality. It is not quite a coming-out piece, because, seventy years after André Gide's *Si le grain ne meurt*, Rodriguez still refuses to say "I." But in his knowing description of San Francisco's gay community, and in his identification with some of its activities—such as body-building—he virtually confesses the truth. Still, "Late Victorians" has to count as an advanced exercise in self-hatred. Its basic theme is that homosexuals are commodity fetishists: most of their energy goes to accumulating decorative things, above all to remodeling the Victorian houses in which they collect their precious artifacts. Their "barren" lives are thus devoted to what he calls "the small effect." At Stonewall they fought not for the right to selfhood but "to defend the nonconformity of their leisure."

Worse than frivolous materialists, they are also unrestrained sybarites. Just like Pat Buchanan, Rodriguez argues that their "covenant against nature" has brought the inevitable retribution of AIDS. He congratulates himself on his own sober Augustinianism, with its doctrine of Original Sin, which has saved him from pursing "an earthly paradise" in the baths, like his now dead friend César. To be sure, Rodriguez occasionally softens his self-congratulation by admitting to a lack of charity, but these gestures are intended to prettify his ugly sentiments. The fundamental message in "Late Victorians" is "I told you so." The essay may come closer to revealing the truth about his sexuality, but his near-confession is, at bottom, monstrously self-loathing.

Only in an op-ed piece of 1994 did Rodriguez make a full-breasted declaration of his gayness. Significantly it came in a defense of the Catholic Church's opposition to abortion. "I am a Roman Catholic—and a homosexual," he writes. And again later, "Yes, yes, I am a queer. I am a fag."[2] But he has yet to tell the story of how he moved from the evasions of *Hunger of Memory*, through the odious half-revelations of "Late Victorians," to the blunt admission of his op-ed piece. I am inclined to say that he owes us a gay autobiography, which ought to be one of the most eloquent and lacerating ever written.

Is there any reason to link Rodriguez's deep repression in *Hunger of Memory*

2. Richard Rodriguez, "In Defense of the Vatican," *San Francisco Chronicle*, September 14, 1994, p. A21.

to his being a Mexican American, as I have linked Samuel Delany's sexual composure to his blackness? I believe there is. The most immediate connection is supplied by religion: the homophobic teachings of the Catholic Church have presented gay Latinos with a formidable barrier to self-acceptance, especially when loyalty to the Church is perceived (as it clearly is by Rodriguez) as a way to maintain their increasingly fragile ties to the family and culture of their childhood. Some scholars have proposed a further source of trauma: the so-called Mexican (or Latin-American) Sexual System, to which immigrant families have remained subject to a greater of lesser degree.[3] These scholars argue that traditional Mexican culture has no category corresponding to the American notion of a gay man. Instead, sexual identity is defined in terms of assertiveness and passivity, so that a man who sodomizes another man in no way compromises his own masculinity, while the recipient, known as a *joto,* is classified as a woman, a singularly abject status in a patriarchal regime like Mexico's. According to the Mexican Sexual System, in other words, true homosexuality is equated with radical effeminacy. As a result, Mexican-American gays must overcome an unusually heavy cultural burden. If they decide to lead a homosexual life or, more rashly, to declare themselves gay, they must break with the deeply held prejudices of their families, above all their fathers. Given Rodriguez's obsession with family loyalty and disloyalty, we might well expect him to be especially vulnerable to this cultural anxiety. If he ever writes the gay autobiography I have suggested he owes us, one would like to see him address the scholarly argument I have just described.

∞ THE CONTRAST I HAVE drawn between Delany's *The Motion of Light in Water* and Rodriguez's *Hunger of Memory* suggests that black homosexuals may stand to the sexual left of the white gay mainstream while Latinos stand to its sexual right. Neither man has written a coming-out autobiography, along with lines of Tobias, Duberman, and Monette: Delany because he doesn't need to, Rodriguez because he can't. This pattern is confirmed by the other minority autobiographies I have read, and it is also supported by the literary record, notably in the novels written by gay African Americans and Latinos.

3. See Ana Maria Alonso and Maria Teresa Koreck, "Silences: 'Hispanics,' AIDS, and Sexual Practices," and Tomás Almaguer, "Chicano Men: A Cartography of Homosexual Identity and Behavior," in *The Lesbian and Gay Studies Reader,* ed. Henry Abelove, Michèle Aina Barale, and David M. Halperin (New York, 1993), pp. 110–26, 255–73.

In *Deep Are the Roots,* for example, the black actor Gordon Heath (1918–1991) speaks of his homosexuality as if it were a benign anomaly rather than a psychic catastrophe. Heath was called a "sissy" as a boy, but more in a joshing than a menacing way. After being "raped" by a couple of older teenagers at summer camp, he quickly decided that the experience, though disturbing at the time, had introduced him to something he wanted and enjoyed. As he puts it, in his typically low-keyed fashion, "I was attracted to men and boys and that was that." His only concern, he says, "was to find someone with whom I could—in E. M. Forster's word—'share,'" which he promptly did the next summer, much to his satisfaction. A few years later he fell in love with a straight young black man, Alex King, who turned him down gently and with whom Heath remained "the best of friends." In fact King was the principal mediator in arranging Heath's first sustained love affair, with the black actor Eddie Cambridge. Eventually Heath lived and worked for thirty years in Paris with another actor, Lee Payant, who was white. He says very little about their domestic arrangement, but he treats it, like everything else concerning his homosexuality, in the relaxed, anxiety-free, manner we are familiar with from Delany.

In *Revelations* Alvin Ailey (1931–1989) is less forthcoming about his homosexuality than Gordon Heath, and we get the sense that it caused him more agony. Above all his story ends rather badly, as he suffered a breakdown after being robbed by an Arab boy he fell in love with in 1979, and he admits to an unhealthy weakness for "young men who take things." The account of his sexual beginnings may lack the carefreeness of Heath's, but rather than the terror we find in the white gay stories he describes something more like low-level depression. Of his sexual initiation at the hands of his "best friend," Chauncey Green, he observes: "He thought it was fun to lie on me and make what amounted to sexual movements. I guess I became a kind of sexual object for Chauncey. I didn't mind, but he introduced me to passivity, to being a kind of sexual object of an older guy." Like Heath, Ailey was called a sissy as a boy, about which he comments laconically, "You were a sissy (*sissy* was a big word back then) if you danced." Even in this rather joyless and circumspect narrative, we get a firm impression that his homosexuality was far from traumatic. "I knew most of the gay people in junior high school and high school," he reports. "I had no qualms about being with one kid named Robert." In other words, though more somber than Delany or Heath, Ailey too adopts a relatively easygoing attitude toward his sexual circumstances.

Perhaps because he is nearly two generations younger than Heath or Ailey,

Ru Paul (b. 1960) is by far the most nonchalant of the black gay autobiographers I have read. Early on in *Let It All Hang Out*, he announces without fanfare, "I have always felt quite straightforward and uncomplicated about being a man who likes other men." Again, like Heath and Ailey, he was called a "sissy" as a boy, but he maintains that the experience was fairly innocuous. "The kids would always tease me about being a sissy and a queer," he recalls, "but they were never vicious." In the same spirit, his parents, especially his mother, took a resigned and tolerant attitude to his sexual preference and his effeminacy. Most of what he tells us about his sex life (which isn't a great deal) is light-hearted, even comic, such as his account of "tucking" his genitals when he dresses in drag or how he once pretended to be a transvestite hooker and turned a trick with a corrections officer. Only at the end of the book does he observe, insightfully, that his romantic life has been sabotaged by chasing after distant men like his father. But even here he sticks to the position that his homosexuality has caused him not the slightest regret. "Being a man attracted to other men has never been a problem for me," he declares. "It's just the way I am."

In sum, the autobiographical evidence suggests that black homosexuals may have been largely spared the Great Repression that made the lives of so many white gays miserable in the central decades of the twentieth century. At the very least their sufferings remained on a more modest scale. In fact the treatment of homosexuality in the memoirs of Samuel Delany, Gordon Heath, Alvin Ailey, and Ru Paul comes closest to the upbeat mood of Donald Vining's *A Gay Diary*, with its full and confident account of homosexual romance and adventuring in the 1930s and 1940s.

By way of contrast, the autobiographies of José Zuniga and Rudy Galindo, both born in 1969, can be easily related to the sexual repression on display in Richard Rodriguez's *Hunger of Memory*. To be sure, Zuniga's book, unlike Rodriguez's, is a garden variety coming-out story, culminating in the public decoration of his homosexuality. Also unlike Rodriguez, Zuniga is comfortably assimilated: though both of his parents were born in Mexico, he describes himself as an "average American boy," and throughout the text his friends call him "Joe" rather than "José." There is not so much as a hint of Rodriguez's patented anxiety about the loss of his ethnic heritage. Zuniga's father is the villain of the piece, but the conflict is explained in terms not of Mexican-American prejudice but of the father's career in the military with its inflexibly masculinist values.

Still, there is evidence that Zuniga suffered from the peculiar repressiveness of his parents' culture. Most strikingly, his sexuality was remarkably belated. When he finally started masturbating, at fifteen, it had, he insists, no sexual significance for him: in other words, it was not accompanied by fantasies. "I knew I enjoyed what I was doing," he writes, "but I had no clue what it meant. . . . I never connected the act with the concept of sex, romance, or relations with others." His ignorance is reminiscent of Julien Green's experience at the beginning of the century, but we have to remind ourselves that Zuniga is writing about the mid-1980s. He didn't have a homosexual encounter until he was nineteen: he lived with the man, another young Mexican American, for a year, but their physical relationship, which sounds very limited, lasted "less than a few weeks." Only when he was twenty-three did he have his first satisfying gay sex. He attributes his long celibacy to his conscientious honoring of the vow he took when he joined the Army in 1989, but he also recognizes that he lived under a distinct cultural burden: "I knew I was gay, but my heritage, my Church and society had all taught me that being gay was wrong." Elsewhere he blames "my father and my Church" and "my strict Catholic upbringing" for having taught him that homosexuality was an "abomination." Even during his first night of love his mind was filled with "thoughts of my father, the religious condemnation of my sin . . . hell and damnation." In the event, his father responded to his public coming out by disowning him, an extreme reaction that may well reflect sexual ideas the father absorbed during his upbringing in Mexico. In sum, there is reason to believe that the Mexican Sexual System played an important, if unrecognized, role in Zuniga's experience.

At first glance, Rudy Galindo's autobiography seems less anxious, more relaxed, than Zuniga's. He treats his gayness, like his effeminacy, as natural and inalterable. At most he considers it an inconvenience. "I was gay and feminine," he explains, "two characteristics that aren't much help to a Mexican-American boy growing up in a working-class neighborhood." He continues stoically: "If I'd had anything to say about it, I would have been straight and masculine. But some things you don't get to choose in life." Still, very much like Zuniga's, Galindo's sexuality was belated and repressed, and, as with Zuniga, the fear of his "cowboy" father's wrath was the main source of his anxiety, especially after his older brother turned out to be gay and was banished from the house amidst screaming and threats. Galindo had sex for the first time just before he turned nineteen (the same age as Zuniga), and later he began visiting gay clubs with his brother. But his only "boyfriend" was a druggie who mooched off him for the better part of a year and with whom "there was never any physical intimacy other than my cuddling up against him." Admittedly, much of Galindo's repression can be attributed to his relentless careerism, which allowed him virtually no time for a sexual or romantic life. His single-minded ambition also stunted his political consciousness, so that when, on winning the U.S. Nationals in 1996, he was asked what it felt like to be the first openly gay figure-skating champion, he responded, "No comment," and was abused by the gay press "for trying to go back into the closet." In a sense Galindo is a post-closet figure. "Anyone who knows me," he insists, "knows that I believe that all gay and lesbian people should be able to live their lives openly and without fear of discrimination. I thought that went without saying." But even in the wake of his athletic triumph and fame, he continued to be plagued by depression and alcoholism, and there was no romance on the horizon. Throughout the book his homosexuality remains strangely disembodied, as if he couldn't escape the shadows of ancient prejudice or the fear of his (now dead) father's rage. In short, Galindo's story is consistent with the sexual pattern we have seen in Richard Rodriguez and José Zuniga. It is utterly without the sense of comfort and enjoyment found in the gay autobiographies written by African Americans.

 FINALLY, THE CONTRAST I HAVE drawn between the gay black and Latino autobiographical traditions is also reflected in the literary record, especially the novel. There is a long and rich history of black homophile writing. It begins with the Harlem Renaissance, which Henry Louis Gates reminds us "was surely as gay as it was black,"[4] and its central figure is of course James Baldwin, the preeminent black and gay novelist of his generation. Five of Baldwin's six novels treat gay themes, and, although suffering and repression are always present, with each book the gay characters grow more self-confident and less at odds with their society. In Soul on Ice Eldridge Cleaver attacked Baldwin for his homosexuality, which Cleaver argued played into the white campaign to emasculate blacks, but, as Henry Louis Gates has again suggested, Cleaver's homophobia, like that of Amiri Baraka, was an aberrant product of the Black Power and Black Aesthetic movements of the 1960s and fundamentally alien to the larger black literary heritage.

4. Henry Louis Gates, Jr., "The Black Man's Burden," in Fear of a Queer Planet, ed. Michael Warner (Minneapolis, 1993), p. 233.

The post-Baldwin years have seen a remarkable efflorescence of black gay writers, including the novelists Randall Kenan, Steven Corbin, Larry Duplechan, Melvin Dixon, E. Lynn Harris, James Earl Hardy, and Darieck Scott. To be sure, much of their work has a critical edge. It addresses the trials of belonging to a double minority, the persistence of white racism (which often sabotages interracial romance), the conflict between the individual gay black man and the broader African-American community, and of course AIDS. But the criticism seldom overwhelms the sense of exuberance and sexual celebration in these novels. A characteristic document is James Earl Hardy's *B-Boy Blues* (1994), appropriately subtitled "A Seriously Sexy, Fiercely Funny, Black-on-Black Love Story," which is raunchy, sex-positive, and often genuinely amusing.

On the Mexican-American side of the literary ledger, by contrast, there is but a single voice, that of Arturo Islas.[5] Islas was the author of *The Rain God* (1984) and *Migrant Souls* (1990), which trace the lives of three generations of the Angel family in El Paso. The books are highly autobiographical, with the figure of Miguel Chico, an English professor who lives in San Francisco, serving as Islas's alter ego.

Arturo Islas was my colleague at Stanford until his death from AIDS in 1991, and I know from first hand that he detested Richard Rodriguez, not only on political grounds but also out a sense of envy for the admiration Rodriguez won by presenting the sheepish apology for assimilation so many white readers wanted to hear. But in fact Islas was more like Rodriguez than he cared to recognize. Admittedly, he shows Miguel Chico in vigorous revolt against his family's superstitious and repressive Catholicism, and he also exposes their homophobia when they fail to defend the memory of Miguel's uncle Felix, a *joto* murdered by a pick-up. But, like Rodriguez, Miguel Chico and his creator remain deeply closeted. The subject of his homosexuality is never mentioned to or by the members of the family. Even more telling, Miguel is textually marginalized: his experience is largely refracted through the eyes of more central figures like his womanizing father or his cousin and confidante Josie Salazar. In *The Rain God* his homosexuality is not even named, only alluded to in the coy fashion of Rodriguez's *Hunger*

---

5. John Rechy is also a Mexican American, but few readers of his gay classics, *City of Night* (1963) and *Numbers* (1967), are aware of the fact, for the simple reason that Rechy generally maintains a firm separation between his gay and his ethnic writings. One might also want to make a case for Michael Nava, the author of a series of mystery novels with a young gay Latino lawyer as their protagonist.

of Memory. When, in *Migrant Souls,* he is finally called "a lover of men,"[6] the identification comes not from Miguel Chico's own lips but from Josie Salazar, and then only in an internal monologue. Later in the novel he discusses his un-happy love life with his brother, a priest, but we are excluded from the conversa-tion. So, although a more liberated and honest writer than Rodriguez, Islas suffered from much of the same repression and embarrassment. We may reason-ably conclude that he too was a victim of the Mexican Sexual System.

Let me finish these brief reflections by mentioning one last book, the late Steven Corbin's novel *A Hundred Days from Now.* It makes a fitting end for my story because its plot turns on the conflict between a gay African-American screenwriter, proudly open to his friends, family, and business associates, and his Mexican lover, who is entirely closeted, in both his personal and professional life. The narrator describes Sergio Gutierrez as "crawling inch by inch out of a twenty-year-long tunnel of closeted homosexuality, laced with homegrown Latin American shame and Roman Catholic guilt, augmented by self-inflicted homo-phobia and self-loathing."[7] Corbin's novel, as the literary critics say, "thematizes" precisely the opposition between black and Latino gay traditions that has been my subject in this Epilogue. Let me hasten to add that the contrast is meant to be suggestive rather than definitive: a handful of autobiographies and novels can't justify any categorical pronouncements about so vast (and contentious) a subject as race and sexuality in modern American culture. Nonetheless I am struck by the pattern that seems to emerge in the texts I have consulted. Perhaps it will be verified by the work of future historians, or contradicted by gay autobiographies yet to be written.

6. Arturo Islas, *Migrant Souls* (New York, 1990), p. 120.
7. Steven Corbin, *A Hundred Days from Now* (Boston, 1994), p. 57.

Sources

The quotations in the text are drawn from the following editions of the autobiographies I treat.

CHAPTER 1

The Memoirs of John Addington Symonds, ed. Phyllis Grosskurth (London: Hutchinson, 1984).

The Autobiography of G. Lowes Dickinson, ed. Dennis Proctor (London: Duckworth, 1973).

CHAPTER 2

Christopher Isherwood, *Lions and Shadows* (London: The Hogarth Press, 1938).

Stephen Spender, *World within World* (New York: Harcourt, Brace, 1951).

Christopher Isherwood, *Christopher and His Kind* (New York: Farrar, Straus, Giroux, 1976).

CHAPTER 3

J. R. Ackerley, *My Father and Myself* (New York: Coward-McCann, 1969).

Quentin Crisp, *The Naked Civil Servant* (New York: Penguin, 1977).

CHAPTER 4

André Gide, *If It Die* [*Si le grain ne meurt*], trans. Dorothy Bussy (New York: Vintage, 1963).

Jean Genet, *The Thief's Journal* [*Journal du voleur*], trans. Bernard Frechtman (New York: Grove Weidenfeld, 1964).

Julien Green, *The Green Paradise* [*Partir avant le jour*], trans. Anne and Julien
    Green (New York: Marion Boyars, 1993); *The War at Sixteen* [*Mille chemins
    overts*], trans. Euan Cameron (New York: Marion Boyars, 1993); *Love in
    America* [*Terre lointaine*], trans. Euan Cameron (New York: Marion Boyars,
    1994); *Restless Youth* [*Jeunesse*], trans. Euan Cameron (New York: Marion
    Boyars, 1996) [*Jeunes années*].

CHAPTER 5

Jeb and Dash: A Diary of Gay Life, 1918–1945, ed. Ina Russell (Boston: Faber
    and Faber, 1993).
Donald Vining, *A Gay Diary, 1933–1946* (New York: The Pepys Press, 1979);
    A Gay Diary: Volume Two, 1946–1954 (New York: The Pepys Press, 1980).

CHAPTER 6

John Reid [Andrew Tobias], *The Best Little Boy in the World* (New York: Ballan-
    tine Books, 1977).
Martin Duberman, *Cures* (New York: Dutton, 1991).
Paul Monette, *Becoming a Man* (New York: Harcourt Brace Jovanovich, 1992).

EPILOGUE

Samuel R. Delany, *The Motion of Light in Water* (New York: Arbor House,
    1988).
Richard Rodriguez, *Hunger of Memory* (New York: Bantam Books, 1983).
Richard Rodriguez, *Days of Obligation* (New York: Viking, 1992).
Gordon Heath, *Deep Are the Roots* (Amherst: University of Massachusetts
    Press, 1992).
Alvin Ailey (with A. Peter Bailey), *Revelations* (New York: A Birch Lane Press
    Book, 1995).
Ru Paul, *Let It All Hang Out* (New York: Hyperion, 1995).
José Zuniga, *Soldier of the Year* (New York: Pocket Books, 1994).
Rudy Galindo (with Eric Marcus), *Icebreaker* (New York: Pocket Books, 1997).

Index

Page numbers in italics refer to photographs.